TRAINING THE BODY FOR CHINA

TRAINING THE BODY FOR CHINA

Sports in the Moral Order of the People's Republic

SUSAN BROWNELL

The University of Chicago Press
Chicago and London

Susan Brownell is assistant professor of anthropology at the University of Missouri, St. Louis.

The University of Chicago Press, Chicago 60637
The University of Chicago Press, Ltd., London
© 1995 by The University of Chicago
All rights reserved. Published 1995
Printed in the United States of America

04 03 02 01 00 99 98 97 96 95   1 2 3 4 5

ISBN 0-226-07646-6 (cloth)
       0-226-07647-4 (paper)

Library of Congress Cataloging-in-Publication Data

Brownell, Susan.
   Training the body for China: Sports in the moral order of the
People's Republic / Susan Brownell.
       p.   cm.
   Includes bibliographical references and index.
   1. Sports—China.   2. Sports—China—Sociological aspects.
3. Sports—China—Moral and ethical aspects.   4. Sports and state—China.   5. Sports—
China—Sex differences.   6. Olympics.   7. China—Social life and customs—1976–
I. Title.
GV651.B76   1995
796′.0951′0*9045—dc20   94-49561
                                                                           CIP

♾ The paper used in this publication meets the minimum requirements of the American National Standard for Information Sciences—Permanence of Paper for Printed Library Materials, ANSI Z39.48–1984.

This book is dedicated to my mother, Claudia Brownell,
because only a mother could read every draft of the dissertation,
and every draft of the book,
and after three years and a thousand pages
still have the energy to argue about every use of
the word "habitus."

CONTENTS

ACKNOWLEDGMENTS

I wish to express my intellectual debt to John Mac-Aloon, who provided me with the opportunity to attend several conferences that completely changed my perception of the Olympic Movement. As the pioneer of anthropological studies of the Olympic Movement, he showed me that it could be done. His reviews of the book manuscript always challenged me to expand my mental horizons, and as a former student of Victor Turner, he understands Turner's influence on my intellectual life. I would like to acknowledge that influence here: I wrote my first paper on sports for Victor Turner in 1981, and I haven't stopped thinking about it yet. Its most recent incarnation is chapter 5 in this book.

Many people on both sides of the Pacific and Atlantic Oceans contributed to this book. My advisor at the Beijing Institute of Physical Education, Guo Jiaxing, expended much time and effort to make my research a success. Qu Zonghu, Vice Director of the Institute, oversaw the arrangements for my productive stay there. Professor Cao Xiangjun's class and my discussions with her were very helpful. Professor Kong Xiang'an at the Tianjin Institute of Physical Education generously shared his manuscripts and ideas with me. In addition, general thanks are due to the administrators, staff, teachers, and coaches at the Beijing institute for their concern and help.

Professors Guan Yushan and Lin Qiwu of Beijing University took the time to discuss their pasts and their work with me. Thanks also are due to my coaches on the track team at Beijing University, Gong Lei, Sun Yulu, and Wang Yu, whose immense efforts made possible my wonderful experience as a college athlete in China. Only they know exactly what it took to get a foreigner onto the Beijing City College Team.

I am grateful to my doctoral committee chair, Donald Brown, and my committee members, Mattison Mines, Charles Li, and Mayfair Yang, for their constant support and encouragement. I would also like to express my gratitude to Stevan Harrell and Helen Siu, who brought me to the University of Washington and to Yale University, respectively, for one-year appointments in intellectual environments that contributed immensely to the development of this book.

Ann Anagnost gave the book manuscript a considered and knowledgeable review that led me to reformulate many issues in a more complex manner. Others read parts of the manuscript or the papers on which they were based and returned insightful comments: Niko Besnier, Vigdis Broch-Due, Deborah Davis, Christina Gilmartin, Richard Handler, William Jankowiak, Deborah Kaspin, Andrew Kipnis, Charles Laughlin, Ralph Litzinger, Thomas Moran, Andrew Painter, Louisa Schein, Frederic Wakeman, Jr., and Rubie Watson. Ren Hai was my able assistant.

Many people took the time to discuss ideas with me and referred me to useful sources: Thea Cremers, Ronald Egan, Stephen Hsü, J. A. Mangan, and Jeff Olson. Dietrich Quanz at the German Institute of Sport Sciences in Cologne directed me to useful German sources and gave me the collection of essays by Pierre de Coubertin published by the Carl-Diem-Institut, which proved indispensable. Anton Blok discussed Norbert Elias's ideas and helped clarify my thinking about the body in social theory. David T. Brent of The University of Chicago Press was very helpful in suggesting ways to improve the manuscript.

My first year in China was partially funded by the Committee on International Educational Exchange. The second year was funded by the U.S. Information Agency through the Committee on Scholarly Communication with the PRC (National Academy of Sciences). The last stage of writing was supported by the Wenner-Gren Foundation for Anthropological Research. I am grateful for their generous financial support.

Jan Möller provided me with friendship in China and a place to stay in Cologne. My brother Rob provided me with rent-free housing, computer room included, while I wrote the initial draft of my dissertation. My father Robert Brownell helped me print out the final manuscript at a time when I was unemployed and had no access to a laser printer. Let me express my gratitude toward the rest of my family—Claudia and Samuel Strite and Lyn Brownell—without whose emotional and financial support I would never have finished this book. My debt to my mother is expressed in the dedication of the book.

Following the Chinese custom, let me state that this is a preliminary investigation. I hope that my readers will bring deficiencies and mistakes to my attention.

PART
•1•

Introduction

CHAPTER ONE

Winning Glory
for Beijing

As I stood with my teammates behind the Beijing City flag, I suddenly felt overwhelmed by the gaze of fifty thousand pairs of eyes converging from around the bowl-shaped stadium onto those of us in the infield. I was one of two Americans (with my teammate James Thomas) among two thousand Chinese athletes lined up behind team flags in the infield of the Dalian city stadium. The shiny black hair of the spectators in the stands merged into a dark, encircling wall. Along one side of the stadium, a bank of ten thousand teenagers in dazzling white held placards over their heads that melded to form a huge bank of Chinese characters: "The Second National College Games Triumphantly Begin!"

I was in the middle of the opening ceremonies of the 1986 National College Games of the People's Republic of China. Twenty teammates and I had left our dorms three hours earlier dressed in our multicolored sweatsuits. We had sweltered under the August sun as we slowly wound our way from the parking lot, along the road, through the warm-up fields, and down to the gates leading into the stadium. There we stood pressed up against the iron bars with the rest of China's student representatives behind us. Finally, the gates were opened, right on schedule, and we were the first to march in, leading the teams from the other twenty-eight provinces and municipalities. We represented the capital city. This was our chance to demonstrate our pride to the nation that, we had been told, would be watching us with interest on television. The large, bright green flag at our head proclaimed, "Beijing City." We moved off down the 100-meter straightaway of the track, passing the rostrum in the grandstand where the high officials sat. The highest among them was Li Peng, chairman of the presidium of the Games. (Two years later he would become premier of the PRC and then lead the crackdown on student demonstrators in Tiananmen Square in 1989.) I was conspicuously placed in the middle of the right-hand column of marchers so that the spectators could see that Beijing City had a foreigner on the team. I did my best for Li Peng. I cradled my plastic flowers in my left arm while my right arm snapped back and forth as we marched along. Nearing the reviewing stand, we began goose-stepping, shouting out slogans in time with our steps. Marchers in the center unfurled small banners inscribed with the slogans at the same time that we shouted them.

> Train the body! [*duanlian shenti!*—This was the chorus.]
> Study diligently!
> Train the body!
> Bravely scale the peaks!
> Train the body!
> Carry out the Four Modernizations!
> Train the body!
> Defend the Nation!

Having passed the rostrum, we furled our banners, down-keyed our goose-stepping into marching, and continued around the curve and into the infield. There we stood for an interminable hour listening to speeches. Those who sat down or got out of line were exhorted by the officials to behave. We were hot, uncomfortable, and did a lot of grumbling. It was at this point that I looked around and wondered if I had actually become Bao Sushan, "the American girl who wants to win glory for Beijing" (as one newspaper headline described me).

Bao Sushan is the Chinese version of my name, which I had assumed on arriving at Beijing University in the fall of 1985 to study Chinese. Shortly after my arrival, I sought out the head coach of the track team, Coach Gong, to inquire about joining the team. I had been a nationally ranked athlete in the United States in the heptathlon and I was hoping to make friends and practice Chinese. I was also testing the first stages of my plan to write a Ph.D. dissertation on sports in China.

Coach Gong was a middle-aged former long-distance runner whose career had been cut short by hepatitis, a not uncommon occurrence in the past. He welcomed me to join the team, so the next day I showed up behind Gymnasium #1. Gymnasium #1 was a beautiful white building with a sloping, gray-tiled roof—a wonderful example, I thought, of "traditional" Chinese architecture. The inside felt very familiar because it reminded me of the old Memorial Gymnasium at the University of Virginia, my alma mater. I was soon told that in fact it had been built by Americans in the 1920s as part of the U.S.-run Yanjing University which originally occupied the site. As a Christian American school, Yanjing had promoted sports, bequeathing to Beijing University two gymnasiums and two dirt tracks—more than most Chinese universities had—but these facilities hadn't seen much repair in the three-quarters of a century since then.

"Where's the track?" I asked Coach Gong, eyeing the cement blocks, dirt, and pipes piled beside a five-foot deep chasm along the rear wall of the gymnasium. Faded characters painted on the wall proclaimed, "Long Live Invincible Mao Zedong Thought!"

"This is it," he said. "There is construction going on just now. But we can run on the backstretch." Slightly distressed, I discovered that even the backstretch was riddled with potholes and chunks of brick from the construction. The rock-hard earth was covered with several inches of red cinder shipped in from a distant volcanic site. "It cost more per *jin* than rice," Coach Gong commented. "Do you believe that?" That fall turned out to be a low point in the life of the sports facilities at the university, but as was true all over China, restoration and revival were in the air. Eventually, the trench was filled in, the weeds in the infield burned off, the cinder raked. And finally a new facility was built in preparation for hosting the city collegiate meet in 1989.

"The door opens, she stands before us: tall of stature, deep-set eyes, prominent nose. Right, it's really her. 'Hello, Bao Sushan! . . .'" That is what I looked like to a freshman reporter for the November 1985 issue of the Beijing University school newspaper. I had attracted some attention at the fall freshman intramural track meet. The image of Bao Sushan took on a life of its own. Over time, articles about me appeared in *Xin tiyu* (New Sports), *Zhongguo qingnian bao* (China Youth News), *Beijing ribao* (Beijing Daily), and *Tiyu bolan* (Sports Vision). I had been in China only one month at the time of the first few interviews and my Mandarin was far from fluent. Interviews often consisted of the reporter asking me a detailed question and my answering briefly, not always understanding the entire question. My simple Mandarin received elaborate interpretation.

A revised version of the freshman reporter's article appeared in *Xin tiyu* (New Sports) magazine, the *Sports Illustrated* of China. In that article, there appeared a statement that I knew I was incapable of formulating:

> There are also people [in America] who like to race cars, climb frozen waterfalls, and do other novel and strange adventure sports. I feel that you shouldn't always use words such as fanaticism, empty pursuit, and thrillseeker to describe them . . . In striving to "die nine deaths in one lifetime," they have cultivated a persistent and dauntless moral character, and they will even more warmly love life and strengthen their will in order to tenaciously continue living amongst the grueling competition of a society with a high rate of unemployment. (Zhang Yan 1986)

Both articles concluded with my saying that in the National College Games, I hoped to "win glory for Beijing University!"

Thus was I assigned the role of critic of my own society, and in places of Chinese sports as well. One reporter wrote an article entitled "The Bystander Sees Clearly," in which I delivered a scathing critique of the Chinese sports system, comparing it negatively with the American system, which (I reportedly said) paid much more attention to sport for the masses and less to elite sports. Fortunately, he let me see a rough draft and I asked that he not publish it. His commitment to journalistic accuracy was evident in the fact that in his handwritten rough draft, he had first put words into my mouth as direct quotes then crossed them out and written different versions above them.

THE SMALL WORLD OF THE BODY
IN THE UNIVERSE OF IDEAS

If at first I didn't say "win glory for Beijing" (*wei Beijing zheng guang*), I soon learned to do so. The world of an athlete is different from that of an anthropologist. The horizons of an athlete's world can never stray far beyond her body. The course of an athletic career entails development of the ability to focus increasingly greater amounts of awareness on increasingly specific parts of the body. In putting the shot, an action that takes about five seconds, I eventually developed the ability to monitor ten different body parts, beginning with the ball of my right foot and ending with the tip of the middle finger on my right hand. The horizons of an intellectual's world lie at the edge of an ever-expanding cosmos of ideas that seems to recede further and further from the body. Athletes are very much *in* their bodies and, as a consequence, are usually very much within the systems that sustain those bodies. Intellectuals are forever trying to escape beyond bodies and the systems that sustain them so that they can gain enough distance to look back and comment on them. Athletes are stereotypically team players; intellectuals, especially anthropologists, are stereotypically rebels.

In the course of the two-month training camp for the National College Games, my world had progressively shrunk until the moment in the infield of the Dalian stadium when I suddenly seemed to realize that I was really there, in my body, in the stadium with two thousand Chinese athletes. The reason my body was there was that I was to win glory for Beijing. The opening ceremonies induced this feeling. After all, the ceremonies were designed to do just that: to place us before the gaze of thousands of eyes and to remind us that our bodies were objects in the service of the people. In the United States, I had never participated in such a formal ceremony before so many people. That night, I found myself lying in bed thinking, "Here I am on the other side of the world, and all I can think about is running faster, jumping higher, throwing farther, beating people." It was with some self-disgust that I realized I had come halfway around the world only to discover I had never left my athlete's body.

In the end, I fulfilled my duty. I won the heptathlon, setting a national college record. In the last event, the 800 meters, I ran alone out front, hearing only the sound of my own footsteps and one singular yell from the stands: "Add gas, foreigner!" I ran on two silver-medal relay teams. Beijing's women placed second overall. I was given a spirit award. A magazine article captured my double identity well when it quoted me as responding, "To use the American formula, I want to say, 'Thank you.' To use the Chinese formula, I want to say I still haven't done enough!" (Chu Zi 1987: 27).

I offer this introduction by way of placing myself in what follows. This book is not about me and it is not about the small world of the athlete's body. Rather, it is about the place of the small world of the Chinese athlete's body within the larger universe of ideas. In a sense, it represents my own attempt to reconcile my two worlds—athlete and social scientist. The chasm between the detachment from the body that characterizes much social science and the limited focus on the body that characterizes sports is difficult to bridge. Pierre Bourdieu states that the different worlds of the athlete and the social scientist have important implications for social theory; he contrasts the teaching of bodily practices, which are learned by a "silent, practical communication from body to body," with the social scientist's theories of behavior, which are "produced for the most part on this side of consciousness." Because the first takes place on *that* side and the second on *this* side of consciousness, "The problems that teaching bodily practices poses seem to me to enclose a number of questions of primordial importance" regarding how a person "seizes awareness [*prise de conscience*]" (1988: 81).

This book discusses Chinese sports from a perspective that is based on three main assumptions. The first is that sports should be analyzed as one set of practices in the entire repertoire of things that people do with their bodies—in other words, sports should be analyzed as part of the entire culture of the body. The second assumption is that the culture of the body is strongly shaped by power relations, including state/society, class, gender, and ethnic relations, as well as the international relations between nations; attention should be paid to the ways in which power affects the culture of the body. The third assumption is that sports occupy an important place within the culture of the body because sports events are one of the main arenas in which the body as a cultural artifact is publicly displayed. Major sports events should be analyzed as cultural performances in which the production of an image of the "legitimate body" is contested behind the scenes and a consensus temporarily reached in the public performance. Hence an analysis of sport must also include the analysis of sporting events as cultural performances produced by self-interested groups.

What follows will serve as a prelude to the rest of the book by first introducing the notion of body culture and its theoretical background and then by suggesting how each of these three fields of analysis will be applied to sports in the Chinese moral order. The chapter will end by placing this discussion within the context of the Olympic Movement.

THE CONCEPT OF BODY CULTURE

Body Techniques and World-Orientations

Marcel Mauss, in 1939, was the first to direct the attention of social scientists to "techniques of the body": "the ways in which from society to society [people] know how to use their bodies" (1979: 97). In his discussion of body techniques, Mauss reminds us that human beings do learn, either consciously or unconsciously, the most seemingly automatic actions. Even walking styles vary from one society to another. Mauss wrote that he could recognize girls educated in convent schools by the way they walked.

Moving through the streets of Beijing, usually at a faster pace than my Chinese fellow travelers, I often noticed that in general people walked further back on their heels with the shoulders pressed downward and rounded slightly forward. When I returned to the Beijing Institute of Physical Education, I was often struck by the fact that the students walked more like Westerners, with their chests pushed out and bouncing off their toes. Western visitors to the institute often commented that the students there looked more European. Once, while training at the Beijing City team center, much to my surprise I saw a group of European women athletes approaching across the field. I watched them until they reached me, when I suddenly noticed their black hair and Chinese faces. Their sudden metamorphosis was as shocking to me as if I had been hallucinating.

It seems likely to me that the typical Chinese walking style has its roots in the traditional forms of physical training such as tai chi and other martial arts. Most people are familiar with these forms and have practiced them at one point in their lives. When play-fighting, little boys often use martial arts moves. These body techniques emphasize solid footing, a low center of gravity, balance, and rootedness in the earth—thus, the feet should be flat on the ground, the shoulders rounded and pressed downward.[1] When one contrasts this with the Western walking style, which is no doubt influenced by Western forms of physical education (and of course within the West there are also vari-

1. Consider this description of the walk of the protagonist in a novel by Lin Yutang:

He walked with a young, steady gait, with slow but firm steps. It was obviously the gait of a trained Chinese athlete, in which the body preserved an absolute poise, ready for a surprise attack at any unsuspected moment from the front, the side, or behind. One foot was firmly planted on the ground, while the other leg was in a forward, slightly bent and open, self-protective position, so that he could never be thrown out of his balance. (1939: 4)

In chapter 2, I quote Lin's comments on the walking styles of foreigners. Lin's attention to walking styles was more than fortuitous. He was among the intellectuals of his day who were influenced by Western social Darwinism, eugenics, and racialist anthropometry (DiKötter 1992: 135, 145). Their arguments for strengthening the Chinese "race" were very focused on the body (see chapter 2).

ations), it is clear that walking styles express broad cultural differences. With their shoulders thrown back and a bounce in their stride, Westerners raise their center of gravity and move as if they want to leave the earth behind. Perhaps rural life has played a role in shaping the relationship of people to the earth in China: to walk with a heavily loaded carrying pole across one's shoulders requires a flat-footed gait and rounded shoulders. This is such a common way of carrying things that it has its own verb in Mandarin, *tiao* ("to carry on the shoulder with a pole"). Almost everyone I knew who was twenty-eight or older had spent some time in the countryside and was well-acquainted with carrying poles. Chinese posture also reflects social relationships: rounded shoulders characterize the bow, which is an expression of humility before superiors, and in the case of athletes, also before audiences. It often seemed to me that the carriage of Chinese women seemed a bit more earthbound than that of the men, which undoubtedly reflected their place in the social hierarchy.

The point is that something as automatic and seemingly trivial as one's walking style expresses an entire orientation to the world. This orientation is simultaneously trained into the body with conscious intent (as through physical education in the schools), acquired through the necessities of daily practice (as through walking with carrying poles), and organized by an underlying symbolic logic that is often unconscious (as with the bow as a sign of humility). This example illustrates that the first step in the analysis of the body is to recognize that attention to the things that humans do with their bodies, however mundane, opens up a whole realm of analysis that has been largely ignored until recently. As Mauss noted, "It is generally in these ill-demarcated domains that the urgent problems lie . . . 'Miscellaneous.' This is where we have to penetrate" (1979: 98).

Body Culture

To delimit this realm of analysis, I use the notion of "body culture" or the "culture of the body." By this I mean everything that people do with their bodies (Mauss's "body techniques") and the elements of culture that shape their doing. Body culture is a broad term that includes daily practices of health, hygiene, fitness, beauty, dress and decoration, as well as gestures, postures, manners, ways of speaking and eating, and so on. It also includes the way these practices are trained into the body, the way the body is publicly displayed, and the lifestyle that is expressed in that display. Body culture reflects the internalization and incorporation of culture. Body culture is embodied culture.

Body Culture versus Habitus

My conception of body culture owes much to Mauss's and Bourdieu's notion of "habitus." For Bourdieu, habitus refers to a system of predispositions, a habitual way of being, that becomes inculcated in the body as a result of the objective conditions of daily existence (for example, economic and class conditions) as well as of more condensed efforts to instill them (for instance, in games, etiquette, rituals, festivals) (1977: 15, 80, 88, 214n. 1, 217n. 40). It is a concept that he developed as a way of overcoming the traditional opposition between objectivist approaches (primarily Lévi-Strauss and Durkheim) and subjectivist approaches (phenomenology) in social theory (Postone, LiPuma, and Calhoun 1993: 3–4). Thus, he writes that

> The source of historical action . . . resides neither in consciousness nor in things but in the relationship between two stages of the social, that is, between the history objectified in things, in the form of institutions, and the history incarnated in bodies, in the form of that system of enduring dispositions which I call habitus. (Bourdieu 1990: 190)

I avoid using the word "habitus" in this book for several reasons. First, it is a jargon word with limited currency. It is my hope that the phrase "body culture" will make for easier reading. Second, I assert that it is not necessary to completely reject the concept of culture in the analysis of these issues. As used by American anthropologists since the early twentieth century, "culture" clearly included body practices, and for English speakers the phrase "body culture" more vividly conjures up the middle ground between the (prelinguistic) body and (institutionalized) belief that Bourdieu wanted to explore. As explained in further detail below, I believe that utilizing a more flexible concept of culture, informed by the current debates on the culture concept in a postmodern world, can contribute a great deal to theories about the body. This allows me to draw on works that utilize a cultural perspective (most important, Geertz, MacAloon, Turner, and the journal *Public Culture*).

Finally, Bourdieu's own work tends to concentrate on knowledge and belief without elaborating in detail the microtechniques of the body associated with them (as, for example, does Foucault). By using the phrase "body culture," I try to maintain a clearer focus on bodily practices. I prefer to discuss habitus as a *process* of habituation and to use "body culture" to delimit the object of my analysis.

At the same time, my ultimate concern, with Bourdieu, is the process of habituation by which everyday practice trains a world-orientation into the body. When my college teammates and I were working out on the sportsfield, we used to joke, "Practice doesn't make perfect. Practice makes permanent." By this we meant that once you learn a sports technique in a certain way, it is very hard to change it later. The essence of Bourdieu's notion of habitus is captured in that bit of sports wisdom, "Practice makes permanent," because of the double meaning of the word "practice." In social theory, of course, it includes more than simply the repetition of sports movements. Marx used it to refer to "concrete human activity." Bourdieu defined practice as the dialectic of incorporation and objectification—that is to say, the process by which the external becomes internal and the internal becomes external (Bourdieu 1977: 72). The sports metaphor illustrates Bourdieu's point that what is first verbally expressed to a person by a voice of authority (in this case, a coach) may, through repetition, become an almost unconscious principle that shapes her movements.

Thus, Bourdieu notes that "There are many things that we understand only with our bodies, on this side of consciousness, without having the words to say them" (1988: 81). For this reason, "[S]port is, with dance, one of the areas where the problem of the relations between theory and practice, and also between language and body, is posed with maximum acuteness" (p. 80).

Constructing a discussion around the French phrase *l'esprit de corps,* Bourdieu suggests that by considering sport (like convents, prisons, asylums, etc.) as a means "of obtaining from the body (*corps*) an adherence that the spirit (*esprit*) could refuse," we can better comprehend the utilization of sports by authoritarian regimes (1988: 82). Although I cannot claim that while I was living and training with my Beijing teammates my body "understood" things in the same way that theirs did, nevertheless I believe that my experiences gave me some insight into the relationship between bodily discipline and consensual belief as structured by the Chinese Communist Party. Though I agree that sports offer insight into the connections between discipline and belief, it is also important to state that the bodily discipline I experienced in China did not *feel* any different because I was in a so-called authoritarian regime.[2] On the contrary, it felt quite similar to the routines I had known as an athlete in the United States, and even more similar to my experiences at summer camp (see chapter 6).

"Practice makes permanent" also reiterates Bourdieu's point that habitus is difficult to change since it is largely unconscious and therefore unquestioned. This durability means that habitus reinforces social order and, in fact, is the ultimate source of social stability (Bourdieu 1977: 189). Since habitus is fairly durable, preexisting habitus will create obstacles for social change. Thus, habitus underpins relatively stable formations such as social class, gender, and nationality. And it must be reckoned with in the shifting contexts of modernization, industrialization, and state formation. In the end, all of these social processes receive reinforcement or resistance from the techniques of the body that are associated with a particular kind of habitus.

In sum, practice theory provides the overall conceptual framework for this book. But rather than reifying the process of habituation through everyday practice by labeling it with the noun "habitus," I prefer to describe it as a process and to delimit my field of analysis as "body culture," which maintains a clearer focus on the body.

The Problem with "Culture"

Bourdieu's attempt to get beyond the subject-object dichotomy is not at all new: Geertz asserts that the central theoretical problem for social science since Parsons has been "how to conceptualize the dialectic between the crystallization of such directive 'patterns of meaning' [as constitute culture] and the concrete course of social life" (1973: 250). Bourdieu formulated his notion of habitus in part as a reaction against the disembodied conception of culture dominant in French anthropology under the influence of Durkheim and Lévi-Strauss. However, some American anthropologists have conceptualized culture in a way that is more amenable to Bourdieu's approach. Certain of the early key figures in American and British anthropology dealt with some of the same issues, such as E. B. Tylor with his emphasis on prelinguistic forms of knowledge (which led him to an interest in gestures, among other

2. Thus, I agree with Richard Gruneau when he takes issue with Bourdieu's emphasis here on totalitarian regimes; he adds, "There is a link between bodily disciplines, beliefs, rituals and power in all societies, not just totalitarian ones" (1991: 170). Gruneau's comparison and contrast of Bourdieu and Foucault as applied to sports resonates with the approach taken in this book.

things) (Stocking 1987: 306–7); Bronislaw Malinowski with his emphasis on pragmatic, utilitarian behavior; and Franz Boas with his emphasis
on the way learned traditions condition individual psychology. Thus,
my use of the word "culture" draws on a long history in American and
British anthropology, in which body techniques, such as manners, dress,
bodily decoration and alteration, have always been considered as elements of culture. This perspective has emphasized the force of habit, the
importance of bodily imitation in "learning" culture, and the nonverbal
nature of much of what comes under the label of culture.

In the United States in the 1970s, Victor Turner was at the forefront
of an attempt to recover subjective experience and resuscitate it before it
was killed off by the Structuralist stranglehold on anthropology (Bruner
1986: 3). He wrote in his foreword to *The Ritual Process* that the book
"represents an attempt to free my own thought, and I hope that of others in my field as well, from grooved dependence on 'structure' as the
sole sociological dimension" (Turner 1969: viii). Later, he emphasized
"experience" (Turner and Bruner 1986) and "performance" (Turner
1988) in an attempt to avoid "reducing all to bloodless abstractions"
(Turner and Bruner 1986: 35). Interestingly, in his attempt to recover
the subject Turner moved in the opposite direction of Bourdieu. While
Bourdieu turned his attention to the practice of everyday life, Turner
wrote, "Cultures, I hold, are better compared through their rituals, theaters, tales, ballads, epics, operas than through their *habits*. For the former are the ways in which they try to articulate their meaning" (personal communication cited in Bruner 1986: 13).

In sum, much of what Bourdieu attempts to do with the concept of
habitus can be done just as well within the framework of the culture
concept. Turner is an example of a scholar who dealt with some of the
same issues through a more traditional cultural analysis, but his work is
limited in that for him everyday life seemed to exist largely as a backdrop for moments of dramatic outburst. Bourdieu, on the other hand,
has little to say about expressive cultural performances. This book combines both approaches; however, because I found subjective "experience" (Turner) particularly hard to research, this book focuses on sports
as daily practice (Bourdieu) and as cultural performance (Turner).

The traditional anthropological concept of culture has been criticized, most notably by Abu-Lughod (1991), because it is used to reify
differences between ethnic groups, especially between "us"—the anthropological experts—and "them"—the exotic subject, at the same
time obscuring other differences such as gender and class. When I use

the phrase "Chinese body culture" I draw a boundary around something that I somewhat arbitrarily define as "Chinese" (does it include non-Han? Taiwanese? etc.). However, I would argue that utilizing this narrower subcategory of culture makes possible a more sensitive appraisal of difference. Let me give an example.

It is common throughout the PRC for members of the same sex to hold hands. The anxiety that most Americans feel the first time a Chinese friend takes their hand indicates a cultural *difference*. Taking this as a starting point, a social scientist can explain (as I do in chapter 8) that this difference stems from the different meanings assigned to holding hands with members of the same sex, meanings shaped through history by social differences between China and the United States—in other words, this difference stems from culture. But removing the analysis to this level of abstraction obscures the fact that in the daily encounters of Americans with Chinese, the more immediate concern is not, say, the influence of the yin-yang logic on sex-linked symbolism; rather, people are concerned with what other people are doing with their bodies. This is where the visceral reactions begin that are the basis for ethnic (or gender or class) hatred. A focus on body culture keeps the social scientist's attention on the daily practices that matter most in the encounter between people and the alien Others in their lives—whether of different ethnicity, sex, or class. I would argue that the concept of body culture can be used to analyze any level of difference—ethnic, national, class, gender, etc.—because it draws our attention to the practical differences that really matter. Bodies are immensely important to the people to whom they belong. Pain, hunger, fatigue, sexual desire, and so on, are central to the people experiencing them. An ethnographic account that overlooks the body omits the center of human experience.

The Problem with "The Body"

While writing this book I worked in three different languages—English, Mandarin, and German. This had the effect of making me acutely aware of the relativity of my key concepts. It is important to touch upon some of the translation difficulties inherent in the concepts of "the body" and "body culture." One cannot talk about body culture in China without dissecting the conception of the body that underlies it. The title of this book, "Training the Body for China," implies that there is one, unified body in the Chinese conception—*the* body—and English speakers will undoubtedly fail to realize that the word poses problems. In fact, there are at least three different root words for "body" in Chinese: *shen*, animate body; *ti*, inanimate body; and *shi*, dead body or corpse. The root characters can be combined in multiple ways, as in *shenti*, body/health; *shiti*, corpse. The difference between *shen* and *ti* is of most relevance to this book.[3]

Sun Lung-kee notes that in thinking about themselves and their relationships with other people, Chinese people use the word *shen* rather than concepts like "personality" or "individual" (Sun Lung-kee 1983: 20). Mark Elvin adds that "in most Chinese phrases that translate into English phrases where the ideas of 'person,' 'self,' or 'lifetime' are used or implied, the word *shen* appears" (Elvin 1989: 275). Examples are the common phrases *an shen* (lit. "to make peaceful one's body" = "settle down in life") and *zhong shen* (lit. "body's end" = "to the end of one's life") (Elvin 1989: 275). The communist system of class labels politicized two phrases with profound implications for people's lives: *chushen* ("family background") and *shenfen* ("class status"). This conflation of self and body leads Elvin to translate *shen* as "body-person." *Shen* implies a lived body, a life history.

Shen is paired with the "flesh-body" (*routi*) expressed in the word *ti*. *Ti* is the character that is used in the words for "physical culture" (*tiyu*), "physique" (*tizhi, xingti, tixing, tipo*), and "physical exercise" (*ticao*). The primary sense of *ti* is that of an individual unit or a closed system; that it is inanimate is indicated by its frequent use in combinations that translate abstract Western scientific phrases like "system," "particle," and so on. One of its important references is also to calligraphy types. However, the inanimate body is also the vessel for lived experience, indicated by the phrases *tihui*, "to know from experience," and *tiyan*, "to learn through personal experience."[4] The Chinese phrase that

3. *Shen, ti,* and *shi* are similar to the German *Leib, Körper,* and *Leiche,* respectively. My discussion of the Chinese words was strongly influenced by works on the history of the German words. In his influential book on the history of *Leib* and *Körper,* Lippe (1988) argued that the transition away from the conception of a living, experiential, subject-body ("the body that one is"—*Leib sein*) toward a dead, instrumental object-body ("the body that one has"—*Körper haben*) was one of the important developments in Europe's march into modernity. *Leib* was the word used in the phrase for "the body of Christ." A *Leib* was a *Körper* plus a soul. It implied purity, morality, identity. But by the turn of the nineteenth century, it was being supplanted in discussions of health and fitness by a concern with the *Körper,* which implied animality, immorality, and instrumentality (Eichberg 1993: 265–66). The difference between the two is illustrated in two words for physical education. *Leibeserziehung* (physical education) implies moral cultivation as well as physical training. *Körperkultur* (physical culture), the science of human physical exercise, does not have as strong a moral implication.

4. The parallels between the two Chinese and German conceptions of the body are not exact; the Chinese does not exhibit as strict a subject-object dualism as does the German. *Leib* was the subjective, experienced body while *Körper* was the alienated object body. In

inspired the title for this book, *duanlian shenti,* "train the body," combines the two kinds of body, implying that one simultaneously trains the body-person and the flesh-body.

Before the advent of the modern science of physical education, references to physical training tended to take moral character and life force as their target. An old phrase for self-cultivation, *xiu shen,* used the word for body but primarily implied the cultivation of moral character. *Yang sheng,* "to cultivate life," referred to the Taoist physical exercises that were supposed to make the body immortal. Thus, there is some evidence that before the absorption of Western concepts of physical education in China, bodily exercise was perceived more subjectively and less as a practice worked upon an objective body that served as an instrumental means to an end.

In Mandarin, the word *tiyu* came into use as a label for the new methods of physical education that Japan and the West brought to China in the late nineteenth century. It was a contraction of *shenti jiaoyu,* "physical education." Before that time, generic words for sports had military connotations (for example, *wuyong, wuyi*). The earliest forms of physical education were introduced by Japanese and Germans, who were themselves developing new conceptions of the body to serve the cause of national strength. German physical education was moving away from the body as subject toward the body as object (Lippe 1988; Eichberg 1993). In the course of its march into modernity, and under Western influence, China also moved away from the Taoist "way of life-cultivation" (*yang sheng zhi dao*) and toward "physical education" (*tiyu*). *Shen* had had female connotations: it could refer to a wife, a prostitute, a woman's loss of virtue; "lower body" was a euphemism for female genitals. The female implications were lost in the move to the gender-neutral, inanimate *ti.* In today's China, the instrumental, gender-neutral body is unquestionably the focus of the culture of the body.

Body Culture, *Körperkultur,* and *Tiyu*

Although "body culture" is not a common phrase in English social science, its European equivalents have a long history. Its main roots extend

---

contrast, both *shen* and *ti* have a subjective, experiential component. *Shen* implies a more abstract life history, while *ti* implies the more concrete imprint that particular lived experiences leave behind in a person. Neither word has the disembodied Western sort of connotation in which a person is somehow *inside* the body that is experiencing life—a body that is separate from the experiencing subject. It appears, however, that with the introduction of Western science and physical education, the linguistic usages of *ti* became much more detached, objective, and instrumental than was formerly the case.

not into the English sporting tradition, but into the alternative traditions that emerged on the Continent in the early nineteenth century—the German Turners, Czech Sokols, and Swedish gymnastics. These movements, in turn, had their roots in efforts at educational reform that began in the late eighteenth century. Forged in the social upheavals of the nineteenth century, the Continental movements linked physical education with character-building, public health, and national self-defense. They advocated gymnastics training for all-around physical and moral development and opposed the specialization and competition that characterized the English model of athletic sports. The debates over "gymnastics" versus "athletic sports" continued into the early twentieth century and spilled over into the United States, where the Turner gymnastics that were quite popular in German communities contrasted with the English-type sports popular in the Ivy League colleges (Barney 1991; MacAloon 1981: 114–25). The relative merits of the German, Swedish, and English systems were debated at the 1889 Boston Conference in the Interest of Physical Training. One of the participants was Baron Pierre de Coubertin, who was then promoting English sports along with his idea of "reviving" the ancient Greek Olympic Games. John MacAloon's analysis of the conference shows that at this time Coubertin was just initiating the process that would eventually lead to the primacy of the English model in international sports due to the influence of the Olympic Games (MacAloon 1981: 114–20).

It was, however, in the alternative gymnastics tradition that the notion of "body culture" was significant. Henning Eichberg locates the origins of the German *Körperkultur* in the "Free Body Culture" (*Freikörperkultur*) movement of the 1900s that advocated diet and clothing reform, nudism, sport, gymnastics, folk dance, abstinence from alcohol and nicotine, and so on. The body was central in this movement, and around the time from 1900 to 1905 the label of "body culture" (*Körperkultur*) appeared (Eichberg 1993: 257–58). Similar ideas were picked up by the German Socialist Worker's Movement and by Karl Marx. *Körperkultur* was translated into Russian as *Fiskultura*, which was in turn translated into English as "physical culture." Physical culture in the Soviet Union was strongly influenced by both the German and Czech schools, but after the 1860s the Czech Sokol system predominated because of its Pan-Slavic associations (Riordan 1977: 46–47). As in Germany, "physical culture" was for a long time conceived of as in opposition to competitive sports in the Soviet Union. Not until 1930 were sports centralized under a sports ministry which established a ranking system for the support of competitive sports. Competitive sports continued to grow in the aftermath of World War II as Stalin further centralized the sports system, utilized sports events to promote national cohesion, and required a spartan lifestyle of the populace. The Soviet Union competed in its first Olympic Games in 1952 and held its first national games, called the *Spartakiad* after the Spartan ideal, in 1956 (Riordan 1977: 82–182). Physical culture lost its connotation of healthy alternative living and came to refer to high-level sports, which was echoed in the meanings attached to *Körperkultur* in East Germany (Eichberg 1993: 258). Although it became somewhat redundant, nevertheless the phrase "physical culture *and* sport" is still used in organization names and sport theory.

In China, the advocates of "gymnastics" and "competitive sports" also engaged in heated debates in the early 1900s, when physical education was mostly taught by foreign teachers. However, as Chinese took control of physical education, this debate was overshadowed by the debate about "Chinese" versus "foreign" sports, as discussed in the following chapter. When the People's Republic of China established its centralized sports system in 1955, it followed the Soviet model, which by that time was thoroughly committed to the support of competitive, specialist sports. As in the Soviet Union, the phrase "physical culture and sport" is common in China, most visibly in the official name for the ministry of sport: the State Physical Culture and Sports Commission (*Guojia Tiyu Yundong Weiyuanhui*), which is nevertheless usually called the State Sports Commission in the English-language Chinese press. Because of its similarity to the Soviet model in both practice and theory, the Mandarin *tiyu* is now often translated as "physical culture," even though it was originally derived from a direct translation of the English "physical education." Chinese sports theory distinguishes the "broad definition" from the "narrow definition" of *tiyu*. Except where established conventions of translation dictated otherwise, in this book I have translated the broad definition as "physical culture" and the narrow definition as "physical education."

A second point in the history of socialist "physical culture" is that the classification of sports as "culture" was part of the socialist endeavor to legitimate a proletarian culture and attack the elitist European conception of culture which included only the fine arts (Eichberg 1977). This effort to culturally elevate sports, however, was never wholly successful in the Soviet Union or the PRC.

In theory, the elitist conception of culture should not have posed a problem within American anthropology, which since Boas has also opposed the elitist definition; but despite "athletic sports" being a human universal (Murdock 1945: 124), the attention given to sports by anthropologists and folklorists cannot compare with that devoted to dance, music, theater, and the other analogues of European high culture. In English, "physical culture" never became common except when used to refer to socialist sports, and "body culture" was never common in any context. In contrast, the German *Körperkultur* underwent a Renaissance in West Germany after 1968, and along with other European equivalents (such as Danish *kropskultur*) has been a key word in a new perspective on the body that has been emerging in the last two decades in Germany and Denmark (Eichberg 1993: 258). This perspective looks at the body primarily as *cultural,* meaning it places its emphasis on the multiple roles of the body in social processes and historical change (Eichberg 1989: 49). It centers on the terms "body," "movement" (c.f. *Bewegungskultur,* "movement culture"), "culture," and "society" seen in a critical perspective (Eichberg 1989: 43).

Like its predecessors, this approach seeks to reconstitute a whole notion of body/self through the concept of body culture. It attempts to overcome the fragmenting effects of competitive sports, with their dichotomies of elite versus mass sport, professional versus amateur, performance versus health, and so on (Eichberg 1993: 52–56). This model serves my purposes because it recombines the field of practices from which sport was singled out in the course of its historical development. However, I extend the use of body culture beyond this tradition by linking it with an understanding of culture that is drawn from American and British anthropology. The *Kultur* in *Körperkultur* connotes the cultivation of the body to political ends. The culture in body culture is meant to refer to a system of meanings and symbols.[5]

"Body culture" is not easy to translate into Chinese. "Physical culture," *tiyu,* consists of two characters: *ti* refers to the body and *yu* means to "raise, cultivate, or educate." *Tiyu* is an overarching term that today refers to three categories derived from an institutional division of labor: competitive sports (*jingji tiyu* or *tiyu yundong*), physical education in the schools (*xuexiao tiyu* or simply *tiyu*), and recreation and physical fitness for the masses (*qunzhong tiyu*). Because these activities are overseen by the State Sports and Education Commissions while health practices are overseen by the Bureau of Health, there is a rather strict division be-

---

5. I wish to thank John MacAloon for clarifying the relationship of my approach to the German and American perspectives.

tween physical culture and health (*weisheng*). Due to its place in communist ideology, *tiyu* is now a highly politicized word with a very specific meaning, hence it is difficult to conceive of it as an analytical
category. In addition, while it captures the sense of "cultivation," its
link with the concept of culture (*wenhua*) is very tenuous. The literal
Chinese translation of "physical culture," *shenti wenhua*, is another alternative. However, it is seldom if ever actually used by Chinese speakers. Perhaps with the popularization and decentralization of sports under the economic reforms, *tiyu*, like *Körperkultur*, might be reconstituted.

SPORT AS A PART OF BODY CULTURE IN CHINA

The Modern History of the Chinese Body

Following this discussion of the concept of body culture it is now possible to return to my original point: that sports should be studied as part
of the entire culture of the body. As Eichberg puts it, "Body culture as
the new paradigm places sport in the context of *culture*" (1989: 49). Although he does not use a cultural framework, Bourdieu provides a more
concrete program for linking sports with their larger context. He states
that "a particular sport cannot be analyzed independently of the whole
of sporting practices . . . one must recognize its position in the space of
sports." Most useful to the analysis of body culture is his argument that
the social scientist can sketch an outline of this "space of sports" by
analyzing "the type of relation to the body that the sport favors or demands." In other words, she should pay attention to the ways in which
particular sports resonate with the tastes of certain social categories
(Bourdieu 1988: 68–69). Through attention to these tastes and disposi-
tions, it is possible to locate the space of sports within the larger universe of practices shaped by forces of supply and demand and socially
assigned meaning (pp. 72–77).

Subsequent chapters show how the history of the body in China reveals the link between sports and body culture as a whole. Continuing
a process begun in the Republican period (1912–49), the communist
body culture replaced a late-Qing (Ch'ing) Dynasty body culture that
maintained ethnic, class, and gender distinctions by dress, hairstyle,
footbinding, exemption from manual labor, participation in rituals, and
other means. In contrast to the Qing body culture, the communist body
culture was more egalitarian and homogeneous, with the working class
and military body culture as its prototypes. Over time, more noticeable
changes in late Qing body culture became common, such as the cutting

of the queue and the abolition of footbinding, but less obvious changes also took place, such as a shift to the international clock and a productivity measured against linear time. There was a move toward a body culture more suited to the needs of industrial manufacture. The sports introduced from the West played a role in these changes because it was impossible to participate in them with bound feet or a long queue, and because most of them were played against a stopwatch.

In the 1980s another transformation got under way. There was a move away from the militaristic communist body culture toward consumer culture. This was expressed in the popular movements of bodybuilding and "old people's disco." These movements took place outside of the state sports system, reflecting an impetus for change that came more from the grassroots level than from the state. State organs also began to loosen their militaristic rules, encouraging less authoritarian coach-athlete relationships and loosening some of the restrictions against the marriage of athletes.

Somatization in Chinese Culture

If we step back a bit, however, in the midst of these changes it is possible to see a rather enduring characteristic of Chinese body culture, a tendency that I call, following the Kleinmans (1985) and Sun Lung-kee (1983), "somatization." This refers to the way in which social tensions are often expressed in a bodily idiom, so that calls for their resolution often center on healing and strengthening the body. Because of this tendency, body culture occupies an important place within Chinese culture as a whole. Since the devastating encounters with Western powers in the last century, Chinese nationalism has been very closely linked with the body, so that the act of individuals strengthening their bodies was linked to the salvation of the nation. In the 1980s, sports victories were said to destroy the insulting label of the "sick man of East Asia," which had gained mythic proportions in peoples' minds. At the time that Western sports were introduced into China, sports were linked with military concerns due to the conditions of Western imperial aggression. This link of sports, the military, and national salvation persisted until recently, reflecting the militaristic nature of communist body culture as a whole. Today, most professional athletes still live closely supervised lives with fixed schedules for sleeping, eating, and training. They also learn marching and slogan shouting. They are not allowed to have sex. Their lives remind us that military discipline has another function: it allows for easier surveillance by state organizations.

Chapter 9 grounds the "somatization" of Chinese culture in practice theory, making the point that somatization emerges out of the patterns of everyday practice. Social tensions are routinely expressed in body symbolism because individual bodies are conceptualized as interlinked; the boundaries between bodies seem fairly permeable. An individual's body is not entirely his or her own but, rather, is subjected to demands and pressures that constantly challenge the notion of individual autonomy. The bodies of athletes belong to the nation in the sense that their bodies represent to the world the health of the Chinese population. The state cultivates them so that they will win glory for the nation. Their bodies also belong to the state, which controls their lives in minute ways, especially in the realm of food. Successful athletes are rewarded with higher food allowances; retired athletes must accustom themselves to less. The act of incorporating the food provided by the state blurs the boundaries between the self and the state. It places athletes in a condition of bodily dependence that makes them feel insecure about food, so that for most of them a constant source of worry is whether they can eat enough to support their training. The families of athletes also have a claim on their bodies. They put athletes under heavy pressure to marry and have a child just at the age when their performances are peaking, so they are torn between their duty to the nation and family. The concern with reproduction leads women to be concerned about affecting their fertility by training during their menstrual periods. Caught in webs of dependency on the state, Chinese athletes focus on food (which is also a part of the dependency on the family). Caught in webs of dependency on family and kin, they focus on the reproductive organs. Diffuse social pressures become focused on specific aspects of physiology—eating, menstruation, and ejaculation—in the process of somatization.

TECHNIQUES OF THE BODY AS SHAPED BY POWER RELATIONS

Discourse and Body Culture

This brings us to the second assumption in my approach to body culture: attention should be paid to the ways in which power relations shape the culture of the body. The main sources of power difference analyzed in this book are the state, class, and gender. The ideas of Foucault prove useful in analyzing these differences. The starting point is Foucault's conception of "discourse." I use discourse as an analytical category which differs from "ideology" (*yishi xingtai*), which I take to refer to what the Chinese themselves recognize as politicized discourses distinguished from everyday speech. Following Manfred Frank's (1992) discussion of Foucault, I understand discourse to refer to the symbolic order that serves as a frame for statements, making it possible for subjects to understand one another because it creates a common understanding of what may and may not be said. Power differences are what shapes this schema, but the shaping process is complex and does not necessarily represent a simple act of censorship on the part of any one group. The concept of discourse reminds us that it is not enough to pay attention only to verbalized expressions: we must look at the expressed, the unexpressed, and the inexpressible. These three categories can be illustrated with examples from later chapters.

The expressed: Statements originating from the state were fairly easy to recognize in 1980s China because the press was rather tightly controlled and generally expressed only state-approved sentiments. Thus, as discussed below, chapter 6 presents a straightforward textual analysis of how official press and Party publications used the words "spiritual civilization" with respect to the body. It also discusses the ways in which educated urbanites used the word "culture" to assert their position over uneducated people. By looking at the way this language was used, it was possible to reveal the power interests that it served.

The unexpressed: The analysis of bodybuilding and disco dancing in chapter 10 makes the point that people generally avoided commenting, especially in a public forum, that the militaristic communist body culture itself was being altered. The State Sports Commission also carefully phrased the approval of the bikini for women's competitions as a case of conforming to international rules. This seemed to be a rather deliberate strategy to avoid censure by the top state leaders.

The inexpressible: In the analysis of gender in chapter 8, I pay attention to the things that could be expressed in English but not in Chinese. I note that "femininity" was generally assessed in a terminology that revolved around social alliance ("it will be hard for her to find a mate") rather than "sexuality" ("do you suppose she prefers women?"). I explain this linguistic difference by noting that the discourse on "sexuality" that Foucault describes for the West, and which has been important in Western sports, is less important in Chinese sports than are considerations of social class, kinship, and marrying up—in other words, an emphasis on social alliance. The state reinforces this emphasis through the birth control policy, which centers on female reproduction. Thus, the Chinese state does not propel the expansion of discourse on "sexuality" in the same way as did the capitalist European states in the eighteenth and nineteenth centuries. The underlying rules of discourse make it possible for Westerners to talk about "sexuality" in a way that is not possible in China because the underlying schema is different.

"Civilization" and "Discipline"

Elias and Foucault also lead us to the ways in which certain symbolic formations accompany an increase in the control of the state over the populace. Elias's concept of the "civilizing process" illuminates the process of state formation in Europe during the sixteenth through the eighteenth centuries. Since its emergence under the absolute monarchs, the discourse on civilization has served to "[sum] up everything in which Western society of the last two or three centuries believes itself superior to earlier societies or 'more primitive' contemporary ones" (1978: 3–4). Elias's work is relevant to contemporary China because the Chinese version of "civilization," *wenming,* is a central moral principle. Like European usages of "civilization," it is used by elites against lower classes. However, unlike Europe during the sixteenth through eighteenth centuries, notions of *wenming* are also strongly promulgated by a modern bureaucratic state.

In the contemporary Chinese state, the discourse on civilization goes hand in hand with the promulgation of techniques of "discipline," of which sports form one type. In Foucault's conception, many of the disciplinary techniques were invented during the expansion of the European nation-states in the eighteenth and nineteenth centuries, when a multitude of minute techniques were invented for exercising a more diffuse, legalistic state power uniformly and at minimum cost (1979: 218–21). This process is relevant to contemporary China because "discipline" (*jilü*) has been an important concept since the founding of the PRC and is currently being promoted by the state in order to shape the potential industrial workforce.

These ideas cannot be transposed wholesale onto contemporary China because, as Elias and Foucault make clear, they are the product of specific cultural and historical trajectories in the West. However, the notions of "civilization" and "discipline" are part of a global discourse that has influenced Chinese culture at the same time that they resonate with Chinese cultural traditions that predated Western imperialism. In contemporary China, "civilization" (*wenming*) is as important as "discipline" (*jilü*) in state discourses about the body, and the state has linked the two principles in new ways in its attempts to shape a modern nation-state. Because these were key principles in the state's effort to train the Chinese body for the 1980s, they were also important in the propaganda surrounding sports.

The way I use the ideas of Elias and Foucault departs somewhat from usual applications. First, I understand them to be describing culturally specific discourses that are useful to a China scholar because of their similarity (but not precise identity) with discourses found in China—a similarity that is at least in part the result of a shared global history. Second, I find that neither Elias nor Foucault, taken alone, describes the workings of Western European state power in a way that completely models the nature of state power in contemporary China. Taken together, however, their discussions of "civilization" and "discipline" complement each other and offer comparative insights into the nature of Chinese state power. I also find that Geertz's (1980) notion of the civilizing center further augments Elias's idea of the civilizing process.

In China as in Europe, "civilization" differed from "discipline" in that it was more clearly a moral judgment emanating from a single elite social class. Western sports were characterized by the harnessing of sports to the cause of nationalism and the establishment of academic disciplines under the rubric of physical culture, *tiyu*. Foucault sometimes uses discipline in the singular and sometimes in the plural. In China, the *discipline* that is imposed on sporting bodies works in tandem with the *disciplines* that study them. This complex of power and knowledge was heavily influenced by the West. However, in Chinese the words for "discipline" are different—*jilü* and *xueke*—but the link between discipline and knowledge is also evident here in that one of the meanings of the character *ji* is "to write down or record" (*A Chinese-English Dictionary* 1986).

The effects of discipline are also evident in the comparison of Qing Grand Sacrifice with the National Sports Games as rituals of state, discussed in chapter 5. In the former case, the rituals emphasized the state hierarchy with the emperor at the top, his chief officials below him, and the invisible masses (who could not even witness the ceremony) below them. All of the officiants were male. In the National Sports Games, the ceremonies are broadcast throughout the nation. Males and females participate equally, and equality is visually represented through the mass calisthenics. At the same time, however, the mass calisthenics represent an equality that is made possible by ordered regimentation and systematic training administered by a centralized bureaucracy. The partiality of this equality is revealed by the presence of leaders of state on the rostrum in the grandstand and the emphasis on their presence in press reports. In the symbols of the National Games, we can see a move away from the social hierarchy and morality that were the essence of Qing civilization toward a construction of the Chinese people as an undifferentiated mass whose main characteristic is their Chineseness. There was a movement away from "civilization" as the focus of the moral order toward something new. While the new morality was labeled "socialist spiritual civilization," a central aspect of it was an emphasis on discipline (jilü). Discipline seemed to refer above all else to a self-restraint that prevented individuals from indulging in acts of violence when they were angry or excited. Thus, the discourse on spiritual civilization reflected an effort by the state to produce "docile bodies."

Chapter 6 describes the disciplinary schedule followed by myself and my teammates during the training camp for the 1986 National College Games. This included military-style roll calls, goose-stepping, slogan shouting, singing, and political study meetings. This discipline was said to aid in the construction of "socialist spiritual civilization." At the same time, it was intimately connected with notions about social class: the emphasis on discipline reflected the general fear that violence would erupt at sports events, a likelihood that is attributed to working-class and peasant athletes and spectators who "have no culture."

The State, Class, and Gender as Sources of Power

The discourse on discipline was not simply generated by a repressive state; the situation was more complex than this. Regional and class differences were also sources of power difference in the discourse on civilization. Beijing, as the capital city, was portrayed as the center of the civilizing process, with the hinterlands learning from its example. Beijing team leaders and athletes took this role seriously. This was seen in the special emphasis on political education for Beijing athletes and in the exhortations reminding them that they must lead the rest of the nation. At the opening ceremonies of the National College Games, Beijing literally leads the other teams into the stadium. At the National Games, the People's Liberation Army leads the way, with Beijing second.

Furthermore, intellectuals engaged in a parallel discourse on "culture" that operated in the same way as the discourse on "civilization" by setting the intellectuals up as examples of self-restraint that should be followed by others, especially unruly workers and peasants. This unofficial discourse was reflected in the concern of better-educated coaches, administrators, and journalists for the low cultural level of athletes, who were said to be predisposed to angry displays and evil habits like smoking and watching pornographic videos.

In China's social hierarchy, athletes stand midway between "mental laborers" and "physical laborers." Sports formed a site of contest between these two groups, with intellectuals trying to assert their anti-physical bias in the dominant culture and sportspeople trying to gain access to the educational system. The success of sportspeople in gaining college admission for athletes was a result of the state's support of sports due to its desire to use sports in the international arena. This contest reveals some of the fault lines that have emerged in the tectonic shifts taking place in Chinese society in the era of reform.

Class also influenced the construction of gender in sports. In the West, sports have played an important role in defining the essential male identity, and women encountered hostility when they entered this "male preserve." In China, women encountered considerably less antagonism because, historically, sports were a lower-class activity and because gender was grounded more in preordained social roles and less in an innate biology. Women in general, and peasant women in particular, were considered good sports prospects because their hard lives prepared them for the "bitterness" of sports training. Sports gave working-class and peasant women athletes a chance to improve their own social status and marry higher-status men than they could have otherwise. This linking of class and gender is another example of the way in which "alliance" is more important than "sexuality" in the construction of gender in Chinese sports.

SPORTS EVENTS AS A PUBLIC DISPLAY OF
THE LEGITIMATE BODY

The third and final aspect of my approach to sport is to recognize that there is something unique about sports compared with other body techniques. Like ritual, dance, and theater, sport is a performance genre with a certain audience appeal, whereas, strictly speaking, things like etiquette, hygiene, and military discipline are not. At the same time that sport can be analyzed along with other everyday body techniques, it occupies a special position because it is one of the most important arenas (sometimes the most important) for the public display of the body. In this kind of analysis, it is important to keep in mind sport's affinity with rituals, festivals, and other public events, as MacAloon (1984) reminds us. Sports practices mediate between the private world of everyday body techniques and the public world of shared performances and, thus, play an important role in the formation of public opinion—and potentially in the political process (Habermas 1992). Sports can be mundane and they can be dramatic; it is this versatility that makes them socially significant and theoretically interesting.

Sport's nature as a public performance makes it a logical tool for regimes and groups that attempt to promulgate new body techniques because they are attempting to effect social change. The behind-the-scene contests over the production of symbols are certainly as important as the finished product. Chapter 4 describes the arguments among choreographers over the type of body that would be displayed in the opening ceremonies of the 1987 National Games—militaristic or artistic? This nonverbal symbolism was juxtaposed against the verbal expressions found in the placard sections. The placard sections, with their political slogans, are particularly subject to contest and had in fact been the focus of a conflict between Deng Xiaoping and Jiang Qing in the past. The debates that precede such public displays reveal the power relations that shape them.

Chapter 3 discusses the many types of public events in which Chinese state and society are brought together face-to-face with athletes playing a mediating role. In publicly staged "congratulatory meetings," athletes returning from recent victories are depicted as both representing the state to the Chinese people and the people to the state. These meetings can be viewed as part of a public culture that was characterized by the use of ritual and symbolism more than by rational-critical debate (Habermas 1974: 51). That sports stars "represented" the nation in international contests, and also often "represented" the people as members of the National People's Congress and other popular organizations, shows a conflation of these two senses of "representation," which are (in theory) perceived to be different in Western democracies.

Chapter 3 also describes a series of incidents that occurred at Beijing University in September through November, 1985, when state leaders and dissident students engaged in a series of moves and countermoves surrounding two important sports victories over Japan in women's volleyball and go. The goal of dissident students was to capture the nationalistic fervor inspired by the teams and direct it toward support of their political position. Thus, the dissident students utilized the "representativeness" of the teams in the same way as the state, never challenging the undemocratic logic underlying the entire public display.

A focus on the sources of public opinion in China forces us to recognize that the state itself is not always a monolithic unity. There is room for maneuver in the cracks between the various bureaucratic systems. For example, the journalist Zhao Yu was able to write and have published a pointed criticism of the Chinese sports system, but he said he did not fear reprisal by the State Sports Commission since he did not live in Beijing and was not a member of the sportsworld. On the contrary, he answered to the literary world.

In another example, the State Sports Commission seemed to promote bodybuilding while the State Council and the Ministry of Culture opposed it, and in the end the other organs had no choice but to allow the Sports Commission to proceed because of the popular support of bodybuilding. A similar case was that of "Old People's Disco," which, since it was not an official sport, was not under the control of the State Sports Commission and, like bodybuilding, arose from popular support. Since people did not describe it as an attack on communist body culture, it was able to slip through the cracks in the Party surveillance system. It finally became an officially legitimate part of body culture when a group of elderly women discoed during the 1987 national telecast of the Spring Festival program.

The debates and conflicts that surrounded such public displays of the body as the National Sports Games, the women's national (bikini-clad) bodybuilding contest, the ceremonies for victorious athletes, and the old people's disco telecast demonstrate the importance of the culture of the body in China. There was a widespread understanding that in order to remake Chinese society one must start by remaking the body. Different groups attempted to shape the body toward their own goals, but in the 1980s the Party maintained a good degree of control over the body techniques that were disseminated. This is why an analysis of the bodily practice of sports can provide important insights into the workings of state power in China and into Chinese society as a whole.

THE IOC: TOWARD ONE WORLD CULTURE
OF BODY TECHNIQUES?

As both everyday practice and as world theater, sports are becoming increasingly widespread around the globe. The Olympic Movement is an unparalleled example of the transnational flow of culture. China rejoined the International Olympic Committee in 1979 after an eleven-year absence due to the unsatisfactory resolution of the "Two China Problem." In 1990 Beijing hosted the Asian Games and in 1993 narrowly lost the right to host the 2000 Olympic Games. The increasing importance of sports within China cannot be considered apart from the increasing international importance of the Olympic Movement.

In 1896, the first modern Olympic Games were held, the culmination of years of effort by Pierre de Coubertin, a French aristocrat and admirer of the British Games ethic (MacAloon 1981). Most of the sports that make up the Olympic Games trace their present form to roots in Northern and Western Europe, especially England. These sports include, for example, soccer, track and field, tennis, boxing, wrestling, and so on. Basketball, baseball, and volleyball were North American inventions intentionally derived from the English model. I call these sports "modern" because their rules moved toward standardization across national boundaries in the second half of the nineteenth century. I use "Olympic sports" to refer to those sports that are or have been on the Olympic program. For the most part, these categories overlap.

The International Olympic Committee (IOC) now has more National Olympic Committee members (nation-states and territories) than any other world organization, including the United Nations (192 and growing). The IOC perceives itself as the leader of the Olympic Movement, which is a movement like many others at the same time that it is one of the greatest ethnological experiments of all time (MacAloon 1981).[6] It has its legendary founder (Coubertin), its heroes and martyrs (Jesse Owens, the Israelis killed in Munich), a well-defined ideology (the Olympic Charter), a propaganda machine (rights to Olympic symbolism, a press), and so on. In its scope, it is perhaps rivaled only by the United Nations and the Roman Catholic Church.

The stated goal of the Olympic Movement is to promote Olympism, a utopian belief that humankind can better itself through sport. An official definition of Olympism was first included in the 1991 Olympic Charter:

> Olympism is a philosophy of life, exalting and combining in a balanced whole the qualities of body, will and mind. Blending sport with culture and education, Olympism seeks to create a way of life based on the joy found in effort, the educational value of good example and respect for universal fundamental ethical principles.

6. In *This Great Symbol*, MacAloon discusses Coubertin's vision of "internationalism," develops a detailed argument for the Olympics as popular ethnography, and reveals links to academic ethnology (see MacAloon 1981: 44–47, 134–36, 217–21, 236–41, 262–69ff.).

The goal of Olympism is to place everywhere sport at the service of the harmonious development of man, with a view to encouraging human dignity. (International Olympic Committee 1991: 7)

A key part of Olympism was Coubertin's concept of "internationalism," by which he meant a respect for each man's (the gender bias is his, of course) country, based on an appreciation of the differences between countries (Coubertin 1967: 20; MacAloon 1981: 189ff.). Coubertin's internationalism, however, has always strained against a homogenizing trend: the Olympic Movement has also been described as "a glorious living demonstration of that hopefully felicitous maxim 'The world is one'" (IOC 1984: 35, quoting Brundage).

The worldwide spread of the Olympic Movement has brought with it a fairly uniform set of techniques of the body. The source of the uniformity is that increasingly they are shaped by the rules of science applied to the momentum, levers, center of gravity, and metabolism of the human body. International journals, congresses, and exchanges facilitate the spread of the sport-scientific worldview. The spread of modern sports can tell us much about the spread of a "modern" body culture, which was in turn made possible by the spread of "modern" science. There is as yet no unified world culture of the body, but there is more unity than there used to be. Whether the spread of sports means that a homogeneous world culture is replacing diverse local cultures can only be answered through detailed study at the level of everyday bodily practice. Thus, the study of the spread of the Olympic Movement can contribute to the debates on the tension between cultural diversity and the world monoculture, tradition and modernity, local and global organizations.

That the study of these important and complex tensions could contribute so much toward reformulating a social science that can keep pace with postmodern society makes it all the more unfortunate that there have been so few fieldwork-based studies of national sport systems—especially non-Western systems—and their place in the global system of international sports (MacAloon 1992). James Riordan's *Sport in Soviet Society* (1977) is the most outstanding exception among non-Western studies. *Training the Body for China* responds at least in part to MacAloon's call for detailed and comparative research on sports that is "historically and ethnographically responsible but also self-conscious that there is nothing necessarily given, natural, or universal (i.e., free of context) about any of its own key terms. And work more devoted to exploring culture rather than simply assuming it or treating it as a servo-mechanism" (1987b: 114).

If the spread of Olympic sports in individual nations serves only the ruling elite, or destroys existing popular culture without adding any-thing useful, then the Olympic Movement's claims for the betterment of humankind should be contested. This book demonstrates that in China sports have been the target of struggles between many different kinds of groups—and the state and elites have not always won. It is easy to demonstrate sport's role in promoting Chinese nationalism and the in-terests of state leaders (women's volleyball victories, the National Games); but there are also many examples of developments in sport in which the Maoist Party orthodoxy was challenged (the glorification of competition and the spread of different forms of the contest), state in-terpretations of sports events were challenged (the student dissident ap-propriation of women's volleyball), the state bureaucratic system was reformed (the implementation of high-level teams in colleges, the use of the contract system on teams), and a practice was popularized against the will of state leaders (the popularization of bodybuilding and legal-ization of the bikini).

On the whole, the Olympic sports better served the interests of the state while popular recreations were a more active forum for social change, but the relationship between the two should not be underesti-mated. And, in the future, the increase in privately funded sports clubs will allow Olympic sports a greater role in social change.

Sport is a part of the utopian striving of humankind because it is a liminal world of "play" that offers an opportunity for controlled experi-mentation with new social structures. A most striking example is the legalization of the bikini for women bodybuilders in 1986: the Chinese government would never have begun by promoting the wearing of biki-nis at pools and on beaches, but bodybuilding offered a controlled realm for its introduction into Chinese society. Sometimes we can watch worldviews unfold in sports that are about to become commonplace in the general society.

As China seeks to "break out of Asia and advance on the world," and to host its first Olympic Games, the rest of the world would be well advised to pay attention.

CHAPTER TWO

Historical Overview

Sports, the Body, and the Nation

I take "sport" to refer to a variety of activities that range outward from an ideal type. The ideal type of sport is found in ball games like soccer and basketball, or in individual contests like boxing and track, which emphasize physical skill and near-total involvement of the body in a contest that is designed to unambiguously separate winners from losers (Lüschen and Sage 1981: 5–6). The ideal type grades into activities that are less clearly "sports" in the Western conception. Chinese martial arts constitute such a gray area because historically they have included a number of activities, some (for example, *leitai*) more sportlike than others (for example, combat skills).

In this book, I speak of sports in China as an identifiable and homogeneous totality. In the West, sports are much more diverse, varying by financial basis (college, club, professional), class, gender, and race. It is possible, however, to lump together Chinese sports in a way that would not be valid for Western sports. The major Olympic sports were introduced into China around the turn of the century by Westerners; hence, Olympic sports as a category are identified as a foreign import. Today, they are labeled "modern physical culture" and contrasted with traditional, popular, and minority physical culture. In addition, they are practiced by state-supported athletes who are recognized as an occupational class, with men and women receiving equal financial support. Sport as an occupation is associated with manual laborers. Some of the Western class associations began to appear under the reforms: soccer hooligans were identified as being working-class, state leaders took up tennis and played on exclusive golf courses that the average Chinese could not afford. Nevertheless, in the 1980s, the class associations of sports were relatively homogeneous.

An ancient proverb is said to characterize Chinese culture even today: "esteem literacy and despise martiality" (*zhong wen qing wu*). Many Chinese people say that sports are identified with the second half of this formula, which explains the historically low social status of sports and sportspeople. Naturally, things in reality have been more complex. Some people admire soldiers and athletes and some do not. If intellectuals express contempt toward *wu*, then it is, in part, an effort to exempt themselves from things physical, especially military training and manual labor. And if people perceive this bias as characterizing Chinese culture as a whole, then it is a measure of the degree to which intellectual ideals dominate public opinion. The long history of intellectual antagonism toward physical exertion is an enduring aspect of the intellectual body culture, which has taken various forms in various epochs.

BODY CULTURE OF THE SCHOLAR-OFFICIAL:
POLO AT THE IMPERIAL COURTS

One example is the role of polo in court life. In ancient times, polo was a popular game at court, reaching its zenith in the Tang (618–906 A.D.). Borrowed from the equestrian nomads of northwest and central Asia, polo in the Tang was played by two teams of sixteen players on horses or donkeys. Dressed in elegant, embroidered jackets, and accompanied by a military band, they hit a leather or wood ball with a stick that had a crescent-shaped tip (Liu 1985: 206–7). The scholars who wrote Chinese histories often confused it with other ball games, leading James T. C. Liu to remark that this reflects "how little their authors knew or cared about athletic games in general" (p. 205).

During the Tang, the game was criticized by the scholar-officials and Taoist clergy because it was dangerous and hurt the "vitality" of the horses and players. Their concern was not unjustified; in the late Tang, polo games were reportedly the pretext for killing an emperor and several generals. During the Five Dynasties period (907–960 A.D.), polo was popular among militarists, who used it to keep their troops fit. In the Khitan empire (947–1125), only aristocrats were allowed to play the game, and officials continued their complaints. An example is the argument presented by a censorial official in 989:

> First, for Your Majesty to compete with subordinates is inappropriate, because when Your Majesty wins they will feel badly and when Your Majesty loses they cannot help but feel happy. Second, during the competition they will fail to observe proper etiquette. And third, if Your Majesty should risk your invaluable well-being for the sake of momentary pleasure, supposing in one chance out of ten-thousand something happens to the bit or the bridle of the horse, what would happen to the state and how would the Empress Dowager feel? (Liu 1985: 210)

The emperor reportedly sighed and commented that the observation was well put, but did not heed the advice. The arguments put forward by the official reveal aspects of the intellectual body culture that seem to have been prevalent in many different time periods. In one short paragraph, he exhibits a concern for appropriate behavior and the observance of social hierarchy, a distaste for failure to observe proper etiquette, a disapproval of seeking momentary pleasure, a fear of physical risks, and a concern for filial piety.

That the scholar-officials considered polo, kick-ball, and other amusements "indulgent and disgraceful" (Liu 1985: 216), while the imperial court continued to enjoy them, reveals a point of conflict between the intellectual body culture and that of the rulers. The rulers' enthusiasm for polo stemmed from their more militaristic orientation. For example, a Jurchen emperor in 1168 countered an official's argument that polo was too dangerous by noting, "Our ancestors conquered the country by military might—should we neglect it in time of peace? . . . [W]e use the game to impress upon the country the significance of the martial arts" (Liu 1985: 214).

Polo fell into disfavor by the Song dynasty (960–1279), and Liu associates this with the political ascendance of the Song scholar-officials, a nonhereditary class of highly educated men (1985: 217). The Song was also headed by Han Chinese, while polo, with its origins among equestrian nomads, seems to have been more popular among the non-Han dynasties. It was briefly revived in the 1160s by an emperor who saw it as a means of military revitalization. A veteran official, however, warned the emperor that drinking, songs, beautiful women, and polo would all interfere with self-cultivation (Liu 1985: 220). By the Southern Song (1127–1279), "the overwhelming majority of scholar-officials paid no attention either to ball games or players" (p. 223). Players were from the army rather than from court circles. Liu concludes that the decline of polo was a result of the transition away from the Tang frontier spirit, ability in the martial arts, and participation in physical exercise toward the genteel, refined, and elegant pursuits of the Song (p. 224). He concludes,

> The non-aristocratic scholar-official class, refined, urbane, and genteel, cared little for the vigorous sports they viewed as inappropriate, pointless, harmful, and even risky. Under their influence, court circles gave up such games as polo. In fact, this negative attitude permeated the culture and persisted until the early twentieth century when modern sports were newly introduced from the West and Japan, as if China had never had them or their equivalents at all. (p. 204)

Though this is an overstatement (other sports were still popular at court and among the populace), it summarizes a trend in Chinese history that reformers have attacked since the turn of the century as the root of the "corrupt, feudal" system that, they believed, disadvantaged China in its encounter with the Western powers. This attack was based on the idea that the historical antagonism toward physical exertion encouraged, even caused, the Chinese people to be physically weak—and because their bodies were weak, their nation was weak. This critique also became a constant theme in Communist Party rejections of the "feudal" body culture and in the construction of an opposing communist body culture.

LATE QING DYNASTY (1840–1911):
LONG GOWNS, QUEUES, AND FOOTBINDING
Changes in Body Culture

Chinese people are still coming to terms with the clash of cultures that characterized the encounter with the West beginning in the nineteenth century. Techniques of the body, including sports, occupied a very important place in that clash. A full history of the body in China's encounter with the West would provide fascinating insights into the very personal and immediate shock that Chinese people felt upon contact with

Westerners. This chapter will only sketch out a few examples as a pre-lude to the discussion of contemporary China.

The treaties that ended the Opium War with Britain in 1842 forced China to open up to the West. This was to have two important repercus-sions with respect to techniques of the body. The first was the emergence of revivalist movements centered on indigenous methods of hand-to-hand combat and meditational exercises. These are the practices known by English speakers as kungfu (in pinyin, *gongfu*). *Gongfu* is the generic word used by at least some of the rebellious sects (see Naquin 1976: 29, 296n. 87). It is a vague word meaning "daily practice" and is not com-monly used by Chinese today; they prefer the rubric of "martial arts," or *wushu,* and I will follow their usage here. The spread throughout the countryside of peasant uprisings, anti-Qing rebellions, and secret socie-ties was associated with the spread of martial arts training in village martial arts halls (*wuguan*). Practitioners trained with traditional weap-ons such as the long spear, the broad sword, and the rake. They also utilized breathing and meditational exercises that traced their roots to the Taoist alchemical and Buddhist meditational traditions. Women as well as men underwent this training and several women became famous for their prowess in battle. Because such movements as the Taiping and Nian Rebellions posed real threats to Qing power, the Qing attempted to suppress martial arts training by outlawing it and executing well-known masters. Their efforts were not successful, however, as the Boxer Rebellion (named for its "boxing" techniques) erupted in 1900–1901, proving disastrous to the Qing court when China had to pay huge in-demnities to the Western powers. The Boxer Rebellion was the last gasp of the martial arts as an effective means of rebellion, but they have re-mained an important part of body culture.

In both the popular rebellions and the subsequent popular concep-tion, the techniques of the body associated with martial arts were con-sidered to be truly Chinese, firmly anchored in ancient Chinese history, and an important means of defining the Han Chinese identity. Most of these techniques are not as ancient as is commonly believed. Of the styles of martial arts practiced today, about 70 percent originated in the Ming (1368–1644) and Qing (1644–1911) (Gu Shiquan 1990: 7). Never-theless, *wushu* methods are believed to continue an ancient, authentic Chinese tradition. Much of this feeling of authenticity derives from the construction of these techniques in opposition to Western techniques of the body.

The second important repercussion of the encounter with the West was the introduction of Western sports through Western-run schools. The reaction of Chinese people to Western physical education reveals the main friction points in the meeting of Chinese and Western cultures of the body.

The first physical education program was instituted in 1875 at the Nanking Military Academy, and other military schools soon followed suit. Military drills directed by German or Japanese instructors constituted the main content of the programs until 1922, when sports became the predominant activity (Kolatch 1972: 4). In 1890, the first modern sports event, a track and field meet, was held at St. John's University in Shanghai. In 1912, the first Boy Scout troop was established, along with its regimented practices. Military discipline and sports formed the two main Western influences on body techniques.

Both kinds of physical education entailed a culture of the body that was directly counter to the dominant Qing culture of the body, which was shaped by intellectual ideals. In the late Qing, dress was an important signifier of social class. Men of high status wore long gowns with long sleeves that covered the hands; this publicly demonstrated that they did not do manual labor, because the gowns would have been too restrictive. Men of the working class wore a short jacket—with sleeves that exposed the hands—over pants (see Strand 1989: 35, 50; Yeh Wen-Hsin 1990: 222–26). The long gown so vividly crystallized the ethos of the scholar-official class that they were sometimes called the "long-gown class" (*changshan jieji*). The contempt with which scholars regarded the Western suit is captured in the feelings of a former Mandarin at the beginning of the Republican period, described in a novel by Lin Yutang:

> Being used all his life to the generous, flowing lines of a Chinese gown, which gave one a leisurely, majestic gate, he conceived with horror a picture of himself wearing pants in public. It was the wearing of pants by foreign gentlemen that made them walk so fast and in so undignified a fashion like laborers and that caused them to be known as "straight-long-legs." (1939: 363)

In his 1917 article, "A Study of Physical Culture," Mao noted that one reason men did not like to exercise was that people respected and admired a flowing gown and leisurely movements so that a man was embarrassed to appear without his gown or to show his hands and feet in public. He therefore had no choice but to exercise within the privacy of his own room (Mao Zedong 1917: 7).

When Chinese students first took up sports at the missionary schools, they wore their long gowns. In 1911, Edward Alsworth Ross, a professor of sociology at the University of Wisconsin, took a six-month tour of China and then wrote a book on *The Changing Chinese*. Ross's book reveals his enthusiasm for the "manliness" that he believed was expressed in Western sports and his contempt for the "effeminate" Chinese intellectual. He describes a scene in which "lissome young men with queues were skipping about the tennis courts, but they wore their hampering gowns and their strokes had the snap of a kitten playing with a ball of yarn" (Ross 1911: 339). Around 1914, Eugene Barnett, director of the Hangzhou YMCA, wrote, "The spectacle of mandarins, department chiefs, and clerks, tearing in scanty attire after a basket or volley ball over the yamen law [*sic*], persuades me that Old China is passing away" (1990: 89).

In the scholar-official view of the world, sports were an activity for the lower classes. To have high status meant to have the authority to command others to perform labor in one's place. This attitude is illustrated by a story that became popular as an example of "the corruption of the feudal dynasty and the absurdity of the ignorance of the officials" (Wang Zhenya 1987: 15):

> At the end of the Qing, in the English consulate in Tianjin, there was a consul who once invited the highest official in the Tianjin administration—the Daotai—to dinner. After the meal, the consul wanted to play tennis to show his guest. This Daotai had never in his life seen tennis, and he was very curious, responding with enthusiasm. It happened to be a time of scorching hot weather, and although the players were wearing shorts and singlets, they were still streaming with sweat. After the demonstration, the consul asked his guest: "How do you think I played?" This Daotai shook his thumb back and forth and said: "Good! Good! Good! It's a pity that you worked so hard; you are so tired that your whole body is covered with sweat. It would be much better if you could hire a man to come play in your place."

This story is also alluded to by James Webster, a professor at Shanghai College (1923: 207), and by Ross (1911: 337–38), which illustrates how Western critiques of China intertwined with Chinese critiques of themselves. If the story is true, it is hard to conceive of the Daotai relating it to others; the source is more likely to have been the English consul, whose version would have spread through the foreign community where it would have been picked up by Chinese and used to critique their own culture.

Another extremely important cultural marker was the queue, which had been required of all men by imperial decree since the Manchu takeover (the original decree in 1645 was so ill-received that it provoked angry Han to renew their fighting against the Manchu) (Spence 1990: 38–39). This hairstyle consisted of shaving the front of the head and braiding the remaining hair into one or several braids. Like the long gowns of the scholars, the queue became an important sign of identity. In the midst of uprisings, rebels could be distinguished from loyalists according to whether they had cut their queues or not. And like the scholar's gown, the queue embodied an entire worldview in the restrictions on behavior that it entailed. Although the braid could be coiled up on top of the head or at the back of the neck, it was still inconvenient. An anecdote from the early history of sports illustrates this point. I cannot tell the story any better than Wang Zhenya does, based on his own recollections, so I will translate his words here:

> In the [soccer] competitions of that time, there is an episode that there is no harm in telling: In the first few competitions between St. John's University and Nanyang University, it was still in the last years of the Qing, and students wore four braids. They were very inconvenient while kicking the ball, fleeing and pursuing, and so they coiled up their braids on top of their heads. Because they were running energetically, the braids would open up, and at that moment it would not be easy to recoil them; they could only leave them hanging loose and dance madly into the wind, at which the spectators roared with laughter. When the ballplayers were each trying to steal the ball, the braids would open up and whip the opponent's face, to the point that he could only stop and rub his eyes, whereupon the player would quickly take advantage of the moment to dribble the ball forward. It's no wonder that at that time, some spectators wisecracked: "They ought to count whipping the opponent in the face with the queue as a foul, otherwise it's too unfair." (1987: 46–47)

This story illustrates how sports vividly and publicly demonstrate body techniques. The incompatibility of the queue with modern sports must have been evident for all of the spectators present, and in this context, at least, they were suddenly forced to perceive this long-established symbol as patently absurd.

The National Games, Queues, and Footbinding

The "National Games" played an important role in the transformation of perceptions of the body that occurred under Western influence. The first two Games, in 1910 and 1914, were organized mainly by the YMCA. The first Games in Nanjing attracted over forty thousand spectators on five days of competition; the second Games in Beijing attracted over twenty thousand spectators in two days (Wang Zhenya 1987: 131–39). Certainly, the huge numbers of spectators must have been due partly to the novelty of the performances to most Chinese.

The format of the sports meet quickly made its way into public life. Jeffrey Wasserstrom notes that practices common at sports meets, such as parading behind school flags, lining up behind the flags in the infield of the sports ground to listen to speeches, raising the national flag and playing the anthem, and swearing oaths, all entered the repertoire of protest tactics used by students in the May Fourth Movement of 1919 in Shanghai (Wasserstrom 1991: 78). In addition, sports teams and other extracurricular associations provided organizational models for the formation of student movements (p. 131). One of Wasserstrom's informants told him that in the December 9th Movement of 1935, the Fudan Volleyball team formed a marching brigade (p. 142). Such tactics remain important in student political life today: it is no coincidence that the main recreation field at Beijing University is named the "May Fourth Sports Field," after the seminal May Fourth student movement of 1919.

At the first National Games, another queue story made its way into the history books. High jumper Sun Baoxin missed twice because the queue coiled up on the back of his neck knocked off the bar even though his body had cleared it. The official, who was a Westerner, yelled out, "Cut it off at once!" and many of the athletes on the field echoed him. According to Wang's interpretation of newspaper accounts, "In that moment, people's hearts became indignant, their revolutionary spirit welled up, and they longed to eradicate the customs that the Qing imperial court forcefully imposed on people" (Wang Zhenya 1987: 136). According to other sources, Sun went home, cut off his queue and returned the next day to win the finals with a jump of 5' 5¼" (Kolatch 1972: 12–13). Though Wang's account is clearly trying to make a revolutionary point, it does not seem unreasonable to assume that Sun's predicament aroused emotions by dramatizing the impracticality of the queue and, implicitly, the obsolete state that prescribed it.

As in the realm of sports, the queue posed problems in the Western-style military schools as well—indicating a common underlying logic in these distinct but related realms of body techniques. Spence notes that the long queue "looked ridiculous in modern combat situations. Soldiers who had first tucked their queues under their caps soon began to cut them off." By 1910, the Manchu court had no choice but to acquiesce (1990: 256).

For women, bound feet constituted the major obstacle to participation in sports. In the 1890s, reform-minded intellectuals began to argue against footbinding. Again, it was exposure to the West that began to present this millennium-old custom in a new light. The leaders of the movement argued that one reason for the superior strength of the Western powers was that since their women did not bind their feet and practiced calisthenics they produced stronger offspring. Qiu Jin, a female revolutionary martyr who became legendary after her death, had bound feet (she was born in 1875) but began to model herself after traditional male military heroes during her studies in Japan. She became an advocate of physical education for women, establishing a gymnasium at the Datong Normal School in Shaoxing and ordering the girls to practice military drills—which was regarded as scandalous by local merchants and gentry (Rankin 1975: 59).

Because of the prevalence of footbinding and the small number of girls who attended schools (Chinese or missionary), and because at that time sports in China were organized by Westerners with similar (though perhaps not as extreme) attitudes, Chinese women did not participate in sports in significant numbers until the late 1920s. Part of the impetus for their growing participation seems to have come from abroad. The

Table 2.1 First Sports for Women in Olympic, Far East, and Chinese National Games

Event	Olympics	Far East	National Games
first sport	*1900**	*1923†	*1924‡
swimming	1912	*1930	1933
track and field	1928	*1930	1930

*exhibition events, not part of official program
**tennis and golf
†volleyball and tennis
‡basketball, softball, and "team ball" (a form of volleyball). Wang Zhenya notes that the meet organizers were very careless in reporting the women's results (1987: 146). Another history fails to record any women's events until the next games in 1930 (Renmin tiyu chubanshe 1985).

Olympic Games included exhibition events for women in tennis and golf as early as 1900. The Far East Sports Games (China, Japan, and the Philippines) first included exhibition events in 1923. Table 2.1 compares the Olympic, Far East, and Chinese National Games with respect to the years in which they first included any sport for women, followed by the two major sports of swimming and track and field.

Unfortunately, Chinese histories of sports do not devote much space to the topic, so the history of the impact of the West on female techniques of the body is still sketchy.

Social Darwinism and the National Body Politic

These changes in body culture occurred in the context of heated intellectual debates about the nature of the Chinese nation and nationalism, in which conceptions of the body occupied a central role. In the 1870s and 1880s, the "Pure View" school was influential at court and among the literati. Benjamin Schwartz describes this school as ultraconservative and belligerent toward the West—a type of "muscular Confucianism." It valorized the martial virtues of the legendary hero Yue Fei and claimed that the martial spirit was sufficient to drive out the Western barbarians without the aid of technology (Schwartz 1964: 15–16). Thus, this school held beliefs about the connection between martial valor and national strength which, as we will see, continued to be an important theme in nationalist discourse for many decades. The notable characteristic of this view was that the focus was on the cultivation of a martial *spirit* more than on the cultivation of a strong body.

It was not until social Darwinism was introduced into China that the relationship between body and nation was conceived of in a new way. The key figure in this development was Yan Fu, who translated Thomas Huxley's *Evolution and Ethics* and Herbert Spencer's *Principles of Sociology* into Chinese at the turn of the century. In Spencer's work, Yan Fu encountered the image of the nation as a biological organism struggling for survival among other like organisms. In his key 1898 article on "The Source of Strength" (*Yuan qiang*), Yan Fu explained this new image of the nation:

> A nation is like a body (*shen*); the arteries and veins are linked together, the system of organs (*guanti*) helps each other. When the head is attacked, all four limbs respond; when the belly is stabbed, the whole body (*ti*) will perish. (Yan Fu 1959: 18)

He argued that the Chinese sense of nationalism consisted mainly of loyalty to the emperor. Because individuals did not identify national interest with self-interest, they failed to realize that an attack on one part of the nation affected the whole nation (Schwartz 1964: 70–71). Schwartz argues that the analogy between the social and biological organism was new to Yan Fu (1964: 57–58). He notes that in the West the analogy goes back to the ancient Greeks, but it is not clearly evident in the Chinese literature. The classical Chinese tendency was to conceive of the body as a state rather than the state as a body. In Taoist and medical traditions, the human body was often portrayed as organized like a state, with departments and bureaus. This metaphor indicated a concern with nourishing the life of the individual rather than ordering the state (p. 255n. 30). Schwartz concludes that "Spencer's biological metaphor, particularly within its Darwinian framework, strikes Yan Fu with all the force of a blinding revelation" (p. 58).

Yan Fu and the other leaders of the Constitutional Reform Movement of 1898—Kang Youwei and Liang Qichao—frequently used the body as a metaphor. A key word in the vocabulary of the reformers was *guoti*, "the national system," which could also be translated as "the national body."

Another key concept was the Pure View school idea of *ti-yong* ("substance-application"), an abbreviation for the idea that "Chinese learning should remain the essence, but Western learning be used for practical development" (Spence 1990: 225). The phrase *ti-yong* was slightly recast by Kang Youwei to express the social Darwinist position. He sometimes used it in a way that is best translated as "body-action." Thus, his student Liang Qichao quoted him as saying, "Take the group as your body and take change as your action" (*yi qun wei ti, yi bian wei yong*). This reflected the social Darwinist position that the group is the basic unit in the competition for survival, and change (or adaptation) is its means of ensuring survival (Pusey 1983: 107–8).

Spencer had discussed the three types of energy necessary for social survival: physical, intellectual, and moral. Translating these into Chinese, Yan Fu advocated the cultivation of *minli, minzhi,* and *minde*.[1]

---

1. Similarly, Coubertin (following his own idiosyncratic interpretation of the ideas of Thomas Arnold at Rugby) advocated "moral development, athletics, and social education." MacAloon argues that Coubertin was not, however, a social Darwinist (1981: 298n. 172). Drawing on this history, the passage from the Olympic Charter quoted in chapter 1 extols the qualities of "body, will, and mind."

However, he was vague on the subject of how to cultivate the "people's physical strength" and had much more to say about intellect and morals. In "The Source of Strength," he urged the abolition of opium and footbinding. He also urged a change in attitudes toward physical fitness, comparing China to an idle man unused to labor, whose death is hastened when he is suddenly forced to exercise. He advocated physical education for women "for if the mother is healthy, then the children will be fat" (*gai mu jian erhou er fei*) (Yan Fu 1959: 27). Kang Youwei and Liang Qichao advocated the same limited measures.

Liang Qichao believed that expectant mothers who exercised could actually strengthen their children while they were still in the womb. He wrote, "All countries that wish to have strong soldiers insure that all their women engage in calisthenics, for they believe that only thus will the sons they bear be full in body and strong of muscle" (Pusey 1983: 102). He opposed early marriage, believing that sexual excess at a young age weakened the seed and led to the degeneration of descendants (p. 213).

The development of physical education in Europe was inseparable from the rise of modern nationalism after the French Revolution (Eichberg 1973: 63). Physical education as a way of linking individual bodies to the welfare of the nation is a historically recent phenomenon and must be viewed as one of the disciplinary techniques that developed with the rise of the nation-state. In China, it developed alongside efforts to turn a dynastic realm into a modern nation-state according to the political ideas of the times.

Once this strain of thought entered the Chinese intellectual milieu, it quickly spread with multiple repercussions for body culture in China. But it is interesting to look at this idea at its inception, because it is clear that while the idea appealed to Yan Fu and the other reformers, they were somewhat at a loss when it came to advocating concrete techniques for linking the body and the nation. The rationalized science of physical education was necessary to complete this link. By looking at the thinking of Kang Youwei, Yan Fu, and Liang Qichao, we can identify a point of transition in ways of thinking about the body and the nation, which eventually led to the well-developed disciplines of the body under communism. In the end, Spencer's conception of a tripartite physical, intellectual, and moral education became central in the communist conception of the role of education in the formation of the socialist person. Sometimes a fourth term, "aesthetic education" (*mei*) is added. In courses on educational theory, Chinese students are taught to rattle off "de-zhi-ti (mei)" (moral, intellectual, physical, aesthetic) as the guiding principles of socialist education. In the beginning, however, Yan Fu used a different vocabulary from that later developed by the Communists. His focus was not so much on the body (ti) as on "strength" (li, tili) and "the people's strength" (minli). His notion of physical exercise was derived from Taoist concepts of physiology: in "The Source of Strength," he argues not for the training of the body, but rather of the "blood-qi-body-strength" (xueqitili) (Yan Fu 1959: 17) and the "body-qi" (tiqi) (p. 27). He calls for "training the people's muscles-bones, rousing the people's blood-qi" (lian min jinhai, gu min xueqi) (p. 27). When the annotated version of "The Source of Strength" was reprinted in 1959, the editor felt compelled to provide a newer word for "body" (tipo, "physique") as a gloss for Yan Fu's by-then obsolete word xinghai (literally, "form and bones") (p. 45). Yan Fu's references to fragmented body parts contrast markedly with the vocabulary of the much more unitary ti that came to dominate later discussions of physical education.

The constitutional reformers were only beginning to grasp a different conception of the body politic. That they did not move far beyond the old conception is especially well illustrated by Liang Qichao's 1916 article on "China's Bushido" (Liang Qichao 1959). This would have been the perfect place for him to discuss the importance of training the body. In it, he argued that the equivalent of the Japanese "way of the warrior" (bushido) was present in ancient China, but that it disappeared during the Western Han dynasty. He called for a return to the ancient martial spirit in order to save China. Although he was very much concerned with strength and weakness, he mentioned the body only in passing and was much more interested in the spirit. Eighteen years after Yan Fu's "The Source of Strength," Liang is still using classical phrases for the body such as "blood-flesh" (xuerou) (p. 44) and "blood-qi" (xueqi) (p. 47). On the whole, however, his vocabulary is slightly different from Yan Fu's: he uses shen and ti in several places, and he also uses tipo ("physique") once (p. 47). "China's Bushido" is essentially an essay on willingness to die for one's country and friends. As James Pusey notes, "he wanted to change attitudes and behavior more than he wanted to change skin and bones" (Pusey 1983: 304). The essay demonstrates that, ultimately, Liang perhaps did not comprehend and certainly did not subscribe to the conceptions of body and nation that had been prevalent in Europe for a century. There, beginning in the late eighteenth century, national physical education programs were designed, popular political movements revolving around rationalized physical training became powerful (for example, the Turners, the Sokols), and the modern Olympic Games were established.

THE REPUBLICAN PERIOD (1912–1948):
BUILDING A STRONG NATION

The 1920s saw the founding of the Chinese Communist Party and an increasing criticism of the Western presence in China by both Nationalists and Communists. Sports came to be particularly identified with the culture of the treaty-port bourgeoisie (Yeh Wen-Hsin 1990: 215), who were viewed as unscrupulous Chinese-Western hybrids. Sports meets also came under attack. For example, in 1925, as part of the broader effort to take back control of the educational system, Nanyang, Southeastern, and Fudan Universities boycotted the annual "Eight University Meet" because the other five schools were Christian missionary schools. By the late 1920s, sports meets were conducted in Chinese rather than English and were increasingly organized by Chinese themselves (Renmin tiyu chubanshe 1985: 107–8).

Communist revolutionaries criticized Western and Nationalist-organized sports for their "medals-and-trophyism" (jinbiaozhuyi). For example, Yun Daiying attacked missionary schools because "sometimes they also particularly cultivate several selected athletes, specially nourishing them with cookies made with milk, so that at sports meets or soccer games they will be a good advertisement for their school" (Yun Daiying 1925, quoted in Renmin tiyu chubanshe 1985: 107). Yun and others attacked the practice of collecting an athletic fee from all students to support the training of a few talented athletes while the average student had few sports opportunities. They argued that some of these athletes were virtually professionals. These critiques did not prevent the Communists from utilizing sports to serve their cause in the revolutionary bases. Sports were recognized as a tool for recruiting young people into the party and a way of improving soldiers' fitness and morale. Also, in the Communist-controlled areas, sports meets seem to have been the most popular means for celebrating significant occasions such as Women's Day, Labor Day, Youth Day, and Army Day.

In fact, in the missionary schools there were athletes who supported themselves with the rewards they received. The personal history told to me by an older sports cadre is a case in point. He was born in 1925. His father and mother were unable to raise him on the money they earned from odd jobs like washing clothes. Since his studies and sports were good, he entered a missionary middle school in Tianjin. The headmaster was Chinese, but the assistant headmaster and a few teachers were American. They believed in "material incentives." He could afford to go to school because he won awards for placing near the top in the annual city track and field competition. First place was four bags of flour—because of rampant inflation, money lost value very quickly, so prizes were given in cloth and flour. He put himself and his younger sister through school with his winnings.

To put things in perspective, however, it should be pointed out that these excesses were nothing like those found in the contemporary United States. Most schools had extremely scarce resources, and the total number of specialist athletes in the country was extremely small. Another sports cadre, Guan Yushan, born in 1908, attended Luhe Christian High School outside of Beijing and then Yanjing University. He told me (in English), "Before Liberation, all athletes were students. They never received any money; the school had no money. It was very difficult even to provide the uniform. But certain famous schools who wanted to be number one, the principal would give a sum of money to buy team members eggs and milk before the meet, shoes, and a shirt. Not even a pullover. There was not even one professional team." He noted that, except in small circles, sports were not appreciated. "You can't generalize about parents. If the parents were athletes, they encouraged their children to participate. My father encouraged me." However, many people thought sports were "just play." "People despised athletic teachers and looked down on them, because many students couldn't pass chemistry or even social sciences, but they could pass the physical education exam. Most parents didn't think sports required brains, just muscle. Also they didn't want to pay for spikes, boats, etc." He also noted that many college students looked down on athletes. There were two reasons: "They were just players in the bad sense of it. They didn't study hard and weren't wise enough to get good grades." And: "The athletes themselves didn't behave properly. They smoked, they bullied others because they were strong. In some universities it was different. It all depended on the athletes themselves—if she or he was good in other things, then she or he was respected, not because he was an athlete."

The communist criticism of "medals-and-trophyism" in sports continued into the Cultural Revolution era, when it was used to denounce sportspeople within the communist system. In the late 1980s, people again began to criticize the practice of lavishing special rewards on athletes, though they did not revive the by now discredited phrase of "medals-and-trophyism." The long life of this critique was nourished, in my opinion, by the Chinese discomfort with the idea of rewarding people for their physical prowess, a notion which goes against a long-standing pattern in the Chinese moral order.

Building on the YMCA tradition, the Republican government continued to use sports in its efforts to create a modern nation-state. The third "National Games," held in Wuchang, Hubei, in 1924, were the first organized exclusively by the Chinese. Their scale was unprecedented, and they included opening ceremonies with a cannon salute from a nearby naval base and an aviation show. Between forty and fifty thousand spectators attended each day for three days. These were the first Games to include women in three exhibition events (Wang Zhenya 1987: 140–47). In the fourth Games, in 1930, four sports for women were incorporated into the regular program. In the fifth Games, in 1933, there were seven regular sports compared with ten for men, numbers which stayed constant through the sixth Games in 1935 and the seventh Games in 1948. Thus, over time the Games dramatized the changes in women's status up to a point of stasis.

In 1935, Eugene Barnett was impressed by the changes in attitudes toward women manifest in their participation in the sixth National Games. After observing the Games he wrote,

> No single feature of the opening parade, or of the contests which followed, was more symbolic of the social revolution which has taken place in China than the presence of the girl athletes, dressed, some in bloomers, some in slacks, and some in shorts. For these girls to travel distances requiring weeks of time (as was necessary for those coming from such places as Yunnan, Szechuan, and Sinkiang [Xinjiang]), and for them to compete before spectators numbering tens of thousands, is a far cry from the bound feet and the accepted seclusion which prevailed among women and girls less than a generation ago. (Barnett 1990: 248)

We can get a good idea of the kind of body culture that was being promoted through the National Games by looking at the list of "Ten Dos and Don'ts of Physiology and Hygiene" that was distributed to athletes at the fifth Games in 1933 (Wang Zhenya 1987: 160):

1. Don't get up late and go to bed late; get up early and go to bed early and have a set time.
2. Don't be greedy for gourmet food (*tantu koufu*); eat less and chew more.

3. Don't be sometimes diligent and sometimes lazy; don't let up before the end.
4. Don't be afraid of difficulty; be undaunted by repeated setbacks.
5. Don't be reluctant to fight for victory, make a genuine effort (*gongfu*), have an honest skill.
6. Don't suddenly make haste; gradually measure your strength.
7. Don't drink wine and smoke cigarettes; don't seek fame and wealth.
8. Don't lust after women and give in to carnal desires (*haose zongyu*); be tranquil.
9. Don't be greedy for money and fine goods, be honest.
10. Don't scheme to break the rules and win by a fluke; be respectful of sporting ethics and competition rules.

This list demonstrates that meet organizers considered the promotion of body techniques alone to be insufficient and that they attempted to link them to moral principles. These organizing moral principles are the essence of body culture because they generate and structure body techniques. The wording of these prescriptions for the 1933 Games indicates the multiple influences of Christianity, Buddhism, and the British games ethic on body techniques in China at that time.

In addition to these periodic national events, the Nationalists also attempted to spread the influence of physical education by instituting programs in all schools. Martin Yang's account of the way in which he was influenced by his physical education class as a child in the 1930s illustrates the effects of such programs on children's bodily habits. He noted that the physical education program in his school in Taitou, Shandong, consisted mostly of military drills like goose-stepping, marching, and saluting. The teachers addressed them with speeches that promoted nationalism and encouraged them to become strong so that they could defend and avenge their nation. Yang notes, "The education inspired [him] so much that he secretly decided to act as a soldier all the time. He began to sit and stand with great erectness of carriage and to walk to school with a marching step" (1945: 224–25).

Wushu and *Tiyu:* National Essence versus New Culture

At the same time that Western sports were being promoted in the schools and through the National Games, the martial arts were undergoing a transformation and revival. These two trends continued the dual pattern in body culture that had begun with extensive Western contact. The earliest expression of this duality had been the outbreak of the Boxer Rebellion, with its roots in martial arts and meditation, in the same time frame as the introduction of Western military training and sports. A decade after the Eight Powers subdued the Boxer Rebellion, there was a revival of the martial arts, or "knight errant" novel (*wuxia xiaoshuo*). James J. Y. Liu believes that the martial arts novel and nationalism developed side-by-side because China was a weakened nation faced by foreign powers with superior military strength. The heroes of the novels appealed to the Chinese imagination because they defeated modern weapons with traditional physical skills (Liu 1967: 135). An important figure in the revival of the martial arts was the novelist and physical educator Xiang Kairan, who wrote under the pseudonym of the "Unworthy Man of Pingjiang" (*pingjiang bu xiao sheng*). Born in 1890, he was a rarity in China—a man talented in both *wen* and *wu* (Ye Hongsheng 1985: 83). He became active in organizing martial arts competitions in his native Hunan. He also became the premier writer of martial arts novels, and his *Lives of Chivalrous and Altruistic Heroes* (*Xiayi yingxiong zhuan*) is perhaps the best of the genre (Liu 1967: 135).

The dual trend in body culture was one element in a more general cultural conflict that began to crystalize around 1915 with the beginning of the New Culture Movement. This was an intellectual movement against traditional Confucian culture. Its leaders advocated the use of vernacular instead of classical Chinese in literature, critiqued the classics, denounced Confucian ethics and superstition, and urged the people to accept Western science and democracy. In attempting to forge a new kind of national identity, they polarized Chinese and Western culture and called for the wholesale rejection of moribund Chinese traditions. The New Culture Movement was opposed by the National Essence School, which was dedicated to preserving the traditional Chinese culture exemplified in the Confucian classics. This debate extended to sports, and by this time intellectuals had much more to say about the link between the body and the nation than had been said fifteen years earlier by the constitutional reformers.

Around 1918, the "New Martial Arts" (*xin wushu*) were developed by Ma Liang, a commander under the Northern Warlords, who opposed Western sports. They included boxing and kicking, wrestling, cudgel, and sword skills (Renmin tiyu chubanshe 1985: 79). The government promoted the New Martial Arts among the troops and in the schools under their control, hailing them as "national essence physical culture" (*guocui tiyu*). They were said to promote traditional martial virtue and valor, and their association with nationalism was evident in Ma Liang's claim that among all the nations of the world, no martial artists could surpass the Chinese. National Essence proponents argued that foreign training methods had no effect on Chinese bodies (Renmin tiyu chubanshe 1985: 79–80).

The National Essence School was countered by proponents of the New Culture Movement such as the important author Lu Xun, who wrote an essay against the New Martial Arts. He argued that he was not opposed to Chinese martial arts *per se*, but that he opposed the way educators picked them up as the latest fad. Further, he stated that the feudal superstitions that were promoted along with the martial arts were downright dangerous (Lu Xun 1973, quoted in Renmin tiyu chubanshe 1985: 79).

Mao Zedong and the New Culture Movement attacked the technique of quiet meditation (*jingzuo, jinggong*), which was also promoted as national essence physical culture. In contrast to the more militaristic and popular martial arts, quiet meditation emerged out of the elite tradition of tranquil study among the Confucian scholar-officials, combined with Taoist life-cultivation practices and Buddhist meditation techniques (Miura 1989: 334). In his 1917 article, Mao argued that quiet meditation was not an effective means of physical training, and he attacked the view of its advocates that vigorous movement could damage the health (Mao Zedong 1917). Quiet meditation was also opposed by the New Culture Movement because it instilled passivity—a characteristic of the corrupt feudal society that was said to be responsible for the current chaos (Renmin tiyu chubanshe 1985: 80–81). By the 1920s, quiet meditation appears to have disappeared from public debate. It was eclipsed by an emphasis on the martial arts.

Ten years after the establishment of the Republic, a "martial arts revival period" occurred in which the martial arts were again linked to nationalist revival, though in a very different way from the earlier millenarian rebellions. This difference exemplifies the unique ways in which body techniques are utilized by a modern state. The martial arts (*wushu*) were renamed the "national arts" (*guoshu*) and reshaped to fit the Western model of sports. A national meet was held in 1923 and men's martial arts were included in all of the National Games beginning with the third Games in 1924; women's martial arts were included in the fifth and subsequent Games. The National Martial Arts Hall was established in 1928, and national tests were held in 1928 and 1933. In brief, the martial arts were categorized, bureaucratized, scheduled into mass displays, and stamped with an official ideology that explicitly linked them with Republican nationalism.

However, the difficulties in making martial arts into a sport illustrate the fundamental differences between the indigenous (*tu*) skills and Western (*yang*) sports. The first National Test consisted of sparring matches. Participants registered and then drew lots to determine the order. The winner of two out of three bouts was the victor, and an elimination series determined the final rankings. There were no restrictions on the blows that could be struck with hand or foot, with points awarded for blows landed and knockdowns. The fighters wore metal-screen face protectors. Except for the face protectors and the point system, this structure was very similar to the traditional *leitai* ("platform fighting") competitions that had been a popular folk entertainment for many centuries. The test also stimulated the same kinds of traditional rivalries between martial arts schools, provoking heated animosity. Because the rules and safety measures were inadequate, there were many serious injuries, including broken bones, knockouts, and gouged eyes (Renmin tiyu chubanshe 1985: 131; Wang Zhenya 1987: 117). The second National Test included other tests and divided the sparring into different types, but the same problems cropped up in the sparring tests. In the preliminary rounds of the fist (*quanshu*) division alone, over sixty people were injured; in the weapons divisions the injuries were even more serious, but a clampdown on the press prevented their documentation (Wang Zhenya 1987: 117). In the end, sparring was never successfully "sportized." As one history book notes, "In regard to sparring, it cannot be said that it was successful as a competitive sporting event. Either accidental injuries occurred, or actual abilities were not fully expressed" (Renmin tiyu chubanshe 1985: 132). Eventually, sparring was abandoned in competitions and the individual performance of the "forms" (*tao*) was judged on a ten-point scale, as in gymnastics.

The problems in fitting the indigenous body techniques into the Western model demonstrate that a different fundamental logic underlay the two types of sport. The martial arts developed primarily as an art of using the most efficient means to kill and injure. Western sports, on the other hand, were not oriented toward killing and prohibited the most efficient means. In boxing, for example, the use of the feet and striking vulnerable parts of the body are not allowed. The difference in the two types of sports, as body techniques and as public performances, embodied the world of difference between Chinese and Western cultural traditions.

Even with the "sportization" of martial arts, the debate over martial arts as opposed to Western sports as a way of strengthening China was not resolved. In the 1930s, the conflict between those who supported each type of training intensified again. As in other areas of culture, this conflict was labeled the "conflict between the indigenous and the foreign" (*tu yang zhi zheng*). The traditionalists consisted of members of the national *guoshu* association and some journalists, while the reformers consisted of Chinese students returned from studying overseas (Xie Lingzheng 1988: 7). In his speech marking the establishment of the National Martial Arts Hall, Zhang Zhijiang argued,

> If we want to quickly train our skills, *guoshu* is the path to start upon . . . Only with a strong body, a strong race, a strong nation will our national spirit develop and expand, and only then will there be hope for world peace. (Xie Lingzheng 1988: 6)

Reformers countered heatedly,

> In cultivating the skills of running, jumping, scrambling, and climbing, indigenous physical culture is completely ineffective. (Wu Wenrui 1932, quoted in Xie Lingzheng 1988: 7)

And again,

> Our nation to this day still has a serious habit of exaggeration, posing as the best in the world at everything, as if our ancestors from the past few thousand years have hogged all of the limelight; even though we unfilial descendants have been like dead dogs after three generations of heroes, we still feel proud. This so-called enriching of our great store of knowledge is nothing more than systematizing a pile of trash. (Xie Siyan 1932, quoted in Xie Lingzheng 1988: 7)

The martial arts survived these attacks and still occupy an important place in Han Chinese identity, as well as in the world's perception of China. Highly stylized forms are practiced by state-supported athletes, who after retirement often star in the ever-popular kungfu films. The promotion of martial arts worldwide and their eventual inclusion in the Olympic Games are an important item on China's international sports agenda. Thus, the martial arts have been incorporated into the sports system along with Western sports.

Unlike the martial arts, quiet sitting was never incorporated into the state sports system. Instead, it seems to have developed into what is now called *qigong* (though it should be emphasized that the classification and historical reconstruction of "indigenous physical culture" is today constantly in flux and is heatedly contested). The first use of the word *qigong* in its current sense is not documented until 1934 (Miura 1989: 343). Over time, and perhaps as a result of the New Culture Movement critiques, more active movements were added (p. 334). By the 1950s and 1960s, *qigong* techniques had become familiar to a large part of the population (p. 335). In the 1980s, *qigong* became a popular movement of astounding proportions, and several of the most popular *qigong* masters were arrested.[2] In view of the 1910s critique of *jingzuo* as feudal, superstitious, and characteristic of the elite scholar-official class, it is significant that these same types of body techniques are now used to express opposition to the communist state. An important part of their appeal is certainly that they are perceived as authentically Chinese.

ESTABLISHMENT OF THE PEOPLE'S REPUBLIC OF CHINA (1949)

The Maoist Body

Chairman Mao brought about the next major transition in the linkage between body and nation. He had a strong, long-term interest in the body, evident in that his oldest surviving piece of writing is his 1917 article, "A Study of Physical Culture." His interest in the body was closely linked to his belief in the human will. Frederic Wakeman suggests that an early teacher, Yang Changji, influenced his thinking about physical education. Yang had studied in Japan, Germany, and Scotland and advocated physical education, including deep-breathing exercises and cold baths, which Mao and his fellow students put into practice (Wakeman 1973: 157–58). The 1917 article contains a clue about the way in which Mao later came to conceive the link between the body and the nation. In the argument against *jingzuo* described in that article, Mao emphasized that "there is nothing between heaven and earth that is not activity" (Miura 1989: 334). The word translated as "activity" (*yundong*) can also be translated as "movement" and "sports." It later came to refer as well to the endless political "campaigns" of the Com-

---

2. For further information on *qigong*, the reader is referred to the work of Nancy Chen (1994), which is based on ethnographic research in contemporary China.

munists. The theme of "motion" (*dong*) as characteristic of the West and "stillness" (*jing*) of China had been a favorite theme of Tan Sitong, a participant in the turn-of-the-century constitutional reform movement who had advocated physical training as a remedy for Chinese people's passivity. An emphasis on "action" also permeated British and American discussions of the male body, forming the rationale for physical training in the late 1800s (Park 1987: 10). Yang Changji was doubtless familiar with these ideas. Thus, Mao's conception of *yundong* probably drew on Chinese and British ideas about the active body. However, Mao linked the training of the body with the strength of the nation in a new way— through the notion of continuous revolution, which was to be carried out by an active body on behalf of a nation that was forever in motion.

In 1952 Mao penned the sports slogan still more often quoted than any other: "Develop physical culture and sports, strengthen the people's physiques" (*fazhan tiyu yundong, zengqiang renmin tizhi*). This ubiquitous slogan, found painted on the sides of gymnasiums and a standard fixture in placard sections at sports meets, was the single major source in the promulgation of the idea of the instrumental body (*ti*). Mao placed a great deal of importance on the health of the people's bodies as a basis for the health of the nation. In addition, he utilized the health of his own body as a sign of his fitness to rule. His swim across the Yangtze River in 1966 stimulated a national swimming craze among young people and demonstrated his fitness to rule at a time when he was losing power. This event continued and perhaps further consolidated Mao's tendency to link the bodies of the people with the strength of the nation in general and the bodies of the rulers with the legitimacy of their power in particular. Since Mao's time, the "fitness" (double meaning intended) of state leaders has been demonstrated through propaganda such as the 1984 feature article in *China Reconstructs* entitled, "How Top Leaders Keep Fit." Premier Zhao Ziyang, aged sixty-four, was reported to jog forty minutes every morning, rain or shine, wearing white tennis shoes and carrying a radio. Every evening after dinner he reportedly took a half-hour walk (Zhu Minzhi 1984: 12–14). Leading cadres participate in sports meets like the 1987 meet organized by the Beijing Party Municipal Committee for high-ranking Party and government officials—described in an article entitled, "Practicing What They Preach, They Take to the Competition Field" (Li Lijiang 1987a). Clearly, the Maoist call for the fitness of the body politic laid the ground rules for the student attacks on the infirmity and age of state leaders in the 1989 demonstrations.

The link between the bodies of the people and leaders with the welfare of the nation and the state were logical outgrowths of the egalitarian, militaristic, and proletarian Maoist body culture. This revolutionary body, drawing on Soviet doctrine, was constructed in opposition to the Western-influenced Republican body as well as to the late Qing body. In the Maoist order, the body was to serve socialism primarily through labor and military service. The goal of physical culture was to promote public health, increase productivity, and prepare the people for national defense. It was egalitarian in that the opportunity to train and to attain good health was to be available to all people, as opposed to the "medals-and-trophyism" of the previous era. The main motivation behind the campaign for public health was an obsession with erasing the label of "Sick Man of East Asia" (*dongya bingfu*) that, it was believed, was applied by Japan and the West to the Chinese body. Maoist body culture was also egalitarian in that, in a sort of twisted logic, *not* engaging in physical training would emulate the privileged exemption from exercise of the feudal elites; thus, people could be under a good deal of ideological pressure to train their bodies. Naturally, in this communist logic, state leaders could also not be exempt. Finally, the Maoist culture of the body was egalitarian in that it was to erase gender distinctions: women and men alike wore short hair and army green, and both did manual labor and broadcast exercises.

The main way in which this culture was trained into the body was through the broadcast exercises instituted in 1951. To Westerners, news footage of hundreds of darkly clad, sexless Chinese exercising in perfect harmony provided one of the enduring images of the Maoist era. At Beijing University in 1986, I was still awakened each morning by the tinny blare of the loudspeakers outside my window shrieking with musical accompaniment, "One, two, three, four, five, six, seven, eight! One, two, three, four . . ." By that time, only a handful of people on campus could be found performing the exercises.

The State Sports Commission System

In addition to this attention to mass physical culture, the Party provided for the training of the top athletes who were to be the vanguards of the new culture of the body. In 1955, the People's Republic of China established the system of sports schools based on the Soviet model that is still in place today.

The sports commission system consists of a hierarchical structure of sports training centers under the ultimate direction of the State Sports Commission, which is equal in status to a government ministry (same-level organizations include the Education Commission and the Ministry of Culture). At the base of the pyramid are the local (county, township, and city) sports commissions; above them are the provincial and municipal sports commissions (in 1988 there were twenty-nine provinces and three municipalities, or federally administered cities—Beijing, Shanghai, and Tianjin); and at the top is the State Sports Commission. The sports commissions at each level control the training centers under their jurisdiction. The State Sports Commission presides over the national team training center (Beijing tiyuguan) located near the Temple of Heaven in the southwest corner of the nation's capital. It also presides over national-team training centers for individual sports located in other parts of the country. In addition, it sets policies for the national-level institutes of physical education located in Beijing, Chengdu, Xi'an, Shenyang, Wuhan, and Shanghai. These are college-level educational institutes. This pyramidal system is designed to recruit promising athletes at the grassroots level and move the superior ones level-by-level up through the system until they arrive at the pinnacle, the national team.

At the grassroots level, training centers may be of several types. One of the most widespread is the "spare-time sports school" (*yeyu tixiao*), where students train before or after their regular school hours. Spare-time sports training is often offered by a regular "sports school" (*jingji tixiao*). This is a training center where students live, train, and attend classes. After they reach a certain age, they may stop taking classes; until recently, many athletes completed only nine years of schooling. These sports schools may be independent or they may be attached to a provincial or municipal training center or an institute of physical education. There are also "traditional sports middle schools" (*chuantong tiyu xiangmu zhongxue*). These are regular middle schools which have traditionally been strong in one or two sports events. I have described here only the bare bones of an extremely complex system in which there are many variations. In addition, the People's Liberation Army has always fielded its own strong teams.

Since its establishment, this system has been responsible for cultivating the specialist athletes who are the main performers in the sports events that publicly display the culture of the body promoted by the Party. As during the Republican era, the National Games are still the most important occasion for dramatizing the politicized body.

The National Sports Games

A summary of the themes of opening ceremonies of past Games shows how they link the body with the politically correct moral order of the moment. The core of all opening ceremonies is the mass calisthenics display performed to music and presented in several acts. Like the broadcast exercises, the mass calisthenics is itself a technique of the body that has had a long and vigorous life under the world's socialist regimes because it so dramatically enacts the socialist principles of discipline and the collective spirit.

The Communists rejected the Western- and Nationalist-organized "National Games" as spurious because they did not truly represent the nation. Hence, they started the numbering sequence of the national games over again. The First National Games were held in 1959, ten years after the establishment of the PRC. They were intended to consolidate the gains made since Liberation and to motivate the people to continue to work for the future. The central theme of the mass calisthenics display was "The Entire Nation Simultaneously Celebrates" and the five acts had corresponding titles. The theme and acts are listed below (Chen Mengsheng 1987):

1959: First National Games
theme: "The Entire Nation Simultaneously Celebrates"
1. Fortunate Children
2. Flowers of Spring
3. Heroes Gather and Match Strength
4. A Beautiful, Healthy Spring
5. Long Live the Ancestral Land

These themes promoted the new communist body and state as youthful, strong, beautiful, healthy, and with a long life ahead of it.

In 1959, China was actually on the verge of disaster due to the Great Leap Forward and the floods and droughts that unfortunately came shortly thereafter. The Games, which were planned to be quadrennial, could not be held until six years later, and even then were greatly scaled down. At that time, China was on the brink of the Cultural Revolution, and this was clearly reflected in the themes for the opening ceremonies of the 1965 Games. As is obvious, the themes were highly military and demonstrated revolutionary fervor. This was an expression of the growing militarism in the culture of the body as a whole:

1965: Second National Games

theme: "A Song of Praise for the Revolution"
1. Lift High the Revolutionary Torch
2. Rely on our own Efforts and Work Hard for the Prosperity of
      the Country
3. Tightly Grip the Gun in Your Hand
4. Red Successors
5. Carry the Revolution Through to the End

The Cultural Revolution lasted ten years, and not until its very end
were the Third National Games held. Only one act is recorded for the
opening ceremonies. The theme is still very revolutionary and meant to
inspire patriotism:

1975: Third National Games

theme: "Ode to the Red Flag"
1. The Flag of Achievement is Fire-Red

The Cultural Revolution ended after the death of Chairman Mao in
1976 and the overthrow of his wife and her cronies, the Gang of Four,
in 1978. The new regime, headed by Deng Xiaoping, celebrated its victory a little over a year later with the largest Games held to that date.
The theme served to remind the audience that, despite the more recent
vicissitudes of his political career, Deng had been tempered by the hardships of the Long March and, thus, was a fit leader for the hardships
ahead.

1979: Fourth National Games

theme: "The New Long March"

By the fifth Games in 1983, the political changes in China had gone
full cycle. The symbolism of springtime, which had been utilized for the
first Games in 1959, appeared again.

1983: Fifth National Games

theme: "A Beautiful Healthy Spring"
1. A Group of Dragons Leaps and Soars
2. Buds Begin to Open
3. Beautiful, Healthy Spring
4. Splendid Tapestry
5. One Hundred Flowers Greet the Spring

Obviously the themes of the National Games are intimately connected with the political winds of the times. To some degree they embody the nation, but at the same time they are a conscious attempt by the Party to alter the nation's body.

CONCLUSIONS: THE INVENTION OF SPORT HISTORY

By now it should be clear that body techniques have occupied a very important position in the arena of cultural contest in China since the late nineteenth century. There are two lessons to be learned from the history of body techniques and their public dramatizations. First, body culture is never as simple as it is depicted to be in such performances as the National Games, and therefore transforming it is never as easy as was often assumed. Chinese people could cut the queue and throw off the long gown and the footbindings, but these were only the more visible manifestations of an entire orientation to the world that was not so easy to transform. Though this orientation has continued to undergo transformation in the century since Sun Baoxin cut off his queue and won the high jump, uniquely Chinese conceptions of nation, class, gender, and social change still shape bodily practice in ways often mysterious to Westerners.

The second lesson is that modern sports have occupied a definite place in the Chinese moral order, but that place has been constructed differently at different times in history. The cultural constructions of sports are reflected in the language used to categorize them. When Western sports were introduced at the turn of the century, the word *tiyu* was introduced to label them. In the early part of the century, they were called "new physical culture" (*xin tiyu*) or "foreign physical culture" (*yang* or *xiyang tiyu*). Reformers and revolutionaries emphasized their newness and foreignness in their attempt to break with the traditions of the imperial past. Modern sports were perceived as being in opposition to the martial arts, which were hailed by traditionalists as essentially Chinese and attacked by reformers as outmoded and feudal. Though the boundary lines between the two and the politics of the debate have shifted in the last century, this opposition has remained.

However, in the 1980s the history of sports was subtly rewritten. What had formerly been "new" or "foreign physical culture" was now labeled "modern physical culture" (*jindai tiyu*). This version of history acknowledged that the phrase "physical culture" had first appeared in the "modern" period of Western contact at the end of the nineteenth century, but it emphasized the continuities between modern and historical sports rather than the revolutionary break with the past. One historian lamented the loss of China's own sports history in these words:

> For a long time, people had many different understandings of ancient Chinese physical activities. In their immediate lives all that people see and hear is modern (*xiandaide*) physical culture, but they see little of ancient physical culture, and hear little. Because of various reasons, particularly because they lack a knowledge of history, people think that ancient Chinese society in fact had no physical culture activities: since ancient China never even heard of this word "physical culture," how could it have had physical culture activities? . . .—I hope that this little book can contribute some material to the understanding and research of our nation's ancient physical culture by the broad masses of educators and physical educators. (Xu Yongchang 1983: vii–viii)

Typically, these histories go on to acknowledge that at the time that modern sports were introduced into China, the country was in a "semi-feudal, semi-colonial" state, with the result that "from the time that 'modern physical culture' was introduced into our nation, it was deeply branded with the character of the times; from the beginning, it never received all-around and complete development" (Wang Zhenya 1987: 1). Physical culture, as this history goes, finally achieved a robust and healthy development under the Communists, despite the setbacks of the Cultural Revolution. This was achieved because the Communists built on the strong base formed by popular and minority sports (for example, Rong Gaotang et al. 1984: 2–5).

Many of the new histories targeted a foreign audience (for instance, *Beijing Review* 1986, New World Press 1986, People's Sports Publishing House 1986). These histories expressed a desire to demonstrate that China had a long and illustrious sports history to contribute to the international sportsworld, a history every bit as valid as the Western one. Martial arts, in particular, were extolled with the goal of promoting their spread worldwide and their inclusion in the Olympic Games, a stated goal of the State Sports Commission. As one history put it,

> [Ancient Chinese sports] have enriched our society and Chinese martial arts constitute a glamorous pearl . . . Through efforts made by the new Chinese government, ancient sports are being unveiled, re-arranged, reformed and improved, then given a new lustre that attracts the world so much so that people around

the world are studying and practising Chinese ancient sports. (New World Press 1986: 6)

An article in the English-language propaganda magazine *China Sports* reinterpreted history in a way that would have astounded the 1920s and 1930s critics of the feudal tradition: it argued that Confucius actually *promoted* physical culture and participated in sports himself! (*China Sports* 1983).

In addition, China's ancient game of kick-ball was described in ways that seemed to indicate it was the ancestor of modern soccer—which is, of course, the world's most popular sport, so that a claim on its past carries more significance than would be the case for other sports. In the Tang Dynasty, the ball was even constructed in a way similar to today's ball, with eight pieces of hide sewn together over an inflated bladder (*Beijing Review* 1986: 32). The *New World Press* leaves the question of the link between kick-ball and modern soccer ambiguous when it states, "Modern football was practically unknown in China until the end of the last century. However, the game in its ancient form can be traced back to time immemorial" (1986: 80).

Around the world, nationalists typically reinvent popular traditions (dances, music, etc.) as "national culture" and promote them as an authentic heritage to foster national pride. Because they were originally constructed as non-Chinese, the relation of Olympic sports to Chinese nationalism is not so straightforward. As we move on to a consideration of contemporary China, it is important to remember the early construction of modern sports as different and foreign and the later attempts to root them in Chinese tradition. This shift was inseparable from China's changing position in the global political economy.

PART
·2·

The Body and
the Nation

CHAPTER THREE

Public Culture

On Sports Clubs, Public Events, and Representation

PUBLIC CULTURE

Sports play an important role in the arena of public events and mass media representations that constitute PRC public culture. My definition of public culture draws equally on the concept of the "public sphere" as formulated by Jürgen Habermas (1974, 1989, 1992) and "public culture" as formulated in the journal of that name (cf., Editor's Comments in inaugural edition of *Public Culture*, Fall 1988; Appadurai and Breckenridge 1988; Kelly 1990). By public culture I mean the realm in which public opinion is formed, national symbols are debated, and a national image is set apart from international and subordinate regional images. It is the realm in which a national consciousness is shaped that occupies the space between state leaders and ordinary citizens. Public culture plays an important role in the political process; it is a facet of political culture. As such, it differs from popular culture, whose defining feature is its demographic extent, not a concern with cultural debate (MacAloon 1990: 62n. 5). The forms of public culture discussed in this chapter include student demonstrations, sports events, ceremonial events that feature star athletes and politicians, and political assemblies. These public events made their way into the national consciousness through a multitude of channels both formal and informal. The most important formal channel was the state-controlled mass media; a secondary channel was the semi-autonomous critical literature called sports reportage (*baogao wenxue*); informal channels included dissident pamphlets, banners and flags, shouted slogans, signatures of endorsement, certificates, posters, publicly read or published letters, and word of mouth.

In analyzing public culture it is not enough to simply look at the cultural forms; we must also consider the people and groups producing them. Following Habermas, a popular Anglo-European approach has been to focus on voluntary associations outside of state control—"civil society"—as important in the formation of public opinion, and this approach has recently been applied to contemporary China by many scholars (Yang 1989a, Calhoun 1989, Strand 1990, Lee and Lee 1990). Habermas himself lists a range of organizations that can contribute an autonomous voice to the political process, which includes everything

> from churches, cultural associations, and academies to independent media, *sport and leisure clubs*, debating societies, groups of concerned citizens, and grass-roots petitioning drives all the way to occupational associations, political parties, labor unions, and "alternative institutions." (Habermas 1992: 453–54; my emphasis)

This chapter begins by describing the proliferation in the 1980s of sports clubs sponsored by individuals and collectives outside of the state sports system; these clubs began to allow some normally silenced groups a small voice in the media. However, a focus on voluntary associations as the locus of production of public culture in China is extremely limiting, so I have chosen not to orient my discussion around the question of the existence of a civil society in China.[1]

1. The concept of "civil society" has a long history in the political-philosophical tradition of the West. Insofar as it illuminates aspects of the political process in Western nation-states, it is because it was a key idea in shaping that very process. To do a similar analysis of the Chinese political process, we need to utilize the philosophical categories that shaped that process rather than abstracting a Western idea out of its context and applying it to China (see Chatterjee 1990). In this and other chapters, I am interested in looking at events from the point of view of Chinese conceptions of the "political"; my comparisons with the West are meant to serve this end. Second, focusing on the existence or nonexistence of a civil society in China ignores the most interesting political machinations, which take place in the cracks and fissures of the Party-state apparatus itself. In this chapter I mention the example of the journalist Zhao Yu, who was able to write a pointed criticism of the sports system because he was not under the control of the State Sports Commission and he did not

The chapter moves on to a discussion of the sports media's increasing boldness in expressing a voice autonomous from the state, culminating in the critical achievements of sports reportage—which, however, was never completely autonomous from state control. Next, the chapter describes public events in which star athletes were utilized as symbolic intermediaries between "state" and "society." "State" and "society" are not analytical categories here,[2] but rather are Chinese categories that reflect people's perceptions of what is going on at public events that bring together state leaders (*guojia lingdao*) with representatives of various social circles (*shehui gejie daibiao*). Such events are an important part of Chinese political culture and are often held in conjunction with important sports events. The athletes involved were not members of sports clubs, however, but were products of the state-sponsored sports system. Nevertheless, the events themselves could be occasions for non-state groups to contest state interpretations. I contend that the symbolic analysis of public events has been neglected in China studies and that a focus on such events will contribute to a more culturally specific understanding of how public opinion is formed in the PRC.[3] By focusing on the tangible channels through which public opinion is shaped, we can in turn begin to understand the sources of a national consciousness. For instance, a theme that runs throughout this chapter is the importance

---

live in Beijing. In chapter 10, I discuss the conflict between the State Sports Commission and other ministries over legalizing the bikini for women bodybuilders. I also discuss the importance of grassroots movements like bodybuilding and disco dancing, which flourish because they are not defined as "political." These examples show that some of the most interesting contributions to public opinion occur in the cracks in the Party monolith— which, after all, is no monolith, but a shifting alliance of self-interested groups.

Because I do not utilize the notion of "civil society," I have chosen not to use the term "public sphere," which Habermas described as the institutional core of civil society (Habermas 1992: 453–54). I find aspects of the public sphere concept to be very useful, however, and have incorporated them into my discussion of public culture. I am indebted to Ann Anagnost for bringing the problems with the civil society concept to my attention and suggesting the public culture concept as a solution.

Habermas's historical work on the public sphere, and the attempts by China historians to apply his model to China, all suffer from the problem that many very important sources of public opinion are not found in the written documents that historians rely on—a point demonstrated in this chapter (cf., Rowe 1990; Rankin 1990; Strand 1990; *Modern China* 1993).

2. As I discuss here and elsewhere, the state/society opposition is too simple when one looks at actual social practice, but it has validity at the level of the symbolic construction of the state. Louisa Schein (1992) has criticized the tendency by China scholars to oppose "state" and "civil society" and to then assume all popular practices are oppositional to the state.

3. Notable exceptions are Esherick and Wasserstrom (1990) and Wasserstrom (1991).

of the world champion women's volleyball team in shaping a sense of Chinese nationhood in the 1980s through a myriad of channels.

THE PROLIFERATION OF SPORTS CLUBS
UNDER THE REFORMS

Corporate and private sponsorship of sports was first called for in Central Document Number 20, issued in 1984. By the late 1980s, corporate and private sponsorship of sports clubs was proliferating, and newspapers reported on many examples of wealthy individuals, mostly peasants and private entrepreneurs, who spent tens of thousands of yuan to fund sports clubs. Families, villages, occupational groups, and strangers could form the basis for these clubs. One cadre from Hebei province recounted that a head of a "ten thousand yuan household" in his county had built a basketball court and ping pong table on his own land. He started a family basketball team consisting of him, his wife, his daughter, and four sons. Each spring he sent invitations to the other villages to participate in a basketball tournament (Peasant Sports Association 1988). Sports clubs founded by and for a family or kin group (*tiyu jia*) are common in rural China.

There are also village-based associations. Another peasant sports cadre told me that in his county, in Heilongjiang, a family had become wealthy by contracting a large orchard. They used some of their money to set up a loudspeaker in their large courtyard. Each morning people went there to work out (Peasant Sports Association 1988).

There are also clubs that do not draw on preexisting social relations. For example, in 1986 a private entrepreneur from Anhui used fifty thousand yuan to found a private workout club, and in 1988 his bodybuilders placed well in provincial competitions (Zhang Yinzeng 1988). The possible influence of this kind of voluntary association on the political process was hard to assess: first, it was such a recent phenomenon; second, since sports clubs were not defined as political associations, their political effects were found in their subtle and indirect influence on public opinion rather than in any direct confrontation with the existing political structure. Of course, it was this nonpolitical appearance that allowed them to exist at all.

There are historical precedents for sports clubs to engage in subversive politics. At the end of the Qing dynasty, sports clubs were formed by revolution-minded people who used them as an open, legal pretext for covert military preparation. Company-sponsored sports clubs in

Shanghai, the National Calisthenics Group in Ningbo, and the Baseball Association in Changsha all participated in local uprisings against the Qing (Renmin tiyu chubanshe 1985: 73–74).

In 1986, a family sports club played a role in shaping state policy by contributing to the state's reversal of its ban on the bikini in women's bodybuilding. In August 1986, before the bikini had been officially approved, the daughter in a "bodybuilding family" wore one in an exhibition during a men's competition staged in Guangdong by her family. Her father was a private entrepreneur and her grandfather was an Overseas Chinese (Yi Chenghong 1988). It seems likely that the family's Hong Kong connection and the father's economic independence from the state as a private entrepreneur contributed to their pioneering spirit. (Bodybuilding as a popular movement is discussed at greater length in chapter 10.)

An example of the use of a sports club by a stigmatized group to gain media attention is the press coverage surrounding the formation of China's first soccer fan club. This club became a channel for publicly expressing a voice of the working class. Soccer fans have an unsavory reputation in China and are viewed with distrust by the state. They have been called "ball game riffraff that don't appeal to refined taste" (*Renmin ribao* 1988). Soccer riots have added to this image. China's most notable example of soccer violence occurred on 19 May 1985, after a World Cup preliminary game in Beijing in which China lost to Hong Kong. After the game, fans went on a rampage, turning over buses and cars and scuffling with the police (Bonavia 1985). Another serious incident occurred in 1988 in Nanchong, Sichuan province, in a semifinal game for the national championships (*China Daily* 1988b). In both cases, most of the troublemakers were identified as male, single, under twenty-nine years of age (most of those detained in Nanchong were eighteen to nineteen years old), with a primary school or lower education, and unemployed or engaged in manual labor. Those who were employed did simple physical labor, and some did heavy labor (Kong Xiang'an and Zhang Zhidong 1987; *China Daily* 1988a). Thus, soccer fans have been stereotyped as being of the working class, and they have been stigmatized by the general feeling among high officials and intellectuals that those who "lack culture" are violent.

In January, 1988, China's first (post-1949) soccer fan club was founded in Shenyang. Officials had resisted efforts to start the club because they worried that China's fandom would develop in the footsteps of the fearsome European soccer hooligans. At its founding celebration, the vice-mayor of Shenyang expressed the hope that it would help "form a civilized social atmosphere." In newspaper and magazine articles, the club's head, Huang Zugang, took the opportunity to attack stereotypes about the working-class soccer fan. He made an attempt to separate Chinese soccer fans from their Western counterparts: "Our innate character is unlike that of the Western soccer fan. We love the ancestral land, love soccer, have feelings, understand aesthetics" (Xie Yanmin 1988).

This man, who was an outstanding Party member and a soldier by profession, became somewhat of a national spokesman for soccer fans and a ubiquitous presence at major soccer functions. His fervent support of Chinese soccer earned him his fame. According to one article, he spent two days trying to get tickets for himself and friends to the final China-Japan game in the Olympic preliminaries. As is typical of such events, the tickets sold out and the "back door" was his only recourse. After being put off by one leader after another, he squatted down by the track near the arena, accompanied by a reporter, and began to shake and moan. According to the reporter, he said,

> I don't remember how long it's been since I've cried. I'm not a weak person, I can carry on a fight, but today I feel suffocated, I feel really humiliated.
>
> We won't make trouble. Among us seven, six are Party members. China's soccer fans really aren't a threat; I admit their economic status is complicated and not a few are outcasts, but most are rather simple young people. They don't have any different, higher-level ways of amusing themselves. They focus all of their interest on the soccer ball. They only have this insignificant little treat as consolation—why are they discriminated against like this? Why is it that as soon as you mention them, people think of "troublemakers" (*daoluan fenzi*)? If you blindly let China's football continue to downslide, what does this indicate about what kind of fate this nation will have? All right, don't even talk of winning and losing, the vast majority of soccer fans drink lemon soda, crack open sunflower seeds, quietly and wordlessly leave the stadium. Isn't this the truly civilized spirit (*jingshen wenming*)? We only want to unfurl two association flags (*huiqi*) and a horizontal banner (*hengfu*), why won't they let us?
>
> We came from the extreme north of the ancestral land to the extreme south. Among us seven, the oldest is 45; we all have

wives, we paid our way, what are we going to do? When we left
Shenyang, tens of thousands of soccer fans sent us off at the train
station, some even held out their hats to collect donations for us.
All for what? I don't care if I don't have any tickets, I can still
find other ways. All we hope to get is a little sympathy, a little
understanding of the soccer fan's heart! . . . (Dong Hua 1987: 4–5)

This article, which may have been somewhat embellished, nevertheless
gave voice through Huang Zugang to the frustrations not just of soccer
fans, but also of the less educated people who have been increasingly
criticized as lacking the "civilized spirit" (see Anagnost 1993). Huang
Zugang's main rejoinder to this criticism, a response that was also voiced
by workers in the Tiananmen uprising of 1989 (Perry 1992), was that
people like himself also love China and care about the fate of the nation.
In this case of the Shenyang Soccer Fan Club, the voice of members of
a subordinate class was incorporated into public culture so long as they
subscribed to "spiritual civilization" and other key values of the dominant culture.

In another article, another stigmatized group—private entrepreneurs—gained some media attention through a sports club. *Sports News*
recounted an incident in which spectators insulted a soccer team
formed by private entrepreneurs from the Jianguo Men area of Beijing
after team members drove fifty motorcycles onto the field for the opening ceremonies of the East City District competition. Again, the point
of attack was the implication that the entrepreneurs were unpatriotic
agents of the Japanese (their motorcycles may have been Japanese im-
ports). After they won the preliminary round, the second round was
canceled without an explanation. In a previous article, *Sports News* had
already criticized such exclusionary tactics. The second article concludes, "But this problem is too big to be solved just by talk" (Ru Qi
1987).

In sum, in the late 1980s, private sports clubs were frequent topics of
newspaper articles. These examples show that such organizations did
have access to the media, offering at least the possibility for the expression of the voices of the stigmatized underclasses. Though sports clubs
were not engaged in a direct critique of the state or contest for public
opinion, they were part of a continuing effort by diverse groups in
China to find a voice in the national arena. These voices, however, were
very small compared to the public attention given to star athletes, who
were supported by the state rather than by privately funded clubs.

SPORTS REPORTAGE: "SUPERPOWER DREAM"

Overview of Sports Media

Sports occupy a very important place in Chinese mass media. A survey conducted in 1987 by China Central Television showed that China had almost 600 million regular television viewers, or 56 percent of the nation's total population. China had more TV watchers than any other nation in the world. Of the regular viewers, 64.7 percent lived in urban areas and 35.3 percent lived in rural regions (Nie Lisheng 1988). Sports programs occupied a significant place in TV viewing habits. In a poll of TV viewers, 50 percent said that sports programs are "an indispensable part of their lives" (*China Daily* 1987c). In his 1986 study of 397 urban Chinese, James Lull found that sports programs (including martial arts) were second only to drama in terms of the number of people who mentioned them as their favorite program types. Altogether, 46 percent of family members interviewed preferred dramas of all kinds, while 17 percent preferred sports and 5 percent preferred martial arts—despite there being far fewer sports programs to watch. Of the subcategories of drama, only "drama series/specials" outranked sports at 21 percent (Lull 1991: 156–57).

Sociological research showed that inhabitants of rural areas enjoyed watching sports on TV. A survey of 306 residents of Baoying, a county in Jiangsu province, showed that 194 of the respondents liked to watch sports, while only 99 liked dramas (13 respondents "don't watch anything"). In addition, 183 said they would "definitely" watch the Chinese women's volleyball team if they were playing for the world championships; 32 would watch if there were no good drama on TV; 76 would watch if they had free time; and only 15 wouldn't want to watch (Bai Guanglin and Ju Shirong 1987: 185).

Only the national Spring Festival program has a larger television audience than major sports events. Over 70 percent of the Chinese television audience watched the 1992 Barcelona Olympic Games on television (*TV Guide* 1993).

In 1984, there were over one hundred varieties of sports periodicals in China with a total circulation nearing ten million (Cao Xiangjun 1985: 118). The major sports newspaper was the daily *Zhongguo tiyu bao* ("China Sports News," until 1988 known as *Tiyu bao*, "Sports News"). The major sports magazine was *Xin tiyu* ("New Sports"). The variety of sports-related magazines at any kiosk was overwhelming. The major newspapers also offered daily sports coverage.

Each year, twenty news agencies sponsor the "Top Ten Athlete" contest, in which sports fans submit ballots to elect China's top ten athletes. Voter participation appears to have peaked in 1983, when 590,000 ballots were mailed in (Cao Xiangjun 1985: 117). In 1987, the ballots cost a small fee and 253,794 ballots were mailed in (Li Xiaofei and Zhang Xiaozhu 1988).

In short, television sports have a huge audience and sports periodicals are numerous and influential. Through these and the other channels discussed below, sports occupy an important place in Chinese public opinion and ultimately in the formation of a Chinese national identity.

"Superpower Dream"[4]

In February, 1988, "Superpower Dream" (*Qiangguo meng* [1988c]), by Zhao Yu, was published in *Dangdai* (Contemporary Times). It was a controversial critique of the Chinese sports system by one of the premier writers of reportage literature—itself an important genre in the democracy movement that led to the demonstrations of 1989. Tom Moran describes reportage as "a form of literary nonfiction that attempts an artistic depiction of fact in order to inform its readers and inspire them to action" (1995: 3). From the late 1970s to the mid-1980s, reportage pieces tended to be about individual people. In sports reportage, this tendency was later characterized as "the literature of champions." Perhaps the best-known piece was Li You's "Proudly Draw Your Sword" (1978), an article about Luan Jujie's second-place finish in an international fencing tournament (Moran 1993b: 9–10; Hong Qingbo 1988: 200).

In the mid 1980s, a few key reportage writers shifted from individuals to social problems and used reportage as a forum for the advocacy of reform (Moran 1995: 1). Magazines were the likely place for this movement because censorship was more relaxed than in other media and because under the reforms they were expected to pay their own way, which meant publishing works that attracted readers. Censorship of magazines was proscriptive not prescriptive; if they published controversial pieces, they were punished only after the fact if the piece came to the attention of the authorities. There was no clear-cut policy: writers

4. I would like to express my debt to Tom Moran, who brought to my attention the importance of "Superpower Dream" as an example of reportage and who generously provided me with his unpublished manuscripts on the topic as well as copies of relevant publications in Chinese that would have been difficult for me to obtain.

were aware of what could and could not be said, and so practiced self-censorship (Moran 1993a). Key figures in the new trend in reportage were Liu Binyan and Su Xiaokang. An important article in the new mode was Zhao Yu's "A Key Issue for China" (1986), which critiqued China's transportation system. In sports reportage, two articles on the May 19 soccer riots of 1985 signalled a move away from the "literature of champions" (Li You 1985, Liu Xinwu 1985). Like these two pieces, Yin Weixing's three-part, 95-page article on "The Chinese Sportsworld" (1987, 1988a, 1988b) also contained a modicum of criticism along with a large measure of glorification of sports.

The publication of "Superpower Dream" in February 1988 was viewed as a "breakthrough" for sports reportage. The result of two months of interviews (including discussions with Lu Yuanzhen at the Beijing Institute of Physical Education) and three months of writing (Hong Qingbo 1988: 196), "Superpower Dream" was a highly critical indictment of the entire Chinese sports system. Zhao's most fundamental criticism was that the emphasis on international victories and Olympic gold medals deprived most Chinese people of the opportunity to exercise for good health, at the same time encouraging them to place far too much significance on international victories to compensate for feelings of national inferiority. Comparing China's fifteen gold medals at the 1984 Olympics (which the Eastern Bloc did not attend) with its prospects at the 1988 Olympics, he concluded that China could win only five golds in Seoul. Several months later, his prediction came true, much to the chagrin of the sportsworld. In addition, he attacked the militaristic, government-operated system that served only a small part of the population, arguing that the system itself hindered the development of top athletes and in many cases damaged them psychologically. The article was not, however, a sustained attack on the sports system. In fact, the tone of the article was relatively measured and distant. The author's points emerged more from the stories he told than in direct diatribe. He described himself as a former member of a provincial cycling team who loved Chinese sports and greatly admired the achievements of Chinese athletes. However, despite what was called its "flat" organization and its lack of climactic moments (Hong Qingbo 1988: 203), the article incited a furor among its readers and in the sportsworld.

"Superpower Dream" was heatedly discussed by the editors of *Contemporary Times* and *Shanxi Literature* who published it. It was reprinted in whole or part by *Xinhua Wenzhai* and over thirty other periodicals

(Zhao Yu 1988a: 217). A few leaders in the State Sports Commission brought it to the attention of the Central Propaganda Bureau, with the result that the large news agencies in Beijing issued documents to limit its circulation (p. 224). The State Sports Commission also repeatedly criticized it in internal publications and threatened to sue Zhao (Zhao Yu 1988a: 224; Su Xiaokang 1988: 214). *Sports News* published an article with the front-page headline, "Superpower Not a Dream, Persevere in the Reforms" (Zhao Yu 1988a: 224). Commenting on the controversy later, Zhao said that the pressure came mainly from top sports leaders, while middle- and lower-level coaches and athletes liked the essay. He also explained that the sports leaders had no way to punish him personally because he was from Shanxi, not Beijing, and because he was a member of the literary world, not the sportsworld (Zhao Yu 1988a: 224).

In June, the editorial department of *Contemporary Times* and the Shanxi Writer's Association convened a "discussion meeting" in Beijing, bringing together writers, critics, and sportspeople to critique "Superpower Dream." This event was an example of the intertwining of the printed and the spoken word in the public realm, a notion I discuss below. One of those present was Zhao Yu's friend Su Xiaokang, an important writer of reportage who was to become a central figure in the democracy demonstrations of 1989. Su was the author of *River Elegy* (*Heshang*), the controversial television documentary that critiqued Chinese civilization and argued for openness and reform. It became an inspiration for many of the student demonstrators in Tiananmen Square.

In his discussion of "Superpower Dream"'s contribution to reportage at the colloquium, Su emphasized that the article was characterized by the spirit of reason (*lixing jingshen*); one is persuaded by the strength of Zhao's logic, not by emotion (Hong Qingbo 1988: 199). Moran identifies the use of "legal arguments" more than "moral suasion" as a general characteristic of post–1986 reportage (Moran 1993b: 15); he notes that Su Xiaokang "[a]ttempts to secure ground on which the critical intellectual can continue to operate" (p. 17). Thus, Su saw "Superpower Dream" as echoing his own effort to carve out a space for rational-critical debate in the Chinese political process—the type of debate that Habermas saw as crucial in the constitution of a democratic public sphere. In this case, however, it was not completely autonomous voluntary associations that made possible the publication of criticism. In China, the different systems (*xitong*) that constitute the Chinese state possess some autonomy vis-à-vis each other, and individuals maneuvering in the cracks between these state organs can carve out a degree of autonomy for themselves. This is what happened in the case of "Superpower Dream."

Su commented that while contemplating Part One of *River Elegy*, "Searching for a Dream," he read a draft of "Superpower Dream" (Su Xiaokang 1988: 211). Right after the opening sequence of the *River Elegy* series, there is a set of camera shots from the May 19 China–Hong Kong soccer match that ended in a riot. The narration states: "A nation which in its heart can no longer afford to lose." This was followed by a scene of the China—U.S. women's volleyball match in the 1988 Olympics and the question, "What if they lose next time?" (Bodman and Wang 1991: 102–3).

Several participants at the Beijing colloquium reiterated the point that, because Chinese sports had been so successful in the past few years, problems in the sports system and the need for reform had been covered up. Lu Yuanzhen commented,

> For a long time half-militarized administration has been implemented, and it has been difficult for criticism and opinions from the outside world to have any effect. This was prominently expressed in the basic fact that sports literature greatly lagged behind other literary creations.[5] (Hong Qingbo 1988: 196)

Zhao stated elsewhere that he felt the sports system lacked a democratic atmosphere. He noted that personnel in the transportation system had been much more amenable to the criticism raised in his article "A Key Issue for China" (Zhao Yu 1988a: 224). The commentators at the Beijing colloquium concurred that the sportsworld had a low degree of "transparency" to the outside world, in part due to the militaristic system, and in part due to the inherently misleading nature of sporting success, which led people to think there were no problems with the system. This last factor seemed to be the most important one behind the furor provoked by "Superpower Dream." It seems to have actually led many people to think about China's sports in a new way.

In December 1988, Zhao Yu published what in my judgment was a less-reasoned criticism of aspects of the sports system. The article's title, "Defeat of the Troops in Seoul," indicated that it would assess the rea-

---

5. Although sports *reportage* may have lagged behind the developments in reportage led by Su Xiaokang and colleagues, sports news media were, in general, more open than other news media.

sons for China's failure to live up to expectations in the 1988 Olympics. In fact, most of the article revolved around the frustrations of young intellectuals employed at the State Sports Commission. Their complaints echoed the complaints of young intellectuals in general. He described the efforts of some young members of the editorial bureau of *Sport History* to form a "salon" to discuss China's failures in Seoul. Each time they posted the announcement of the organizing meeting on the wall, it was torn down by a Party official. Finally, the organizers hired a lawyer and threatened to take the Party officials to court. When one official was confronted, he explained that he thought the notices were "big character posters," that he did not know what a "salon" was, and he asked what law he had violated. The point of Zhao's story was that a vast cultural gulf separated young intellectuals from their superiors, and the result was that their skills were wasted.

The small space for rational-critical debate carved out by Su Xiao-kang, Zhao Yu, and others was all but shattered in the aftermath of the 1989 crackdown. According to Asia Watch, Zhao headed the intellectuals' contingent in Tiananmen Square and recruited other writers. For this he was imprisoned for three months, although the Chinese government stated that he was never accused of any offense (Asia Watch 1994: 492). The history of my own encounter with "Superpower Dream" is indicative of how small that space was even at its apex. Although I was at the Beijing Institute of Physical Education at that time, I never heard the article mentioned. Neither did I hear mention of it on the Zhejiang Provincial team when I spent time there shortly after the article's publication. Perhaps this was only a chance oversight, but it was also noted at the colloquium that the essay had considerably more impact on the State Sports Commission than on the sports teams themselves (Hong Qingbo 1988: 197). I was given a copy of the article by Jaime FlorCruz at the *Time Magazine* Beijing bureau, who told me it had created quite a stir. Accustomed as I was to critical American journalism, I did not even recognize "Superpower Dream" as particularly controversial when I first read it, though it clearly gave much more detail about problems that other newspapers and magazines only alluded to. The coaches and athletes I knew commonly discussed most of the problems raised by Zhao. However, within the context of the "literary world," Zhao's article was something new and different. That it was brought to my attention by a writer for the American press illustrates that the literary world in China maintains close links with foreign intellectuals and the press. The sportspeople among whom I did my research did not move in these social circles and were often unaware of the issues being debated in them.

"IRREGULAR CHANNELS" FOR PUBLIC OPINION: ON VOLLEYBALL, GO, AND STUDENT DEMONSTRATIONS

At Beijing University in September through November of 1985, state leaders and dissident students engaged in a series of moves and countermoves surrounding two important sports victories. This series of events illustrates some of the concrete techniques by which a group of people sought to shape the national consciousness by utilizing the nationalism inspired by international contests. On one night in November, the Chinese women's volleyball team played the Japanese team in Japan for their fourth straight world title, and the final game of the first-ever Sino-Japanese Go championship was held in Beijing. The incidents described here were the first of the student demonstrations that, four years later, culminated in the Tiananmen Square incident of 1989.

Go and women's volleyball are both important in Chinese popular culture. Go is the oriental version of chess; more than just a popular game, it is regarded as an important part of the cultural heritage of both China and Japan.

The phenomenon of the Chinese women's volleyball team requires some explanation. Their story began in 1981, the year that the team won the World Cup in women's volleyball. This was China's first world championship in a major sport. The victory had special patriotic significance since China defeated Japan in the final match. The Japanese women had reigned over the volleyball world for many years, and the match was played in Japan. The championship became much more than a volleyball match: it was a victory over China's longtime Asian rival, the country which had invaded and brutally oppressed parts of China from 1931 to 1945. When the live broadcast of the Chinese victory came to an end, spontaneous demonstrations erupted across China. People flooded the streets, setting off firecrackers and weeping openly. A peasant sports cadre from Hebei province recalled to me that in her village, everyone shouted and set off firecrackers. "Some people even cried. Some people were so agitated that they were unable to eat and skipped several meals . . . The team won glory for China and showed the world that China is also good. Peasants also care about China's world reputation." Raising her thumb in a "number one" gesture, she said, "We felt like, 'Now we're even!'"

Approximately thirty thousand letters were sent to the women on the team, along with money, gifts, and proposals of marriage. Many of the letters were written in blood, a customary way of expressing deep sentiment. Many people mark the victory as the beginning of the revival of Chinese patriotism after the devastation of the Cultural Revolution. It was possibly the most significant event in the realm of public culture in the time period after the death of Mao and before the Tiananmen Uprising. It aroused more optimism than the event that was officially supposed to have done so: the Party Congress in 1978 during which the Cultural Revolution was declared at an end and the era of reform begun.

Yuan Weimin, the male coach who led the team to its first three world championships, began a meteoric rise to power with his appointment as Vice-Director of the State Sports Commission. In 1987, he was selected as a member of the Central Committee of the Chinese Communist Party, making him one of the top 175 Party members in China. He was also one of the most well-liked public figures in China. In a survey of women at Beijing University, he was most often named as the ideal male (Xie Baisan and Zhang Ming 1985). The string of victories by the volleyball team and Yuan's rise to power aided the State Sports Commission in its struggles for a greater share of the national budget and national prestige vis-à-vis its closest rivals, the Ministry of Culture and the Education Commission. China's successes in international sports stimulated other ministries to look at the Sports Commission for solutions to their own problems (*Zhongguo tiyu bao* 1988).

"Democracy '85": Dissident Appropriation of Women's Volleyball[6]

Ritual has always permeated Chinese politics (Esherick and Wasserstrom 1990: 848). One ritualized aspect of Chinese politics is the fixed schedule for student demonstrations. For a half-century, student demonstrations have regularly taken place on four occasions: September 18th, December 9th, May 4th, and during the funeral ceremonies of important state leaders.

On 18 September 1985, student unrest had already manifested itself

6. This section owes much to my discussions with my Anthropology 530a students at the University of Washington: Lisa Hoffman, Kevin Laycock, Kathryn Libal, David Tatman, and especially Peter Moran.

in a demonstration at Beijing University that protested the Chinese handling of the anniversary of the "September 18th" Incident, the day in 1931 when the Japanese began their invasion of the northeast. Several thousand Beijing University students had gathered at the South Gate of the University to protest Japan's so-called economic aggression against China in the 1980s. Big-character posters around the university used the occasion as a springboard to protest the lack of democracy in China.

After the September 18th demonstration, the anniversary of the December 9th Movement was widely rumored to be the target date for the next demonstration. This movement had occurred in 1935; it was a demonstration by Beijing students calling for resistance to Japanese aggression. University leaders began making plans to forestall another incident on December 9th.

However, some student dissidents attempted to preempt them. Copies of a letter were pushed under dormitory doors during one night in early November, calling for students to demonstrate in Tiananmen Square on November 20. This was the date on which the women's volleyball team would play Japan for their fourth straight world title, and Go champion Nie Weiping would play the final game against a Japanese player in the Sino-Japanese Go championship.

The letter hinted (probably falsely) that its authors were from Taiwan as it began:

Fellow Students (*tongxuemen*) of Beijing University:
We salute you, we raise our arms and shout out salutations. Despite the fact that we are not far apart, we are only able to use irregular channels (*fei zhengchangde qudao*) to become acquainted with you.

The letter concluded with the following paragraph:

In order to make the outside world comprehend the facts and the real situation, and in order to make the central government face up to our opinions, go to Tiananmen on the eve of November 20! On this day, Nie Weiping will do all he can to overcome the Japanese Go player, and the Chinese women's volleyball team will defeat Japan for the fourth straight championship. This is a day in the history of contemporary China-Japan contacts on which to feel proud and elated, and the patriotic enthusiasm of the entire Chinese people will show an unprecedented upsurge. Go to Tiananmen and stage a new operation—"Democracy '85." Commemorate "December 9th" ahead of time, complete the unfulfilled duty of the "September 18th" assembly.

The letter set the campus buzzing. School leaders advised the students not to allow foreigners to see the letter. An acquaintance of mine loaned it to me to copy by hand, warning me that local xeroxing facilities had been given the word not to copy it. I took it to my room and fortunately copied it right away, as my friend returned the next day in a panic to say he needed it for a political study session that had been convened to discuss it. The Communist Youth League of Beijing University had distributed its own letter in response to the first one, asking its various branches to convene meetings to discuss the subversive letter. The authors understood quite well why the dissidents had invoked the women's volleyball team:

> In fact, they are attempting to exploit the influence that Beijing University students have at home and abroad, and to exploit our patriotic enthusiasm. They are taking advantage of the chance that the women's volleyball team may win their fourth consecutive championship, and are adopting a strategy of preemption [literally, "defeating slowness with speed"].

As November 20th approached, students discussed whether or not they would go to Tiananmen Square. They had been told that students who were absent from their dorm rooms that night would be reported. When the evening arrived, the school gates were locked and students had to show their IDs to get onto the campus. Almost all of them elected to watch the games on televisions set up in the auditorium and in common spaces, however. As it turned out, the Chinese won both events, but only a few hundred students showed up in Tiananmen Square, as did a multitude of Western journalists who had gotten hold of the dissident letter. The students sang the national anthem and shouted slogans for two hours until they dispersed as ordered by security officials with bullhorns (*Time Magazine* 1985: 50). Although it never was clear who had printed and distributed the letter, the rumor around campus was that two graduate students were arrested and carried off into the night a few months later.

The state responded with its own publicly displayed interpretations of the sports victories. In the next week, there were no less than six state-sponsored occasions on which the volleyball and go athletes were brought together with Beijing University college students and students from other local colleges for ritualized exchanges.

First, at the closing ceremonies of the go championship on 21 November, Vice-Mayor Chen Haosu represented Beijing University students in handing over a letter of congratulations (*hexin*) from them to the Japanese team (Li Lijiang 1985c).

Also on 21 November, a "welcome ceremony" (*huanying yishi*) was conducted for the volleyball team when it arrived at the airport. In attendance were "representatives of various social circles" (*shehui gejie daibiao*), a group of college students, and a number of high officials (sports cadre Rong Gaotang, Sports Commission Director Li Menghua, Vice-Mayor Chen Haosu). Yuan Weimin "briefed [the audience on] the warm feelings of the Japanese audience towards the Chinese athletes during this competition, the friendly situation." Beijing University students read aloud (*xuandu*) a letter of congratulations expressing that they "want to learn from the team's spirit of fighting for the ancestral land, to work hard to obtain greater results in studies and work, to make greater contributions" (Li Lijiang 1985c).

On 22 November, the go team attended a "report meeting" (*baogao hui*) in the Beijing University gymnasium before an overflow audience of several thousand students. There was a ritual exchange of gifts as students presented to the team a silk banner (*jinqi*) inscribed with a poem: "One chess game erases a thousand marks and fulfills a long-cherished wish." They also presented a work of calligraphy that read "Superstars of Intelligence" (Zhong Yang and Yi Xianhe 1985). Speeches by the coach and by star player Nie Weiping emphasized the cooperation and friendly relations between the Chinese and Japanese players. The go team visited nearby Qinghua University the next day (Li Lijiang 1985b).

On 26 November, the volleyball, go, and gymnastics teams were received in the Great Hall of the People at a "tea and talk meeting" (*chahua hui*) convened by the State Sports Commission and the All-China Athletic Federation. In attendance were at least fourteen high officials from the Party, the National People's Congress, and the State Sports Commission. There were also 400 representatives of the sportsworld and other circles, Beijing University, Qinghua University, the Beijing Institute of Aeronautics, and the Iron and Steel Institute. The highest-ranking official present was Bo Yibo, vice-chair of the Advisory Committee of the Central Committee of the Communist Party, who gave the athletes an inspirational 24-character saying (Yang Mali and Huang Weikang 1985; Li Lijiang 1985a).

Finally, on 27 November, the women's volleyball team visited Beijing

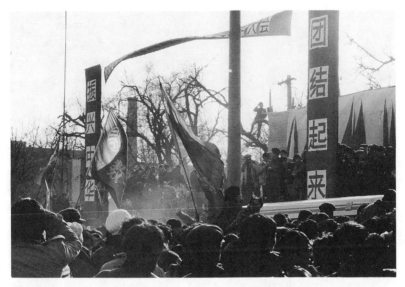

"Welcoming Meeting" for Chinese Women's Volleyball Team at Beijing University (1985). They are standing on the rostrum in the grandstand, which is decorated with banners and flags. In the foreground, students hold department flags.

University for a "welcoming meeting" (*huanying hui*) consisting of four hours of speeches and presentations on the rostrum in the grandstand at the "May 4th" athletic field (named for the famous student uprising).

The rostrum was decorated with a row of red flags before a backdrop of white cloth behind. The team members, coaches, and university president, all wearing their down coats, were seated behind a long table. Pots of red flowers decorated the front of the rostrum, which was framed by two vertical banners (*jufu biaoyu*) reading "Vitalize China" and "Rise Up and Unite." A horizontal banner across the top read "Mass Rally for Beijing University to Warmly Congratulate the Chinese Women's Volleyball Team on their Consecutive World Cup Championships." Poking up out of the throng of students were red flags bearing the names of departments and Beijing University in yellow writing. The team members and coaches gave speeches, and students read congratulatory letters. As on previous occasions, there was a ritual exchange of gifts: the Beijing University women's volleyball team gave the women fresh flowers, and Young Pioneers from the Beijing University Attached Primary School tied red scarves around their necks. In return, the women

Beijing University students watching the welcoming ceremony for the Women's Volleyball Team.

were asked to sign a volleyball to be mailed to the frontline soldiers on the southwest border in order to "express their common fighting spirit, their desire to win glory for the nation" (Xue Tongshe 1985).

Several thousand students braved the infield crush to watch the ceremonies. The situation was potentially dangerous, as the crowd was nearly out of control. I wandered around the periphery of the crowd taking photos and attempting to avoid being trampled when the outer edges of the crowd expanded and contracted according to whether the margin was pressing inward or the core was fighting back. A few days later I gathered that such zeal was common when I told a teammate that I had been at the ceremonies and she asked me, "How many people got hurt?" I later heard that two students suffered leg injuries from being trampled.

On the borders of the crowd, I encountered a reporter for the Beijing school newspaper, who asked me if we had such events in the United States. My negative reply was later reported in the paper's account of the event in such a way as to imply that Americans do not support their athletes as strongly as Chinese do.

CHINESE PUBLIC OPINION: A "MAZE OF CHANNELS"

This series of events illustrates several points about the ways in which public opinion is formed in China. It illustrates Stuart Hall's assertion that there are a "maze of communicative channels which support the formation of *public opinion*"; and that "many of these lie, in the first instance, outside the formal channels of the public media altogether" (Hall et al. 1988: 135). A meeting between representatives of the state and society in China is a dangerous thing. Hence it is not surprising that the culturally demarcated realm in which it takes place is highly choreographed. Many of the channels through which criticism can take place have a long cultural history; however, despite their cultural importance in China, they are often passed over perfunctorily by Western analysts who fail to recognize their importance (a notable exception is Esherick and Wasserstrom 1990). By concentrating on the formal channels of the public media, and by looking for the forms of critical debate characteristic of Western public culture, Western observers have often failed to recognize the distinctive institutionalized forms of Chinese public culture.

One of the main informal channels for shaping public opinion in China is to convene in Tiananmen Square. For nearly a century now, the square has occupied an important symbolic position as China's main public space for representations of the state and displays of public opinion. As Craig Calhoun has noted, since the communist takeover the square has straddled two modes of authority: one epitomized in the ritual displays of the Maoist period and the other in the nascent critical discourse of the 1989 demonstrations (1989: 56, 69). Celebrations or demonstrations in the square usually follow nationally significant sports victories; these are not always occasions for contesting official ideology.

Given the fixed calendar for student demonstrations, the students' deviation in 1985 from the ritual script shared with the state should be recognized as an important innovation. Another innovative feature of these demonstrations was the way they combined the traditional strategy of assembly in a public space with a modern mass media event. The motivation for the assembly was a *media event* received in private and semi-public contexts, which was then translated into assembly in a public locale.[7] This is an important characteristic of public culture in China. It is not enough to simply observe important events on the television; media events are often followed by gatherings in which the key symbols are publicly displayed and interpreted. This strategy was utilized by the students as well as by the state.

A second point that is evident in the above accounts is the multitude of forms that public events can take. There are opening and closing ceremonies, welcoming ceremonies at the airport, report meetings, tea and talk meetings, welcome meetings, and also send-off meetings (*huansong hui*). These are all occasions during which state officials share a space with representatives of society. Such public events are attended by selected "representatives" of the various social circles or worlds (*jie*), the most frequently mentioned *jie* being the literary world, the sportsworld, the arts world, and the educational world. This shows how the state organizes its subjects into occupational groups and choreographs the interactions between them and representatives of the state. These are not merely symbolic groupings, however; the *jie* are also represented in the national mass political organizations, and Chinese people consider these groups responsible for voicing political concerns. That the public events mentioned above were occasions on which the state was accountable to the people was reflected in the labeling of some of the events as "report meetings." Implying that the purpose of the meetings

7. Thanks to Andrew Painter for this insight.

was to transmit information, newspaper accounts emphasized that the coaches and athletes "briefed" (*jieshao*) the audience or "reported on" (*baogao*) the conditions of the competition.

One of the notable features of the public events described here is the importance of written forms.[8] These included silk banners; association, department, or school flags; horizontal banners; large banners with slogans; works of calligraphy; letters of congratulation; and signatures of endorsement. These genres are part of a whole repertoire of written forms that mediate between superiors and inferiors, including state leaders and common people. Other forms are described in later chapters: big-character posters, posters of commendation (*biaoyangshu*), posters of criticism (*piping bao*), self-evaluations, self-criticisms, certificates of commendation (*zhengmingshu*), etc.

One particularly important example of the use of writing in mediating between superiors and inferiors is the practice of "offering words on behalf of" an event (*wei . . . tici*). These endorsements are often published in the media in the leader's own calligraphy with his signature. The most famous example in sports is the phrase penned by Chairman Mao in 1952 in endorsement of the Second Congress of the All-China Sports Federation: "Develop Physical Culture and Sports, Strengthen the People's Physiques." These phrases are considered extremely important indicators of a leader's position on a particular matter. Mao's phrase became the guiding slogan of sports policy for many decades. Particularly catchy endorsements are sometimes used as slogans (*kouhao*), which are shouted aloud on ceremonial occasions, painted on walls, and utilized in placard sections. Mao's endorsement underwent this transformation.

During an interview with a reporter at the 1986 National College Games, I was asked to offer words for the Games. Since I had no idea what he was talking about, I had to receive a quick cultural lesson from him and my teammates. Not only did I not understand what he intended to use it for, but also I did not know what kind of phrase was appropriate, and when he suggested one I could not write all the characters. I finally ended up copying down his own suggestion: "Best Wishes for the 1986 National College Games to Open Victoriously!" My words were never published; perhaps his editor did not consider me important enough, or perhaps my handwriting was too atrocious.

In my analysis, the prevalence of written forms is a way of circumventing the more dangerous give-and-take of verbal discourse. Writing

8. I am grateful to Stephen Hsü for clarifying these categories and practices for me.

is easier to choreograph. This sort of choreography has always been important in the construction of the Chinese state and has an ancient history in the discourse of *li* (ritual, etiquette) (see Zito 1984; Esherick and Wasserstrom 1990). Writing as a channel between state and society is epitomized in the form of the petition. For many Chinese, the most climactic moment of the 1989 student demonstrations occurred when state leaders emerged from the front of the Great Hall of the People and were confronted by a student who was kneeling and holding a petition above his head that contained the students' demands. The leaders' failure to even take the petition from him had great symbolic force for many Chinese.

This sort of choreography is undemocratic if measured by Habermas's ideal of rational-critical debate. However, the search for such debate should not blind Western scholars to the multitude of genres that do exist for the formation of public opinion in encounters between state and society.[9]

LETTERS, DIARIES, AND SUBJECTIVITY

Another channel which utilized writing consisted of the various kinds of letters that managed to make themselves public. Private people attempted to make their opinions publicly known through letters to newspapers as well as through the thousands of letters mailed to the women's volleyball team. Some of these letters became quite well known and even made their way into the official histories. China's public figures are expected to respond to private people, giving the whole process the feel of a dialogue. Nie Weiping and his coach personally replied to every letter written to him that asked a question about go (*Tiyu bao* 1985b). The senior members of the women's volleyball team wrote letters that were published in China's main sports newspaper (*Tiyu bao* 1985a), and the "diary" that the star spiker kept during the competition was published in the main sports magazine (Lang Ping

9. Thus, I take issue with Myron Cohen's statement that in the absence of a shared cultural framework, political relationships in China are "largely expressed in the form of naked commands" (1991: 130). It seems to me that a rather elaborate cultural framework is interposed between those issuing commands and those receiving them. The slogans and posters he mentions are just two (actually more, if one considers the variety of Chinese practices that are translated as "slogan" and "poster"). Moreover, these messages do not come just from the top down; they are also offered from the bottom up. Calhoun remarks on the amount of creativity in the slogan shouting and chanting during the Tiananmen demonstrations (1989: 69).

1985). In 1988, Coach Yuan Weimin published a book that he said was a response to the many letters he had received asking for advice (Yuan Weimin 1988). There were also the ritualized letters of congratulation from delegations of students that were read during the congratulatory ceremonies. State leaders also sent telegrams to the volleyball team in Japan that were published in newspapers the next day and later recorded in the official history (Rong Gaotang et al. 1984: 199–200).

In this light, it is important to consider that the dissident students chose the letter as their medium for expression, and the Communist Youth League responded with a letter of its own.

The function of private letters in Chinese public culture can be compared with their function in the "literary public sphere" of eighteenth-century Europe as described by Habermas. Letters and diaries played an important role in the period preceding the emergence of the bourgeois public sphere because through them the subjectivity developed in the intimacy of the family attained clarity (Habermas 1989: 49, 51). The ideas that developed in this domain were later used to defend the interests of the privatized market economy from the incursions of the state (p. 51). In China, as in eighteenth-century Europe, the intimate and the public are curiously conflated in this practice of publishing letters; many of the letters and diaries were written for an audience in the first place, although they "were to be written in the heart's blood, they practically were to be wept" (p. 49). A most evocative example was a letter written to the women's volleyball team in 1981 by a formerly disillusioned university student:

> For ten long years I've been drunk, I've been numb; I had already lost enjoyment and sorrow, and even that golden October [the founding of the PRC] had faded to a mere thread of a pale shadow of a smile, and hadn't left much of a mark. But today, you have aroused again the love of country in the bottom of my heart. Your resolute stance, your fighting spirit, your utter loyalty to the nation, have lit the flame of my love which had already died out. To my surprise, I discovered, on that moving night, that I had suddenly taken leave of the past with joy and tears . . . In ten years this was the first time I felt my heart beating—along with the strong rhythm of the pulse of the nation; in ten years this was the first time I felt the honor of being human—China's pride. Perhaps there are some people who won't believe that an insignificant little round ball could have such great power that it could turn

around a person's life path. It's true. It has certainly dropped a heavy bomb on a teenager who was hesitating at a crossroad, shook his numbed spirit, aroused his awareness of loving the Party and the nation! (Cao Xiangjun 1985: 137)

This letter illustrates the linkage of the subjectivity of the privatized individual to a national consciousness (cf., Habermas 1989: 50). Due to the state's control over the Chinese press, this subjectivity, which is "always already oriented to an audience" (p. 49), must necessarily express a *positive* unity of the private individual with the nation. Sports are curiously suited to mediate between a private and public subjectivity because they allow people to talk about the most intimate details of the bodies and minds of other people while at the same time linking these to a shared concern for the welfare of the nation. In the letters written to the volleyball team, unlike in the European case, there was no movement toward delimiting a subjectivity autonomous from the state. In fact, since high cadres were some of the most important letter-writers, a kind of melded private-state subjectivity was constructed. Based on the emotions expressed to me, I believe that many people experienced a feeling of unity between themselves as individuals and the nation as embodied in the volleyball team. The Party attempted to formulate this as a unity with the state, but for most people I believe identification with the party-state was overshadowed by an overwhelming sense of being Chinese.

SPORT AND REPRESENTATIVE PUBLIC CULTURE

In the importance of the face-to-face encounter between state officials and members of "society," and in the highly choreographed nature of such encounters, there is a similarity with what Habermas called the "representative public sphere" of pre-seventeenth century Europe. By this he meant a public culture in which state rulers represented their power *before* the people rather than *for* the people (Habermas 1974: 51). Representative public culture is tied to the personal; it is created by the presence of leaders of state (p. 51n. 4). Because the symbolic construction of the state is wedded to discrete locations, events, and people, public authority is constructed more as a status attribute and less as a permanent and continuous force (1974: 51; 1989: 18). Following this logic, I would argue that despite the ability of the media of mass communication to transcend the public/private distinction, Chinese public culture is still strongly linked with the sharing of a locale. The mass media clearly played a role in creating a national consciousness in the case of the women's volleyball victories, but this consciousness would not have been nearly as intimate and emotional if people were not watching the games together, celebrating in the streets, personally welcoming the returning victors, writing letters to newspaper editors, and attending congratulatory ceremonies. Television and the print media were only one rather sterile aspect of an entire lived experience.[10]

The importance attached to the face-to-face encounter with public officials, and the use of writing to mediate such an encounter, is illustrated by an interaction that occurred during preparations for the 1986 National College Games. China People's Airline demanded foreign exchange currency for the tickets to Dalian for me and the other American on the team, James Thomas. They also demanded four times the price of the other athletes' tickets. Despite showing the airline documents from the Central Communist Youth Group, the State Sports Commission, and the State Education Commission, and despite the fact that the Beijing City Education Commission was paying for the tickets, my coach could not convince them to accept People's Money. He realized the problem was that he was dealing with the Beijing City branch of the airline and therefore required the aid of someone in the Beijing City government. He came up with a plan. He would wait until Vice-Mayor Chen came to review the goose-stepping and slogan-shouting that the team had been practicing for the opening ceremonies, and at that time he would slip him a note. I asked him why he didn't just go to the vice-mayor's office with his request. He replied that the vice-mayor was very busy and perhaps he would not have time to see him. This plan was more certain, though it might be tricky to get the note to him at the right time. When the day came, my coach managed to get the note to

10. Thus, I would argue against John Thompson (1990: 241) that the mass media transcend spatial separation; the sharing of space is too important in Chinese public culture to be dismissed. I would also argue that print media are not as singularly important in forming a national consciousness as Benedict Anderson (1991) suggests; what is equally important is the social relations that determine how the media are read and how the interpretations flow from person to person.

Comparative studies of Olympic media coverage have revealed great cultural variability in the transmission and interpretation of a single event (see Larson and Park 1993; Rivenburgh 1992, 1993). In the large international project on the opening ceremonies telecast of the 1992 Barcelona Olympics (outlined in Rivenburgh 1993), the Chinese telecast was distinguished by the fact that it related *less information* than any of the twenty-seven other national telecasts studied (Moragas Spa 1993: 43).

Chen while he stood behind the reviewing table as we marched by on the infield. The note was phrased as if it were written by our teammates, though since Chinese requires no explicit subject for verbs, it was hard to ascertain who was doing the asking. It read:

> Vice-Mayor Chen:
>   How are you!
>   Let [us] [report?] something to you: our Beijing team has two foreign students from America, who are also the only foreign students in this meet; but when [we] arranged for the plane tickets to proceed to Dalian, the comrade at the China People's Airline office requested that these two classmates pay foreign exchange currency. Otherwise, they would not be allowed to take the plane and must take the train. Consider that we are a group, further that these two are also going to Dalian for the honor of Beijing; therefore, we team members all feel that this action is not proper, but none of us has a way to persuade the comrade at the China People's Airline office. Therefore, toward this end [we] ask that you give us a little help in solving this problem.
>
> Beijing Team
Group A Classmates 7/25/86

In the margins, Chen wrote in a barely legible scrawl:

> Would the China People's Airline office please study [this], I consider that the fees of these two foreign students ought to be collected according to the standards of Chinese people. Please co-operate promptly in handling this accordingly.
>
> Chen Haosu 7/25

The airline office head reluctantly acquiesced, though he caused my coach as much trouble as possible before relenting.

Vice-Mayor Chen was present at all of the major meetings leading up to the Games. As an athlete in the United States, I cannot recall ever shaking the hand of any politician, but I shook Chen's hand twice. The first time was at an awards ceremony, and the second time was when he made a personal visit to the dormitory in Dalian. As I sat in my dorm room one day, my coach and the team leader came rushing in to tell me that the vice-mayor was coming and that I should get ready. As I was unsure what I should do to get ready, they explained that I should stand and prepare to shake his hand. They left me standing in the middle of the room for fifteen minutes. It turned out to be a false alarm, and he never reached my room. A day or so later my roommate rushed into the room to say that he was coming again and that I should stand up. I argued that I had stood there for fifteen minutes the last time and he had never come. If he did come, I could hear him outside of the door in enough time to stand up before he reached the room. With a note of panic, she started to argue with me but we were interrupted by a commotion outside and he indeed entered the room to shake our hands.

"REPRESENTATION" IN THE CHINESE POLITICAL PROCESS

In the role of athletes as intermediaries between the people and the state, it is possible to draw out an important point about the concept of "representation" in China. As in English, in Chinese the same word (*daibiao*) is used to mean political representation and the act of representing a group of people in a sports competition. In Western society, despite the congruence of terminology, there is generally an understanding that political representation is very different from athletic representation (though even in the West the two are sometimes confused). In the West, the act of political representation theoretically entails verbal debate on behalf of one's constituents, while in athletic representation the whole group partakes vicariously in the victories of one of its parts, the athlete. Both cases imply a process of metonymy whereby the speaker or athlete is a part that represents the whole and can do so because she shares a fundamental likeness with the entire group.

A second kind of representation is more common in China. It is grounded less in a shared sameness and more in a hierarchical order. In this kind of representation, someone who stands out from the crowd (who has a lot of "face") is in a position to *endorse* various endeavors on behalf of subordinates. Endorsement implies placing the force of one's "face" or reputation behind an organization, a plan, or a symbol. This is the logic behind the practice of "offering words," and it was the logic behind getting Vice-Mayor Chen's signature on a piece of paper. It also explains why, when I asked one of my teammates if I, a foreigner, could "win glory for Beijing," he replied that I could win even more glory for the team than a Chinese. This confused me until I realized that I would not be perceived so much as a product of the Beijing college sports program (which I was not) as I would be perceived as endorsing Beijing's programs by casting in my lot with that of the team. That an outstanding foreign athlete would voluntarily choose to do this was more note-worthy than that a Chinese would, who after all had considerably less choice in the matter.

The conflation of the metonymic and the hierarchical types of representation is obvious in the role of Chinese athletes in public culture. On the one hand, athletes are taken as metonymically representing the Chinese people as a whole. For example, when the women's volleyball team won the World Cup in 1981, a group of Chinese students studying in West Germany wrote a letter to them that said,

> Open-minded and magnanimous, open and aboveboard, you have simultaneously demonstrated before the eyes of the world the modesty and goodwill of the Chinese people, the traditional virtue of Chinese women, the fighting spirit of today's young people, and superlative ball skills. You've told the world, "These are the Chinese!" (Cao Xiangjun 1985: 139)

On the other hand, many famous athletes are designated as representatives to the National People's Congress (NPC), the People's Political Consultative Conference (PPCC), and other political organizations. The stars of the 1981 women's volleyball team were so rewarded over the next few years: three of the women were appointed as representatives to the NPC, one to the National Party Congress, and one to the PPCC. Coach Yuan Weimin's rise to power has already been discussed. Among the two hundred mostly male, white-haired members of the presidium of the 14th Party Congress in 1992 sat Gao Min, winner of gold medals in diving in the 1988 and 1992 Olympics (Kristof 1992). In 1988, a total of fifty-six sportspeople were elected to the NPC and PPCC. Reporters at the meetings discovered that only thirty of the representatives were present, most of them coaches; the majority of the athletes had not come, or had left early. Those present explained that it was an Olympic year, and training took precedence over the meetings. However, the reporters seemed to agree with one NPC representative who said that "it is more important that they carry through their duty to the end" (Zeng Hong and Zhou Meng 1988).

That athletes are chosen as political representatives stems less from a perception of them as parts representing the whole and more from the idea of rewarding them for their achievements. This practice is said to demonstrate that "the state (*guojia*) has not forgotten." In this construction, athletes and "the state" seem linked in an alliance that sets them apart from the common people.

SPORTS IN CHINESE PUBLIC CULTURE

Athletes' representation of the people is thus multilayered and contradictory. On one level, they are to represent the Chinese nation in international competitions and their qualification for doing so is their unity with the people, a unity that many people actually feel. On a second level, they are to represent the Chinese people through critical debate in the political organizations that the state labels "democratic." This they have perhaps not done very well. On yet a third level, they also represent the state to the people at public functions, where they are seen sitting on the dais and giving speeches alongside important state officials while "society" forms an appreciative audience. Certainly they often appear to act as mouthpieces for the state, as in the series of events surrounding the 1985 student demonstrations when they never failed to emphasize the Sino-Japanese cooperation that the State Council was working hard to promote.

In all of this, athletes are caught up in the contradictions that permeate public culture in China. Unlike in Habermas's model, public culture is not conceived of as being in opposition to the state, yet neither is it entirely controlled by the state. It functions mainly as an arena to contest and defend representative rather than economic interests. For this function athletes are admirably suited.[11]

Because sport is primarily nonverbal, it is characterized more by representation than by rational criticism. However, the examples of "Superpower Dream" and the dissident student appropriation of women's volleyball show that even sport is not entirely free from critical debate. On the whole, sport is perhaps less threatening to authoritarian governments than other forms of popular culture. Its ceremonial nature suits the choreographed nature of Chinese public events. In the name of sport, one can get away with a lot. A Chinese professor told an American

11. MacAloon (1990) describes a Canadian public event in which the political dynamic seems both like and unlike the events described in this chapter: the 1988 Dubin Commission inquiry into steroid use by sprinter Ben Johnson. In this media event, he argues, responsibility for *wrongdoing* was shifted from institutions to individuals, thus *exonerating* the Sports Ministry, the Canadian Olympic Association, and SportCanada. In the events I describe, responsibility for *success* was shifted from individuals to institutions, thus giving *credit* to the sports ministry and other state organs. The similarity is that in each case the state seemed to use individual athletes to its own benefit. However, I do not think that the Canadian logic is typically applied in China when things go wrong; the blame is not shifted from the state to individual athletes. Rather, it is directed at the State Sports Commission. After the failures of the 1988 Seoul Olympics, government cadres were criticized, and Li Menghua was replaced by Wu Shaozu as head of the Sports Commission.

reporter in 1989 that the best approach to the Chinese press was to "Trust the papers only for sports" (Kramer 1989: 66).

In order to understand Chinese public culture, we must get beyond the verbal expressions and look at the nature of representation and symbolic action in public events from the Chinese cultural perspective. The distinctive character of China's public culture results in a predictably different conception of public events. In public events in which state and society come together in a highly choreographed display, their conjuncture is circumscribed by codes of etiquette and communication; a large part of the communication takes place through symbols and written forms. Critical debate is limited or nonexistent. The ritualized nature of public events is reflected in the architecture of sports stadiums (with a rostrum in the grandstand from which leaders and athletes address spectators), in the prominence of written communicative forms, and in the practice of reviewing the athletes in the opening ceremonies. Despite international influences, this is a distinctively Chinese public culture with a structure that reflects the broader Chinese culture and history. This public culture will no doubt continue to undergo structural transformation in the future, but the structure that is already there will prevent it from closely following the Western model.

CHAPTER FOUR

Body Culture and Consumer Culture in China's 1987 National Games

The official title of the PRC's biggest multi-sport event is the National Games of the People's Republic of China (*Zhonghua Renmin Gongheguo Yundonghui*). The Games include almost all of the summer Olympic sports plus acrobatics, martial arts, chess, go, and some other non-Olympic sports. Like the Olympic Games, they are supposed to take place once every four years. The 1987 National Sports Games in Guangzhou were the first national games of the PRC in which economic modernization appeared as the central theme. They were also the first games in which the choreographers debated doing away with mass calisthenics in the opening ceremonies. These two events were connected. In 1987, the policies of economic reform and opening-up were rapidly changing the shape of the Chinese economy and the Chinese body. Militarism was on its way out. Consumerism was on its way in. The Guangzhou Games almost marked a turning point, but not quite. In the end, consumerism reached

Portions of this chapter were published previously in much more abbreviated form as "The Changing Relationship between Sport and the State in the People's Republic of China," in *Sport . . . The third millennium,* edited by Fernand Landry, Marc Landry, and Magdaleine Yerles, pp. 295–301, Proceedings of the International Symposium, 21–25 May (Quebec City: Les Presses de l'Université Laval, 1990).

unprecedented heights but the mass calisthenics were kept. Placing the debate over the mass calisthenics within the economic context of 1987 demonstrates the links between the body and the changing economy in contemporary China. The Party considers the link between the economy and the body important, therefore the way in which it is publicly dramatized in the National Games is tightly controlled.

COMMERCIALIZATION IN THE 1987 NATIONAL GAMES

In the 1980s, thoughtful Chinese were realistic enough to realize that China's ascension in international sports had outpaced its ascension in the world economy. As Cao Xiangjun put it, "China stands lower than place number 100 in the world economic situation; how is it able to produce world-class athletes? How could they get 15 golds in the Olympics when there are still people who can't eat enough?" (Cao Xiangjun 1987).

The state physical culture budget is comparatively small. The expenditure on physical culture was 0.17 percent of the total state expenditure in 1952; except for the Cultural Revolution era, it increased gradually until it reached 0.36 percent of the budget in 1982 (Guojia tongjiju shehui tongjisi 1985: 287). After China's successes in the 1984 Olympics, the physical culture expenditure increased to around 0.4 percent of the total budget, which was still judged inadequate. Zhang Caizhen, deputy director of the State Sports Commission, noted that "even India" spends 1.0 percent of its annual budget on physical culture, and more sports facilities and equipment were badly needed in China. The national teams often complained about their lack of facilities (Qu Guangli 1988). Before 1987, China's success in international sports, despite the low state expenditure, was attributed to the advantages of a centralized socialist economy:

> [T]he progress of China's physical culture endeavor, comparatively speaking, has been rather quick. This precisely demonstrates the superiority of the Chinese socialist system . . . [T]he decentralized economy generated by a system of private ownership, where everyone does things his own way, intent only on profit, causes them to be unable to effectively realize their economic strength through unity. (Cao Xiangjun 1985: 96–97)

In 1987, the virtues of centralization were no longer touted. On the contrary, the state's monopoly over the organization of sports teams was criticized for stifling the development of sports. The 1987 Games opened less than a month after the 13th Party Congress. Though it was not planned, the timing was perfect for propaganda about the success of the economic policies, the correctness of which had been reasserted at the Congress. The propaganda surrounding the Games made continued reference to the guidance of the Party and the Basic Road laid out at the Congress. One of the main policies reasserted at the Congress was decentralization. As in other sectors of the economy, the sport system was encouraged to rely less on subsidies from the state.

The 1984 Los Angeles Olympics, held in the wealthiest capitalist nation in the world and relying on heavy commercialization, were acclaimed worldwide for turning a huge profit.[1] The extent of commercialization was regarded with some consternation by the West: Greece even threatened to refuse access to the flame in Olympia to protest the selling of the right to run on the torch relay (see MacAloon 1987a). The Los Angeles Games were the PRC's first Olympic Games since 1956 and they made a profound impression. Paradoxically, the most populous socialist nation in the world sent representatives to learn from the Los Angeles Organizing Committee how to turn sports into a moneymaking enterprise. The head of the Guangdong Sports Commission, Wei Zhenlan, was one of the representatives. He later reported that

> he received enlightenment from the Los Angeles Olympics, and formed the concept of support coming from all sectors of society. From the first moment when lottery tickets were issued, to the product and advertising rights to the meet emblem and mascot, it developed in the end into the organization of sports tour groups. (Ping Yuan 1987)

As a result of the enlightenment he and others gained in Los Angeles, the Sixth National Games in Guangdong were characterized by five new policies: corporate sponsorship through sale of advertising rights to the meet mascot, emblem, and song; lottery tickets; tour groups; and business management of gymnasiums rather than administrative management (Cao Yuchun 1987).

Corporate sponsorship was the biggest innovation for the Games, one directly related to the economic reforms. Advertising rights for the meet emblem and mascot made a profit of about 20 million yuan. One

---

1. As MacAloon points out, however, the $90 to 120 million in taxpayers' money that went into the Games was conveniently overlooked in calculations of profit (1987a: 125).

Guangdong observer remarked, "Right now, sports is like a pretty and charming girl; a lot of enterprises are coming to 'court' her!" (Huang He 1987b). Although this led to some complaints about commercialization, the reception was generally favorable. People commented that in the past corporations had not earned enough profit to be able to afford a great deal of advertising. Only under the economic prosperity of the times was it possible, and only under the new policies for the Games was it allowed.

Increased corporate sponsorship was attributed to three conditions, described in one newspaper as follows:

1. The 1984 Central Document Number 20 called for the socie-tization [*shehuihua*—public sector support] of sport, causing many enterprises to see that sport benefits the nation, the people, and themselves. This changed their concept of sports and made them realize that making a contribution to sports is within the realm of enterprises.

2. Sport "brings the competitive spirit into the factories and shops."

3. Sponsorship can increase the name recognition of the enter-prise. This is the most direct element. The head of the Hengdao River Seed, Fruit, and Wine Factory remarked, "Sports competi-tions are most full of competitiveness. Any entrepreneur with a brain will want to make thorough use of the special position sports have in people's hearts and minds to expand and influence his enterprise's development." (Huang Zhenzhong 1988)

At the National Games, such well-known corporations as Fuji, Kodak, Coca-Cola, Pepsi, Xerox, Boeing, Seiko, Polaroid, Sharp, Olivetti, and NEC, and joint enterprises such as 555 and Gold Lion prominently dis-played logos and billboards all over the city, outside of the main sports complex and inside the arenas along the railings. A total of over one hundred enterprises advertised at the Games. While the largest contri-butions came from two Chinese companies (Wanbao refrigerators gave three million yuan and Jianlibao sports drink gave 2.5), the majority seemed to come from foreign companies. Contributions from corpora-tions and wealthy Overseas Chinese reached 20 million yuan. The open-door policy that encouraged foreign investment was a large factor in the financial success of the Games.

Lottery tickets were a new phenomenon in the PRC, and the Chinese people's love of gambling was reflected in the lottery's success. Over a

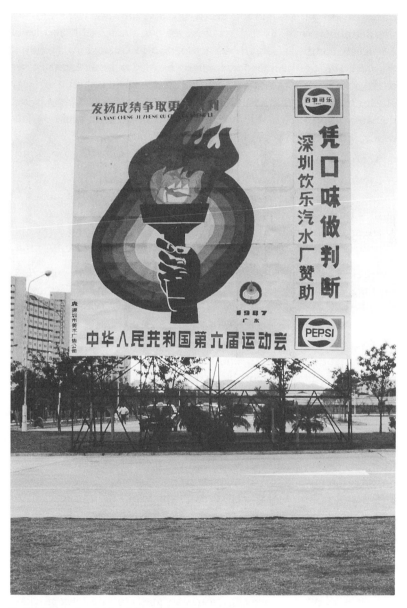

Pepsi billboard outside of the 1987 National Games gymnastics competition in Shenzhen. It reads, "Rely on taste to decide." These were the first national games at which sponsorship by foreign corporations occurred on a large scale.

three-year period, 169 million tickets at 0.50 yuan each were sold, raising 30 million yuan. By the end of November, a remarkable average of 2.5 tickets had been bought by each person in Guangdong Province! (*Tiyu bao* 1987c). This practice, formerly banned as being capitalist, received a warm welcome. It was said that people saw it not only as a way of winning money (five million yuan for each one-month period), but that they also felt that if they lost, it went to the good cause of Chinese sports:

> People consider that a losing ticket is equivalent to making a contribution to the National Games. The lottery tickets that we issued are not the same as lottery tickets issued by capitalists. The money they earn goes into the money bag of a private individual, but we are taking the money from the people, spending it on the people, using it to develop sports, so people are willing. (Huang He 1987a)

Prices of gate tickets brought gasps from the Chinese: 15 yuan (U.S. $4) for opening and closing ceremonies, 5 yuan for key events, and 3 yuan for less-popular events like track and field. People from other parts of China were amazed; spectators from the capital joked that at those prices, the stadiums in Beijing would be empty. Even so, the crush was so great that tickets to the opening and closing ceremonies and the soccer finals were almost impossible to get. People outside of the gates were offering up to 200 yuan with no takers, and fights erupted among the mobs waiting in line to buy the few tickets offered for sale. Since the stadium of 60,000 people consisted of an 8,000-member placard section, and the majority of the tickets were apparently given out to officials and their friends and relatives, the gate profits for the opening ceremonies probably did not amount to much, and this was true of the soccer events and closing ceremonies as well. Perhaps the total gate receipts came to a few million yuan. The figures were not made public.

The profits made from tour groups and other sources were also not made public. In any case, the Sports Foundation felt it could meet all operating costs. Whether or not it turned a profit was unknown by all except the cadres at the highest administrative levels.

Even with this commercialization, state and local subsidies provided the bulk of the funding for the Games. Within the city of Guangzhou and in the surrounding counties, forty-four new gymnasiums were built and fifty-five old ones repaired; the total cost of building and renovating facilities was 500 million yuan. The operating costs (costs of competi-

Table 4.1 1987 Chinese National Sports Games Expenditures and Revenues (by million yuan*)

	Expenditures	
Facilities construction	500	
Operating costs	50	
Total Expenditures	550	(U.S. $149 million)
	Revenues	
Facilities construction	300	(Guangdong subsidy)
	200	(local subsidies)
Operating costs	22	(state subsidy)
Lottery tickets	30	
Corporate sponsorship	20	
Partial Revenues**	572	(U.S. $154 million)

*At 1987 exchange rate, 1 yuan = U.S. $0.27.
**Gate receipts and other unknown.
SOURCE: Figures from *Tiyu bao* 1987a; Huang He 1987a; Ping Yuan 1987; *China Daily* 1988c.

tions; the Games committee members' rooms, board, and transportation; the costs of the opening ceremonies; and apparatus of all kinds) came to 50 million. Together, then, the facilities and operating costs totaled 550 million yuan (U.S. $149 million). The state gave a subsidy of 22 million, a little less than half of the operating costs. Guangdong province contributed 300 million, and the various localities contributed a total of 200 million. Thus, a total of 522 million came from state, provincial, and local subsidies. The breakdown of expenditures and revenues is shown in table 4.1.

Clearly, large sums of money are needed to produce a sports event of this size. Guangzhou was able to do it on an unprecedented scale because of local investment in sports facilities and corporate sponsorship, neither of which would have been possible before the economic reforms because localities and Chinese corporations did not have enough money, and foreign companies were not doing intensive business in China.

Guangdong, with its extensive ties to Hong Kong, is the wealthiest province in China. Whether the same policies could be so successfully implemented in another province was unclear. The quadrennial schedule was to be reset so that there would be three-year intervals either side of the 1990 Asian Games in Beijing; this suggests that the government perceived major sports games as a net drain. Originally, the 1993 Games were set for Chengdu in Sichuan province; they were to be the first Games ever held in an inland province. The Chengdu Games were to symbolically mark the progress of inland provinces as they followed the coastal provinces into prosperity. However, shortly after the Guangzhou Games, leaders began to fear that Chengdu could not live up to the standards set in Guangzhou. Chengdu gave up its assignation, which proved a bad omen. In the years after, the economic gap between coastal and inland provinces widened. The 1993 Games returned to Beijing.

China's national industries were also more visible than in previous Games. The People's Liberation Army had always fielded a strong team outside of the sports commission system, but in 1987, for the first time, many national industries fielded teams. These included the "Locomotive" team from the Railway System, the "Silver Eagles" from the Banking System, the "Advance Guard" of the Water and Electricity System, and teams from the Petroleum and Coal Mine Systems. This was seen as an encouraging development because it provided competition for the state sports system, which had had a monopoly on the organization of sports teams in the past. Under the policy of decentralization, such competition was hailed for stimulating progress. It was expected that such teams would become more numerous and reach a higher level in the future. That sports development was closely related to the economic base, especially foreign trade, is demonstrated by a comparison of the standings of the provinces in the National Games with the top ten exporters of 1987. Export values are only one measure of a province's economic development, but the results, shown in table 4.2, are still remarkably close.

Foreign export was directly a product of the policy of opening up to the outside world. It was an important source of the money necessary to develop sports. Thus, the open-door policy benefitted sports in China; it follows that the continued improvement of China's athletes could be cited as proof of the success of Party policies.

Another unique feature of the 1987 Games was that substantial economic incentives were offered to coaches and athletes for the first time. Although small bonuses of up to several hundred yuan had been standard for years, the changes in the economy at large led to astronomical increases in 1987. This development was not viewed positively by everyone. The press complained that on some teams,

Table 4.2 Athletic Standings in Games Compared with Export Rankings, by Province/Municipality

Province/Municipality	Standing in Games	Export Ranking
Guangdong	1	1
Shanghai	2	2
Liaoning	3	3
Beijing	4	10
Shandong	5	4
Sichuan	6	—
Hubei	7	9
Jiangsu	8	5
Zhejiang	9	8
Hebei	10	7
Tianjin	19	6

SOURCE: Figures for standings in the Games are from *Tiyu bao* (1987b); figures for export rankings are from *China Daily* (1988e).

there was too little talk of winning glory for the nation and making a contribution to the cause; instead they were greedy for comfort and talked about enjoyment; there was an increase in the mindset that fears hardship and fatigue; 'everything was focused on the money'; if the material incentive was low, 'activism' was not stimulated. (Huang Yawen 1987)

According to the press and to accounts told to me personally, some athletes had threatened to boycott the Games if their bonuses were not increased. In general, poorer provinces offered higher bonuses because they expected to win fewer medals. When other teams heard what they were offering, the athletes were unhappy. For example, Beijing originally offered 1,300 yuan for a gold medal, but was later pressured into raising it to 3,000; this was still under discussion a month later. All of this was seen as detrimental to the "spiritual civilization" that the meet was supposed to promote. While athletes and coaches were generally supportive, less involved commentators felt that "China is a poor nation" and must rely more on spiritual than material incentives. They considered it especially inappropriate that the poorest provinces offered the largest bonuses, since they could least afford them.

No one, however, seemed to doubt that material incentives did motivate people. This was brought home to me one day during track practice at Beijing University. My coach had measured one of my long jumps and come up with a surprisingly large number. I later expressed my dis-

belief to a teammate. I had previously explained to her the concept
of amateurism in the United States. She explained my outstanding
performance by saying, "It's probably because this year you get
bonuses."

THE CONSUMER BODY IN THE 1987 NATIONAL GAMES

Changing perceptions of the body were at the center of the growth of
consumer culture. During this time period, the "pursuit of beauty" was
officially acceptable and much discussed in the media. Fitness, beauty,
and fashions played an increasingly important role in people's lives, and
they were also promoted in state discourses (see Honig and Hershatter
1988: 41–80). During the Games, local businesses conducted special activities, and their sales figures were tracked in the press as carefully as
were the sports performances. The official sporting goods store of the
Sixth National Games was the New Yitai Sporting Goods Company, a
hundred-year-old company that was the largest sporting goods company south of the Yangtze. According to *Sports News*, it averaged ten
thousand yuan of sales daily during the Games and was patronized by
many of the star athletes. The main products sold, it was reported, were
clothing, shoes, balls, and paddles (Shi Chunming 1987). Athletes and
spectators to the Games got carried away in the wave of consumer enthusiasm. The Chinese people with whom I attended the Games made
multiple shopping trips into the cities of Guangzhou and Shenzhen to
buy goods unavailable in Beijing. After their competitions were over, I
accompanied several Zhejiang team athletes to a downtown street market and we came home with our arms full.

Although foreign sporting goods companies at that time concentrated on exports, some of them were just beginning to try to move into
and shape the domestic market in China. Through the media, they began to teach Chinese people how to consume. The China marketing
manager for Nike International, Michael Della Ratta, told me that Nike
had been featured in a spot on a lifestyles television show produced by
a local TV station. These sorts of programs were literally how-to guides
to consumer culture in the 1980s. On the show, he had demonstrated
high-technology shoes that were not then available in China, with the
goal of introducing the concept of shoe "technology." Because Nike was
not at that time interested in exploiting the domestic market, he was
more interested in introducing a concept than in selling shoes. Nike
could reap the rewards many years later. He noted that there was no

concept of the fitness lifestyle in Guangzhou: sports shoes were used for walking and standing in line. However, they were also popular for disco dancing, and a scene in the lifestyles show depicted this. Another Nike employee, Kevin Grolsey, commented to me that when Nike had held fun runs to celebrate the opening of factories, masses of people turned up in everyday clothes and street shoes to run the five miles; they weren't used to the concept of special running clothes and shoes—and couldn't afford them in any case.

Nike imagines that it promotes more than shoes: it promotes a way of life. As the leading American sporting goods company, Nike played a leading role in disseminating the concept of a "fitness lifestyle" in China, and other companies were not far behind. Part of Nike's strategy involved outfitting the national track and field team in Nike shoes and clothing.

The Chinese were just as interested in creating a consumer culture of the body. During the Games, an exhibition of sports and fitness products was held at the International Exhibition Hall. The Cantonese salesman at a booth selling American weight machines said that his equipment was beyond the means of all but factories of 500 or more people. The salesman at one of the Chinese booths told me that their equipment cost one-quarter of the foreign equipment. He sold to trade unions of fifty or more people. He commented that their machines were not as pretty on the surface as the foreign ones, but they worked just as well. Both salesmen agreed that business was growing each year.

CHINA, THE OLYMPIC MOVEMENT, AND COMMERCIALIZATION

The Olympic Movement as a whole encompasses political messages, economics, and entertainment, as well as sports, but only some aspects of these are incorporated into the official ideology of the IOC. Two sticking points in the official discourse have been the politicization and commercialization of the Olympic Games. Historically, China has been pragmatic about accepting the reality of the Olympic Movement and ignoring the ideological discourse. In the period after the founding of the PRC, Chinese representatives repeatedly angered the IOC by overtly mixing politics with sports when this was explicitly forbidden by the Olympic Charter (Kanin 1978: 36, 44–45, 62–63). The IOC's insistence on separating the two in its official pronouncements occurred at the same time that Cold War maneuvering and the "Two China Question" dominated the organization's politics. The ill feeling between China and the IOC led to China's severance of all contact with the IOC in 1958. Over the years, the IOC became less dogmatic about separating sport and politics, and in the 1970s it loosened its strictures against commercialization, banning the word "amateur" from its publications (MacAloon 1991b: 268–69).

The link between business and sport was incorporated into the meaning of China's 1987 National Games as a symbol of "modernity," but in a way that departed from Olympic practices. The commercialization of the Olympic Games is still popularly perceived by many Westerners as devaluing the "true meaning" of the Games (witness Greece's threat to withhold the flame for the torch relay of the 1984 Los Angeles Olympics in objection to the commercial exploitation of the symbol).

There was opposition to such commercialization in China, but on different grounds. In China, the opposition came from committed communists who felt that sports should primarily serve socialist spiritual civilization and that the incursion of materialism had corrupted the patriotic values the Games were supposed to embody. The Games gave the overall impression of an attempt to symbolically link economic modernization, Chinese nationalism, and Communist Party legitimacy into a meaningful and even moving totality. Some people were not comfortable with the inclusion of economic modernization in this formula. Thus, the growth of consumer culture occurred within an ambivalent political context.

The nationalistic link of sports and commercialism also exceeded even the more relaxed standards of the IOC in the late 1980s. The state's explicit praise of the Games as promoting market growth would have been equivalent to the IOC hailing the Olympics because they increase sales for Nike, Coca-Cola, Fuji, and so on, thus contributing to the growth of the world economy. The IOC does not yet go so far.

Mike Featherstone comments of consumer culture that "[t]he basic freedom within the culture is the freedom to consume" (1991: 176). It was easy to become intoxicated by this freedom during the Guangzhou Games and to overlook the absence of some other freedoms. Chinese visitors from other parts were overwhelmed by the abundance and quality of goods available in the markets, the multitude of ultramodern high-rise hotels and office buildings, the wealth of the inhabitants. Guangzhou city is an Oz shining on the horizon like a beacon for the rest of China. The dreamlike vision of Guangzhou as a metonym for China struck one reporter during the opening ceremonies (titled "Great

Aspirations") when he overheard a young person comment, "It was just like a fairytale!" The reporter later wrote,

A fairytale is an amazing scene that could not possibly appear in real life; it is nothing more than an ideal. Today Guangdong people, at the front ranks of reform and opening up, are using creativity and labor to turn ideal into reality step by step. "Great Aspirations's" success—can't this count as an example with symbolic significance? (Zhao Lihong 1987)

REVOLUTION AND DEMOCRACY IN THE TORCH RELAY

A consideration of the symbolism of the torch at China's 1987 Games reveals the tension between communist revolution and free-market democracy that was already in motion within Chinese society a year and a half before the Tiananmen Incident of 4 June 1989.

The torch has become one of the most closely guarded symbols of the Olympic Games, although the first torch relay was not held until the Berlin Games of 1936. Since the torch that starts the Olympic relay is lit in ancient Greece, the event could be interpreted as a representation of the light of Western civilization spreading throughout the world (and entrusted to non-Western nations for further enrichment—see Kang Shin-pyo 1991: 54–56). Once it reaches the site of the Games, the cauldron is lit during the opening ceremonies and the flame burns brightly until the closing ceremonies, symbolizing the period of world peace that is supposed to characterize the Games.

Before the Great Hall of the People in Tiananmen Square, on 11 November 1987, at 6:30 p.m., the mayor of Beijing, Chen Xitong, declared that the torch-lighting ceremony for the Chinese National Games had begun. On both sides of the platform a drum corps composed of one hundred Young Pioneers sounded their drums while groups of dancers with flower garlands and colored scarves performed a dance. Vice-Premier Wan Li lit the torch and passed it to the Secretary of the Communist Youth League Central Committee, who then lit five more torches. Altogether, the six torches symbolized the Sixth National Games. The ninety members of the torch relay team then lit ninety small torches. He Zhenliang, vice-director of the Sports Commission,[2] gave this speech:

2. He Zhenliang was then the IOC member in China and would later become IOC vice president and executive vice president of the Beijing 2000 Olympic Bid Committee.

Today, the youth of the capital receive the flaming torch lit by the comrade leaders of the Central Communist Party and take it to the City of the Rams [Guangzhou]. This torch symbolizes the ardent expectations of the Party and State for the masses, and especially for the vast numbers of young people. We want to lift high the revolutionary torch lit by the older generation, continue and carry through our party's glorious revolutionary tradition, follow the Basic Path of the first stage of socialism advocated at the Thirteenth Party Congress, struggle arduously, unite in the fight, struggle to build our nation into a wealthy, democratic, civilized, socialist modernized nation! (Yang Xuewei 1987)

Among the state and sports commission leaders present, there was one person who must have appreciated this invention of ritual: Fei Xiaotong, China's premier anthropologist.[3]

The runners, carrying the six large torches and ninety small ones, then led the way out of the square, followed by another hundred runners. The runners were composed of Beijing athletes and the "Old People's Long March Distance Running Team." The latter is an officially sanctioned group of runners that consists mostly of men over the age of sixty (Rao Hu 1982). The long "dragon" formed by the torch lights was destined for the Mutianyu section of the Great Wall outside of Beijing.

He's speech resembles speeches given at previous National Games' torch-lighting ceremonies and sets forth the official interpretation of the torch. The state leaders designated the torch as a symbol of the communist revolution and, in a Confucian manner, associated it with the duty of the younger generation to carry out the will of their elders. The revolution was begun by the older generations and handed on to successive generations in a never-ending relay. It was the duty of the next generation to carry on the revolutionary torch lit by their predecessors. The transfer of tradition across generational bounds was emphasized by the selection of two groups of athletes—one youthful, one elderly—to carry torches toward that archetypical symbol of Chinese identity and national defense, the Great Wall. The relay involved movements along

---

3. Unfortunately, I do not know whether Fei had a hand in designing the ritual. A former student of Bronislaw Malinowski, he is now best known for his work on small-town development. He may simply have attended as a high-ranking member of the Central Committee of the Party; however, this is the first time I have seen mention of his attendance at a sports event.

two major symbolic axes. The first movement, the run from the Great Hall of the People to the Great Wall, united a modern symbol of Party legitimacy (which, in theory, stems from the will of the people) with an ancient symbol of an unchanging Chinese identity. The second movement, the passing of the torch from state leaders to elderly males and young males and females, traced the contours of the social hierarchy in today's China.[4]

A week later, the torch was conveyed by airplane to Guangzhou, where it was carried into the stadium by star diver Tan Liangde. At the moment before the cauldron was lit, one reporter was moved to record his thoughts:

> [T]he torch held high in the hand of a Chinese sports star is like a symbol of a new age that is already upon us! . . . Give your hopes over to the torch, give the torch over to the future! . . . The torch, the symbol of modern China! (Yang Yingming 1987)

This image conflicts with the official ideology. In the official imagery, the emphasis was on the past revolution and filial duty to the elders who came to power during that revolution. In opposition, the reporter emphasized a new age: it is almost as if he is exhorting the state leaders to let go of the torch and allow the new age to take shape.

The shape of a torch formed the dominant element of the official emblem of the 1987 Games, but the official explanation of the emblem does not mention what the torch itself signified in the context of these Games. The base of the torch was formed by a running track that was also in the shape of the character for "ram," a reference to Guangzhou's nickname of the "City of Rams" (*yangcheng*). The flame was shaped like a "6" to indicate the Sixth National Games. Each of the six Games had its own emblem, but the only other emblem that contained a torch shape was the one for the 1979 Games (see figure 4.1). This was the Games that celebrated Deng Xiaoping's rise to power, an ascension that was facilitated by the Democracy Wall Movement of November 1978 to March 1979. These emblems were chosen by the organizing committee in an open competition and were to capture the essence of the Games. It can only be considered coincidence that the two games symbolized by torches were those that followed the 1979 Democracy Wall Movement and preceded the 1989 Democracy Movement.

4. The similarities with the hierarchies played out in the torch relays for the 1986 Asian Games and 1988 Olympic Games in Seoul are striking. Compare with MacAloon and Kang Shin-pyo (1990).

Figure 4.1. Emblems of past National Games (*Shenghui bolan* 1987: 40–41).

A year and a half after the torch of the 1987 Games was extinguished, the "Goddess of Democracy" was erected in Tiananmen Square with a torch held high in her hand, like a symbol of a new age. This string of symbols may be pure coincidence—but if the torch symbolized the communist revolutionary tradition as it was officially supposed to, then why would it appear during these key breaks with the revolutionary tradition? This may reveal how symbols enter into public circulation and are then selected out and foregrounded when they resonate with key historic moments in a way not anticipated by their official promoters.

The Olympic flame burns throughout the Games, a fact that is often exploited in television camera shots of the flame burning away in the night while the Olympic Village sleeps. At China's 1987 Games, a malfunction in the torch base meant that the flame was extinguished for most of the Games (though a flame was kept burning elsewhere). Workmen, banging noisily away on the cauldron during the track and field events, finally restored it to working order just in time for the closing ceremonies, when it was to be extinguished. This rough treatment was, of course, due to an unfortunate technological breakdown, but to an American accustomed to a more reverential treatment of the flame it seemed profane, or ludicrous—or worse, a bad omen. During the closing ceremonies, the flame would not go out when it was supposed to and ended up sputtering down and then rising up again, like a phoenix from the ashes, for at least ten minutes after its exit cue.

THE DEBATE OVER THE MASS CALISTHENICS

The clash between consumer culture and committed communism manifested itself in a heated debate about the type of body culture that was to be represented in the opening ceremonies for the 1987 Games.

The opening ceremonies consisted of the elements that have become common internationally: marching bands, the Parade of Athletes, the raising of the national and Games flags and playing of the national and Games anthems, the lighting of the torch, the Opening Addresses by state leaders, the Athletes' and Officials' Oaths, the mass calisthenics, and fireworks (in that order). The centerpiece of the ceremonies was the mass calisthenics.

A choreographer explained to me that the theme for the opening ceremonies is a combination of what the organizing committee wants and what the choreographers think is possible. The budget for the 1987 opening ceremonies was two to three million yuan. After they have decided on the themes, the designers report to the leaders of the organizing committee. In 1987, the organizing committee was chaired by Vice-Premier Wan Li; the two vice-chairmen were Director of the State Sports Commission Li Menghua and Governor of Guangdong Province Ye Xuanping. Yuan Weimin was the Secretary-General. I asked a choreographer if the top state leaders had to approve the content of the opening ceremonies, and she replied only that they were aware of it. In the past, top leaders have fought over the content of the ceremonies, including Deng Xiaoping's famous fight with Mao's wife Jiang Qing over a placard section for the 1975 Games (Rong Gaotang et al. 1984: 24).

The mass calisthenics designers had a tricky task because preparations began two years ahead of time and they had to be able to predict the direction of the political winds. The designers made an effort to choose general themes that would not become politically sensitive, and empty pages were left in the book that guides the placard section in case last-minute changes were needed. The placard sections cause more trouble than the mass calisthenics themselves because they are more concrete and contain many slogans. Two placard backgrounds for the 1987 Games were changed during the two-year course of preparations because the designers decided they were inappropriate. Even so, the designers remained in suspense until the last minute, since the 13th Party

Congress could have produced an eleventh-hour shift in the political winds.

Several people told me that there had been a very heated debate over the type of opening ceremonies that would be created. Inspired by the Hollywood-type show presented in Los Angeles in 1984, the Chinese choreographers had considered discarding the mass calisthenics type of performance—which is a standard fixture of socialist sports events, and which was the only type of show the PRC had ever had in its national games. Instead, some people advocated an "artistic" performance with more singing, dancing, and gimmicks. The Hollywood-type of performance, it was felt, was more modern, more festive (*renao*), and better able to produce a good atmosphere. One of my informants commented that he knew Western nations did not go in for mass calisthenics in a big way because they perceived it as too "rigid" (*siban*). The opening ceremonies were supposed to reflect the "feeling" (*ganqing*) and fit the "conditions" (*guoqing*) of the times. Many of the choreographers apparently felt that the "feeling" of the times would be best expressed by an artistic performance.

However, they ultimately decided the "conditions" would not allow it. They had more experience in mass calisthenics so they were less likely to fail. They had tried some artistic elements in the Fifth Games and didn't quite succeed. Hollywood-type shows demand a higher level of technology, particularly acoustic technology, which would have been difficult to properly employ. If the acoustics had gone wrong, the opening ceremonies could have been a failure. The Los Angeles ceremonies had utilized the skills of many famous artists, but China, according to one informant, didn't have that many good singers—there just weren't that many people in China that specialized in the arts. And they would need large numbers in order to create a proper atmosphere. Another argument was that the opening ceremonies should reflect the characteristics of physical culture rather than the arts, in order to encourage the growth of physical culture. As one informant phrased it, why would you want to encourage the arts at a sports meet? This attitude was one manifestation of the competition for popular support between the arts and sports in China, a competition which can perhaps be traced back to the rivalry between the State Sports Commission and the Ministry of Culture over state funding and policy-making.

The choreographers felt that they had not entirely discarded the arts. In the end, they decided to combine "traditional" art forms with mass calisthenics to produce an innovative show. In my discussions with the choreographers, it was clear that in their way of thinking there was a clear distinction between the "traditional" (*chuantong*) and "modern" (*xiandaihua*) elements in the show. Traditional elements were pre-Communist imperial or non-Han practices. Some of the traditional elements included the martial arts and dancing in the second act, the pole dancing in the fourth act, and the dragon dance in the final act. These were all drawn from local Guangdong practices: the martial arts were the "Southern Fist" style, dragon dancing is a Cantonese tradition, and the pole dancing is a southern minority practice. The modern elements were those that utilized "technology," such as the glowing rods and placards in the last act, the fireworks on the dragons' bodies, and the electronic music. I also thought I detected breakdancing moves in the fourth act, perhaps another idea borrowed from Los Angeles.

One reporter compared these ceremonies to those of the Los Angeles Olympic Games, which even three years later were fresh in many people's minds because they had made a deep impression.

The mass calisthenics at the opening ceremonies of the 23rd Olympics in Los Angeles . . . expressed America's history, and vividly exhibited America's arts and culture. But if you had those 10,000 smiling, energetic young Guangdong boys and girls perform a show of American-style group gymnastics, they'd probably be neither fish nor fowl. "Great Aspirations" expressed modern Chinese people's sentiments, character, and ideals; the designers sought modern flavor in costumes, movements, formations, music and overall conception, but they also paid attention to preserving the "Chinese flavor." When the four dancing dragons suddenly spouted dazzling flames in the darkness, the entire stadium was full of joyous voices and thunderous applause. These were the ancient Chinese dragons that could not be extinguished, these were the exuberant Chinese dragons that leap and fly, these were the symbol of China's athletes, these were the symbols of today's China. (Zhao Lihong 1987)[5]

CONCLUSIONS: NOT QUITE A TURNING POINT

The 1987 National Games were widely appreciated as a demonstration of the success of the economic reforms: the amount of money they re-

5. Los Angeles as an "anti-model" was prevalent in the public discourse. However, John MacAloon brought to my attention the similarities with the South Korean ceremonies for the 1986 Asian Games and 1988 Olympic Games. These similarities must have been due to

Milky Way Stadium, Guangzhou, site of the opening ceremonies for the 1987 National Games. Banners, suspended from balloons, are printed with slogans. The Games emblem stands above the main entrance and below it is a large statue of the Games mascot, a ram.

quired was well publicized, and the grand visual scale of the opening ceremonies proved to the huge television audience that they were more expensive than any past Games could have been under past economic conditions. Everyone I spoke to enjoyed the opening ceremonies, describing them as "magnificent" (*jingcai*), "moving" (*dongren*), and "beautiful" (*mei*). However, their expense in itself aroused some cynicism. Many people in the sportsworld, for example, saw the money spent on the opening ceremonies as somewhat of a waste, noting that if it were spent on grassroots sports development it would have a stronger effect on the progress of Chinese sports. One coach commented on opening ceremonies in general: "You give all that money to them and they prac-

---

a shared cultural logic, because the choreographers did not consciously use the Seoul Games as a model, as they did with the Los Angeles Games. Compare descriptions of the 1988 Opening Ceremonies in Kang Shin-pyo (1991) and Dilling (1990). An important difference between the Chinese and Korean ceremonies, however, was that the Korean ceremonies drew more directly from traditional Korean cosmology and mythic plotlines; the Chinese ceremonies only faintly suggested mythic allusions, and even this slight link to "tradition" was considered innovative.

tice for months just for that ceremony, and what does it mean? It doesn't develop sports any. But that's the way the government does things in China. You always have to have a big ceremony."

A taxi driver sitting outside of the stadium during the rehearsal for the opening ceremonies echoed the most common sentiment among Guangdong residents about the National Games: their major advantage was that they brought business. Secondarily, the system of roads was improved for the Games, reducing the traffic problem. "But in general, the average person's life hasn't been affected."

From a more distant perspective, it was evident that things were changing in China. This transformation took concrete form in the series of new economic measures adopted for these Games. In the more abstract realm of public symbols, the transformation manifested itself in the conflicting interpretations of the torch and the debate over doing away with mass calisthenics. Although the mass calisthenics were kept, it was evident that there had been a slow movement away from a militaristic revolutionary culture of the body toward an aesthetic consumer culture of the body. The lack of technology and skills, however, prevented the choreographers from fully realizing the shift from the conformity of mass calisthenics toward the Hollywood-style showcasing of individual talents. This is a thought-provoking metaphor for the current state of Chinese public culture and its ability to borrow from the West.

CHAPTER FIVE

Qing Dynasty Grand Sacrifice and Communist National Games

Rituals of the Chinese State?

PUBLIC EVENTS IN CHINESE CULTURE

A Note on Method in Studying Public Events

Chapter 3 argued for the importance of nonverbal representation in the Chinese political process and chapter 4 discussed the social context for a very important Chinese public event, the National Sports Games. This chapter analyzes the symbolism of the 1987 National Games in more detail to demonstrate the role of the Games as a public event in the formation of a national consciousness and the consolidation of state power in the PRC. A comparison with the most symbolically important public event of the imperial state—the Grand Sacrifices—illuminates the significant differences in the nature of the PRC national consciousness and state compared with what existed a century prior.

I stated in chapter 3 that the analysis of ritual and symbol in modern Chinese politics was underdevel-

A different version of this chapter was previously published as "Qing Dynasty Grand Sacrifice and Communist National Sports Games: Rituals of the Chinese State?" *Journal of Ritual Studies* 7, no. 1 (Winter): 45–64. This chapter has been expanded in parts and the central argument altered. I wish to thank Charles Laughlin and Deborah Davis for their comments.

oped and argued that this deficiency could be partly remedied through greater attention to public events. Here, I would like to advocate a method for studying public events. It is my contention that the starting point for any study of public events should be an analysis of the native categories that are used to classify them. MacAloon (1984) brought to our attention that public performances come in various types and that the analysis of the relationship between the types can provide as much insight as analysis of the individual events themselves.

Among sports scholars, failure to appreciate the importance of native categories has led to a question that has never been satisfactorily resolved: "Is sport a form of ritual?" This riddle has been leading sports scholars in circles since the publication of Allen Guttmann's *From Ritual to Record* (1978), if not since the founder of the modern Olympic Games, Pierre de Coubertin, declared in the early 1900s that "modern athletics is a religion, a cult, an impassioned soaring" (Coubertin 1967: 118). My answer to the question is a simple one: sport is a form of ritual if the people who practice it think it is. In the Chinese perspective, sport is not classified as ritual. If Western social scientists are capable of asking whether sport *is* a form of ritual, then it is because for the past century in the West people like Coubertin have extolled sport as a new kind of religion, in part because of their own political agendas and in part because the sociocultural history of sport in the West allowed them to liken sport to ritual. Christianity and the ritual traditions of the French Revolution were the primary forces that shaped this tradition in the West.

This chapter compares the premier ritual of state of the late Qing dynasty—Grand Sacrifice—with a major sports event—the Chinese National Sports Games. The last Grand Sacrifice was performed some fifty years before the first Communist National Sports Games. In the intervening years, China had changed from an imperial state ruled according to traditions believed to be ancient into a socialist state ruled according to communist principles oriented toward modernity and the future. My use of the words "traditional" and "modern" in this chapter echoes the categories that the Chinese themselves use and refers to the use of either adherence to custom or pursuit of the modern to legitimate state power. The point of comparing these two national events is not to demonstrate that the National Sports Games *are* a ritual, but rather to show how the changing types of public events have been part of a broader change in the symbolic construction of the state in China. What has *not* changed is that large-scale public events are very important in this construction because such events dramatize and reinforce a world-order that organizes human bodies in space and time, with the state portrayed as the keeper of that order.

A Typology of Chinese Public Events

At a linguistic level, Mandarin Chinese distinguishes five types of public performance; three of them are significant in contemporary Chinese political culture. They are expressed in characters which, when appended to descriptive phrases, designate particular types of public events: *hui* ("gathering, assembly, meeting"), *shi* ("ceremony"), *jie* ("festival"), *li* ("familial ritual"), and *dian* or *dianli* ("celebration, nonfamilial ritual").

The word "gathering" is used for most political assemblies (for example, National People's Congress) as well as for the genres discussed in chapter 3: report meetings, tea and talk meetings, welcome meetings, send-off meetings, and many others. It is a neutral term most often applied to events with no religious associations (an exception is the temple fair, or *miaohui*). Sporting events take the character *hui*. The Chinese National Games are called a "sports meet" (*yundonghui*) or a "solemn gathering" (*shenghui*).

Shi is the character used in the words for the opening and closing ceremonies of sports meets, which literally mean "opening the curtain ceremony" and "closing the curtain ceremony." *Yishi* also describes the welcoming ceremonies for victorious teams. In general, *shi* has both religious and political uses.

The words that are usually translated as "festival" (*jieri, jieqing, jieling*) all contain the character *jie*, which implies a link to the seasonal calendar—the literal meaning of *jie* is something divided into segments.[1] Its original references were to the celebrations embedded in religious practices and associated with the cyclical agrarian calendar (for example, Spring Festival, Qing Ming, Duanwu, Zhongyang). As secular celebrations were added to the Chinese calendar, other uses were added: *jie* is used for political events such as National Day, Labor Day, and Women's Day. *Jie* is not applied to sports, though sports meets have often been held to celebrate National Day, Labor Day, and others, and Duanwu is celebrated with dragon-boat races. Festivals are supposed to be voluntary, spontaneous, and joyful. In Chinese, they should be *renao*—full of activity and excitement.

---

1. I am indebted to Ren Hai for researching and discussing with me the Chinese concept of festival.

Li and *dian,* by contrast, imply events which are organized, formal, and solemn. *Li* is most frequently used to refer to the different wedding rituals and is thus associated with the family and gift exchange. While *li* implies private, familial rituals, *dian* refers to large-scale official rituals: a ritual that celebrates the founding of a new state is a "great *dian*" (*kai guo da dian*). In combination, *dian* and *li* mean "ritual" or "celebration." Grand Sacrifice was called a *dianli.* Today, neither is commonly used to refer to sports events.

To this brief typology of public events, we might also add the notion of the "market" (*shi*), which is used to describe country fairs (*jishi*), street markets, night markets, and so on. This category, however, in-cludes a range of activities, not all of which are formally organized, peri-odic events. Market activities *are* commonly linked with sporting events.

Festivals and Sports: Symbolizing Public Culture

In a cultural analysis of the role of public events in the West, festivals deserve special attention, but in China the relationship takes a different shape. Habermas has been criticized for neglecting the link between citi-zenship and public festivals while overemphasizing public discourse (Garnham 1992: 360). Monique Ozouf's study of the festivals of the French Revolution and John MacAloon's studies of the festivals of the Olympic Movement suggest the ways in which national festivals and sports festivals in the West were and are conceived of as performative expressions of bourgeois public culture.

In the West for the last century, festivals and sports have had a close relationship. Since the French Revolution, Western festivals have sym-bolically expressed the ideals of bourgeois public culture—though not, of course, without contestation from other social categories. For the French revolutionaries, the democratic festival must above all allow "'that which despotism had never allowed'—that is to say, the mingling of citizens delighting in the spectacle of one another and the perfect accord of hearts" (Ozouf 1988: 54). In order to represent democracy and equality, the revolutionary festival was to take place in open, public spaces and involve women and children as well as men from all occupa-tions except the aristocracy (pp. 17, 19). And in opposition to the Ro-man Catholic heritage, it was to utilize dehistoricized classical symbols such as Reason, Liberty, and Equality. The revolutionary festival embod-ied the ideals of freedom of assembly in public spaces, freedom of ex-pression, equality, and secularism.

Sports have often been contested within the frame of the festival in the West. The link between sport and festival was reinforced in the Olympic ideology developed by Coubertin, whose concept of festival seems heavily influenced by the French revolutionary tradition. He often referred to the Olympic Games as a sporting or youth festival. As MacAloon (1984: 248) has pointed out, Coubertin felt that a festival atmosphere was central to the Olympic Games: "If anyone were to ask me the formula for 'Olympizing' oneself, I should say to him, 'the first condition is to be joyful'" (Coubertin 1967: 57). The notions of carnivalesque democracy and equality are also central to MacAloon's descriptions of the role of festival in the contemporary Olympic Games. He argues that Coubertin's ideal of "internationalism" is more nearly achieved in the street festivals that take place during the Games than it is in the formal and sometimes repressive festival constructed by the authorities (MacAloon 1987c: 27–29). During his speech in the opening ceremonies of the 1992 Barcelona Olympics, IOC President Juan-Antonio Samaranch intoned, "The greatest festival of our contemporary society, the Olympic Games, is about to begin."

The influence of Coubertin's Olympic ideology on American sports is illustrated by the choice of the name of "National Sports Festival," later changed to "U.S. Olympic Festival" for the American national sports games.

As might be expected, major sports events in China are not designed to be a symbolic acting out of bourgeois public culture with its principles of freedom of assembly and speech. The emphasis on solemnity is echoed in the reference to events as a "solemn assembly" (*shenghui*) and in the formulaic use of *longzhong* ("grand, solemn") to describe major sports events and their opening ceremonies. In the China Central Television broadcast of the Barcelona opening ceremonies, Samaranch's statement about the Games as a world festival, not surprisingly, was mistranslated in the following form: "This is our nation's greatest festival day."

At the Chinese events that I participated in and observed, "joy" took a back seat to "civilization" as the mood that was officially promoted. The 1987 National Games were portrayed as a showcase for socialist spiritual civilization at its best. A constant attention to obeying rules took much of the joy out of the occasion and was intended to imprint Party ideology deeply into the minds of those who watched the telecast or were present at the event. The most joyous group that I saw was a band of male college students who, wearing papier-mâché lion heads and carrying banners and large drums, roamed the walled-in Milky Way sports complex (the French revolutionaries denounced walls as symbols of despotism). They appeared to be enjoying themselves despite their solemn banners proclaiming them to be the "Guangzhou College Student Civilized Cheering Squad." One banner read, "Soar up in the World, Win Championships, Obtain the Double Harvest of Outstanding Performances and Civilized Spirit." The other banner contained a poem which they also chanted along with the beat of the large drum: "Lion of the East Awakens, Heart of China." One of the students explained to me, "The Awakening Lion represents the Chinese people's spirit, because the Lion is the King of the Ten Thousand Wild Animals." These students were out for fun, but their fun was not carnivalesque in that it stayed within the bounds of official ideology. They were also delegated by their colleges to attend the competitions and were allocated tickets to spread the civilized spirit.

The solemn atmosphere that surrounds major sports meets in China makes them similar to rituals, even though they are not classified as such. Both rituals and sports constitute important techniques by which an orientation to the world is instilled in individuals, in the first instance through the bodily manipulation of symbols and in the second through the symbolic manipulation of the body. They make use of a principle recognized by Confucius fifteen hundred years before Bourdieu: when structured body movements are assigned symbolic and moral significance, and are repeated often enough, they generate a moral orientation toward the world that is habitual because the body as a mnemonic device serves to reinforce it.

MacAloon argues that the Olympic Games are a "ramified performance type" composed of many different performance genres (1984: 268). The Chinese National Games also embrace several types of public events. Though the street festival is practically absent, the National Games have often been held in conjunction with official national festivals. The first five National Games overlapped with National Day (*Guoqingjie*) or concluded just before it. At the 1987 National Games, the bustle of the street did not revolve around festival activities, but around the street markets downtown, which were frequented by crowds of visitors from elsewhere eager to purchase goods unavailable in the rest of China. This, of course, was a distinctive feature of these Games. Artistic events were held in conjunction with the Games, including a special "Evening Show of Culture and Arts" that brought together many top performers to celebrate the opening of the Games. And although the Games were not labeled as a ritual of state, the emphasis on athletes and spectators being civilized and polite so that the Games became an "exemplary center" of Chinese civilization echoed the central ideas in the ancient logic of *li,* which will be discussed further here and in subsequent chapters. As a *system,* the National Games are not as complex a set of "Chinese boxes" as the Olympic Games.

Pre-Communist Theory of Ritual: *Li*

Today, the word *li* refers to small-scale rituals, but it is also a word with a long history in the Chinese political philosophy. This philosophy formed the rationale for the official rituals of the Qing, which then influenced the cult of the state under the Nationalists and Communists. In Chinese theories of statecraft, there is an idea with an ancient pedigree that if you wish to control Chinese society you must start by controlling the body. Confucius crystallized this notion in the concept of *li* ("rite, ritual, etiquette"), which referred to the proper observance of the rituals and etiquette dictated by social hierarchy. *Li* was oriented more toward proper ritual performance and less toward the intentions and feelings of the performers—hence, it was "the embodied expression of what is right" (Wechsler 1985: 24, quoting Legge's 1967 translation of the *Li ji*). It "came to be regarded as the very principle upon which Chinese civilization was based" because it instilled moral values and regulated social conduct (Wechsler 1985: 24).

According to J. G. A. Pocock, Confucian thinkers recognized that the problem with words is that when you tell a person to do something, you call into his mind the possibility of not doing it (Pocock 1964: 4). The Confucian emphasis on *li* could be interpreted as an attempt to circumvent the resistance that is generated by verbal commands, which were not classified as *li,* but rather as *fa*—a system of decrees backed by punishments. Since *li* was performed, it did not call to mind counter-arguments (Pocock 1964: 4–5).[2] The bodily nature of *li* is illustrated in a metaphor employed by Xun Zi (298–238 b.c.), who compared *li* to dancing. "How do we know the meaning of dancing?" he asked, and concluded that the dancer "exerts to the utmost all the strength of his body to keep time to the measures of the sounds of the drum and bell, and has no rebellious heart" (p. 6).

Though *li* disappeared from theories of statecraft with the fall of the

---

2. Pocock's insightful analysis of *li* and *fa* brings to mind Foucault's conceptions of power and discourse. In my opinion, Pocock's article portrays an ancient Chinese political philosophy that was more elegant, practical, and subtle than Foucault's rendition.

Qing (1911), the importance of the body was recognized by Republican reformers and by the Communist Party. Since its inception, the Party has utilized bodily performances as a way of transforming old thought patterns and instilling new ones. Revolutionary techniques focused on the body have included class-struggle sessions, revolutionary dramas, labor reform, mass calisthenics, civilian military training, and—of course—sports. What follows is a concrete description of the world-orientations instilled by the Qing state cult and Communist National Games.

"GRAND SACRIFICE" IN THE QING DYNASTY

The Qing State Cult

The Qing Dynasty was founded by the Manchu, who in 1644 succeeded in wresting the remnants of control from the fading Ming Dynasty. The Confucian theory of ritual was put into practice by the Manchu rulers. "The most subtle attempt at ideological control made by the Qing rulers was their extensive application of the ancient principle, 'instruction through worship'" (Hsiao 1960: 220). The state religion they adopted was based in large part on Ming precedent, which itself was based on the ritual of previous dynasties. The ritual procedures were set forth in *The Statutes of the Qing (Da Qing Huidian)*.

The *Statutes* divided official sacrifices into three types: Grand, Middle, and Common. Grand Sacrifices were conducted by the emperor himself at the temples in the capital and its suburbs. Middle Sacrifices were conducted by the emperor or delegated officials in the imperial and lower-level capitals. One of the Middle Sacrifices in Beijing was performed at the Temple of Xian Nong, patron god of agriculture, located just west of the Temple of Heaven; this site later had an important connection with sports, as discussed below. Common Sacrifices were performed by local officials at all capitals (Feuchtwang 1977: 585–86).

The Grand Sacrifices were most critical to the maintenance of the imperial order. There were four: to Heaven, Earth, the Imperial Ancestors, and the Land and Harvest. The most important ritual was the emperor's worship of Heaven, which he performed on the winter solstice at the Temple of Heaven in the southern suburb of Beijing. The Earth was worshiped on the summer solstice at the Temple of Earth in the northern suburb. The Imperial Ancestors were worshiped in the first month of each of the four seasons and at the end of the year in the Temple of the Ancestors within the walls of the Forbidden City. The

Land and Harvest were worshipped in the middle month of spring and of autumn at the Temple of Land and Harvest in the western suburb.

The timing and location of the sacrifices imposed a distinct order onto time and space. Temporally, they marked important junctures in the lunar calendar that regulated the practice of agriculture. Spatially, the temples were major landmarks that structured the landscape of Beijing, as they still do today. Blending space and time, the Grand Sacrifices linked the four directions, the four seasons, and the four great sacrificial altars (Zito 1984: 59).

E. T. Williams (1913) gives a detailed account of the performance of the worship of Heaven based on the *Statutes of the Qing* and his own personal observations in the waning years of the Qing. Three days before the sacrifice, all government offices (*yamen*) posted an imperial announcement on a table outside of the main door. A notice that he observed read,

On the —— day of the —— year, being the winter solstice, WE shall reverently sacrifice to the Great Ruler of Imperial Heaven at the Altar to Heaven in behalf of you, OUR people. The purity of the ministers depends upon their hearts, their righteousness upon the determination of each to exalt his office, lest by neglect to discharge their duties calamity be visited upon the State. Be reverent. Let there be no carelessness. (Williams 1913: 17)

The date was also announced in the Peking Gazette (p. 28).

On the day of the sacrifice, the way from the palace to the Temple of Heaven was cleared by guards, the side streets were roped off, and the shops were closed and shuttered. The emperor in his sedan chair and his retinue proceeded to the Temple of Heaven between rows of kneeling soldiers. The common people were not allowed to observe the procession or the ritual.

At the temple, the ritual was overseen by an officer of the Court of Sacrificial Worship, who functioned as the master of ceremonies by announcing the beginning and end of the service and by requesting the emperor to worship, change locations, receive the sacrifice, and so on. Another officer carried a tablet which was used to mark the spot where the emperor should stand. The emperor followed the verbal directions of the master of ceremonies and the guidance of the officer bearing the tablet. The emperor seems to have been a passive participant. He did not speak; even the prayers were read by a special officer (Williams 1913: 36).

The entire ritual was choreographed in minute detail. The center of the ritual was the offering of fourteen slaughtered bullocks. Other offerings included cups of wine, all sorts of cooked and uncooked food, jade, silk, incense, sheep and goats. The service was accompanied by music and dancing, directed by a bandmaster who announced each musical piece and signaled the dancers to start and finish. The end of the music signaled the end of the ritual. The dancers were divided into two groups, one of sixty-four civil dancers who danced with plumes and wands, and another of sixty-four military dancers who performed military movements with spears and battle-axes. The musicians and dancers rehearsed the ceremonies ahead of time in a hall for that purpose on the temple grounds.

The Grand Sacrifices continued to be performed until just before fall of the Qing in 1911. Meanwhile, beginning in the late 1800s, the American YMCA and the missionary schools had introduced the performance genre of the sports meet. Building on this tradition, the Republican Government (est. 1912) conducted seven small-scale "national sports meets" between 1910 and 1948. The Communist Party came to power in 1949 and conducted its first National Games in 1959, some fifty years after the last Qing sacrifice.

THE CHINESE NATIONAL SPORTS GAMES
The Structure of Time

Like the Olympic Games, the PRC National Games are supposed to take place once every four years. The timing of the National Games is (in theory) dictated by the timing of the Olympic Games; they were held in the year before the Olympic Games in order to choose China's Olympic team (until 1993, when the schedule was again changed). Thus, the Games follow an international cycle. The most immediate and striking difference with Grand Sacrifice is that the National Games are not scheduled by the lunar calendar and reflect nothing of the agrarian cycles. As Bourdieu notes, the calendar is one of the most codified aspects of human existence (1977: 97). The lunar calendar is still very important in Chinese peoples' everyday lives because it orders the celebrations that have the deepest popular meanings (for example, Spring Festival, Mid-Autumn Festival, and Duanwu). The disjuncture between the importance of the lunar calendar to the people and its lack of importance in ceremonies of state is one of the major disjunctures of the modern era (Cohen 1991: 128). The main holiday of state, National Day, is held on

1 October in the international calendar. National Day was celebrated in the midst of the First National Games, and the next four Games concluded just before it (on 28 or 30 September).

The Structure of Space

The stadium locations for the National Games do not exhibit the close connection with cosmic order that the Grand Sacrifices did, but they nevertheless map out the modern history of state development in China from the Qing to the PRC. At the end of the Boxer siege of Beijing in 1901, the Temple of Heaven and the Temple of Xian Nong were occupied by the British and American relief troops, who bivouacked there "for want of a better spot" because of the open green areas and the fresh well water (Landor 1901: 253). Although the temples were chosen for practical reasons and not specifically in order to desecrate the sacred sites of the Qing state, once they were inside the troops were quite aware that they had penetrated the *sanctum sanctorum* of the Qing (see Hevia 1990). The temple complexes were looted, furniture destroyed for firewood, grass used for grazing horses. At the Temple of Agriculture, the soldiers used the emperor's throne as a barber's chair until their commanding general took it into his own possession (Landor 1901: 248, 267). Sports were common in garrison life and the British instituted regular field hockey, polo, and gymkhana events on the grounds at the Temple of Heaven that drew participants from several of the other Eight Powers (Steel 1985: 63–67).

The irony of the victorious troops playing sports at the most sacred Qing temple is especially acute when one considers that one of the first events of the Boxer siege of Beijing was the Boxers' burning of the grandstand at the international horse racing course six miles west of the city wall. According to the British reporter Landor, it was with this outrage that "all the young men of a sporting disposition in Pekin [sic] began to realise how serious matters were getting . . . They could hardly believe that Boxer villainy could reach so far" (1901: 19). The Boxers may have been more conscious of the significance of their act than we might think: before the introduction of Western sports, the one large-scale spectator sport in Beijing appears to have been horse racing. Races at the Chinese race course outside of the Western Wicket Gate were an occasion for the Manchu nobility to display their horses and finery. They were not "races" in our understanding, as the riders merely rode their horses up and down for the enjoyment of the spectators, occasionally displaying their speed at a gallop (Gamble 1921: 229). The point is that the Boxers had the cultural background to recognize horse racing as a display of aristocratic privilege and power, and their attack on the international race course may have been motivated by this recognition, just as the international outrage was. By playing sports on the grounds at the Temple of Heaven, the victorious international troops had their revenge.

When one traces the history of large-scale sporting events in Beijing from this point on, one traces the history of state power. After the founding of the Republic, the American YMCA utilized an area next to the Temple of Heaven as a sports field. In 1914 the Second National Games of the Republic, organized by the YMCA, were held there, with temporary bleachers erected for the occasion. After the founding of the PRC, the National Team Training Center was located on this site and a small stadium was built along with many other facilities. The Temple of Heaven itself is more or less intact and is maintained as a tourist spot.

The Temple of Xian Nong, however, is today completely replaced by the Beijing Municipal Team center. In 1918, the South City Amusement Park, a group of concrete buildings with theaters and restaurants, was built in the northeast corner of the temple (Gamble 1921: 239). In later decades, sports fields and a sports institute were built on the grounds. The first modern stadium in Beijing was built there in 1937 with a capacity of ten thousand and a dirt soccer field in the center (Rong Gaotang et al. 1984: 479).

The Republican government established its capital in Nanjing from 1928 to 1948 so that Beijing lost its importance as the center of government. For the Fifth National Games in Shanghai in 1935, the Nanjing government built what was the first large-scale modern stadium in China, the River Bend stadium. The last Republican national games were held there in 1948. With the return to Beijing as the national capital under the Communists in 1949, the city regained its importance as the site for celebrations of the new state.

Right after Liberation, the stadium at Xian Nong Temple was enlarged to a capacity of nearly thirty thousand, lights were added, and the infield was covered with grass. The first large-scale sports event in the PRC, the First National Worker's Games, was held there in 1955 (Rong Gaotang et al. 1984: 479; Zhou Yixing 1989: 260). In order to celebrate the tenth anniversary of the PRC in 1959, the Worker's Stadium was built on the eastern side of the city. This remains the PRC's largest stadium. It occupied over seventy thousand square meters and could seat eighty thousand people (Zhou Yixing 1989: 261). In 1959, the opening ceremonies of the First National Games of the PRC were held in the stadium. The Worker's Stadium was the site for the opening and closing ceremonies, track and field events, and soccer games for the first four National Games of the PRC in 1959, 1965, 1975, and 1979. After two absences in 1983 (Shanghai) and 1987 (Guangzhou), they returned in 1993. The Worker's Stadium was also the central site for the Asian Games of 1990.

In sum, the history of state power in China since the end of the Qing can be read from a map of the locations of large-scale sporting events starting with the Boxers' destruction of the international race course, followed by the British polo games at the Temple of Heaven, to the YMCA-organized Republican national games next to the Temple of Heaven, and finally to the PRC national games at the Temple of Xian Nong and the Worker's Stadium. That the two most important early sports sites in Beijing were located on the grounds of two important temples in the Qing state religion exemplified the process by which a nation-state inspired by the Western model was superimposed over the ruins of the Qing Dynasty.

Today's National Games show very little of the spatiotemporal orientation that was so important in Qing rituals. The modern state does not place much importance on establishing collective social rhythms of the cyclical, agrarian kind. Though the sites for national games are significant, the stadiums are not oriented toward the four directions in the traditional manner. The spatiotemporal structure inherent in modern sports events is at once more subtle and more complex than that in Qing ritual.

The Legitimation of Power

The quadrennial schedule of the PRC National Games has been repeatedly disrupted by social and economic turmoil. Still, the timing of the Games that have been held (in 1959, 1965, 1975, 1979, 1983, and 1987) shows that, like Grand Sacrifice, they are utilized to legitimate the group in power. There was a ten-year gap between the 1965 and 1975 National Games precisely because this was the period of the Cultural Revolution when no one faction had enough legitimacy to stage them.

The Cultural Revolution ended with the death of Chairman Mao in 1976 and the overthrow of his wife and her allies, the Gang of Four, in 1978. The new regime was headed by Deng Xiaoping, who proved as skillful as Mao in utilizing the symbolism of sports. In 1644, within a year of assuming power, the first Qing emperor went to the Temple of Heaven to sacrifice and announce to Heaven that he had ascended the throne (Williams 1913: 12–13). Deng Xiaoping celebrated his rise to power a little over a year later with the grandest National Games held to that date.

As in the Grand Sacrifices, the head of state is present at the Games. Chairman Mao and Premier Zhou Enlai attended every Games held during their lifetimes. Though Deng Xiaoping was not present at the 1987 Games, Premier Zhao Ziyang was. Speaking, however, is delegated to lesser officials. The usual format is for the vice-director of the State Sports Commission to declare the Games open and the vice-premier of the State Council to give the opening speech. This is a significant departure from the Olympic Games format, in which the head of state of the host country declares the Games open and the president of the International Olympic Committee gives an address.

The opening speech by the vice-premier is printed verbatim in all major newspapers the next day, much like the announcement of the Grand Sacrifices. In 1987, Vice-Premier Wan Li's speech was as follows:

Comrades, Friends:

The Sixth National Games of the People's Republic of China now begin. I represent the Party Central Committee and the State Council in expressing warm wishes to all the athletes, coaches, and personnel staff. I express warm welcome to the overseas Chinese, Taiwan compatriots, Hong Kong and Macao compatriots, and foreign guests invited to attend this grand occasion! To convene this National Games, Guangdong Province, Guangzhou City, and the Army stationed in Guangzhou have put out a great effort. We also express thanks to them!

The National Games are a big event in our nation's sporting life. This meet will reflect the achievements of the reform, opening-up, and modern construction in our nation, test the level of sports, further promote sports among all people. The Party Central Committee and the State Council place a high value on the clear achievements of the vigorous development of our nation's sports, solidly support the comrades on the sports battlefront who have put out a huge effort on behalf of breaking out of Asia and advancing on the world, and building China into a sports power in this century. We hope sportspeople from every area and every system participating in the National Games will work ceaselessly, engage in fair competition, unite in their struggle, display good sportsmanship, realize their potential, strive to obtain the twin harvest of sports performance and spiritual civilization!

Sport is a component part of the socialist construction endeavor in our country, it is an active means of improving the mental and physical fitness of the entire people, it is beneficial to the development of the social forces of production, it strengthens the friendship between the different minorities of our nation and the people of every nation. Comrades on the sports battle-line should thoroughly recognize the honor of their profession. Under the guidance and encouragement of the Party's Basic Road of the Primary Stages of Socialist Construction, let us carry through the Four Basic Principles, carry through reform and opening-up, stand on our own two feet, build the enterprise through arduous effort, further develop the new face of the sports undertaking, make a contribution towards building a wealthy, democratic, civilized, modern socialist nation!

May the National Games be a complete success! (Wan Li 1987)

The Grand Sacrifice announcement quoted earlier seems directed mainly toward imperial ministers and officials, who are warned to be righteous lest dire consequences result. Wan Li's speech is directed specifically toward the international community and the Chinese sports community and more generally toward the Chinese people as a whole. The length of the speech seems due in part to an effort to make clear what the Games ought to mean in the face of possibly ambiguous interpretations; presumably the Grand Sacrifices required no such exegesis because everyone knew what they were supposed to mean.

Another major difference between Qing Grand Sacrifice and the Chinese National Games is that the former were forbidden to common eyes, while the latter are deliberately disseminated through the media to as much of the populace as possible. The Qing rituals were widely announced but not publicly viewed. This is because "the objects of control were not so much the populace at large as the bureaucracy and the local elites" (Feuchtwang 1977: 581). In the absence of modern communication technologies, Qing emperors had first to control their own officials before they could control the populace. By contrast, the television audience for the 1987 National Games was probably over 500 million, or half of the entire population of China (*China Daily* [1987a] estimated an audience of one billion, but this is certainly an exaggeration).

Because the Games, in particular the Opening Ceremonies, were replayed repeatedly for many months afterwards, this figure is not implausible.

At the same time, there is evidence that the National Games were as much intended to impress a handful of rival state officials as they were to impress the popular audience. Articles about the Games always begin with a list of the thirty or more leaders of state, in order of importance, who sat on the rostrum at the Opening Ceremonies to review the Parade of Athletes. It is not unusual for the Games to become an arena for battles over symbols. In 1974, when Deng Xiaoping succeeded in revising one of the placard sections requested by Mao's wife Jiang Qing, his victory was characterized as "a head-on blow to Jiang Qing and the handful of counter-revolutionary bandits" that "aroused the fighting will of the people" (Rong Gaotang et al. 1984: 24).

The Structure of Symbolism

Another similarity between Grand Sacrifice and the National Games is the use of multiple sensory channels: music, speeches, banners, bright colors, fire, the procession, dancing, and so on. The opening and closing ceremonies of the National Games are the main occasions on which these similarities may be observed. In both Grand Sacrifice and the National Games, the dancing and singing were rehearsed beforehand, thus revealing the close relationship between ritual and theater. Both events were directed by a master of ceremonies. Both were choreographed ahead of time in minute detail; however the Qing ritual was based on a long historical tradition, while there is no effort to ground the format of the National Games in ancient tradition. Instead, the format is derived from the Soviet model and from the Olympic Games format. The symbolism is grounded in the Revolution and in communist history; for example, officially the torch symbolizes the Communist Revolution.

The 1987 Games closely followed the 13th Party Congress. During the Games, frequent reference was made to the guidance of the Party and the Basic k. .d laid out at the Congress. At that time, the main area of uncertainty for China as a nation was the effect of the economic reforms. This situation played into the official interpretation of the Games, which aimed to inspire confidence in the reforms.

The part of the Games that was most densely packed with symbols was not the sports competitions themselves, but the Opening Ceremonies. This was an occasion for symbolizing the Chinese nation; the ceremonies were a Party-orchestrated representation of the nation to the Chinese people. This differed from the Qing ritual, which primarily represented the emperor's link with Heaven, not the nation.

The centerpiece of the opening ceremonies was the mass calisthenics show. I will describe the show in some detail to demonstrate how it was designed to imprint a habitual way of being onto the Chinese people, in particular a linear and forward-looking temporal orientation. It was divided into five acts. The show took us back to the past, and then by stages brought us forward into the future.

The title, "Great Aspirations," captured the feeling that the choreographers attempted to express in the show. The choreographers stated their intent in the official program, which was distributed at the ceremonies. Similar statements were read aloud during the ceremonies by the emcees, with a musical accompaniment.

> *thematic concept:* Expresses the infinitely deep love of the Chinese people for the great ancestral land, brimming with hope for the future, determined to carry on the spirit of the Foolish Old Man who moved the mountain. The great aspiration of uniting in the struggle to make China soar to the heights. (*Lingyunzhi* 1987: 1)

The first act, entitled "Welcoming the Guests," invited the audience into the liminal world of suspended disbelief. It involved 768 boys and girls in brightly colored clothes, 213 small children dressed as white rams, and 600 children with balloons and fresh flowers circling the track. Rams and flowers are signs of Guangzhou, which is called "city of the rams" (due to a foundation myth) and "city of flowers" (due to the abundance of flowers in its temperate climate). The choreographers described its meaning as follows:

> *central thought:* Expresses the people of Guangzhou fervently wishing for the Sixth National Games to convene victoriously, warmly welcoming the top athletes from all parts of the ancestral land and the guests from China and abroad.
> The style is warmhearted and youthful. (*Lingyunzhi* 1987: 1)

The second act, entitled "Pride," took the audience into China's mythical past. It involved 768 girls wearing varicolored gauze dresses and scarves and 578 boys dressed in black-and-white martial arts costumes. The boys performed vigorous kungfu movements in unison, accompanied by shouts which rang throughout the stadium. The placard section flashed various scenes from China's history, such as the Great

Wall and the Yellow River. The program set forth the guiding theme as follows:

central thought: Expresses the infinitely deep love and strong national pride of the people of the nation for the great ancestral land. The style is lyrical and heroic. (*Lingyunzhi* 1987: 2)

In the third act, "Hope," we were brought forward to the modern era, to the creative time of childhood. In it, 1,200 primary schoolchildren formed patterns and objects with large multicolored blocks. The theme:

central thought: Conveys our country's people brimming with hope for the future, and that they place their hope on the next generation. The style is innocent and lively. (*Lingyunzhi* 1987: 2–3)

In the Fourth Act, "Struggle," 720 boys formed patterns with long painted bamboo poles, then 628 boys and girls unfolded specially designed high bars and balance beams and performed on them in unison. We had moved from the insulated world of child's play to the real world of risk and hardship. The choreographer's conception:

central thought: Reflects that the Chinese people don't fear hardship and danger; they are determined to carry on the fighting spirit, arduously struggle for the future of the ancestral land. The style is resolute and strong. (*Lingyunzhi* 1987: 3)

In the fifth act, "Soar," we moved into a mythical future, a world of high technology with electronic music and fluorescent colors that lit up the stadium, which had been suddenly darkened by extinguishing the lights. In this section, 784 boys and girls performed in the dark, swinging rods with glowing white and red balls on the end.

central thought: Expresses the bright future of the great ancestral land as it takes off under the guidance of the Party's policies of reform and opening-up. The songs and dance inspire people's spirits, sing out the song in the hearts of hundreds of millions of people: "Soar, Great Dragon of the East! Soar, Great Ancestral Land!" The style is ardent and bold. (*Lingyunzhi* 1987: 3–4)

Following this, 200 boys composing four dragons performed a dragon dance. The bodies of the dragons spouted fireworks that sent up a huge cloud of smoke, so that the dragons were almost totally obscured, except for the glow of their bodies writhing in and out of the cloud. These dragons were described in one newspaper as follows:

Act I, "Welcoming the Guests," opening ceremonies of 1987 National Games. Children dressed as white rams symbolize Guangzhou.

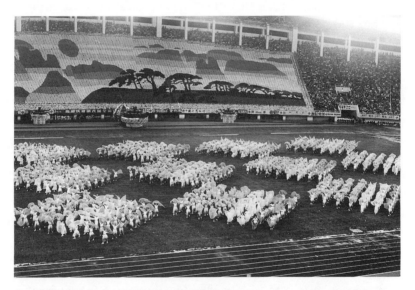

Act II, "Pride." Girls in gauze dresses dancing, waving scarves as part of the choreography.

Act II, "Pride." Boys perform southern-style martial arts. Placard section shows the Great Wall. Note the marked gender difference in Act II compared with the other acts.

The dragon, symbol of the Chinese nation. The twisting and soaring of the dragon, his spirited dance, reveal that the Chinese nation begins to fly! (Li Lijiang 1987b)

The passage through time had gone full cycle: we had been returned to the legendary past, then brought back to the modern age, and when we opened our eyes, we beheld a new China, embodied in the dragon, prancing into the modern era. It represented a China transformed by the rite of passage it had just undergone. The future China will not be the prehistoric dragon of the past—it will be a high-technology dragon. This was explained to me by one of the choreographers, who showed me one of the dragons before the show. The design involved "a bit of technology," consisting of tubes of gunpowder, fuses, and battery-powered sparks lit by pressing a button. She noted that the addition of sparklers to the body of the dragon was their own innovation—a conscious combination of the traditional and the modern.

"Great Aspirations" invited the audience to cross the threshold into a world of suspended disbelief, and then to reconstitute their worldview in a way that would enable them to make that world real. Guangzhou

Act III, "Hope." Primary schoolchildren build human shapes out of white blocks.

Act IV, "Struggle." Bamboo pole dance inspired by a minority custom.

Act IV, "Struggle." Girls and boys perform on balance beams.

became the liminal world, a metaphor which was highly appropriate, because the city leads China in its economic modernization. Its extensive ties to Hong Kong and overseas Chinese have made Guangdong the wealthiest province in China. The people I interviewed were very conscious of Guangzhou's symbolic significance. Guangdong province also won the Games according to the official point system.

The ceremonies concluded with a fireworks display that ended the liminal period of the rite of passage and marked the return to everyday life, bringing all of us back to the real world, the modern world. This is the world that China's leaders hold up as the utopia toward which they are leading the nation. This idea was echoed by the reporter who wrote, "'Great Aspirations' success—can't this count as an example with symbolic significance?" (Zhao Lihong 1987).

Unlike the Grand Sacrifices, the National Games show very little grounding in the cosmology or history that still have deep symbolic appeal to the Chinese people. The appeal to history could be more effectively used in the Opening Ceremonies. There seemed to be widespread agreement that the most moving act of the Opening Ceremonies was Act Two, "Pride," which utilized symbols of China's past (namely, martial arts, the Great Wall, and the Yellow River). The martial arts were

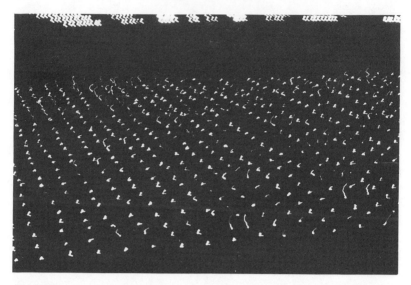

Act V, "Soar." In darkened stadium, students swing rods with glowing balls on ends. Placard section is also lighted.

Dragon dance finale. Fifty boys carry a dragon with fireworks spouting from its body.

considered the most exciting. When I asked one person why he liked Act Two best, he replied, "Because it was China's traditional sports." Despite the popular appeal of this cultural history, the majority of symbols were not drawn from it (see Cohen 1991: 113).

LANGUAGE AND PERFORMANCE

Grand Sacrifice was embedded in the official discourses on astronomy and ritual produced by the Imperial Board of Astronomy and the Ministry of Rites against the background of a centuries-long philosophical tradition. The National Games are embedded in the official Chinese Marxist discourse produced by the leaders of the Communist Party and secondarily by the State Sports Commission (which oversees the organization of the Games) and the Ministry of Culture (which controls the organs of the press).

Media coverage of the Games is saturated with slogans. Key slogans from past and present political campaigns are printed on the banners hung behind the rostrum, suspended from large balloons around the stadium, flashed by the placard section, and sometimes shouted by athletes as they pass the rostrum. All are then reprinted in the reports on the ceremonies.

Charles Laughlin, John McManus, and Eugene d'Aquili (1979) suggest an explanation for the relation between ritual and its conceptual background. They separate ceremonial rituals from other kinds of ritual behavior. What is distinctive about ceremonial rituals is that they are always embedded in a web of meaning (d'Aquili and Laughlin 1979: 160): this is because humans have a need to give order to unexplained experiences (p. 161). The realm of religion is found in the conceptual models that explain the zones of uncertainty in human life (Laughlin, McManus, and d'Aquili 1979: 40). Whether or not a ceremonial ritual is "religious" depends on whether the participants conceptualize it as such (p. 41). D'Aquili and Laughlin do not consider a football game to be a religious ritual because it does not have a religious consequence (p. 40).

However, the amount of ideology, propaganda, and ceremony that surrounded the National Games reflected the Party's attempt to give order to the zones of uncertainty in Chinese life at that time. The conceptual model that forms the official backdrop for the Games is Chinese Marxist ideology, and the results of the events are interpreted according to this ideology. One characteristic of ritual is that it "invokes religious or sacred forces or, in Paul Tillich's phrase, the locus of a people's 'ulti-mate concern'" (MacAloon 1984: 250). In the PRC, the national locus of concern has changed through time, requiring the constant rewriting of ideology; in the past, the chief concern was "revolution," while in 1987 it was "economic modernization." While the 1987 Games were not explicitly classified as "religious," they nevertheless addressed two of the concerns formerly addressed by state and popular religion—namely, the quest for prosperity and social order. It is very difficult to distinguish the "religious" from the "secular" in this comparison.

Thus, the external structural relationship of the Games to a concep-tual model of the world is similar to that of religious ritual. In addition, their internal structure is similar to the internal structure of ritual: there are numerous rites and ceremonies, an invocation of sacred forces, and a meaningful spatiotemporal structure (in the 1987 Games, imitating the individual life cycle). In sum, the Qing ritual resembled the Commu-nist games in the linking of language to action and in the internal sym-bolic structure. This is because they both made use of time-worn meth-ods for inculcating a world-orientation into bodies beyond the grasp of consciousness and of integrating the body space with cosmic space (Bourdieu 1977: 91).

TRANSFORMING THE SOCIAL BODY

Ritual action is designed to bring about a social goal; it effects social transitions or spiritual transformations (MacAloon 1984: 250). For one of the most noted scholars of ritual, Victor Turner, this is the defining element of ritual. It is transformative; it "does work"; in many societies, ritual is described as "work" (Turner 1988: 26). On this basis, Turner denies a Brazilian soccer game the status of ritual. Instead, he prefers the label of "ceremony," which describes a process that confirms or ratifies existing hierarchy rather than reshaping it (pp. 26–27).

The quintessential transformative ritual is the life-crisis rite of pas-sage. Among the Ndembu, it was easy for Turner to observe that a boy's initiation ritual was "transformative"; a boy looks, acts, and is treated one way before the ritual and another way afterwards. His body is also permanently altered by circumcision.

There is a second kind of rite of passage which, although perceived as transformative by the participants, is less clearly observable as such to the outsider. This is the collective ritual performed to mark a whole group's passage from one culturally defined season to another in the annual cycle (Turner 1988: 101). Qing Grand Sacrifice is closer to this type. The sacrifice to Heaven each year renewed the contract between the emperor and heaven (the Mandate of Heaven), thus perpetuating the cosmic-human hierarchy. This renewal may not have been immediately evident to the outside observer, but within the Chinese cultural framework it was very real. The ritual was believed to accomplish something.

The National Games are more similar to a periodic collective ritual. They do not effect the same sort of clearly identifiable transformation as, for example, an Ndembu initiation ritual. They do not even effect the same sort of renewal of cosmic order as the Qing Grand Sacrifice. Still, there is plenty of evidence that the Communist Party attempts to use sports to effect transformations in accord with its goals. The 1987 National Games were designed to bring about a spiritual shift toward greater unity and the pursuit of excellence in order to facilitate China's movement toward modern nationhood.

From this angle, the Qing Grand Sacrifices and the Communist National Games shared a similar underlying political philosophy. The idea of shaping the people to serve the polity through a cultural performance was fundamental to both. It was the social and cosmological effects that differed.

The tricky question in all of this is, of course, what sort of social effects Grand Sacrifice or the National Games actually had. Grand Sacrifice was not even seen by the populace, while the National Games were observed in person by several hundred thousand people and on television by a half-billion. In the Qing, the problem of popular participation was partly remedied by the execution of similar events on a lesser scale at the grassroots level. The Middle Sacrifices performed at the capital were mirrored in those performed at lower-level capitals, and all administrative capitals down to the county seat conducted the Common Sacrifices (Feuchtwang 1977: 586–92). Funerals and weddings also contained the same basic elements throughout the social hierarchy, from emperors and empresses to commoners. This standardization of ritual was crucial in the creation of a unified Chinese culture (Watson 1988: 3, 18; Rawski 1988: 32). But outside of the imperial religion, there were also numerous local deities, and heterodox religious practices proliferated beyond the control of the local officials throughout the Qing. "Literally thousands of deities were worshipped in temples of every conceivable description throughout the empire" (Watson 1985: 293). Though the state attempted to standardize popular religion by promoting the most popular deities to official status, there was a great disjuncture between the ritual practices that were important in people's everyday lives and those that were important to the state.

In the case of the 1987 Games, concern about the problem of popular involvement was revealed by the choreographers' own understanding of the effects of their opening ceremonies. As discussed in chapter 4, they had engaged in a heated debate about whether to stage a mass calisthenics show, such as is typical of socialist sporting events, or an "artistic" show more similar to American sporting events (the Los Angeles Olympics were fresh in their minds). One of the reasons they settled on the traditional socialist mass calisthenics was that it involved large numbers of young people in the production, while the American model involved larger numbers of professional performers. "Great Aspirations" included a total of 6,455 performers, and a placard section of 8,028 members (*Lingyunzhi* 1987: 1–4). A high degree of organization and discipline was required to produce the show; it demanded two years of cooperative effort from the Guangdong school system, the Guangdong sports system, and a national team of choreographers. It had involved over 14,500 students in thrice weekly practice for over half of a year, and the Games organizers believed this would help inculcate socialist values. The Third Act, "Hope," was considered by the choreographers to have been the most difficult act to successfully complete because it was extremely difficult to get 1,200 primary schoolchildren to perform movements simultaneously and in straight lines.

Anyone who has seen mass calisthenics of this scale cannot doubt that this is an example par excellence of the synchronization of the rhythms of the social body (see d'Aquili and Laughlin 1979 and Bourdieu 1977 and 1988). This was my first opportunity, and I confess that chills ran up and down my spine.

In contrast to the discontinuity of popular and imperial ritual practice in the Qing, the practice of sports in contemporary China is remarkably homogeneous. Sport is only one of a number of state-promulgated performance genres: one might also include political campaigns, national holidays, military displays, and the mass broadcast exercises, for example. In addition to these homogenizing efforts, heterodox popular religion is now undergoing revival in the countryside. But sports are also becoming increasingly popular.

When I interviewed six Peasant Sports Association cadres, they all agreed that in the past few years sports have become much more important in the countryside, especially since the state document issued in 1984 that gave specific guidelines for the development of mass sports. They stated that the popularity of sports is a grassroots phenomenon that is not imposed from above, only encouraged. Sports meets have been incorporated into traditional festivals, such as harvest festivals or temple fairs (*miaohui*). One peasant sports cadre noted that in his county in Heilongjiang, "They don't want the traditional temple fairs. They have a lot of sports instead. They have businesses circling the field and sports in the center. They want big opening ceremonies like the National Games, with mass calisthenics. They all want to drive their motorcycles [in the opening ceremonies]. The competitions last four to five days, but the businesses keep going on for over ten."

Another cadre noted that sports meets last longer than any other kind of get-together and are better-attended. Meets in her county, Shanghai county, commonly attracted 100,000 spectators. She said that the head of the County Sports Commission had become a well-known figure. "Everyone recognizes the Sports Commission Director. As he sits in the stands, spectators point him out. It didn't used to be this way. The lower levels call him 'teacher' [*laoshi*—a term of respect], and other sports cadres [are called that], too." The cadre from Heilongjiang asked me if an American governor would go to a sports meet. I told him, "Not necessarily." He replied, "If you ask the provincial director or vice-director, they go right away. The government asks them to attend meets."

The emulation of the National Games Opening Ceremonies extends the homogenizing effects of the Games to the grassroots level. Opening ceremonies, complete with a parade of athletes, opening speeches by officials, and performances by marching bands or flag teams, are a necessary component of almost every sports meet, including city primary and middle school championships, city college meets, interdepartmental college championships, and the National College Games. In 1988, the Beijing University Sports Meet opening ceremonies included a mass calisthenics performance by 224 staff members, and the Beijing City College Meet had a performance by 600 Qinghua University staff members.

The preparation and practice for the opening ceremonies is the time when the techniques of military discipline are imparted to all Chinese children. They learn goose-stepping and slogan shouting from a young age. I represented Beijing City in the 1986 National College Games and took part in a training camp beforehand. The team practiced its goose-stepping and slogan shouting every morning after six-thirty roll call. My goose-stepping proved to be an object of great amusement to my

Parade of Athletes, opening ceremonies of the 1987 National Games. Placard section reads, "Develop physical culture and sports, strengthen the people's physiques."

Parade of Athletes, closing ceremonies of Beijing City College Track Meet, 1988.

Drill team, closing ceremonies of 1986 Haidian District Middle School Track Meet.

teammates. One of them finally asked me, "Didn't you ever learn how to goose-step?" I explained that I had not and asked where they had learned. They had all learned in school from the time they were small.

Before the era of reform, and especially during the Cultural Revolution, sports were chiefly promoted as a means of military preparation. As mentioned, in addition to military discipline, participation in sports helps inculcate a body culture that is suited to the needs of the industrial nation-state. This is the "micro-physics of power" that Michel Foucault makes symptomatic of the modern state (Foucault 1979, esp. pp. 135–41). This sort of training of the body is far more continuous, detailed, calculated, and normalizing than the Qing official rituals ever were (see Mayfair Yang 1988: 421).

HIERARCHY, EGALITARIANISM, THE STATE, AND THE NATION

If the Communist Party did not succeed in transforming China into an economically advanced nation-state through the National Sports Games, then it was not for want of trying. Don Handelman points out that transformation in a modern state is perceived to be accomplished through bureaucratic channels rather than performative ones (1990: 77–81). This is an overstatement for China, whose leaders have always appreciated the value of performance. Still, since the end of the Cultural Revolution the onus of change has been mainly assigned to bureaucratic management and secondarily to performative genres. However, a closer analysis reveals that a different kind of transformation is effected through events like the National Games. It does not occur at one time and is not immediately obvious, but the National Games are one aspect of a whole system of technologies of the body by which Chinese body culture is slowly but surely altered. In fact, this transformation is probably more successfully accomplished in the modern Chinese state than it was in the Qing.

The Qing state religion was segmented by the agrarian calendar into periodic rituals. Its effects were discontinuous through time. They were also discontinuous through space. The Grand Sacrifices performed by the emperor were witnessed by only the highest officials—who, in fact, constituted the primary target of the ritual's effects. The ritual actions that the common person was able to observe and perform were considerably different in form and content. Watson notes that all Chinese were subject to the same set of death rites, which says something about the egalitarian nature of the late imperial class system (1988: 18). Nevertheless, the effects of the entire set of rituals were conceived of as hierarchical and unequally distributed among unlike, unequal people. One of the main functions of ritual was to maintain the social distinctions that made the Qing state possible (Rawski 1988: 27). It was not the state's goal to impose total conformity (Cohen 1991: 122). State rituals marked class and gender distinctions: they were carried out by elite officials, who were male. They also set apart the emperor: throughout history, there was only ever one Temple of Heaven in all of China, and only one emperor at any given time who could sacrifice there (Feuchtwang 1977: 595).

The effects of the National Games are more continuous through time and space. Through the media, they are witnessed by hundreds of thousands of Chinese people. Lower-level sports meets imitate closely their form and content. The moral effects of the Games are for the most part conceived of as evenly distributed between essentially like, equal people (see Tocqueville 1956), although some of the symbolism of the Games is directed toward the thirty or so high officials who are sitting on the rostrum in the coliseum for the opening ceremonies.

MacAloon (1995) argues that while "nation" may be a global category, there is cultural variability in constructions of "nationalism," and that interpretations of Olympic Games ceremonies provide insight into the variability of these constructions. In particular, interpretations of the ceremonies reveal beliefs about hierarchy, egalitarianism, and the relationship between the nation and the state. The symbolism of the Chinese National Games reveals a complex combination of egalitarian and hierarchical symbols that conflict in the realm of the nation-state relationship. On the one hand, sports as a popularized technique of the body have a leveling and equalizing effect and are promoted by the Party as such. Chinese victory ceremonies, which are celebrations of hierarchy, are simple and do not get nearly as much attention as opening and closing ceremonies, which emphasize a homogeneous "Chinese" identity. Roberto DaMatta (1988) has suggested that in a society whose primary cultural logic is hierarchical, the dramatically interesting performance is one that displays egalitarian ideals. In the epilogue, I argue that hierarchical ideals are still very strong in Chinese sports, therefore DaMatta's hypothesis may be correct for China. On the other hand, there is a display of hierarchy among state leaders at the national games, so that representations of the undifferentiated "masses" that constitute the nation conflict with representations of the individuated leaders that constitute the state. At the same time, state leaders are not represented as "morally encompassing" the Chinese people in the way characteristic of hierarchical representations of the state elsewhere (Kapferer 1988: 7). In theory, these leaders are also subject to the leveling effects of sports, symbolized by their participation in fitness activities and sports meets (see chapter 2). Thus, conflicting messages about the relationship between state and nation are evident in the symbols of the National Games. These conflicts are, of course, symptomatic of tensions in contemporary PRC political life.

CONCLUSIONS: THE MODERNITY OF POWER IN SPORTS

Mayfair Yang's characterization of "the modernity of power" in contemporary China summarizes the difference between the nation-state relationship represented in the Grand Sacrifice and in the National Games: "[S]ociety, the people, and the population became the new telos of power. Power was now understood, not as serving the state or the Party, but as the way to effect an economic, occupational, and cultural leveling and uniformity of society" (1988: 421).

The nature of the power relations underlying the Grand Sacrifice is substantially different from that underlying the National Sports Games. The latter exhibit a more strategic employment of power, one based less on the personal sovereignty of the emperor (see Foucault 1978: 102) and ultimately more ingrained in the bodies of the subjects. However, the processes by which the principles of the modern state are embodied are so minute and subtle that they "are placed beyond the grasp of consciousness, and hence cannot be touched by voluntary, deliberate transformation, cannot even be made explicit" (Bourdieu 1977: 94). That is why "transformation" is so hard to observe and assess, though when it occurs it is probably more stable and permanent.

This is the modern nature of the power that is exercised through sports in China. That this power focuses on the body—its movements and postures, its harmony with cosmos and humankind—is similar to Qing ritual, and perhaps to any ritual; but the modern practice is more uniform, continuous, specific and refined in application, and more generalizable in its effects. The specific applications of power on athletes and the generalizable effects that are expected to result in the nation's construction of socialist spiritual civilization are the topics of the next chapter.

PART
•3•

Class Culture and
Body Culture

CHAPTER SIX

Training the Body
for China

Civilization, Discipline, and Social Order[1]

The microtechniques of state power are more carefully
applied to the minds and bodies of top athletes than
they are to most other groups in the PRC. Athletes are
categorized and studied; their movements, diets, and
bodily functions are monitored; they give up the
"truth" in their confessional, written self-evaluations.
The discourse that justifies the disciplinary program is
equally concerned with their "thoughts" and their
bodies: it is impossible to judge whether the thoughts
are the medium and state control over bodies the ultimate goal, or the body is the medium and control of
the thoughts the ultimate goal (cf. Foucault 1979, esp.
pp. 14–24). Both bodily and mental discipline are to
serve the needs of the state—in the words of the official discourse, they are to serve the construction of socialist spiritual civilization. Thus, the most minute disciplines of the body are conceived of as having
civilizing effects with very general consequences for
the fate of the nation. This combination of disciplinary techniques with the call for a civilized morality is
a way in which PRC political culture differs from its

1. I would like to express my intellectual debt to Ann Anagnost. Her work on the "civilized village campaign" suggested to me the idea of organizing this chapter around the discourses on "civilization" and "culture."

Anglo-European counterpart. Like the other disciplinary technologies described by Foucault (prisons, asylums, military barracks, etc.), physical education came into existence with the rise of European nation-states in the eighteenth and nineteenth centuries in order to meet the needs of a more diffuse, legalistic kind of state power—a power that was to be exercised uniformly and efficiently (1979: 218–21). This rationalistic exercise of power to some degree superseded the earlier importance of a moral order revolving around the absolute monarch, who embodied the standards of civilization. PRC political culture differs from this model in that the notion of an "exemplary center" (Geertz 1980) is as important as the bureaucratic disciplinary technologies. Leading by moral example is regarded as seriously as leading by the uniform application of rules. The two conceptions of power are evident in the disciplinary schedules and political education of athletes—who, after all, are to embody the best of the political system.

CIVILIZATION AND CULTURE

Wenming, here translated as "civilization," can refer to China's glorious past. It is also used in the Marxist distinction between material civilization (*wuzhi wenming*) and spiritual civilization (*jingshen wenming*). Civilization implies progress along a scale from less civilized to more civilized (Anagnost 1993: 6, 8; Elias 1978: 5). It is often identified with the advanced industrial nations, in comparison with which China is perceived as less civilized, though it was formerly more so (Anagnost 1993: 6). The discourse on civilization in contemporary China implies a continuing effort to push the Chinese people toward greater civilization, expressed in the important goal of *jingshen wenming jianshe,* "the construction of spiritual civilization." As Ann Anagnost has demonstrated, the concept of civilization is a flexible one that can be made to serve state policy in various ways. Its polymorphous character means that its effects are "generalizable." Cadres in the Jiangsu township where she did research used "civilization work" (*wenming gongzuo*) to refer to the creation of a disciplined, docile labor force that would appeal to foreign capitalists (p. 2). In the discourse surrounding sports as well, discipline (*jilü*) and civilization are intimately related, and civilization is oriented toward the international arena. In speeches and in the media, China's 1987 National Games were described as a display of socialist spiritual civilization to the world, which was described as watching the Games with interest.

Disciplinary techniques are instruments for fashioning people to suit an already existing social hierarchy (Elias 1978: 84). Like factory discipline,[2] sports discipline involves a political investment of the body with the "micro-physics of power" oriented toward the needs of the state (see Foucault 1979: 28–29). This, at least, is the ideal according to Chinese Marxist theory:

> [I]n service of socialism, physical culture ought to ultimately be expressed in the cultivation of the individual; it should insure that the members of society are all "both red and expert," that they become individuals with ideals, morals, culture, discipline, and good health; it should develop qualified, capable people for the construction of socialism. (Cao Xiangjun 1985: 196)

The reality, of course, is more complex. By analyzing in detail the disciplines of athletes' daily lives, it is possible to uncover the ways in which they are shaped by the power relationships in Chinese society as a whole. These power relationships do not just emanate from the "state" as a kind of monolithic force; they are also the product of shifting tensions within Chinese society. In fact, the official discourse on "civilization" is paralleled by an unofficial discourse on "culture." The interpenetration of the two is reflected in the similar ways in which they reflect a bid for power: in the first instance, on the part of the Party apparatus that claims responsibility for civilizing the populace; in the second instance, on the part of the intellectual class that claims responsibility for instilling culture into the populace. After the argument for the relationship between civilization and discipline has been set out, the parallel issue of culture will be discussed.

TECHNIQUES OF DISCIPLINE ON SPORTS TEAMS
Criticism and Self-Criticism

All teams have a system of sanctions and controls on the behavior of athletes. Criticism and self-criticism are standard methods of social control in all work units. The most minor infractions result in criticism and self-criticism. More serious rules violations result in expulsion from the team and transfer to a job. In the most serious violations that I heard of, athletes who had violated the law were taken to the local public security bureau and punished according to the law.

2. See Rofel (1992) for a discussion of factory discipline in the PRC.

Yang Duo, vice-head of the Beijing City Team's Sports Technique School, commented that "problems" with violence and pornography are more widespread in the more backward areas and less severe in Beijing. He noted that there are always conflicts between athletes and coaches; this is a natural part of the training process, often resulting from the athlete's frustration when his or her progress is not fast enough. He noted that in the 1960s, coaches relied on their authority. They shouted slogans to motivate athletes, and when they got angry they tried to force them. These days, things have changed. They know that they shouldn't rely on their authority; they emphasize that the athlete should voluntarily obey. This is called the "democratization of education" (*jiaoxue minzhuhua*). The coach shouldn't get angry in a minor conflict; he should sympathize and compromise a little. "After you have done a little self-criticism, saying 'I was excessive' and things like that, the athlete should come around. If he doesn't, you can criticize him and have him do self-criticism" (Yang Duo 1988).

One way of carrying out criticism is the "Notice of Criticism" (*piping tongbao*). An example is the one that was posted during our training camp for the 1986 National College Games. Two of the team members had missed the 10:00 P.M. evening curfew and one had missed morning practice. As a result, the coaches hung a big-character poster on the wall inside of the dormitory entrance, where everyone who went in and out could see it. It read (the names are pseudonyms),

> Yesterday evening, the two teammates Zhu Yaohua and Li Jianmin, without seeking permission, did not return to the dormitory. Gu Yuji did not come back from the break and did not participate in morning practice. We direct special criticism toward the three above people. Consider the group, your fellow students, and strictly follow all rules.

This poster did not seem to have much actual effect, and some of the team members scoffed at the entire idea.

Mr. Yang said that if criticism doesn't work, then "self-criticism" (*ziwo piping*) may be employed. This begins with the student writing down a self-examination in which he acknowledges in detail the wrong he has done and asks his leaders for forgiveness. This procedure was employed against a foreign student at the Beijing Institute of Physical Education while I was there. Because the student had no experience in writing self-criticism, the leaders felt his letter was not contrite enough, which added fuel to their flame and almost led to the student's expulsion. By my American standards, Chinese letters of self-criticism were so obsequious as to seem excessively humiliating to the writer. However, one writer that I knew was considerably more accepting because she knew it was a formula that she would have to follow. Her letter, which asked for release from a team, contained phrases like, "The Comrade leaders have shown such concern for me, and I feel deep regret that I have not been able to repay their concern. Instead, I was very incautious, and as a result injured myself and am no longer able to represent my team . . ." In fact, these same leaders were indirectly responsible for the injury because they had made her compete three days in a row against her will, and on the third day—probably due to fatigue—she fell on a poorly kept cinder track and injured herself.

Yang Duo (1988) said that criticism work usually solves most discipline problems. However, if the conflict continues, there are three options: the athlete can change events if another coach wants him or her, or the person can go to another coach in the same event if there is more than one coach; or, if the athlete is older, he or she can be released from the team and transferred to a job.

Labor Reform

My findings differ from the account given by the tennis player Hu Na, who defected to the United States and was awarded political asylum in 1982. Hu entered the Chengdu City sports school at the age of fourteen and defected to the United States at the age of nineteen. She had been to the United States twice before the trip on which she defected; on her second trip she had been seen wearing jeans and makeup. She told Taiwanese players she met that after returning home from these tours, she had been criticized for being too bourgeois and Westernized, apparently because she was too carefree and wore her long hair loose instead of in a braid (Taylor 1983: 10). (The rule against wearing long hair loose over the shoulders was one of the dress code rules during our 1986 training camp in Beijing.) Hu asserted that party cadres were pressuring her to join the Party, and that if she refused, "my tennis life would end— even ordinary [noncompetitive] tennis—and I would be sent to a factory in the countryside to do very low labor" and would face charges of disloyalty to the nation (Ostrow 1983: 17). She told the story of an 18-year-old tennis player from her school who lost his temper at a match in Romania and threw down his racket in front of spectators. Hu said the Party concluded he had been influenced by capitalism and sentenced him to one year of hard labor (Ostrow 1983: 17).

Labor reform for rules infractions and political incorrectness seems to have been more common before and during the Cultural Revolution. In "Superpower Dream," Zhao Yu describes one such event that occurred in 1962. A female table tennis player cut her hand with a knife in order to avoid a competition and lied that a burglar had attacked her in her room; she served three to four months of labor reform before being recalled to the national team (Zhao Yu 1988c: 171). During the Cultural Revolution, of course, large numbers of people who stood out for their achievements or high status were sent to the "cattle pens." Today, labor reform is a possible punishment for criminal acts committed by anyone. However, none of my informants had ever heard of an athlete being forced to do labor reform since the Cultural Revolution. Expulsion from the team was generally the worst sanction for noncriminal acts, but even this was followed by a state-assigned job. This was the punishment meted out to a decathlete who threw a heavy medicine ball at a groundskeeper's head, knocking him out and sending him into temporary paralysis. His coach told me that if the groundskeeper had not recovered, the athlete would have gone to jail. Since he did recover, the athlete was expelled from the team, even though he was a national record-holder. It was difficult, however, to find work units to accept him. Eventually he became a security guard.

Liu Zheng, whose story is recounted later, assaulted a coach several years before the time of Hu Na's defection, but he was not sent off for labor reform—nor, for that matter, even taken to the police. He did not fear reprisal for speaking to me because he had married a non-Chinese and would soon be leaving the country. (Even so, I have used a pseudonym here.) Since he was very bitter toward his former coaches, I believe he would have told me if there were more serious punishments for athletes, but he said that transfer to a factory job was generally the worst punishment. In fact, coaches say that a top athlete may get off lightly for rules infractions since his performance is valuable to the team. Hu Na was certainly a valuable athlete. As far as I have been able to ascertain, Hu Na's assertions were exaggerations. This also seems to have been a widespread sentiment at the time she received political asylum; the decision of the Immigration and Naturalization Service required eight months and much discussion.

Thought Education

"Thought education" (*sixiang jiaoyu*) is an important part of the preparation of both athletes and spectators for any major competition. During the training camp for the 1986 National College Games, in which I participated, correct ideology was emphasized at frequent meetings, which were held almost every day in the last two weeks of the camp. Handbooks setting guidelines for behavior were published by the committee in charge of the Games as well as by the Beijing College Sports Association. This mental training was the other half of the bodily discipline that we observed.

On 2 June, at 9:00 A.M., selected representatives of the track and field team of the Beijing City College Team rode their bikes to the new dormitory at the Beijing Institute of Aeronautics and Aviation to check in. We returned the next day for our first team meeting. Team leaders introduced the basic information about the team and the meet. We formed the Group A (regular colleges) track and field team. There were three other groups in the Games: physical education departments in teaching colleges (B), physical education institutes (C), and technical institutes (D). Basketball was the one other sport. Beijing's Group A track and field team consisted of eight coaches and thirty athletes (sixteen men, fourteen women). They informed us that they had already selected our team officers: a team captain, two assistant captains, a Communist Youth League branch secretary, and a Party group head. They told us that notes on our political thinking would be sent to our work units for inclusion in our dossiers, which would help us in the future when we tried to find jobs. I was surprised to learn that I also had a dossier: my coach told me that my dossier from the Foreign Students' Office at Beijing University had included the appraisal, "She is friendly toward China."

Later, the team hierarchy was confirmed on a large poster near the dorm entrance that listed each team member's name, school, political affiliation (*zhengzhi mianmu*), sex, competition events, and dorm room number. Under political affiliation, six students were listed as Party members and the remainder as Communist Youth League members; the two Americans, James and I, got blank spaces. I jokingly offered my American party affiliation, but they wouldn't allow it.

We were informed of our daily schedule:

6:20	roll call
6:30–7:00	morning exercises
7:00–7:30	eat breakfast

Beijing City group A relay teams, 1986 National College Games track and field meet. Games mascot is in background. The author stands in the middle.

8:30–10:00	train
12:00–12:30	eat lunch
3:30–5:30	train
6:30–7:00	eat supper
11:00	lights out

Showers were allowed Tuesday through Saturday between 3:00 and 8:00 P.M. We were allotted twenty tickets per month for the communal shower hall.

On 7 June, we attended the "Mass Rally for the Establishment of the Sports Team to Represent Beijing in the Second National College Games," as announced in large colored characters on the chalkboard. Present were Vice-Mayor Chen and a number of other officials. Vice-Mayor Chen began by urging us to try to win a spirit award. These awards for good behavior are an important part of all major sports competitions. The title literally means "spiritual civilization athlete (or team)" (*jingshen wenming yundongyuan* or *daibiaotuan*). In track and field, these would be awarded to six of the twenty-nine participating track and field teams and one out of every ten of the athletes. Later in his speech, Chen reiterated that spiritual civilization was our most important goal. The slogan for the Games was to be "Civilization, Unity, Learning, Vigorous Progress" (*fenjin*).

Back in the dorm a few days later, we were given a questionnaire to fill out. It was being administered by the Investigative Group of the Preparatory Committee of the Second National College Games. In addition to requesting basic information, including names of family members who participate in sports, it asked for detailed questions on sports performances, the effects of sports on studies, and costs of training. One teammate's reaction to the form was vehement: "Who wants to fill out this form? It's just like a residence permit survey! And it doesn't have the least bit of advantage to you!" She most resented the request to list family members' names. The team captain had a very difficult time collecting any forms from anyone.

On 28 June, we had another team meeting. We were given a copy of a pamphlet, entitled "Things to Know Before the Meet" and printed by the Beijing College Team Secretariat, and instructed to study it. My friends only looked it over briefly. The team leaders introduced the catch phrases contained in the pamphlet. The goal of the meet was a "proper competition atmosphere, strict and impartial discipline, good performances, a whole new look." It repeated the guiding slogan of the Games: "Civilization, Unity, Learning, Vigorous Progress." Our assignment was to "increase knowledge, improve friendship, receive education."

The rules listed in the pamphlet included a dress code, one of the restrictions being against long, loose hair; curfews; rules against eating food from street vendors; rules about obeying coaches; and rules against smoking, drinking, and fighting. So many of the male athletes and coaches smoked, however, that this prohibition was impossible to enforce. At a team meeting in which the air was opaque with smoke emanating from the cigarettes of the coaches, the team leader acknowledged that they had found that some people simply could not stop, therefore they only asked that athletes not smoke on the track. He also acknowledged that many people liked to drink beer (a weakness to which my coach confessed) and that they should try not to do so excessively.

We memorized the official meet song and practiced it so that we could sing along with gusto at the opening ceremonies and other occasions. The meet song expressed the spirit of the meet, helping to imprint its message into our brains:

As majestic as the dragon,
As brave as the tiger,
Our mother is China.
Facing the world, facing the future,
We give our best in the struggle for national unity.
We give our best in the struggle for national dignity.
Civilization, learning, unity, progress,
Our banner glistens beneath the sun's rays,
College students of the '80s,
Carry out your great task.

In addition, we made a special trip to the Beijing Institute of Physical Education for a preliminary review of our marching technique for the Parade of Athletes in the opening ceremonies. We were to shout slogans in time with our goose-steps as we passed the reviewing stand where the high officials sat.

Train the body! [This was shouted out by our march leader,
followed by a response by the rest of us. Our responses were:]
Study diligently!
Bravely scale the peaks!
Carry out the Four Modernizations!
Defend the Nation!

Our performance, as far as marching displays go, was a technically difficult one because it entailed carrying flowers, shouting slogans, and unfurling banners, all while goose-stepping. Our successful execution of this level of difficulty was an important part of our bid for a spiritual civilization award. As we were reminded by a cadre speaking down to us from the reviewing stand at our first dress rehearsal, we would be representing Beijing's 138 thousand college students before an audience of many thousands. The opening ceremony was our opportunity to show our spiritual attitude (*jingshen mianmao*), so we must be very serious. Despite his injunctions, the column of women behind me laughed nonstop at my marching form.

Later, a young coach commented, "Why do you always have to shout slogans? Of course we all want to 'win glory for Beijing.' But do you think Beijing really cares whether you win points for it or not? Most of Beijing doesn't even know who you are. If you do badly, is Beijing going to console you? No, but you have to live with it. So we're all really performing for ourselves." This sentiment was shared by many of the athletes, who were more cynical than the older coaches. However, I later came to realize that the athletes were not as concerned with Beijing's watching them as they were with other provinces watching them represent Beijing.

On 15 July we had another meeting. Our team leader noted that in all we were required to have ten meetings; they would get more frequent as time went on in order to create the proper atmosphere for the meet. Also, the rules would get stricter. This would help us "enter our roles" (*jinru jiaose*). After today, we were required to stay at the dormitory, and there would be a bed check at 10:30 each night and a sanitation check once a day (fruit peels and sunflower seed husks should be swept outside of the door). Every other day, the 6:20 roll call would be followed by marching practice. One of the coaches pointed out that in attendance at roll call, "the men have been consistently worse than the women. Last time only five men showed up; this morning, we waited ten minutes for the men. They should be on time."

Self-Evaluations

Around this time, self-evaluation (*ziwo jianding*) forms were distributed. These were to be the basis for selecting the recipients of the individual spiritual civilization awards. Self-evaluations are a frequent requirement in everyday Chinese life; most work units require their regular submission. The style is highly formalized and full of key jargon words. Since I was unfamiliar with the proper language, I asked two teammates to help me. They quite enjoyed the process. One of them began by reeling off the phrase, "Under the correct guidance of the Party and the leaders . . ." The other interrupted him, pointing out that I was a foreigner and not a Party member, so I didn't have to say that. He agreed, so they deleted it and proceeded as I wrote down:

> Since joining the Beijing City collegiate group training, I have been able to obey the directions of the leaders and coaches, actively join in on all the activities organized by the team, train strenuously, and assiduously improve my sports technique. I have respected the coaches and made many friends, despite the fact that I wasn't accustomed to the food and drink and other aspects; but I was able to overcome the difficulties. As a foreign student, I very much want to work hard to improve the friendship between college students of the two nations of America and China, and I am determined to spread the fighting spirit during this college student meet, and to win glory for Beijing's college students.

These self-evaluations were later examined during a meeting of the team leaders, captains, and officers, and six semifinalists were announced at the next meeting of the entire Beijing team. During the College Games themselves, all of the Beijing semifinalists' self-evaluations were submitted to the national committee and finalists were selected. Perhaps not surprisingly, I was one of the finalists. The names of the finalists were read out at the closing ceremonies, and six teams with the largest numbers of finalists were designated "spiritual civilization teams." Individuals were awarded certificates and teams were awarded trophies.

As one might imagine, the entire process is open to manipulation. Of the six chosen from our group, I was the only one who was not a team officer and thus was not present at the selection meeting; except for me, the participants at the meeting selected themselves. Athletes who were not team officers complained that the officers chose themselves because they were looking forward to the time after graduation when they would be assigned jobs, and they thought it would look good in their dossiers.

As a team, we experienced a range of the disciplinary techniques mentioned by Foucault (1979: 148). We were classified and organized spatially, temporally, and hierarchically and it was all posted on a chart on the wall for everyone to see. We each then had the necessary information to determine if the others were in their proper place. Our coaches held us accountable for this information, as when I was asked if my roommate was "often in the room" by a coach who knew full well she had missed several curfews. I replied that she was in the room "fairly often." Since she performed well in the meet, she was never criticized, but after the meet I heard two coaches commenting that it was fortunate for her that she had done well. The survey that was distributed made us an object of study; the self-evaluations forced us to make at least superficial confessions. Our disciplinary model was the military; this was reinforced by our marching practice. This production of "docile bodies" (Foucault 1979: 136) was accompanied by a set of practices for shaping the thoughts: songs, slogans, exhortations, political study meetings.

This is the theory. If it sounds Orwellian, then I should point out that the experience was not dissimilar from the various American summer camps I attended in my childhood.[3] I confess that I often felt impa-

---

3. During the training camp for the college games, I was often reminded of a girls' sailing camp I attended one summer at the age of sixteen. This camp also had morning roll calls, curfews, sanitation checks, a talent show, and inspirational singing after lunch and dinner. As the "oldest" cabin, we were told it was our duty to lead by example. The camp explicitly

tient with the notion that the singing, marching, slogan shouting, and weekly meetings would contribute to my performance. My coaches believed that it would, but my teammates were less sure. I felt a great deal of pressure to perform well in the meet, and I wanted to be sure that I was ready to do so (by that point I had practically lost all of my distance as the participant "observer"). Nevertheless, I obeyed the rules more strictly than most of my teammates, mainly because I had nothing better to do. The main problem with the regime of discipline was boredom. As my roommate complained to me, it seemed like all we did was sleep, eat, train, and sleep again. My teammates violated discipline mainly when they had more important things to do. The main sanctions were criticism and the threat of a negative entry in the dossier, but evidently a good performance in the meet would override them.

The athletes seemed more cynical than the team leaders. A coach of another team expressed to me an opinion that the older coaches on the Beijing team might have shared: she said students are really hard to control these days, not like in her youth. Now young people love freedom too much.

CIVILIZATION AND DISCIPLINE

Our last important meeting was our send-off party on 25 July. First our marching was reviewed by the vice-mayor and other top officials, then

---

promoted, not communist ideology, but rather the ideology of "Jane Achiever." I distinguished myself by achieving the third of five ranks in only one summer, which was viewed as highly difficult. Ranks were marked by differently colored elastic bands worn around the neck at all times, which functioned as status symbols. Much to my surprise, while writing the final draft of this manuscript I learned that the camp was founded and run by the YMCA. Far from being the exotic brainchild of isolated oriental despots, communist discipline has roots in the Christian missionizing of the early twentieth century and is linked to transnational cultural flows and global modernization processes.

The national heptathlon training camps that I attended at the U.S. Olympic Training Center in Colorado Springs utilized somewhat different disciplinary regimes. Although we did not sing songs and shout slogans, we ate every meal surrounded by the flags of the world strung around the cafeteria, and every time we left the front gate we passed under the American and Olympic flags. There, our ideology was "science," and instead of interminable political study meetings, we endured even more interminable sessions in which our bodies were weighed underwater, tested on machines, and measured. We analyzed videotapes of our training sessions, publicly dissecting our own bodies according to the principles of momentum, levers, center of gravity, and so on. I found this process far more invasive and humiliating than the self-evaluation I wrote in Beijing: science is such an ultimate voice of authority that one feels absolutely defenseless under its gaze. If, according to the principles of biomechanics, my high jump form is all wrong, how can I argue with that? Our sessions with the

The author, after winning the 1986 National College Games heptathlon, standing with the silver medalist.

we were treated to a banquet, and finally we went to the auditorium for speeches and a talent show. At my banquet table, one of my teammates spoke about the importance of spiritual civilization for Beijing. He hinted that there were things Beijing could not do because it was the capital city and must set a good example. Representing Beijing was a serious matter for him. This was reiterated in a speech made by one of the cadres. She commented that we shouldn't think people don't care about Beijing. At some previous competition, Beijing took only a few medals, and people asked, "What's wrong with you?" If it were Zhejiang province, she asked, do you think they would have even noticed? Another cadre pointed out that there would be television coverage sent back each day to Beijing, and several speakers made a great deal of the fact that we would be representing Beijing's 138,000 college students.

On 29 July, we left for Dalian, where we won glory for Beijing by placing second overall in Group A track and field. I contributed my share by winning the heptathlon, setting a national Group A record, and running legs on the two silver-medal relays.

---

sport psychologist were hardly enough to overcome the "paralysis by analysis" brought on by the biomechanics lectures.

Everyone involved with the Beijing team seemed aware of Beijing's importance as an example of the correct implementation of state policy. The team leaders took Beijing's image seriously and, at our meetings, often reminded us that, unlike the athletes on other teams, we were all legitimate students who had taken the college-entrance exam. As discussed in the next chapter, the practice of lowering admission standards for athletes was just beginning. Within the Beijing team, Beijing University in particular considered itself the moral guardian, and Qinghua University was just behind.

I believe my teammates took seriously their duty to represent the capital city to the other provinces. As an American, I did not understand what it meant to represent Beijing and why spiritual civilization was important in doing so. As Lisa Rofel reminds us, "we should be cautious about assuming a bourgeois subject, with its attendant consciousness, as the site of all disciplinary regimes" (1992: 106). I was always skeptical of sport sociology surveys which showed that one of the main motivations of athletes was to win glory for China and that when they had their first big performances they thought of the Party, the people, and the nation (see Ma Mingshan 1984). Athletes I talked to spoke of concrete conditions as their main motivations: mostly, this meant bonuses and better food. However, I think there is a sense in which both are true. On a day-to-day basis, they probably thought of mundane rewards. When they were marching into the stadium with their team or receiving a medal before an audience of tens of thousands, they probably thought of more spiritual rewards. Such thoughts are an almost inevitable product of the symbolic structure of such public events (MacAloon 1995: chapter 1).

I came to realize that my teammates' duty to represent Beijing with style received its importance from two elements in the construction of state power in China. The first is that Beijing, as the center, should exercise a civilizing influence on the periphery. The second is that the civilizing process occurs mainly through the force of example. This is similar to what Geertz calls the "doctrine of the exemplary center" in his description of the nineteenth-century Balinese state—except that in China it is practiced by a modern bureaucratic state: "the theory that the court-and-capital is at once a microcosm of the supernatural order . . . and the material embodiment of political order" (1980: 13). Beijing houses the Party, not the court, and the Party is supposed to be the moral exemplar of communist ideology, not a supernatural order. But like the Balinese state, the Chinese Party-state is in large degree an expressive state oriented toward spectacles and public dramas, as was shown in the previous chapters.

But what, exactly, is "civilization," and to what "uncivilized" practices is it opposed? Upon rereading "Things to Know Before the Meet" and reviewing the rhetoric of our meetings, I realize that one concern, above all else, seems to be linked to the concept of civilization: control of physical violence.

"Things to Know Before the Meet" consists of a sequential unfolding of the argument for civilization and how to achieve it. After listing the meet goals and slogans, the pamphlet moves right to the section on "Competition Ethics," which begins with the following paragraph:

> On the competition field, you should not only demonstrate consummate technique, you should also express a superior sportsmanship style, strive to do the "three respects": First, respect the referee; when the referee makes a mistake or lacks judgment, be forgiving, don't get tangled up in it, look at the big picture. Second, respect your opponent, be brave and resolute, and at the same time don't act boorishly, or go so far as to intentionally hurt someone; even if your opponent is aggressive toward you, you should adopt a restrained attitude, and don't exchange "a tooth for a tooth." Humbly learn from stronger teams and opponents, help weaker teams and opponents, and by no means may you put on airs of superiority. Third, respect the spectators and compete conscientiously; you may not be lax and undisciplined. In addition, athletes must also spread the communal spirit and the heroic revolutionary spirit, spread the fighting spirit, compete with style and compete to potential, have a civilized bearing, be natural and generous. (*Beijing daxuesheng daibiaotuan mishuzu* 1986: 1–2)

The immediately following paragraph is addressed to coaches. It reiterates:

> Coaches ought to set an example in obeying the decisions of referees, be polite to the athletes and spectators on each side, pay attention to civilization [*jiang wenming*], be even more respectful and polite to other coaches. (p. 2)

"Spirit" is said to be "More Precious than Gold Medals." The section entitled "'Loss of Control' Is Not Permitted During Competitions" analyzes why loss of control (*shikong*) occurs. The ultimate reason given is that when coaches and leaders have lost control, or don't exercise strict enough control, their athletes don't take the issue of control seriously enough. The section concludes that whether or not athletes have self-control hinges on the concrete conditions of their spiritual civilization (p. 5). The discussion then moves on to discipline. "All persons are equal before the face of discipline," it notes. Therefore leaders cannot overlook infractions by their top athletes because they are afraid of having their names "smeared black." "Especially when a top athlete violates discipline, it is even easier for 'big things to become small and small things to disappear' due to the fear of influencing performance and placing" (p. 6).

This is followed by a section on "The Cultivation and Construction of Spiritual Civilization." It notes, "The athlete's construction of spiritual civilization is a strict requirement that is important in everyday life." It further notes, "The concrete demand to set an example [*biao-shuai*] is put upon Party and Youth Group members" (p. 6).

The sequence of this argument illuminates what spiritual civilization meant in the realm of sports in the 1980s. First of all, it referred to self-control, especially restraint over angry reactions to competitors and referees. Discipline is the way in which this control is inculcated and maintained. The people who are ultimately responsible for inculcating this discipline are the coaches, team leaders, Party and Youth Group members. A breach on the part of their athlete implies that they themselves have been inadequate models. It causes them to lose face. Their fear for their own reputations helps to explain what often seems like an exaggerated fear that "something will happen," especially an outbreak of violence.

The same logic was evident in the discourse on civilization during the 1987 National Games. Banners and speechmakers proclaimed that the goal of the Games was to "win the double harvest of outstanding performances and spiritual civilization." The ideological preparation on the sports teams was intensified for the Games. As reported in the press, the Beijing team had special study sessions after they arrived in Guangzhou. They not only studied the rules and regulations published by the organizing committee, but also continued studying the handbook specially printed by the Beijing team, "The Civilized Manners Handbook." Many provinces instituted systems of punishment and reward, so that even a gold medalist who didn't show a suitably civilized spirit would be fined (Zong He 1987).

"Spiritual Civilization" awards were also given out at the closing cere-monies of the National Games in Guangdong, and these were regarded by team leaders as quite important. *Sports News* wrote that the Games should "reflect the civilized manner of Chinese people who are a prod-uct of the era of opening-up and reform" (*Tiyu bao* 1987d). Those ath-letes who chased only gold medals were said to lack the proper spirit of the Sixth Games, reportedly because they were concerned only with placing in domestic competitions and did not hold to the policy of "Ad-vancing on the World." If they broadened their horizons, realizing that the Games were a window through which the world watched China's behavior to see if it was civilized, they would not engage in improper behavior (*Tiyu bao* 1987d).

Initially, I was confused at the way in which the rhetoric was directed at the spectators as well as the athletes. During the National Games, at a gymnastics competition in Shenzhen, for example, the announcer called upon the spectators to "be a civilized audience, win honor for Shenzhen, win honor for the nation." I was also skeptical that both aspects of the "double harvest" were equally important. However, I found that Guangzhou residents echoed the state's concern that with "the world" and most of China watching, something unseemly would happen. A Cantonese driver told me that Guangzhou people had all been very tense because they were afraid something would go wrong. They had all been very conscientious, he added. From the state's point of view, a mishap would subvert its goal of demonstrating the peaceful, "civilized" coming together of various peoples. From Guangzhou resi-dents' perspective, it would also reflect badly on Guangzhou. Finally, I realized that the discourse of civilization formed the background for Guangzhou residents' perception of themselves vis-à-vis the rest of China, and Chinese people's perception of themselves vis-à-vis the rest of the world. Thus, for people who cared about Guangzhou's and Chi-na's reputations, it actually was important that both athletes and specta-tors be civilized and that they obtain "the double harvest of outstanding performances and spiritual civilization."

Clearly, "civilization" is a concept in the name of which the state can invade the most minute actions of the body, because it is so polymor-phous that "there is almost nothing which cannot be done in a 'civi-lized' or 'uncivilized' way" (Elias 1978: 3). It provides a rationale for the state's permeation of everyday practice, which spirals out from Beijing, the center of the civilizing process. In the name of civilization, the state can also appeal to feelings of nationalism and patriotism. The discourse on civilization is both inward- and outward-looking.

CULTURE AND SOCIAL ORDER

The importance of "civilization" in state discourse is mirrored in the unofficial discourse on "culture" (*wenhua*). The two discourses also overlap and merge in places. "Culture" plays a role in a class structure in which those who "have culture" attempt to solidify their position over those who "lack culture." Thus, "civilization" and "culture" are involved in a complex relationship which reflects shifting power relations both within Chinese society and in China's positioning of itself in the world. Both discourses shape the disciplinary practices of athletic institutions and the subjectivities of individual athletes who also work to discipline themselves.

In contrast to civilization, "culture" in 1980s China had most relevance to class relations within China. "Culture" expressed primarily a social antithesis rather than a national one (Elias 1978: 29–31). In this sense, it was similar to the concept of *Kultur* in Germany in the eighteenth and early nineteenth centuries, before it underwent a transition "from its place within the oppositional ideology of an intellectual elite to a mass-mobilizing substitute religion in the context of the rise of a nation-state" (Bleicher 1990: 97; see also Elias 1978). In the late 1980s, a "culture craze" and "search for roots" among Chinese intellectuals shifted the emphasis toward the international arena in which Chinese culture was set apart from other cultures—again with intellectuals as the rediscoverers of the new Chinese culture. The effects in the realm of sports events are discussed in the Epilogue, but the discourse on culture described below was still mainly a domestic discourse.

The Chinese word, *wenhua*, implies education and literacy. A very frequently used phrase is *wenhua shuiping*. While this phrase is best translated as "cultural level," in some contexts it refers to "educational level," or number of years of schooling. "Low cultural level" is often used to describe backward peasants, athletes, rowdy African exchange students, and other people who do not conduct themselves according to the urban Han sense of decorum. It is also possible to speak of these people as "lacking culture" (*meiyou wenhua*), as opposed to others who "have culture" (*you wenhua*). These linguistic formulae reflect the class structure; workers and peasants are to a large degree ignorant of the elite "culture" created by the dominant classes (see Bourdieu 1984: 505). When "culture" is taken to mean the dominant tradition, the lower classes really do not "have culture."

Athletes are often said to "lack culture." Predictably, it is those people who "have culture" who are most likely to accuse athletes of lacking it.

A freshman at the Shanghai Institute of Physical Education, a retired javelin thrower, explained why she had entered the institute. "I want to learn a little knowledge because if you don't, people look down on you. Here, everyone looks down on the professional team athletes because they think they're dumb. I want to study hard so I can do my job better after I graduate and also to show them that I'm not dumb." Many elite university students do consider that athletes have "four developed limbs and an undeveloped brain" (*sizhi fada, tounao jiandan*). For example, a derogatory joke about students at the Beijing Institute of Physical Education circulated at Beijing University, which is located nearby. The joke was a pun based on two Chinese characters which look very similar but are pronounced differently. The joke went like this: "Did you hear about the student from the Beijing Institute of P.E. who wrote a letter to the American embassy (*dashiguan*)? Instead, he addressed it to the 'American shithouse' (*dabianguan*)." A student from Qinghua University, himself an athlete, told me, "I don't like p.e. institute students. Their educational level is low. I don't like their language; it is vulgar (*cu*). And they don't have any manners. They don't treat people well."

When I mentioned to an athlete at the Beijing Physical Education Institute that Beijing University students looked down on students at her institute, she said,

> It's true, they do. They think they're really intelligent, know all these things, and that sports institute students don't have culture. But these years it is better than before, because they have seen that athletes do a lot for society. And it is true that athletes make a great contribution to society. It is not clear what sort of influence getting a college degree has on society. So in recent years regular college students don't look down on them as much; it is much better.

She also stated that "Athletes are very easygoing with each other. Whatever they want to say, they can say. Not like with other people where you always have to watch what you say. Athletes are open-minded (*kailang*). Students at the institute all prefer to be with athletes." The idea that athletes are more "open-minded" is a widely held one, even among nonathletes. It is said to be a result of striving together on the competition field. This acknowledgment is perhaps indicative of the fact that an open mind is not a necessary accoutrement of "culture" in the Chinese scheme of things.

College-educated cadres and coaches often mentioned the low cultural level of athletes as a major obstacle to China's progress in sports. One coach told me that sometimes the questions players ask are laughable; there are a few running jokes on the subject. For example, you tell a player to shoot the basketball at a 45-degree angle, and he asks, "What's an angle?" Or you tell a runner to "run the curve" and he tries to run bent over like a hunchback.

More important than these mild forms of contempt was the belief of educated urbanites that those who lack culture are violent. This linking of a lack of "culture" with violence parallels the state's linking of a lack of "civilization" with violence. Because athletes and many sports fans are stereotyped as lacking culture, they are said to be prone to violence. It is hard to judge whether there is, in fact, a high degree of violence in Chinese sport or whether it can be attributed to a low cultural level. As discussed previously, soccer violence has been attributed to working-class hooligans (Kong Xiang'an and Zhang Zhidong 1987). A riot during a basketball game was reported in the press. In a worker's basketball game in Xi'an, one team was losing 20 to 0 and became so frustrated that the number of fouls escalated quickly and, despite cautions by the wary referees, one member finally punched an opposing player in the face. The teams began fighting, throwing chairs, benches, and soda bottles. The audience left quickly without becoming involved. The article stated that such brawls had been rare for many years (Qiu Zutai 1988b). When, after reading this report, I asked a few urban sportspeople if such incidents were rare, however, they told me that one cannot know, because they aren't reported in the press; probably they occur in isolated rural areas all the time.

A low cultural level is also used to explain the proclivity of some (mostly male) athletes to pick up "bad habits" (*exi*) such as smoking, watching pornographic videos, and engaging in premarital sex. Sportspeople acknowledged, however, that besides working out there was very little else to do, and "bad habits" alleviate the boredom. This problem was said to be worse in the isolated provinces, especially Guizhou, which was mentioned more than once to me as the most lawless province in China (even by an athlete who grew up there, although her family was from Beijing). I was visiting a less isolated provincial team when a handful of male athletes were caught watching pornographic videos from Hong Kong that one of them had bought in Guangdong. This athlete even recorded and sold them and also recruited other athletes to pay him money to watch. Word got around the dormitory and they were caught in the act. Three athletes were dragged off to the police station, and two were expelled from the team immediately. The athlete who instigated it was not only expelled but also sent to prison, possibly for as long as three years.

Violent outbreaks among individual athletes were usually attributed to a low cultural level. For example, a young female track athlete from an isolated mountain village was described as "really being able to fight." She was reported to have engaged in fisticuffs with boys over a space in line at the ticket window of the local movie theater. Her coach was known for being extremely tough. Even one of his athletes told me that he could be really "ferocious" (*xiong*) and "ruthless" (*hen*) in practice, though she said she thought it was best that way. An athlete from another team claimed she had once seen him throw a (shotput) shot at the head of one of his athletes. The man himself was a college-educated urbanite. When I mentioned to him that I had heard he was very tough, he said, "Let me tell you, Bao Sushan, I do that on purpose. It is the only thing these athletes understand; they don't understand anything else."

The story of a martial artist whom I knew well sheds some light on motivations for violent acts. Martial artists are said to be very fierce. There is a tradition of students challenging their masters, which is one reason that masters traditionally retained a few secret techniques for themselves, passing them on only on their deathbeds. I was told that occasionally *wushu* athletes attack their teachers. Such an incident was recounted to me by a former national champion, Liu Zheng (a pseudonym), who had had a bitter childhood. During the Cultural Revolution, his father, a doctor, was denounced as a capitalist element and the entire family was sent to a poor rural village. His father's disposition had always been bad, but now it became even worse, and he often beat his son. At the age of eighteen, in 1975, Liu Zheng joined the provincial team. There was a coach on the team who wore straw sandals and always carried Mao's Little Red Book in his pants pocket, constantly whipping it out to read from the book and yell at students for "incorrect thinking." For this, Liu Zheng recounted, all of the athletes hated him. Liu Zheng enjoyed painting very much and once painted a picture of a "goddess," but when this teacher saw it he accused Liu Zheng of painting "beautiful women" and called a meeting where he was publicly criticized for his "thought problems." The next year, Liu Zheng injured his lower back and aggravated the problem by training despite his injury, with the result that he finally had to use crutches for a year. During this period, he felt extremely angry and frustrated. People often criticized him behind his back, especially the coach he hated so much, who wanted to remove him from the team. One day, after such criticism, Liu Zheng lost his temper. What kind of person would vilify a young person on crutches? He lay in wait where he knew the coach would pass and jumped him, beating him until he had blood coming out of his nose. Years later, Liu Zheng still laughed to think that, even on crutches, he could beat the man so badly. He said the teacher was short and stiff and his *wushu* was uninteresting. As a result of this incident, Liu Zheng was brought before a meeting of the team leaders and coaches and they almost decided to send him to the police station; but because there were people who sympathized with him and disliked the teacher, he wasn't sent. He and that teacher never spoke to one another again, however.

In a later incident, Liu Zheng was angered at the selfishness of the coaches and confronted them. This incident ended with him throwing a long spear across the room and punching out the glass window in a door, threatening to do the same to his coach. A long sliver of glass sliced into the inside of his forearm and he had to be taken to the hospital, where it was sutured with three stitches. He said, "I was very sullen in those days and hard to get to know. For anything you did, you could be criticized for capitalist thinking: long hair, bright clothes, everything." He said that the leaders are the problem with Chinese sports—they are too conservative and they look out for their own interests, not those of the athletes. They stress political thinking too much—what does that have to do with your performance? In fact, the worst people were the Party members; they thought that because they were Party members, they were better than everyone else. The coach that he beat up used to say, "I represent the Party. So I'm right."

I told him that in the United States if an athlete doesn't get along with his coach, he changes coaches. Liu Zheng said, "China's system is to change athletes." He said conflicts between coaches and athletes are many. If an athlete doesn't get along with his coach, he gets sent off to do factory work. On the other hand, he noted that athletes don't always learn how to use their brains. The Chinese tradition is to listen to everything the coach says; they don't teach athletes to think for themselves.

These stories illustrate that motivations for violence are more complex than simply a low cultural level. Liu Zheng's bitter childhood was not at all atypical of the generation of athletes who experienced the heights of the Cultural Revolution during their formative years. The authoritarian relationship of coach over athlete was the norm until the mid-1980s, as discussed above by Yang Duo. Most athletes are not as well-educated as their coaches, especially those who missed out during the collapse of the educational system during the Cultural Revolution. There are many possible explanations for athletes' tendency toward violent outbreaks, if it in fact exists. I am inclined, however, to think that there is less violence in Chinese sports than there is, for example, in American sports. Certainly the sports fans, including the soccer fans, that I observed were much more subdued than American fans are. The athletes were under such pressure to demonstrate socialist spiritual civilization that they seemed more restrained than American athletes; as an athlete in China, I felt the pressure myself more than I ever had in the United States.

A SELF-CONTROL THAT PREDISPOSES THEM TO CONTROL OTHERS

If there is, indeed, less violence in Chinese sports than in American sports, then the reasons for what seemed to me an almost obsessive concern with violence must be sought elsewhere. I propose that the explanation is found in the parallel efforts of the Beijing-centered party-state and urban intellectuals to assert themselves as examples of "civilization" and "culture" fit to rule the unruly masses.

Bourdieu reminds us that the ethic of sportsmanship in the West began as an aristocratic ethic because it embodied the greater cultural constraint on "natural" functions that the dominant classes attributed to themselves—"a self-control that predisposes them to control others" (1978: 324). Efforts similar to the Chinese party-state's civilizing project surrounded the popularization of sport in the period from 1837 to 1939 in the West, though in this case it was primarily the capitalist sponsors of sporting events who promoted ideals of good behavior rather than the state. In Victorian England and America, fair play, good sportsmanship, and gentlemanly spectatorship were promoted in the schools, the media, and juvenile literature in an attempt to transform the ticket-buying masses into a well-behaved crowd (Guttmann 1986: 121). Ironically, the upper classes ended up promoting the same aristocratic ethic among the masses that they had originally developed to set themselves apart from the masses.

In China, the state promotes "civilization" among the masses, while intellectuals use "culture" to set themselves apart from the masses. Both discourses share the fact that they construct the masses as inherently violent, a strategy that plays on the widespread fear of social disorder. Sportspeople are caught in the middle of a conflict between the two discourses. They are used by the state as examples of the "civilization" it claims to promote, but they are ridiculed by intellectuals as lacking culture. The state is propelling them upwards in the hierarchy, while intellectuals attempt to hold them below themselves. The tensions in this situation of flux are emblematic of the tensions in Chinese society as a whole as official state discourses conflict with the discourses produced by shifting alignments in the social structure—a social structure itself produced in part by the discourses and policies of the state.

CHAPTER SEVEN

"Those Who Work with Their Brains Rule; Those Who Work with Their Brawn Are Ruled"

In the late 1980s, Chinese sportspeople were caught in the middle of a shift in alignments in the social structure. This shift involved a reassertion of the value of education and a concomitant move away from the glorification of manual laborers and peasants that had characterized the preceding eras. Sportspeople found themselves positioned in the gap between "mental laborers" (*naoli laodongzhe*) and "physical laborers" (*tili laodongzhe*). It seemed that the state's promotion of sports was the major support for their position above manual laborers, but the renewed importance of education placed them below intellectuals. They were thus positioned at a major fault line in the social structure. It was the friction along this fault line that contributed to the discourses on civilization and culture that characterized state and intellectual assessments of the restless masses described in the previous chapter. Here, I will examine this fault line more closely by analyzing the political and social machinations that occurred along it.

Portions of this chapter were published previously in much more abbreviated form as "The Changing Relationship between Sport and the State in the People's Republic of China," in *Sport . . . The third millennium,* edited by Fernand Landry, Marc Landry, and Magdaleine

SOCIAL RANKING

Studies of social prestige in China concur that professional athletes tend to rank somewhere near the middle of the social scale. Here I use "professional athlete" to refer to those on municipal, provincial, or national teams. These state "shamateur" athletes are officially amateurs, but the English-language *China Daily* newspaper calls them professionals, so I will follow its example here.

In a 1983 study of 1,632 Beijing residents, Lin Nan and Xie Wen concluded that, in terms of occupational prestige, athletes ranked eighteenth out of fifty occupations (1988: 805). They found that athletes generally ranked below "mental workers" (doctors, engineers, scientists, writers, teachers, officials, accountants, secretaries, and librarians) and above "physical workers" (mechanics, jewelers, machinists, and typists were fairly close categories). Lin Nan and Xie Wen also found a significant difference between the attitudes of "manual" and "nonmanual" laborers toward sports. Out of the fifty occupations they examined, eleven were rated significantly lower by nonmanual laborers than manual; one of those was sports (1988: 815).

Interestingly, athletes ranked above elementary school teachers and actors. The category of "athlete" is difficult to rank because the status of its members ranges from the rich and famous to the fairly anonymous. In this sense, they are similar to actors. It is interesting that the Lin and Xie survey showed athletes as ranking higher than actors; this may be a result of the greater media attention given to their performances on behalf of the nation.

Less detailed Chinese surveys support Lin and Xie's findings. Kong Xiang'an, China's premier sport sociologist, told me he had concluded that athletes rank above those who do "physical labor" (peasants, *getihu*, and workers), below those who do "mental labor" (college graduates, administrative cadres, skilled technical personnel), and about equal with service personnel (*fuwu renyuan*) in "clean" jobs, such as hotel employees and drivers. In contrast to Lin and Xie, he felt they ranked just below middle and elementary school teachers, which is what many of them will become; Kong argued that physical education teachers are generally not accorded as much respect as teachers of academic subjects (Kong Xiang'an 1988). He noted that since the vast majority of China's

Yerles, pp. 295–301, Proceedings of the International Symposium, 21–25 May (Quebec City: Les Presses de l'Université Laval, 1990).

Table 7.1 Percentage of Parents Favoring Their Children's Participation in Sports, by Parents' Occupations

Head of household's occupation	Favor their children becoming athletes
soldier	53.0 (%)
service personnel	48.3
worker	35.8
doctor	20.5
administrative personnel	19.5
teacher	13.0
scientific and technical personnel	10.0
coach	2.2

SOURCE: Data from Niu Xinghua, Li Shuyi, and Su Lianyong (1986: 63).

population are workers and peasants, who rank below athletes, this is regarded as a fairly high social status in Chinese society.

Niu Xinghua, Li Shuyi, and Su Lianyong used different occupational categories in their study of differences in parental attitudes, according to the various occupations of the parents, toward their children's engaging in sports, but they also found that the division between people engaged in "mental" and "physical" labor was significant. The results are summarized in table 7.1. They also concluded that those engaged in "mental labor" were less favorably disposed toward sports than those engaged in "physical labor."

The social status of athletes is also reflected in their marriage patterns. Social status is the central consideration in mate choice for most young people; it is generally considered best if "doors match" (*mendang hudui*)—in other words, if spouses are of similar status. Young members of the Beijing City team, especially the unmarried women, had very clear ideas about what sort of mate an athlete could expect to find. They agreed that athletes are able to find mates among groups whose social status is fairly high in China: this included other athletes or college students, drivers, or hotel employees. They said that athletes who marry workers are few, although a boy will marry a worker if she is pretty. Most athletes marry other athletes since their statuses are similar and they have more opportunities to meet each other (Beijing City Team 1988).

Star athletes also sometimes marry up, especially women. If a sportswoman marries a man with an advanced degree, this is considered an improvement in status. The star spiker on the women's volleyball team, Lang Ping, married a Qinghua graduate student. Marrying up seems to be almost synonymous with marrying a college graduate, although other options are conceivable, such as marrying the son of a high cadre. Another member of the women's volleyball team made such a match. This does not seem to be a general aspiration, however, perhaps reflecting the endogamous practices of high-ranking families. Generally speaking, the most desirable man is an educated one.

LIVING CONDITIONS[1]

What did a "fairly high" social status entail in the Chinese society of the late 1980s? To Americans, the word "professional" calls to mind the outlandish salaries of American pros. In China there may have been a few sports stars—less than ten—whose salaries were just as outlandish relative to the average income. However, the majority had unremarkable living conditions and salaries—in absolute terms, theirs constituted a tiny fraction of the salary of even an average American. In this sense, they resembled the majority of amateur athletes in America. The only area in which the sportspeople's standard of living far exceeded even the average Chinese was in nutrition, as is discussed in chapter 9.

Athletes on professional teams lived in dormitories with four to six people in a room, which was slightly less crowded than the average college dorm room where roommates commonly numbered five to eight. The dormitories themselves were standard for China: bare cement floors, whitewashed walls, on each floor one communal toilet room and a washroom with cold running water. Athletes had access to the communal shower hall six times a week, whereas the average college student was given shower tickets for only once or twice a week. Even this was a luxury compared with the opportunities for many urban Chinese. Showers were considered a necessity for athletes because they sweat a lot.

There is usually a medical clinic at the training center, so sportspeople could often get immediate medical attention, unlike other people who might have to wait in line for hours or even days. Obviously, medical treatment is more important to sports than to other careers. Training centers often have a relationship with a hospital, which expedites treatment for more serious injuries.

Many famous athletes had their own apartments. These were either

---

1. This section is based on data from the publication *Selected Physical Culture and Sports Documents 1949–1981* (Guojia tiwei zhengce yanjiushi 1982: 780–817), as well as from interviews, observations, and newspaper reports.

given to them as bonuses or were bought by the athletes who had enough money. These apartments were also within the average range, which means they consisted of two or three rooms plus a kitchen and bathroom.

Athletes' wages, too, were unremarkable. National team athletes might receive a total of about 90 yuan per month, which included about a 70-yuan basic wage and 20 yuan in subsidies for shoes, showers, housing, and other things (at the 1988 exchange rate of $1 = 3.7 yuan, 90 yuan converted to $24). Even the most famous athletes received no more than 150 yuan per month, about what an associate professor made. Top junior athletes at regular sports schools received about 60 yuan per month. The lowest wages were about 30 yuan per month.

Wages are set by each province or municipality according to its particular cost of living. There is a fourteen-grade wage scale set by the state. An athlete's position on the wage scale depends on performance and age. Performance levels are divided into grades according to the standards set for each sporting event. At the top of the scale is the "International Master Sportsperson" (guoji jianjiang); second is the "Master Sportsperson" (jianjiang); third is the "First Grade"; fourth is the "Second Grade"; fifth is the "Third Grade"; and last is the "Junior Athlete." Each jump in grade is accompanied by certain benefits: a one-time bonus, an increase in wages and food subsidies, and/or the addition of points to the National College Entrance Exam score. In addition, coaches who have worked with the athlete receive a bonus. This applies to all of the coaches at the various levels who have at one time or another been designated as the athlete's main coach. Coaches themselves are also divided into grades, which are determined by the number of athletes they have coached who have reached high grades. This practice results in a very complex situation. When an athlete achieves notable success, coaches who worked with him years before, when he was a beginner in the spare-time sports school, may have a claim to a bonus. Sometimes coaches will try to claim an athlete when they were not actually his main coach. To resolve disputes, one province was forced to require all coaches under consideration for a promotion in grade to post a list of athletes they were claiming, and these lists were later debated publicly in order to resolve contradictory claims to the same athlete.

Since athletes are issued nutritional supplements, sweatsuits and workout clothes, and are sometimes given other products by companies as a means of advertising, they may actually spend less of their wages on necessities than most people.

Bonuses were more significant than wages, but even these could not compare with those awarded to "amateur" athletes in the United States, who may have contracts with corporations. For example, for the 1984 Olympic Games, one American shoe company awarded $40,000 to track and field gold medalists who were enrolled in its incentive program. In China, bonus money varies by province. At the 1987 National Games, the highest bonus given for a gold medal was 10,000 yuan ($2,700), and this much was given by only a few "backward" provinces (Xinjiang, Guizhou, Gansu) in order to promote sports development. There were also other perks. Gansu gave a three-room unfurnished apartment. Most provinces, however, gave only about 3,000 yuan ($810) for a gold medal, in addition to color television sets and other appliances. National and Asian records were said to be slightly more valuable than gold medal bonuses. An Olympic gold medal was the most valuable, of course, at around 10,000 yuan ($2,700).

He Zhuoqiang, the star of the 1987 National Games after breaking a weightlifting world record, was said to have been awarded an apartment, a set of furniture, and home electrical appliances worth 30,000 yuan (*China Daily* 1987b). He was from Guangdong province, the wealthiest province in China, which can afford to give greater financial rewards, so this probably represented the top of the scale. Two of China's most popular stars were said to earn a great deal, although figures were not public. Gymnast Li Ning, for example, donated several thousand yuan to his hometown, and ping-pong star Jiang Jialiang purchased a house in Guangzhou for 80,000 yuan (Kang Bing 1988b).

Athletes had other sources of income, such as patriotic Overseas Chinese who gave them a few hundred to a thousand American dollars for doing well in international competitions. Foreign currency was not available to the average person, so it was a valuable possession. It could be used to buy imported appliances at duty-free shops, which were considerably cheaper than regular shops where import taxes raised the original prices as much as threefold. Also, there were restrictions which made it hard to buy imported appliances even for those who had the money. Athletes who went abroad could either buy appliances abroad and bring them in duty-free (with a limit of four), or they could use their foreign currency to buy them when they returned. Televisions and VCR's were the most coveted. While abroad, athletes and coaches saved foreign currency from meal allowances. Sometimes they even changed money on the black market in China and took it out of the country only to bring it back in again. When they reentered the country, they declared the amount of foreign currency they possessed and were then allowed to spend that much at the duty-free shops. Even the certificate specifying how many items they were allowed to buy and how much currency they were allowed to spend at the duty-free shop had value; it could be sold for as much as 300 yuan. This practice was illegal, needless to say. Clearly, international competitors exploited many possibilities, both legal and illegal, for improving their material existence.

Lower-level athletes received bonuses, too. For example, in the 1986 National College Games and the Beijing City College Championship meet, athletes received as much as several hundred yuan for breaking records and winning gold medals.

So much for the material conditions of athletes' lives. What is the cultural context surrounding these conditions?

BODY CULTURE AND THE CLASS-IFIED BODY

Bourdieu suggests, "We can hypothesize as a general law that a sport is more likely to be adopted by a social class if it does not contradict that class's relation to the body at its deepest and most unconscious level, i.e., the body schema, which is the depository of a whole world view and a whole philosophy of the person and the body" (1984: 218). If we look at the relation between social class and the body in China, we discern the circulation of ideas that clearly function as currency in the ongoing struggles between occupational groups for symbolic capital (that is, prestige). The main players in this contest are those classified as "intellectuals," "workers," and "peasants."

The Intellectual Body: In Need of Strengthening

In the late 1980s, just as the educational system was beginning to recuperate from the Cultural Revolution and intellectuals were beginning to find their voice, a topic of widespread concern was the sickliness of intellectual bodies and the ill effects of education on health. The discourse ranged from young school children to college students to older intellectuals. This discourse was both an official one discussed by cadres and in the press and an unofficial one discussed by intellectuals themselves. This 1980s critique of the frailty of the intellectual body echoed the critiques of the 1890s to 1930s made by the constitutional reformers, Chairman Mao, and the New Culture Movement (see chapter 2). These two time periods were similar in that the critiques both recognized intellectuals as key contributors to national strength—which was not true of the intervening period, when manual laborers were to be the revolutionary vanguard.

In the 1980s, college entrance was determined by a student's score on the National College Entrance Exam, a gruelling three-day examination which requires incredible amounts of memorization. Because a small fraction of middle-school graduates went to college, the competition was very heated. Japanese students are world-renowned for their hard studying, but in 1986 a joint China-Japan survey of almost ten thousand primary- and secondary-school and college students showed that while Japanese students spent an average of thirty-five minutes per day at home studying, Chinese spent one hour and thirty minutes (Qu Beilin 1987). That the respect for education had permeated even those most excluded from the dominant culture was indicated by a 1988 survey of 10,939 peasants which showed that 66 percent hoped their children would get a college degree (Liu Fuhe and Sun Zhonghua 1988).

In the late 1980s, it was observed that middle-school students' physical fitness levels dropped markedly in their last year when they were studying for the college-entrance exam. An example was the study reported by the Education Department of Shandong Province: in the physical examination for the 1987 College Entrance Exam, 35 percent of the students had passed and 64 percent were classified as "restricted" (unable to participate in military training, physical education class, etc.). The proportion who passed had dropped since 1986, even though standards had been relaxed (*Tiyu bao* 1987e). When physical examinations were given to the entering class of 1,200 students at the People's University in Beijing, 19 students were found to have hepatitis, tuberculosis, or other illnesses, and one was sent home. Surveying the new freshmen, one official reportedly commented, "For the most part, this year's freshmen have rather inferior physiques, not even as good as the physiques of youth of the same age in Beijing society" (Liu Shun and Lei Wenbing 1987). Another cause for concern was that 74.67 percent of Chinese college students wear eyeglasses (Wu Jingshu 1988).

Because of the alarming number of middle-school children in poor health, the Education Commission in 1988 enacted a set of physical standards that students must meet in order to pass from lower- to upper-middle school and from there to college. The basic purpose of the document was to require students to participate in physical education classes, scheduled morning and rest break exercises, and the "National Physical Culture Training Standards" test (the equivalent of the U.S. "President's Physical Fitness Test"). The goal of the document was clear:

to force students to engage in physical activities. Students who failed to fulfill these requirements would not be allowed to participate in the test for the next highest school (upper-middle or college); they could not be awarded the title of the "three good" student (good health, good studies, good work); and a card recording their physical condition would be inserted into their dossiers or report cards (Wu Dong 1987). This ruling shook up the middle schools. One student at a top middle school was reported to have burst into tears and said, "Our physical culture level is so bad! Is one year enough time to remedy it?" (Liu Shun and Lei Wenbing 1987).

The ill health of older intellectuals also became an issue when a state survey of over twenty thousand intellectuals showed that they had a life expectancy almost ten years lower than the national average, with over half of them dying between the ages of forty and sixty. Almost 40 percent of those surveyed suffered from diseases of the heart and circulatory system (He Zhenliang 1988). Popular opinion attributed this to intellectuals not getting enough physical exercise because of the nature of their work and because they fail to see that exercise is important. This was also the officially given reason for their bad health, and the State Sports Commission urged "each bureau . . . [to] actively lead and organize them to participate in physical culture activities, to improve their health conditions . . ." (He Zhenliang 1988).

Beijing City Team members mentioned that there were fewer children of intellectuals than other statuses on the team, and high-level intellectuals were fewer than lower-level, although there were a few children of full and assistant professors (Beijing City Team 1988). According to the head of the Beijing sports technique school, the most widespread attitude toward athletes in Chinese society is contempt, due to the old stereotype that they have "four developed limbs and an undeveloped brain." These people think that athletes "jump around all day." He said this attitude is especially prevalent among college professors and scientists (Yang Duo 1988).

In sum, at the same time that education was becoming more important and intellectuals were gaining in prestige, a popular discourse was circulating that portrayed education as physically weakening and intellectuals as physically inferior people who considered themselves too good for physical exercise and, by implication, manual labor. This discourse followed the long period of the glorification of manual labor and the proletarian body that had characterized Communist Party propaganda since Liberation. During this period, the state excluded intel-

Table 7.2 Physical Culture Participation according to Educational Level (by Percent)

Educational Level	Rate of Direct Participation
primary school	3.5
lower-middle school	37.2
upper-middle/vocational school (*zhongzhuan*)	15.2
technical school (*dazhuan*)	2.9
college and above	4.9

SOURCE: Adapted from Niu Xinghua and Feng Jianxiu (1986: 12).

lectuals from the system of sports games that was to forge strong bodies for a strong nation: there had been regularly held National Workers' Sports Games since 1955, but the first National College Games were held in 1982. It seems that the discourse on the sickly intellectual was generated by the state's increasing emphasis on education. It was a working-class counterdiscourse asserting itself against the intellectual class. As Bourdieu points out, the working classes valorize physical strength because their position in the labor market tends to reduce them to a labor power characterized mainly by sheer muscle power; thus their physical strength is the most important thing they have with which to oppose the other classes (1984: 384). With the increasing importance of education, workers could still cling to the notion of their physical superiority, which had counted for so much more in the preceding decades.

At the same time, the characterization of intellectuals as uninterested in developing their physical strength was not an empty critique. Sociological studies seemed to support the claim. A study of 1,029 enterprise personnel in the cities of Tianjin, Hangzhou, and Dalian showed that employees with a lower-middle (grades 7 to 9) school level of education participated directly in physical culture at a higher rate than any other group.[2] The average rates of participation are summarized in table 7.2, in which educational level is ordered from lowest to highest (I have combined the rates for men and women).

The figure for "college and above" is actually slightly higher than it should be, because the figures for Hangzhou included only college students, who, because of physical education classes, had a much higher participation rate than the people from other occupations surveyed in

2. The researchers were not able to obtain controlled samples; hence, the results were not statistically reliable.

Tianjin and Dalian (Niu Xinghua and Feng Jianxiu 1986: 11). Removing them from the calculations reduces the participation rate for the college-educated to 2.1 percent, with college-educated females from Tianjin having a rate of 0. With this adjustment, the participation rate of the group with the highest education level would be the lowest on the scale. The study concludes, "In China's large and small cities, whether in direct or indirect participation, those with a lower-middle school level of education have the highest rate. After that, as education level increases, participation shows a progressively decreasing trend" (Niu Xinghua and Feng Jianxiu 1986: 11).

China contrasts markedly with other countries in this respect. John P. Robinson (1967) and Gerald S. Kenyon (1966) showed that, in the United States, frequency of participation in sports tends to increase with educational level, with the highest rate of participation for those with some college schooling (Robinson 1967: 81). Citing a number of studies, Guttmann states that managers and professionals participate in sports more than the working class, and educated people more than uneducated people. He finds that this is true of both communist and non-communist countries and is more true of highly competitive sport than recreational sport (Guttmann 1978: 79–80). Robinson discusses a cross-national survey of time expenditure on sports in ten nations (Belgium, Bulgaria, Czechoslovakia, France, Hungary, Poland, USSR, USA, West Germany, and Yugoslavia), which showed a general trend for the better-educated to be more active in sports. However, this trend was not evident in all nations and was more true for men than women (1967: 76).

In Japan, one might suspect that the emphasis on education would lead to a pattern similar to China's. This appears not to be the case. From his 1961 survey of 638 males and 45 females who used the Tokyo YMCA Athletic Center, Takenoshita Kyūzo concluded, "In general, the higher rate of sports participation is found for groups of higher educational background" (Takenoshita 1967: 10).

In sum, there is some evidence that, unlike much of the rest of the world, higher levels of education do contribute to less participation in physical exercise in China. But why? If we accept the popular discourse, we would attribute it to a general antagonism of the educated toward anything implying manual labor and would trace this antagonism to the traditional Confucian ideology of *laoxinzhe zhi ren, laolizhe zhiyu ren* ("Those who work with their brains rule, those who work with their brawn are ruled"). But this would be too simple. Intellectuals proved quite able to cast aside the Confucian ideology when their children could gain advantages through participation in sports. This occurred during the period of Western imperialism, when they sent their children to missionary schools; during the Great Leap Forward, when they wanted the food subsidy; and during the Cultural Revolution, when they wanted to help their children avoid being "sent down."

In addition, there are other possible reasons for the sickly bodies of intellectuals and their disinterest in exercise. Perhaps they do not exercise because they are in poor health, rather than the other way around. The older intellectuals who are dying at such a rapid rate are the people who suffered most during the Cultural Revolution, when intellectuals were sent to the countryside to do manual labor. Many of them have lifelong health impairments as a result of the beatings they endured and the hard lives they led. I vividly remember various teachers that I knew showing me the scars on their heads and faces, the aching knots on the shoulders and knees that they were always massaging. Today, they continue to live under heavy stress because their salaries are comparatively low, they are subject to strict surveillance, and the anti-intellectualist rhetoric of the Cultural Revolution era is not entirely dead. These explanations for their poor health were not discussed in the media.

The issue of physical education in the schools also proves to be more complex on closer examination. Again, the information cited in support of the bodily sickliness of college students does not logically imply that disdain for physical activity is the problem. Exercise could not have cured the tuberculosis and hepatitis discovered in the entering class at the People's University. And I would not be surprised if 75 percent of American college students also wear eyeglasses, even though they participate in sports at a high rate.

In addition, physical education in the schools was clearly a site for a contest over social power between the regular teachers and the physical education teachers, who felt they were seen as inferior. Sportspeople were quite excited about the State Education Commission's decision in 1988 to strengthen physical culture requirements in middle schools because they thought their status would improve if physical education became as important as academic achievement for students who hoped to go on to college.

Complicating the actions of administrative organs was the student culture in the schools, where the well-rounded person was not a prevalent ideal. College students recollected that in the middle schools there is usually a clear division between students who are good at the books

Official at a 1986 Haidian District Middle School Track Meet.

and good at sports. Seldom are students good at both. One graduate student at Beijing University commented, "Athletes are thought to be dumb. So they don't study hard because they are sure they will fail. Chinese don't believe you can be good at sports and studies at the same time. So nobody expects them to study hard. Chinese put things into categories like that."

Nevertheless, in the midst of this complexity, one point remains: since the restoration of the National College Entrance Exam, intellectuals have demonstrated increasing resistance to their children's involvement in sports. This resistance is found to a lesser degree among other classes, but the reason seems to be the same: education is again perceived as the way to get ahead in life. This perception persists despite widespread complaints about the economic successes of uneducated peasants and private entrepreneurs (*getihu*) whose success is not considered legitimate by intellectuals—a dominant ideology to which other classes subscribe to varying degrees.[3]

In China, educational level articulates with sports participation in a way that is different from many other nations. In view of the social position of Chinese intellectuals, this is no trivial point. The National College Entrance Exam seems to have replicated the influence of the Imperial Examination System in many ways. Rather than perceive the intellectual body culture, with its opposition toward sports and manual labor, as an outmoded remnant of imperial times, it is more useful to view it as part of a strategy for maintaining a social position that is perceived as worth defending.

The Worker's Body: A Strong Body for a Strong Class

If the intellectual culture of the body is maintained by a nexus of social and cultural tensions, then so is that of workers and peasants. In some ways they represent reactions against each other. The class culture of the "mental workers" is characterized by a different orientation toward

---

3. An important point that is relevant to the Tiananmen Square student demonstrations of 1989 is that my ethnographic research and the surveys cited here all pointed to a widespread and profound respect for education among many social strata—a finding that contradicts the picture of intellectuals in the Western press during the period leading up to and following the uprising. It is my opinion that the Western press exaggerated the plight of intellectuals because its main sources were the intellectuals themselves, who were obviously interested in gaining Western sympathy. The demonstrations were in part due to the feeling among intellectuals that they were not benefitting from the reforms to the degree that they were entitled to—and they felt entitled to benefit because of their own high opinion of their place in Chinese society.

the body than that of the "physical workers," but there are also differences within the class of "physical workers." The vast majority of the population of China falls into this category, which refers mainly to factory workers and peasants. Under the economic reforms *getihu*, or private entrepreneurs, increased in number so that they became a recognized category in this class as well.

The head of the Beijing sports technique school felt that there were few people in China who had a "correct understanding" of sports—who appreciate the techniques and respect athletes for their hard-won skills. He believed that most of the people who respect athletes idolize them simply because they are famous but lack a real understanding of their skills and contribution to society. He stated that this attitude is mostly found among the lower classes (Yang Duo 1988). Workers, *getihu*, and peasants are notorious sports fans. Wealthy *getihu* are known for spending their newly acquired money on sports spectating and clothing.

In the 1980s, the children of workers formed the backbone of high-level sports. Most athletes were children of workers; for example, informants said the majority of athletes on the Beijing City team came from working-class backgrounds (Beijing City Team 1988). The survey cited previously by Niu, Li and Su found that parents who were laborers were more supportive of their children becoming athletes than were parents from more skilled categories (Niu Xinghua, Li Shuyi, and Su Lianyong 1986: 63). China's emerging soccer fandom was characterized as working-class (Kong Xiang'an and Zhang Zhidong 1987), and bodybuilding spread as a popular movement among workers and peasants (see chapter 10). The working-class support of sport is not surprising, given the position of athletes just above workers and *getihu* in the social hierarchy. Working-class parents encouraged their children to become athletes because it was an attainable step upward in the social hierarchy. Also, unlike for the intellectuals, sports conflicted neither with their own orientation to their bodies nor with the state's portrayal of their bodies. In the official and unofficial discourses on sport and social class, there was no portrayal of the worker's body as sickly and in need of immediate intervention. The strong and healthy worker body was a metaphor for the strong and healthy working class that the state wanted to promote.

The Peasant's Body: Finally Eating their Fill

Because of the lack of proper facilities and coaching in the countryside, peasants were not represented on professional teams in proportion to the 75 percent of China's population that peasants occupy. In the late 1980s, however, increasing prosperity in the countryside allowed peasants to make a growing contribution to China's sports. According to 1988 official statistics, half of China's counties had held different kinds of peasant sports meets; and of China's 80,000 villages and small towns, 60,000 had "cultural" centers (*wenhua zhan*) or "cultural and physical culture" centers (*wenhua tiyu zhongxin*). In addition, seventy-eight counties had been designated as "advanced physical culture counties" (*tiyu xianjin xian*) in the campaign to encourage rural sports (Dang Li 1988). Eighteen provinces, municipalities, and autonomous regions had founded peasant sports associations, and the first national peasant games were held in November 1988 (*Tiyu bao* 1988). A significant number of China's very best athletes were from peasant backgrounds. In the Ninth Asian Games in 1986, twenty-six of China's ninety-four golds were won by peasants.

I was told that peasants were formerly antagonistic toward sports; reporters were fond of summarizing this attitude in sayings commonly attributed to peasants mocking those engaged in sports:

"He's eaten his fill and has nothing to do" (*chibaole mei shi gan*).

"He's eaten more than he should have" (*chibaole chengde*). (This phrase implies that a person is fat and happy and has the leisure time to engage in useless activities. An acquaintance explained this phrase to me by noting that, in the Chinese view, "Everything you have over there in America is *chibaole chengde.*")

"If you can eat your fill and avoid getting beaten up, that's good enough" (*chibaole bu ai da jiu xingle*).

"Grain, oil, and cotton all / don't come from playing ball" (*da qiu dabuchu liang mian you*).

The head of the Beijing City sports school commented, "Before we solved the problem of basic food and shelter, peasant brains simply did not even have the concept of physical culture" (Yang Duo 1988). With the improvement of economic conditions, they learned to like sports. He noted that in the 1960s he often went to the countryside to give exhibitions. "Now that peasants have money, what do they want to do? They want to do sports themselves."

The advent of television has played a large role in changing the old attitude. Many peasants like to watch international sports contests and can name all of China's top sports stars. "They worship top athletes," said a peasant sports cadre. Exposure to the outside through television has stimulated the desire of peasants to see the wide world; a strong motivation of peasant athletes is to go abroad. "When I was at the spare-time sports school," wrote weightlifter He Zhuoqiang, "I heard that if you practiced hard, you could travel around the world, see the wide world, and I secretly vowed to train until I achieved something" (He Zhuoqiang 1988).

A student who did a teaching practicum in a very poor part of Hebei province described the conditions under which he worked. He said that the county was so poor that there were only three black-and-white televisions per village. "They had never seen volleyball except on TV, and they thought tennis balls were fun for little children to play with. The sports they played were basketball, and ping pong on a stone table. But even so, they liked sports a lot." He said that the peasants avidly followed sports on television and were very eager to learn from him and his classmates. The local cadre was enthusiastic about building up sports, but the student felt there was no way that good athletes could come out of such conditions—they were still worried about eating enough food. "Even the young men had such gnarled fingers from laboring with tools with handles that they couldn't straighten them out. So they had to hit the volleyball with bent fingers." Although he had lived in the countryside himself during the Cultural Revolution, he found the conditions in Hebei hard to believe: "They are very simple and naive; sometimes you have to laugh, but you don't know whether to laugh or cry. It is really pitiful, actually."

I interviewed six cadres from the Peasant Sports Association (nongmin tixie) who were all from "advanced sports units." As might be expected, all of them came from areas which ranged from extremely wealthy, such as Shanghai County, to fairly well-off. They presented a more optimistic picture and stated that peasants are the future of Chinese sports. This is because sports are a "way out" (bentou) for peasant athletes who have the chance to change their residence permits to the city and to enter physical education institutes or colleges for higher education. One cadre stated that the countryside was giving much attention to sports and studies: some counties gave the family 1,000 yuan if a child tested into a university or was selected for a provincial sports team. A survey of 306 peasants in Baoying County, Jiangsu, showed that 47.71 percent of them would support their children in becoming athletes (Bai Guanglin and Ju Shirong 1987: 186), a percentage that is similar to the highest percentages recorded by Niu, Li, and Su (53 percent for soldiers and 48.3 percent for service personnel).

I was told that peasants are envious of athletes because their physiques are strong and healthy and because they are issued sweatsuits which look very nice. After athletes have been in the city for a while, they start dressing up more, and when they go back to their homes, it is as if they are foreign. This is reflected in a rhyme that was said to apply to peasant athletes: "One year later—rustic, two years later—foreign, three years later won't acknowledge Dad and Mom" (*yinian tu, ernian yang, sannian buren die he niang*) (Yang Duo 1988).

Sports cadres contrast the peasant ethos with urban parents who are reluctant to allow pampered only children to engage in hard training. "The cities have more only children who don't want to participate in sports as a career," noted one peasant cadre. "For peasants, sports are a way out: they can test into a college, get a higher education. The countryside has talent. They can eat bitterness because their economic situation is poor. They have the chance to change their residence permits to the city . . . The future of Chinese sports lies in the countryside. They are the bulk of China's population . . ."

In sum, peasants are said to be increasingly enthusiastic about sports, and this is well covered in the press. Their enthusiasm for sports is said to have several reasons. One is that they are acutely aware that they are to a large degree excluded from the dominant, "legitimate" culture, but they are eager to take part in it and emulate it. Since major sports events are constructed in the media as a symbol of participation in the dominant national and international cultures, peasants are eager to join in (as discussed in chapter 5). A second reason is that they eagerly exploit opportunities to leave the countryside to take part in the dominant, urban culture. Third, they are accustomed to hard labor and do not feel that sports are below them, though they may regard them as an unnecessary waste of energy when food is in short supply. For all of these reasons, sports cadres are confident that the countryside will continue to provide peasant athletes for years to come who will be willing to "eat bitterness" in order to improve their lot in life. This construction of the peasant body culture is obviously one version of the state's construction of the countryside as a vast reservoir of inexpensive labor that is being led out of its poverty by the Deng regime.

THE EDUCATION PROBLEM

The tectonic social movements of the 1980s opened up a number of fissures in the social terrain upon which China's top-level sports were grounded. Two of the more important gaps were labeled the "education problem" (*jiaoyu wenti*) and the "exit problem" (*chulu wenti*). As upwardly mobile sportspeople pressed against the "mental laborers" above them in the social hierarchy, new arrangements had to be made in order to accommodate them.

The problem began with the restoration of the College Entrance Examination in 1976 and gradually worsened. In the intensely competitive atmosphere associated with the National College Entrance Exam, schoolchildren who participated in sports were at a disadvantage. Training takes time and energy away from studies, and they fell behind when they went away for competitions. An example is a seventeen-year old member of the national junior track and field team. She told me that she had studied English in middle school, but not very well, because every week she went to a competition for a few days, and when she got back she wouldn't feel like studying. So she never made any progress.

When an athlete entered a boarding school, she might spend only a half-day in class, and the academic demands were not very rigorous. Many athletes stopped schooling altogether at a young age, some going no further than sixth grade. This was the case with a talented young track athlete who came from a mountain village. Her coach often complained that she "doesn't understand things" (*bu dong shi*), that he had to be a "nanny" for her. He said that although he had arranged classes for her, she refused to take them because she thought it was enough to do sports, and her brain was incapable of learning anyway. When I showed her a photo of the American heptathlete Jackie Joyner-Kersee, whose name she knew well because Joyner-Kersee held the world record in her event, she commented in surprise, "She's black! I always thought she had yellow skin like us." Her coach commented, "She thinks everyone has yellow skin like her."

A 24-year-old fencer said that he had been in a spare-time sports school until after ninth grade, when he joined a professional team, and then he had no classes at all. He said that on the team his only free time was in the evening, and then he was too tired to study. He was able to test into the Beijing Institute of Physical Education because of the lower admission standards for professional athletes. However, he said, "I can't learn as fast as the younger students in my class who graduated from middle school. Especially English . . . I don't know how to study. My brain is slow."

With such a poor educational background, it is impossible for athletes to score well on the College Entrance Exam, and thus they may have sacrificed their education for sports.

There were athletes who attempted to study on their own. This depended on their family background: those from well-educated families tried to keep up with their studies. One example was a young man whose parents were well-educated teachers (a grandfather had studied abroad). He had wanted to study computer science at a regular university, but the provincial educational commission decided to send him to the institute of physical education in his province because they felt they needed some better students to study sports. He had some outstanding performances as a junior athlete before a serious injury ended his competition days, but he had never been interested in pursuing sports as a career. He did not learn that he had been assigned to the provincial physical education institute until he received his letter of assignment. His parents were very disappointed and he was very angry. "The leaders shuffle your dossier around just like they are playing cards," he said. He had no recourse because he didn't know who had made the decision; but then he thought that his studies would be relaxed at the institute and it would be easy for him to be first in his class. The English teacher there wasn't very good: he took an English test and they decided his level was higher than the teacher's, so he was exempted from English. Instead, he studied on his own from records. His classmates all criticized him for studying English so hard, but in the end he had the last laugh because he received the best job assignment when he was sent to work for the State Sports Commission in Beijing.

An athlete from the Guizhou team was the child of educated administrators. After ninth grade, she joined the provincial team and had to study on her own in the evening. She commented that some subjects are easy to study on your own, like anatomy, where you just have to memorize muscles and bones; but some, like physiology and biochemistry, really require a teacher. Her teammates used to tease her and ask why she always lay on the top bunk reading. "But I always thought, now all they think about is their sports performance, but later on what will they depend on to eat? You can't just think about your performance, because after you retire it won't count for anything." She was able to test into the Beijing Institute of Physical Education because of the lower admission standard for professional athletes.

These stories were typical of the education of athletes. They often stopped going to classes and began to train full-time after ninth grade,

Table 7.3 Levels of Education Attained by Top Athletes, 1983

Educational level	Women	Men	Total	Percentage
primary school	8	17	25	36.8
lower-middle school	17	12	29	42.6
upper-middle school	9	3	12	17.6
college	0	2	2	2.9
Totals	34	34	68	100.0%

SOURCE: Adapted from Ma Mingshan (1984: 115).

and only those who were motivated to study on their own continued to learn. The results of a 1983 survey of sixty-eight of China's best athletes in all sports showed the educational levels indicated in table 7.3.

The low educational level of athletes is often mentioned as a major obstacle to China's progress in sports and is one reason for the stereotype of athletes as stupid and lacking culture. This problem reached an extreme during the 1970s due to the effects of the Cultural Revolution.

THE EXIT PROBLEM

The "exit problem" refers to the troublesome transition into the working world. Sport is a high risk/high gain career that is particularly unreliable because an athlete must retire at some point and take on a new job. On retirement, one may find oneself lacking in education and behind younger people who have already engaged in the career for many years.

In the 1980s, most professional athletes were assigned jobs by the government on retirement. The majority of those who did not go on to further schooling were retained in the sports system as assistant coaches, cadres, or office workers. One of the most desirable jobs was to become a coach, but the number of coaching jobs was limited and the competition intense. A common job assignment for the average athlete was in a factory. This was especially true of soccer, volleyball, and basketball athletes, who could represent the factory in competitions for a few years before becoming regular workers or helping to run the recreation program. Athletes in more obscure sports might become simple workers. However, factories became more reluctant under the reforms to accept athletes because productivity became more important. The athletes had no factory experience, but often had worked their way up the state wage scale so that they had to be paid the same wages as more skilled workers. Some sports events were considered appropriate background for other jobs. For example, judo players were often given positions as police or prison guards.

More options were open to famous athletes. They became high-level cadres in the sports commission system, movie stars (especially martial artists), or went abroad to study or coach. This last option became increasingly popular, creating problems for Chinese sports as many of the best athletes retired and went abroad to coach instead of contributing to the development of Chinese sports. The main reason they did so was that the salaries, living, and working conditions abroad were much better.

Increasingly, the most desired post-retirement option for professional athletes was to go on to a physical education institute or regular college. With an education, there were many more career options. Graduates of physical education institutes had a better chance of becoming coaches, physical education teachers, or researchers. Graduates of a regular college had access to an entirely different world.

PARENTAL OPPOSITION TO SPORTS

In the mid-1980s, it became apparent that many parents were reluctant to send their children to sports schools. A 1985 survey by the State Sports Commission showed that only 2 to 3 percent of parents favored the idea of sending their children to spare-time sports schools, and a 1986 survey in Nanjing showed that only 5.96 percent were supportive. A poll in Shanghai in 1987 showed that while 65 percent of parents said their children loved sports, only 1.2 percent would send them to spare-time sports schools. By way of comparison, 10 percent of parents in a national survey said they would want their children to pursue careers in fine arts and literature (Shen Yanping 1988a). Their reluctance was related to the growing number of families with only one child. A 1985 survey of 1,039 parents from twenty-eight provinces and cities showed that a total of 37 percent of parents in families of multiple children would support their children's efforts to become athletes, but only 13.8 percent of single-child parents would (Niu Xinghua, Li Shuyi, and Su Lianyong 1986: 61). Only 2.2 percent of the parents who were sports coaches were in favor of their children becoming athletes, the lowest of any group (p. 63). These figures vary quite a bit and were not always the results of rigorous research methods, but they do illustrate a trend with effects that sports cadres could see on the ground. There was a widespread recognition that most parents opposed their children's involvement in sports. Almost all of the athletes I interviewed said that their parents had been reluctant at first to allow them to participate; after the fear that it would hinder their studies, the second most-frequent objection, usually raised by mothers, was that it was too "bitter" (ku). Except for one athlete whose father was a military man, none of my informants mentioned a desire on the part of their parents to inculcate moral character through sports. When they saw that the child liked sports, and after he or she had some success, they realized there were definite benefits to be gained. In most cases, parents hoped the child would become a famous sports star. All parents agreed on one advantage of attending a sports school: "At least he can eat well."

The head of the Beijing sports technique school (Yang Duo 1988) said that parents generally fall into three categories. The first type do not want their child to do sports, and the coach who recruits the athlete has to do "mobilization work" (dongyuan gongzuo). He visits the parents to do a bit of persuading; he tells them the child can win glory for China and that she can gain a chance to go to college. In the second type of case, the child is only average in academics, and the parents know he won't be able to get into a university. They say, "Forget it; if you want to do it, then do it." The final type simply "can't bear the sight of" (kanbuguan) their children. They may be so busy with their jobs that they cannot take proper care of the child. This was the case with the parents of the five-year-old gymnast featured in Sports Illustrated (Reilly 1988), whose father confided that he hoped she would be accepted into the full-time sports school because then he and his wife, both of whom worked full-time, wouldn't have to take care of her.[4]

Part of the explanation for parental attitudes is found in class differences. Parental antagonism toward sports varied according to educational level. The lower the educational level of the parents, the more they were in favor of their children becoming athletes. In the survey conducted by Niu et al., educational level correlated strongly with the percentage of parents who hoped their children would become athletes (see table 7.4).

Also in the mid-1980s, it became apparent that Chinese sports were undergoing a transitional period with respect to the social backgrounds of those who entered sports schools. The age cohort that was in its late

---

4. I overheard this remark while working as an interpreter for Sports Illustrated during the photography session for Rick Reilly's article (Reilly 1988). Although I relayed it to Reilly, he did not allow it to intrude into the idyllic family scene depicted in his article.

Table 7.4 Educational Levels of Parents Favoring Their Children
Becoming Career Athletes

Educational level of head of household	Percentage who hoped children would become athletes
primary and below	41.5
lower-middle school	35.8
upper-middle school	24.5
vocational school (*zhongzhuan*)	22.5
college and above	8.8

SOURCE: Data from Niu Xinghua, Li Shuyi, and Su Lianyong (1986: 64).

twenties to early thirties was retiring, or had recently retired, from active training. Many of them had begun their careers during the Cultural Revolution era. A large number confessed that they would have chosen other careers if there had been others to choose. They had always wanted to go to college, and when the college entrance examination was restored in 1976, they tested into physical education institutes. Even so, they wistfully said, "If I hadn't been an athlete, maybe I could have tested into Qinghua or Beijing University."[5] The reinstitution of the entrance exam marked the beginning of a downward spiral in grass-roots support of the sports schools due to the return to an emphasis on education. By 1988, this trend had led to a crisis in Chinese sports as teams had insufficient recruits to replace their aging stars.

In response, state leaders began to forge closer links between the sports system and the educational system. The most natural link was between professional teams and physical education institutes. There was a lower admission standard at physical education institutes for professional team athletes. However, the step from sports team to physical education institute was not always easy. Sports teams were often reluctant to let athletes go if they might still have a few good years left. One athlete had been forced to give up serious training due to an injury, so she decided to attend the nearby physical education institute. First she went to the institute, took the tests, and was accepted. Then she returned to the provincial team to get permission to leave. "This is really the only way to do it," she explained, "because otherwise they won't release your dossier." For ten days she made daily visits to the leaders of

5. Rofel notes that women workers at the silk-weaving factory where she did research often insisted that they might have become intellectuals if not for the shutdown of schools during the Cultural Revolution (1992: 102).

her team; they kept delaying and telling her to come back later. They asked her to write a self-criticism, in which she was to ask forgiveness for wrongly going to the physical education institute before talking to her leaders and to explain that she wanted to study so that she could return and be a better coach for the team. She felt that if she had taken a "gift" worth "about 20 yuan" to the team head, he would have released her sooner, but she refused to do so as a matter of principle. Finally, her coach talked to the party secretary and asked him to intervene with the team head. After more time had elapsed, and she had missed two weeks of her first semester, she got permission to leave. Her roommates at the sports institute agreed that her case was typical: "None of them want to let you go." Since each of them had debilitating injuries, their team leaders had no choice.

Although entering a physical education institute is a desirable option after an athlete leaves the professional team, it is clearly not the most prestigious choice, for the general public still esteems a regular college education more than a physical education degree. The most prestigious option would be to enter a regular college. After 1984, when China's success at the Los Angeles Olympics spurred enthusiasm for sports, this option became increasingly easy for athletes to pursue. In preparation for the Second National College Games in 1986, increasing numbers of regular universities began recruiting professional athletes and accepting them without their taking the National College Entrance Exam, or with lower scores. The first collegiate games had been a small-scale event held in 1982, but it grew in scale and importance long with the overall sports boom. Since the founding of the PRC, outstanding accomplishments in sports had been rewarded with the addition of points to the entrance examination score, but in 1986 some colleges had gone far beyond this point by recruiting athletes who scored hundreds of points below the minimum and, in some cases, who reportedly had not taken the test at all.

At the beginning of the 1985–86 academic year, those universities which had not given in to the practice panicked when they realized they were going to "lose face" in the national meet. Even such universities as Qinghua and Beijing University, which had high academic standards to uphold, gave in and hurriedly recruited a batch of athletes into the class of 1985. Meanwhile, the State Education Commission postponed action, although there were constant rumors that a document was about to "come down" which would restrict the participation of those athletes in the national meet. Finally, only months before the meet, the document appeared. It declared athletes in the entering class of 1985 who had not entered school through the proper testing route to be ineligible for the National College Games. This amounted to penalizing Qinghua and Beijing Universities and others who had waited until 1985 to recruit athletes while other colleges had been doing it for several years. Beijing University's leaders were fairly indifferent, but Qinghua had a long tradition of excellence in sports to uphold (see Yeh Wen-Hsin 1990: 213–15). Its leaders lobbied to keep the former professional athletes out of the city championships as well, since, if they participated, Qinghua's placing would be lower than the first or second it had always attained in the past. After two months of negotiations, a compromise was reached: two meets would be held on consecutive weekends. The first would be the selection meet for the team to represent Beijing in the National College Games, and only the eligible athletes would compete; the second meet would be an "invitational" in which all athletes could compete, but it would not count as an official city championship. That would be postponed until the fall—enough time, some people claimed, for Qinghua to recruit new athletes into its ranks.

The battle was not over. There was pressure on all sides for regular colleges to accept former top athletes. The State Sports Commission saw it as a vitally necessary measure to solve the "exit problem" in sports, recognizing that due to this problem Chinese sports were losing vast numbers of potential recruits. Figures from Liaoning Province are an example of how severe the problem could be: the province each year had around two thousand graduates of spare-time sports schools, but only five hundred could be accepted by national, provincial, or municipal teams (Kang Bing 1988a). It was thought that college teams could take in some of the surplus. As it turned out, not much of the surplus was taken in. The problem with recruiting middle-school graduates was that their level was usually far below that of older professional team athletes—so colleges were more eager to lure older athletes away from professional teams than to take younger ones. There were many people in colleges and universities who were eager to receive the athletes in order to bring honor to the school in major sports meets. Some individual departments were eager to accept athletes to represent the department in the yearly interdepartmental competitions, which aroused more interest on campus than those between colleges. This depended on whether the department had a tradition of winning the school championships and whether professors in the department liked sports.

The situation was complicated by a general uncertainty about where the Education Commission stood on the issue. Schools were unsure whether the professional team athletes they had recruited would be eligible to compete. At the Fall 1987, Beijing Collegiate Track Meet, an athlete described the situation:

> The Education Commission doesn't restrict it and also doesn't support it; they haven't said anything. It's as if they haven't seen it. So all over the nation professional athletes have been recruited, and now the A group [regular universities] is maybe even better than the B group [physical education institutes] . . . My school recruited a former shotputter from the Beijing Institute of Physical Education . . . He is studying for a second degree. So I have stopped training seriously. I just play around. My goal is gone—I have no chance to participate in the national college meet next year. There is no significance in improving my performance.

Shortly thereafter, the Education Commission gave outright permission to fifty-five colleges nationwide to create "high-level sports teams" by recruiting former professional athletes. Several options were available to help them catch up in their studies: they could have a year of tutorial classes before they joined the regular students; they could take a longer time to graduate; they could attend middle schools affiliated with the college for a period of time; or they could study special majors just for athletes, such as sports psychology at Beijing University or biomechanics at Qinghua.

An example of the special arrangements made for athletes was that of the women's volleyball players accepted by Beijing University. They were said to be so hopelessly behind in their studies that they couldn't keep up with the other students even with tutoring, so they were sent to the Beijing University middle school. "So you can see this two-meter tall girl, who is also rather ugly, going to school with her books under her arm along with the middle school students. They are all afraid of her," said a college athlete. "It must be embarrassing for her because she is in her late twenties." At the same time, my friend acknowledged that one should admire her perseverance and courage in getting her college degree.

The "double degree" system was another way for athletes to enter regular colleges. This referred to those who had already earned a degree in a sports-related program. Beijing University accepted ten track and field athletes from the Beijing Institute of Physical Education into the psychology department to study sports psychology. According to word-of-mouth, the school leaders had given funds to the psychology department to pay for their food and other subsidies. One of the athletes said, "Beijing University is going to hold the city college meet next year and wants to give a show of strength . . . We were recruited because our performance was good, not because our studies were good."

Many colleges simply recruited entire teams of professional athletes. The Tianjin Institute of Finance and Economics "just snapped up the entire Tianjin women's basketball team, even helping them pass the entrance exams. It plans to get a coach from Oklahoma State University, something the Tianjin team would find hard to do" (Kang Bing 1988a).

Given the choice, most outstanding athletes would choose a regular university over a physical education institute. A teacher at the Beijing Institute of Physical Education discussed the heated competition he encountered on recruiting trips. Recruiting trips are a normal part of the enrollment process for national-level universities (universities which enroll students from all over China, as opposed to provincial universities which take only students from that province). At a certain date, the recruiters convene in a given province to meet students and give presentations about their schools. In the case of physical education institutes, students are required to pass certain sports tests to establish that the performances they claimed were valid (sometimes schools accepted athletes only to discover that they had falsified their marks). The Beijing teacher said that nobody wanted to go to physical education institutes after regular colleges established high-level teams. The competition to steal students away was very fierce. He complained, "Those teams sometimes have even lower standards in the liberal arts than this institute. Some of them even carry a letter of admission with them and pull it out on the spot and give it to an athlete. All I can do is to say I must wait and see how they did on the test. Between a sure chance to go to Qinghua or Beijing University and a 'maybe' for the Beijing Institute of Physical Education, of course they'll choose the university." He did note, however, that some students liked sports and wanted to pursue a career in them, so they signed with him.

One young woman that I met was the child of two teachers. They had hoped for her to do well in her studies, but she said, "I liked sports and didn't like to sit still to study." She explained that she had no regrets about engaging in sports, because now she was able to go to college; if she had concentrated on her studies, she might not have been able to do so. "Many students are very serious but still can't get into college. They spend all day studying. Also the social pressure is very great. The neighbors always ask how it is going. If the student fails to get into college, she hardly dares to go out of the house and show her face. A lot of my classmates were good students and studied very hard but failed to make it."

These changes have not occurred without resistance and debate. There are accusations that China is simply imitating the West (Zhang Xiaozhu 1988). Strictly speaking, they are imitating not the West, but the United States—the only country in the world in which the majority of top athletes are trained in the college system. There are others who say the Western system has its advantages. In 1988 there were very few national-class athletes in China who were also college students. In fact, there may have been only one: a Beijing University student who was also a national-class swimmer. He had discontinued his spare-time sports school training when he was fifteen in order to concentrate on his studies. He tested into Beijing University and later achieved the remarkable feat, for a college athlete, of winning a bronze medal in the 1987 National Sports Games. He said, "I only want to break a path as a college athlete in becoming a full person; I don't want to drop my studies, and at the same time want to be able to achieve something in my sports performance. Foreign athletes are able to do both, why can't we Chinese?" (Cai Dengbiao 1988b).

The state of affairs changes so rapidly that the system described here will surely be vastly different in the 1990s. New doors were being opened up for athletes every year; in 1988 there were over four thousand athletes on college and industrial enterprise teams outside of the sports commission system (Kang Bing 1988b). The situation will no doubt continue to change rapidly until the conflict between education and sports is perfected to a degree that makes sports an attractive career option to athletes and parents again.

CONCLUSIONS: THE TECTONICS OF SOCIAL CHANGE

A complex social history is succinctly summarized by a simple list of the dates on which the first national games were conducted for the three main occupational classes in the PRC: The first workers' games were held in 1955, the first college student games in 1982, and the first peasants' games in 1988. This sequence marked the emergence of each class as an economic and social force with state approval. Echoing a theme that runs throughout modern Chinese history, the healthy body was displayed as a metaphor for the healthy collectivity.

Athletes were caught in the middle of the tectonic shifts that were taking place in Chinese society in the 1980s. They were poised along two major fault lines in the social landscape. The first was the line between mental and physical laborers. The strength of the intellectual body culture as a dominant ideal was revealed in the intellectual contempt for sports as a career, an ideal to which other social classes subscribed to some extent. This ideal was one aspect of the intellectual contempt for manual labor that evoked an official and popular counterdiscourse about the frailty of the intellectual body. The state's support of sports played a role in this backlash against intellectuals by increasing the prestige and status of athletes, who eventually obtained a position of strength from which to claim a share of the educational system for themselves. Since athletes were largely drawn from the working class, and increasingly from peasant backgrounds, the strong social pressure to allow athletes to enter colleges revealed that worker and peasant parents still subscribed to the intellectual ideal for their children when it was within reach.

The second fault line along which athletes were poised was that between top state leaders and the State Sports Commission on the one hand, and other ministries and popular opinion on the other. State leaders and the Sports Commission had a certain agenda for change in which athletes were figured to play a role by winning glory for China in international competitions. However, they ran up against the obstacles erected by the restoration of the college entrance exam, which strengthened the relative position of the Education Commission and made sports a less prestigious career option. Faced with the growing force of the intellectual ideal, state leaders were forced to construct new bridges to allow athletes to cross the gap between physical and mental laborers—a gap which was in part the product of their own educational policies. State policies were as much shaped by the tectonic shifts going on among occupational classes as the other way around. In the end, the complexities of the relationship between the state and occupational classes described here illustrate that even in a totalitarian state like the PRC, the state is as much a reactor as an actor in social change.

PART
•4•

Sex, Gender,
and the Body

CHAPTER EIGHT

Sex, the Body, and History in Chinese and Western Sports

Once, while I was watching a women's shotput competition with a Chinese coach, he remarked that "it will be hard for them to find a mate." He explained that Chinese don't think large women are attractive; as a rule they don't like "fat" (*pangde*) people. He surmised that the women's one hope would be to marry men on the national team who were bigger than they. At the time, I thought it strange that he had called the women "fat" rather than "masculine" or "muscular," which I had come to expect in the United States. Wondering if such an athlete might be concerned about damaging her prospects for a husband by becoming too muscular, I asked a robust, former javelin thrower if she felt it was hard for "muscular" (*zhuangde*) women to find a husband. She was married to a man smaller than herself. She commented nonchalantly, "Some men like muscular women." I had expected this to be

I wish to thank Vigdis Broch-Due, Margaret Nelson, William Jankowiak, and Ann Anagnost for comments and suggestions. Special thanks to Niko Besnier and Ralph Litzinger for clarifying key issues and suggesting some of the key phrases. Drafts of this chapter were presented before the Harvard Council on East Asian Studies, China Gender Studies Group, 29 April 1993, and the Berkshire Conference of Women Historians, Vassar College, 13 June 1993. Rubie Watson and Christina Gilmartin, respectively, were the thought-provoking discussants. The chapter also benefitted from the comments of several anonymous reviewers at *Signs: Journal of Women in Culture and Society.*

a loaded question, as it would be in the United States, but to her it was not. During two years of fieldwork among Chinese sportspeople, I often caught myself expecting the comments about masculinity or lesbianism that Americans frequently make about athletic, muscular women; but I never heard them. In fact, the words "masculinity" and "femininity" are not easy to translate into Chinese, and their closest equivalents (*nanxing, nanzi qi, nüxing, nüzi qi*) are not commonly used in everyday conversation.

My interest in Chinese gender thus began with my vague feeling that things weren't quite the way I expected them to be. I began to realize that I had been thoroughly socialized into an American view of gender in which women in many sports are problematic and that the Chinese view was different. In the United States, I competed in track and field beginning in the mid-1970s, when sports opportunities in schools and colleges were first opening up for women. I was a member of my high school's first girl's track team, which was added under the pressure of Title IX. I believe the situation has changed somewhat, but in those days women in sports excited a good deal of discussion about the "meaning" of femininity and masculinity; and as the first female star athlete to emerge in my small town, I encountered ambivalence from peers, parents, and teachers of both sexes, as well as from my school's football coach/athletic director. I received a scholarship to college just as colleges began offering scholarships to women and went on to compete at the national level through the year that I finished my Ph.D. As a student at Beijing University in 1985–86 I trained daily with the track team and I lived with the other members of the Beijing City Team during our two month-long training camps for the National Collegiate Games. I spent 1987–88 at the Beijing Institute of Physical Education, where I also trained several times a week with the track team in addition to pursuing my dissertation research on sports in general. Since I spent so much intimate time with so many sportswomen from different parts of China and different class backgrounds, I began to sense how their experience as women in sports differed from my own. In this chapter, I attempt to answer the question that has occupied me since my first year in China: Why would Chinese women gain acceptance in the realm of sports more easily than American women did?

I had erroneously assumed that Chinese concepts of gender would be more "traditional" than American (which to my mind implied they would be more restrictive of women) and that therefore I would find strong feelings against women in sports. In retrospect, my concept of

Primary school track meet, Beijing University (1986).

"the traditional" was, of course, a particular one based on American tradition. It took me quite a long time to realize that my Chinese friends were not simply being polite in their refusal to joke about the "sexuality" of female athletes; they were using a cultural map of gender that had very different landmarks from my own. My coach's comment about the female shotputters was typical in that his ultimate reference point was their ability to find a husband, not their appearance, which he characterized as "fat," not "masculine." Rather than bring up the abstract notion of "sexuality" that is so important in the West, he characterized the gender of the shotputters by reference to an ability to achieve a particular role in life—that of wife.

In this essay, I borrow Foucault's distinction between "alliance" as a technique of the body that is characteristic of societies oriented by kinship and "sexuality" as a technique of the body that is characteristic of the modern Western state (Foucault 1978: 106–13). Foucault has been criticized for portraying the effects of a (despite his disavowals) monolithic power on an essentially passive body (McNay 1991: 133–34). In contrast to Foucault, I am more concerned with the question of individual agency: of showing that individuals choose to "act out" their sex in ways that allow them to take advantage of the opportunities offered to them within a given set of power relations. The performance, the "acting out," is gender.[1] In any society, a person's assigned biological sex shapes her or his strategies for getting ahead in life. Within the Chinese sociopolitical context, women choose to "use" their anatomical sex to achieve goals that are somewhat different from those usually expected in the American context.

One of the most important formations of power that shapes gender is the class structure. Thus, after I have discussed the relevance of Foucault to China, I will consider the importance of the symbolism of social class in shaping the presentation of Chinese gender. Sports provide an excellent takeoff point for this analysis because in the West they have been such an important arena for the public performance of gender for the last century and have often reinforced class divisions. By contrasting the Chinese case with selected examples from works on sports in the West,[2] I will show the interrelationship between history, concepts of the person, sex-linked symbols, and social class that produces the construction of gender in Chinese sports. I will also touch on the implications for notions about homosexuality and about complementarity between the sexes. These interrelated elements ultimately converge in the practice of sports, shaping the way in which athletes experience their female or male bodies.

THE HISTORY OF WESTERN GENDER: "ALLIANCE" AND "SEXUALITY"

Many scholars agree that sometime in the eighteenth century, concepts of human sexual nature changed in the West (Foucault 1978; Laqueur

1. I find the sex/gender distinction problematic for several reasons. As Laqueur (1990) shows us, anatomical sex can be just as culturally constructed as the social behaviors associated with it (gender), and it can be hard to tell where one ends and the other begins. In this chapter, I use "sex" to mean anatomical sex, "gender" to mean cultural beliefs and social behaviors, and I note when I find the distinction more confusing than helpful. Rubie Watson and Christina Gilmartin brought to my attention the second problem with the sex/gender distinction: the dichotomy is itself made possible by a Western social-scientific dualistic thinking that doesn't seem to apply in China where, as this chapter shows, sex and gender are inseparable because reproduction is so central to both. The idea that one might "put on" and "take off" one's gender is harder to comprehend in the Chinese cultural framework, in which gender is more closely tied to durable traits like social class and less tied to changeable traits like appearance. For this reason I do not subscribe to Judith Butler (1990) as my authority on the sex/gender distinction, as is currently common: in my opinion, much of her analysis makes universal what is actually specific to the Anglo-European tradition.

2. I realize that my use of the word "West" sounds like a simplification and essentialization here. However, I do not know a better word. As an example, as a track and field athlete,

1990; Illich 1982; Hausen 1981). Before this time, sexual difference was a matter of degree rather than of kind. "To be a man or a woman was to hold a social rank, a place in society, to assume a cultural role, not to *be* organically one or the other of two incommensurable sexes" (Laqueur 1990: 8). For example, a 1735 German encyclopedia contained this definition: "The female or woman is a married person, who, subject to her husband's will and rule, runs the household, and in the latter is the servants' superior" (Hausen 1981: 57).

These views of male and female were consonant with what Foucault calls "alliance," which he defines as "a system of marriage, of fixation and development of kinship ties, of transmission of names and possessions" (Foucault 1978: 106). In itself, Foucault's definition of "alliance" does not go beyond Lévi-Strauss (1969), and he uses it only as a vague characterization of what existed in Western Europe before "sexuality." I am not claiming that Western European "alliance" was the same as Chinese; rather, I wish to take Foucault's suggestion that "alliance" has different effects on the body from "sexuality" as a takeoff point for describing the specific case of contemporary China. Neither am I claiming that this is a mutually exclusive binary opposition; rather, it is a question of cultural emphasis. Foucault points out that even in Europe, "sexuality" was superimposed on the old system of alliance, never completely obliterating it (1978: 106–7).

Foucault's notion of "alliance" gives us an important point to consider with respect to gender in China. It is widely accepted among Sinologists that in China reproduction is a key goal of almost all young adults, that most marriages are contracted based on considerations of social alliance and attempts to "marry up," and that these practices continue despite the presence of a state that frequently attempts to alter them (for example, Croll 1981; Honig and Hershatter 1988; Jankowiak 1989; Lavely 1991; Whyte and Parish 1984; Wolf 1985). This is true in both rural and urban areas, though the emphasis may differ. It was also true up to and after 1949: the principles have remained the same, though the content has varied. The importance placed on alliance has effects on techniques of the body and on the construction of gender in China, and these effects are evident in the practice of sports.

---

over the years I knew and trained with athletes from Canada, Britain, New Zealand, West Germany, Finland, Sweden, Switzerland, and elsewhere. I also lived in Germany for five months after leaving China in 1988. I felt that the constructions of gender among these nationalities were all fairly similar, and considerably different from what I experienced as a college athlete in the PRC.

As described by Foucault and others, the transformation of European gender began in the last third of the eighteenth century, when writers began to insist that between the sexes there were fundamental, essential differences with a biological basis (Laqueur 1990: 5). Over the next century, much Western thinking about sexual difference involved an effort to locate a "true essence" of masculinity and femininity in a fixed, unchanging, "natural" biology that was either male or female and was given at birth (Fuss 1989: xi, 2–3). This naturalized, essentialized view of sexual difference was one manifestation of "sexuality," a technique of power that enabled the state, medical institutions, and academic disciplines (working in tandem) to penetrate the family and private bodies in a way not found when considerations of "alliance" prevailed in family life. In the old system, the body's main role was to reproduce. "Sexuality" did not center on reproduction; instead, it was linked with the exploitation of the body as an object of knowledge, as a producer, and as a consumer (Foucault 1978: 106–7). Knowledge about the body was produced by a growing number of legal, medical, and social institutions that concerned themselves with "the sensations of the body, the quality of pleasures, the nature of impressions" (p. 106). "Sexuality" as a cultural construct became imbedded in bodies, a mark of individuality (pp. 44, 146).[3] Hence, it was closely linked with an individualistic concept of the person.

CONCEPTS OF THE PERSON: CHINA

Many scholars have argued that the Chinese conception of the person differs from the Western individualistic concept and can instead be characterized as holistic or relational. Mayfair Yang states that "Chinese personhood and personal identity are not given in the abstract as something intrinsic to and fixed in human nature, but are constantly being created, altered, and dismantled in particular social relationships" (Yang 1989b: 39). Sun Lung-kee, a Western-educated Chinese, writes, "A Chinese is the totality of his social roles. Strip him of his relationships, and there is nothing left" (1988: 163). The relational concept of the person

---

3. For Foucault, desire is culturally created, hence he rejects the role of biology or psychology in shaping sexuality. I cannot accept this extreme view; however, this chapter focuses on sexuality in Foucault's sense of a disciplinary technique inseparable from the kinds of power/knowledge that appeared with the modern Western nation-state. Thus, I place quotation marks around the word "sexuality" to remind the reader that I am using it in the unique Foucaultian sense.

is another facet of the emphasis on alliance in Chinese society; of course, this concept of the person has implications for conceptions of gender and the body. Gender is only one aspect constituting a person's social identity; it is embedded in a larger construction of personhood whose key landmarks include class, generation, and kin relations.

In the context of this relational concept of the person, "woman" cannot exist as a transcendent, essentialized category. This argument is made for Imperial China by Tani Barlow, who argues that "sex-identity grounded on anatomical difference did not hold a central place in Chinese constituting discourses before the early twentieth century" (Barlow 1991: 147). She notes that in an influential eighteenth-century work by Chen Hongmou, "Advice Handed Down for Educating Women" (*Jiao nü yigui*), gender is primarily acted out in the context of specific kin relations (p. 152n. 21). Of course, it was this restriction to kin roles that gave women a very limited social space compared with that available to men. William Rowe, in another article on Chen Hongmou, notes that Chen and his contemporaries began any discussion of women with a "construction of social roles (*fen*) which included, but was not limited to, gender roles" (Rowe 1992: 2). By conforming to the social roles ordained by Heaven, a person realized her or his "essential nature" (*zhixing*) (p. 3). Thus, Chen Hongmou reversed the relationship of social role to "essential nature" that was described in the Western literature of the eighteenth and nineteenth centuries: instead of using a biologically preordained "essential nature" to explain the social roles allotted to the sexes, Chen Hongmou used the social roles preordained by Heaven to explain the "essential nature" of men and women. This may be essentialism, but it is not the form of essentialism usually meant by the feminist discussions of it. The essentialism is grounded in a different terrain, but it is still used to limit women's possibilities for action. The Western model is only one of the possible solutions to the search for the "true essence" of sexual difference.

SEX-LINKED SYMBOLS

The relational nature of this gender-embedded-within-personhood also influenced the structure of sex-linked symbolism. In Western symbolism, the male/female opposition is often a crucial principle that organizes other symbols (Strathern 1980: 174–223). During the late eighteenth century, Western writers on the topic of gender began to generate whole series of binary oppositions, with one side of the series being male and the other female. Male/female oppositions set out in German tracts included public life/domestic life, energy/weakness, independent/dependent, and reason/intuition (Hausen 1981: 56). The oppositions were seen as inherent in both mind and body; for example, an 1815 encyclopedia explained, "Thus in the male form the idea of power prevails, in the female more the idea of beauty" (p. 54). These dichotomies, which presented male and female nature as if they were polar opposites, were intended as a universalistic typology of the general natures of men and women (p. 55). During the nineteenth century, these principles were reinforced by "science" (for instance, the principle of the "conservation of energy"), and an increasing portion of the population accepted them as the standards of "masculinity" and "femininity" (pp. 56–57).

The Western tendency to spin off lists of opposing terms from the basic opposition of male/female has made sex-linked symbolism seem particularly amenable to structuralist symbolic analysis (for example, Ortner 1975). However, this sort of analysis may demonstrate a Western bias among scholars who assume that the female/male distinction will always be an irreducible organizing principle in any symbolic system. In non-Western systems, sex-linked symbols are often secondary to other, more fundamental principles of moral and social life (as argued for the Hagen by Strathern 1980 and for the Ndembu by Turner 1966).[4] The structure of sex-linked symbolism mirrors the social structure, in which gender is situated within a broader network of social relations that take precedence over the dyadic sexual relation.

Traditional Chinese cosmology is one such symbolic system. Westerners typically misunderstand the yin/yang dichotomy, assuming that yin "means" female and yang "means" male. In fact, yin and yang originally connoted shade and light, but later had no fixed meaning (Black 1986: 175). They were a way of describing relationships between things. In Taoist cosmology, yin was identified with nature and female—principles which were more highly valued than yang, culture, and male. As they were used in Confucian orthodoxy, yin and yang referred to hierarchical human relationships. A wife was inferior to her husband as yin to yang—but a subject was also yin in relation to the yang of his ruler. Yin and yang expressed complementary, hierarchical relationships

---

4. Like myself, Turner realized he had a preconceived bias when his findings countered his expectation that the "the opposition between the sexes would secure ritual and symbolic representation" (1966: 49).

that were not necessarily between males and females (Anagnost 1989: 321). Yin and yang "are not consistently sex-linked" but "may be situationally specified to represent the opposition of the sexes."[5] Rather than being an irreducible polarity in traditional Chinese cosmology, sex[6] was one concept caught up in a network of other, perhaps more basic, concepts; the polarity of unity/diversity may have been more central (Black 1986: 185, 189). This was because sex was simply one principle among many (such as kinship, generation, age, and class) that determined a person's position in the family and in society.

In Chinese sports, the yin/yang construct shaped concepts of the body in a way that is quite different from the action of Western gender symbolism on concepts of the body. This difference is apparent in a comparison of martial arts, the main form of indigenous physical culture to survive into the twentieth century, with Western sports. In the martial arts, the yin/yang dichotomy is a central principle, particularly in the "soft arts" exemplified by tai chi. These arts are guided by principles such as "there is yin in yang and yang in yin," "there is hardness in softness and softness in hardness," and "there is strength in yielding." These principles translate into a style of continuous motion that alternates the use of opposing principles. Because of the alternation of opposing forces, martial arts are not perceived as an arena exclusive to virile young men (whose yang, hardness, and strength might be exalted in the Western system). It is widely believed that women and wizened old men, if they are masters of technique, are capable of defeating young men. For example, a former national champion martial artist once told me that he had noticed female martial artists were not as quick and powerful as male athletes. He was somewhat confused, because "in theory" sex should make no difference. The figure of the woman warrior (*wudan*) has been popular for centuries and is a stock character in martial arts novels and operas. In this respect, China contrasts with the West, where from ancient Greece until recently most sports were considered a specifically "masculine" type of performance. Since the Enlightenment, this has correlated with a philosophy that depicted male and female as immutable, mutually exclusive principles.

To summarize, I have outlined a distinction between a Chinese emphasis on alliance and a Western emphasis on "sexuality" and suggested

5. The phrasing is borrowed from Turner's statement about sex in Ndembu color symbolism (1966: 49).

6. This is one place where I am unclear whether the word "sex" or "gender" is best. Black uses "gender," but I believe she is primarily talking about the cultural construction of sex.

that they are associated with different concepts of the person and symbolic systems. I will now move on to a more specific discussion of the history of sports.

WESTERN SPORTS AS A "MALE PRESERVE"

The development of modern sports was interwoven with the structure of power between the sexes. "It is widely agreed that nineteenth- and twentieth-century sport served as a major vehicle for defining and reinforcing gender differences, at least among the middle and upper classes" (Mangan and Park 1987: 3). Why sports in the West became so strongly interlaced with the construction of middle- and upper-class masculinity is a problem that has yet to be fully unraveled. Eric Dunning's (1986) work on modern rugby and soccer suggests that their development in Britain was closely related to a change in the power balance between the sexes. Rugby became a game for adults in the 1850s and was at first exclusive to the upper and middle classes (p. 274). Its emergence coincided with the emergence of the Suffragette Movement in the mid-1800s. Dunning states that sports obtained significance because the arena of "combat" sports (sports that represent mock combat between individuals or teams) presented opportunities for the socially acceptable expression of ritualized, controlled, physical violence. Urbanization and industrialization were changing the nature of the family. Men were drawn more closely into the family, and male and female spheres of activity increasingly merged (p. 273). Sports were one of the few realms where men had what was perceived as a clear, biologically based advantage, and they were hostile when women began to invade this realm, too. Rugby clubs strongly resisted admitting females. The female threat and fears of male inadequacy were expressed in traditional rugby songs about sexually insatiable women and songs insulting homosexuals (pp. 274–75). Sports became a last bastion of exclusively male activity. Dunning calls this the notion of sport as a "male preserve." Though Dunning himself does not ground his discussion in the feminist critique of the "naturalization" of gender, his history illustrates that sport was an important way in which the assumed biological basis of "masculinity" was publicly displayed, performed, and consumed. The hostility expressed toward women reminds us that gender constructs were not abstract concepts floating around "out there," but, rather, they were strategies used in real conflicts over social territory. Sports reinforced the then-current notions of gender because they were effective at sorting biological males from females and demonstrating the inferiority of females in a seemingly objective way, according to the standards internal to the sports themselves. Of course, those standards were partly designed to separate men from women in the first place. The major English sports, unlike Chinese martial arts, were not designed to be impartial to men and women, young and old.

Social class was another facet in the complex social relationship between sport and gender. J. A. Mangan argues that by the mid-nineteenth century, sports and anti-intellectualism were on the rise because the British upper class (the titled nobility and landed gentry) desired an educational system that socialized young people to suit the needs of imperialism—by producing a physically strong, patriotic, and preferably religious "team player" who would be an able soldier, missionary, or leader of men on imperial frontiers. The gentry admired active muscle and held learning and "bookworms" in contempt (Mangan 1981: 106). The strongest pressure to develop organized sports in the schools came from parents and alumni who saw them as a means of character training. Again, the convergence of class and "masculinity" demonstrates that sports were one tactic in maneuvers for social power as the social structure in England and Western Europe changed under industrialization. The body was a focal point of conflict in these changes as the state and medical institutions asserted their claims on it (through the "deployment of sexuality"), and the medical claims were then picked up and used by upper- and middle-class males to exclude females from sports (see Smith-Rosenberg and Rosenberg 1987). Lower-class males were excluded on sociomoral grounds. The British male "games ethic" diffused throughout the Empire and was also influential in Western European and American sports. This history was very different from that of China until the point that they converged in the late nineteenth century.

CHINESE SPORTS: NO "MALE PRESERVE"

There is some evidence that, in China, sports were a part of the education of the male elite until the Song Dynasty (960–1279 A.D.). The early educational curriculum for men was said to have included the "six arts" of archery, charioteering, music, writing, mathematics, and ritual (Cleverley 1985: 2). Confucius himself was said to have taught archery and charioteering (p. 6). Polo was a popular pastime among emperors and generals until the Song. However, from the Song onward, it appears that elite education increasingly emphasized literary knowledge. The scanty historical evidence gives us no reason to assume that after the Song sports ever occupied more than a peripheral place in the overall education of the future ruling class. By the Qing (1644–1911), many scholars ruined their health and contracted tuberculosis in the effort to memorize the vast amount of knowledge necessary to succeed in the Imperial Examinations and thereby advance their social status (Chen, Jun, and Wang 1981: 106, 120). The last of the ball games that had been popular in imperial courts throughout Chinese history died out, leaving wrestling as the only court-sponsored sport—and even then, members of the court were only spectators. So, by the mid-nineteenth century, the situation in China contrasted markedly with that in Britain, where sports and anti-intellectualism were on the rise among the upper classes rather than in decline.

The influence of China's long history is evident in that, despite the efforts of the state, sports still do not play an important role in the educational system. Chinese parents do not like their children to devote too much time to sports because they perceive education as the way to a better life. The traditional attitude of parents toward children is embodied in the saying "hoping your children become dragons" (*wang zi cheng long*), which refers above all to academic achievement. The attitude is reinforced by the National College Entrance Exam, as discussed in the previous chapter. This means that sports are essentially perceived as an activity engaged in by lower-class, uneducated people, in contrast to the valorization of sports for men among the Anglo-Saxon upper classes.

Because of the intellectual bias against sports, they are not well represented in the Chinese historical texts. Many of the surviving depictions are of women. They demonstrate that from as early as 123 A.D. through the mid-Qing, women of the imperial courts played the popular games of the time, including versions of polo, soccer (kick-ball), and field hockey (New World Press 1986; People's Sports Publishing House 1986). The Ming Dynasty (1368–1644) poet Li Yu wrote a poem about young women playing kick-ball that began, "The sweat on their powdered faces is like dew on flowers . . ." (People's Sports Publishing House 1986: 238, plate 76).

In the Song Dynasty, the balance of power gradually shifted from the monarchy and aristocracy toward the scholarly bureaucracy, and *wen* (letters) gained ascendancy over *wu* (militarism) in elite ideals (Levenson

1964: 37). Footbinding, which appeared among the upper classes during the Song, is reminiscent of the appearance of the corsetted, frail female among the Victorian bourgeoisie. However, an interesting contrast is that the popularization of footbinding was not associated with a withdrawal of women from sports; during the Song, kick-ball apparently became more popular than ever for women, even with bound feet, spreading from the court attendants to the general populace (New World Press 1986: 84). Wrestling by both men and women was a popular court entertainment. Men wrestled wearing only shorts and the women adopted this attire also. Sima Guang, a minister, considered women's wrestling morally offensive and submitted a petition to the emperor asking him to prohibit it. The petition failed (Chen Jia 1986). However, that the best women wrestlers became quite famous (New World Press 1986: 131) suggests that the events were more than a Chinese version of mudwrestling. For men, polo, kick-ball, and wrestling were regarded as important methods of military training. Though there were certainly gender differences in the ways these sports were played and the meanings assigned to them (there were no memorials against the nudity of male wrestlers), that women also played seems to demonstrate that throughout Chinese history these sports were not regarded as an exclusive "male preserve."

Dunning's notion of sport as a "male preserve" does not appear to apply to China during the Republican period (1912–49) and after the Communist takeover (1949), either. Because Western sports were introduced into China through Western-run schools, and especially by the YMCA, the Western bias against women in sports was reflected in the limited participation of Chinese women from the turn of the century until the 1930s. Women were not included in the National Games organized by Westerners in 1910 and 1914. After this time, the Chinese took over organization of the Games. There were three exhibition sports for women in the third Games in 1924; and, finally, in the fourth Games in 1930 four sports for women were added to the program—track and field, volleyball, basketball, and tennis (Wang Zhenya 1987). Again, one is struck that Chinese women did not particularly lag behind men in sports that are strongly identified with masculine identity in the West. Female athletes participated in the Second National Martial Arts Test in 1932 despite large numbers of athletes being seriously injured due to inadequate rules (Wang Zhenya 1987: 117—he does not state whether any of the injured were women). In the Seventh National Games in 1948, women's wrestling was an exhibition event (p. 176).

At the time of their introduction into China, modern sports were understood to be a Western cultural form. Participation in them implied Westernization and polarized those who favored the indigenous (*tu*) martial arts against those who preferred the Western (*yang*) sports. Male-female polarization was subsumed by the larger issue of nationalism. As discussed in chapter 2, reformers who advocated physical education for women did so because they thought that it was one of the sources of the superior strength of the Western powers. The link of strong women/mothers with a strong nation is a trend that continues in present-day China.

In the communist period, women and men had fairly equal opportunities in sports since the establishment of the sports schools in 1955. Only two years after that, a Chinese woman bettered the high jump world record, and many other women attained world-class levels. If one takes the passage of Title IX as the point when American sportswomen began to achieve legal parity with men, then 1972 was the year when the American situation approached the Chinese. That means American women lagged seventeen years behind Chinese women. If one considers the actual situation (including professional sports) rather than the legal ideal, then American women have nowhere near the parity that Chinese women have.

According to the Chinese, the difference is that socialist ideology promotes equality between men and women, while capitalist ideology does not. In my view, the socialist ideology of equality cannot completely explain the relatively easy acceptance of sportswomen. This ideology has even today failed to eradicate sexist attitudes and practices in other areas of life. Also, China, like the Soviet Union, has had significant difficulty in promoting sports for women among its Muslim groups and in Tibet. This shows that where custom strongly opposes women in sports, socialist ideology alone is not enough to overcome it. Another significant point is that parity does not extend very far off the playing field: most of the important administrative and coaching positions are still held by men. While the socialist state has been important in implementing sports for women, apparently there was not an overwhelming resistance among the Han majority to the idea of women participating in sports. Naturally, there was some resistance, mainly due to a parental fear that excessive exercise might affect a girl's childbearing abilities. However, even in the face of this widespread belief, many sports clubs for women were formed by private initiative in the Republican and post-

Liberation periods in both the cities and countryside (see Wang Zhenya 1987: 109; Rong Gaotang et al. 1984: 121–22).

China's sportswomen have, overall, performed better than the men in the international arena. The most outstanding examples are the women on the Chinese volleyball team, who became national heroes and a focal point for the revival of Chinese patriotism when they won the world championship in 1981. They went on to win five consecutive world championships. I have noticed that when I mention the team's patriotic importance to uninformed Westerners, their first reaction is surprise that Chinese *women* could throw off their shackles to become champion athletes in an aggressive sport; presumably they would not have been as surprised about Chinese men. To the Chinese, by contrast, the women were Chinese first and women second. Their successes seemed to evoke surprisingly (to an American) little reference to sex. An example is a letter to the team from Chinese students abroad who wrote, "You've told the world, 'These are the Chinese!'" (Cao Xiangjun 1985: 137). In the wave of patriotism ignited by their victory, their Chinese identity was more important than their gender identity. Any potential polarization of females versus males was overwhelmed by the intense popular feelings about "China versus the world."

The women's volleyball team is the most luminous example of champion sportswomen, but there are many others. In almost every sport, the women have ranked higher in international competitions than the men: volleyball, basketball, soccer, track and field, swimming, judo, weightlifting, softball/baseball, and so on. In classical Chinese iconography, the dragon represents the male and the phoenix the female; a frequent topic of discussion among sportspeople is why "the phoenix has taken off first" (*feng xian fei*). This situation contrasts with that in America, and most other capitalist nations, where the sportsmen tend to gain higher world rankings in men's sports than the sportswomen do in women's sports, which have until recently been dominated by socialist women (probably for reasons similar to those outlined below).

To return to my original question: Why would Chinese women gain acceptance in the realm of sports more easily than American women did? A large part of the answer lies in the different class structures of China and the West. Since sports in China were a lower-class activity, women were accepted into them fairly easily, just as they were accepted into hard labor in agriculture and construction. Men are not likely to prevent women from doing something that is relatively unimportant to men in the first place. This lower-class stigma has implications for the way in which gender articulates with class in sports practice today.

WORKERS AND PEASANTS

In the West, most middle- and upper-class women ceased to engage in hard labor during the Industrial Revolution. The idle bourgeois woman was one of the first figures, according to Foucault, to be "sexualized" in the deployment of sexuality (Foucault 1978: 121). However, working-class and rural women did not conform to the elite pattern. There were efforts to persuade workers to adopt the "correct" sense of family in the nineteenth century (Hausen 1981: 67). A German encyclopedia of 1878 noted that among male and female peasants, "occupation is in many respects the same . . . the voice, facial features and behavior of both sexes in this lower class are very similar, thus the characteristic difference clearly only unfolds in the atmosphere of more educated circles" (p. 67). Working peasant women presented a clear challenge to the attempt to polarize the essential natures of men and women. It is therefore informative to compare peasant women with women of the urban classes in China. Compared with the West, there was and is a much larger number of Chinese women who participate in agricultural labor, and this must have some effect on the popular ideology of women. Rural women are a clear example to everyone that women are physically and mentally strong. Because communist ideology glorifies labor and the lot of the oppressed, women's suffering has been well-represented in Chinese propaganda, and the notion of women's strength has probably penetrated all social strata to a greater degree than was true before Liberation. Chinese sportspeople believe that women in general are more able to "eat bitterness and endure hard labor" (*chiku nailao*) than men, and peasant women more so than urban women.

The majority of Chinese sportswomen come from urban working-class or rural peasant families (Kong Xiang'an 1988). Sportspeople recognize that the greatest reservoir of sports potential lies in the countryside, but it was not until the mid-1980s that could they begin to tap it. At that time, the economic reforms began to raise the rural standard of living so that more sports facilities were constructed and nutritional levels improved. Increasing numbers of sportswomen were recruited from among peasants, and in recent years a growing proportion of China's most outstanding athletes have come from the countryside. The low status of female peasants makes them superior prospects for sports training because they are accustomed to physical hardship and are highly motivated to take advantage of sports opportunities in the face of limited options.

This view was expressed quite vividly by one of the sports cadres I interviewed. I asked him, "Why have China's women athletes improved faster than the men?" He answered,

> This has a political element. For thousands of years Chinese women were oppressed by male chauvinism. In the '50s a woman singer used to sing a folk song about women. One line went "women are crushed beneath many layers." When this pressure was removed, it was as if they had seen the sky again. Women's ability to eat bitterness is good. They seized the opportunity. For example, Gao Fenglian won the world judo championship after practicing for only three years. Before that she engaged in labor. Truly women are more able to eat bitterness, endure hardship, endure labor. For thousands of years they did all the housework. They got up very early and worked all day long, then slept and got up again. That ability, that tradition, persists because they did hard labor for years. They are more disciplined and obedient than men. If you're working with three women and three men athletes, you have to watch the men a lot closer. They always sneak off and cheat on workouts.
>
> Wang Xiuting [a world-class long distance runner] originally worked breaking up stones to pave roads. She only practiced two years and got eighth in the world championships. Whatever you ask her to do, she does. She trains very hard and fears nothing . . .
>
> In the peasant village, women work from morning to evening. This is the historical perspective. It trained their labor ability. It is related to heredity. Their sports performances reflect their endurance . . . (Yang Duo 1988)

This cadre clearly lacked the polarized notion of women as biologically weak and men as strong, and I believe his views are widely held. Instead of using an innate biology to explain women's social position, as has been common in the West for three centuries, he used women's social position to explain their innate biology. The logic of this construction is similar to that of the eighteenth-century moralist Chen Hongmou described above. Laqueur's observation on pre-seventeenth-century Europe might apply equally well to this cadre's viewpoint: sex is "a sociological and not an ontological category" (Laqueur 1990: 8).

CROSSING BOUNDARIES:
HOMOSEXUALITY AND COMPLEMENTARITY

The rigid, immutable Western conception of gender has important implications for those people who are perceived to cross the boundaries between female and male. Women and men who violate the deeply held cultural categories of "femininity" and "masculinity" have often aroused the shock and revulsion typically inspired by culturally anomalous objects. When a woman seems "masculine" or a man seems "feminine," observers immediately doubt their "sexuality." These feelings seem to have emerged as "sexuality" became the dominant discourse of gender in the nineteenth century. Once a normal "sexuality" was delimited by the legal system and medical institutions, the logical result was that those who did not conform were regarded as perverted.

Historically, the male/female conceptual boundary has been a central preoccupation in popular perceptions of Western sports. Because sportswomen entered a realm previously identified with the masculine character, they were often suspected of lesbianism. The Chinese attitude contrasts markedly with that of the West: in China, a woman who plays soccer might be considered "vulgar" (*cu*), but she is never considered "butch." In other words, the primary axis for moral evaluations is based on class rather than "sexuality." The state-propagated and publicly expressed opinion is that homosexuality does not exist in China, or that it is extremely rare. I once observed an event which brought home to me the striking contrast between China and the West in this respect. I spent a few days living with Chinese athletes in the dormitories at the Shanghai Institute of Physical Education. During the rest hour one day, two big, strong females—a javelin thrower and a shotputter—were lying one on top of the other in their underwear, stroking each other and whispering in each other's ears. This behavior aroused not the slightest degree of interest from their three other roommates. The conversation I later had with one of the roommates followed a typical course for this topic. I asked her what kind of relationship the two girls had. "They are good friends," she replied. Trying to lead her on, I noted that in America, when two women lie together like that, people sometimes think they are homosexual (*tongxinglianren*—literally, "person who loves members of the same sex"). "We don't have homosexuals in China," she replied. The notion that there are no homosexuals in China is a widespread one and is a result of the idea that the natural course of life is to marry and have a child soon after. Chinese people gossip as much about couples who choose not to have a child as Westerners do about supposed homosexuals. In the 1980s, most heterosexual Chinese that I talked to were not offended or disgusted by the idea of homosexuality; instead, they wondered, "Why would someone want to do that?" The idea was not as emotionally loaded as it is in the West (though this may be changing now with exposure to Western ideas). As a result, relations between members of the same sex often involve a good deal of physical contact (hand-holding, stroking, sitting on the other's lap). At student dances in 1985–86, it was more common to see men waltzing and fox-trotting with men, and women with women, than it was to see mixed-sex pairs. In communal showers, my Western mind was at first shocked to notice women straddled against the wall (in the position we associate with being frisked by the police) while their girlfriends scrubbed their backs. For them, same-sex physical contact was a source of comfort rather than anxiety.

A second preoccupation generated by Western essentialized gender is that of maintaining a clear distinction between males and females. Westerners often think that there should be a degree of complementarity between a woman and a man on an abstract, symbolic plane. We might assume that a woman who was herself slightly "masculine" would choose a husband who was even more "masculine" so that he would make her "feel like a woman."[7] For example, we might expect that a female athlete would be most attracted to a male athlete, and this often seems to be the case.

Chinese athletes were not nearly so concerned with these abstract notions, which reflect the concerns promoted by the "technology of sex." Instead, in accord with the emphasis on alliance, social status was the prime consideration in choosing a mate. The proverbial wisdom was that husband and wife should be of similar social status; but, given the chance, many young people also aspired to "marry up," women more so than men. Top female athletes aspired to marry not male athletes, but men with advanced degrees from distinguished universities. An oft-cited example was China's star volleyball player, Lang Ping, who married a master's degree student from Qinghua University. One of my friends explained, "Women want to marry someone with academic attainments (*xueli*) . . . Famous male athletes usually marry other athletes. Academic attainments aren't that important. The women want some-

7. Margaret Mead comments that even the notion of "feeling like a woman" is peculiar to the West (1963: 301).

one who is better than them, but the men don't." In her eyes, education was what made a person "better," and her notion of complementarity was based on education and social status.

The women I interviewed did not find anything unusual in the idea of a robust sportswoman hoping to marry a malnourished college student. The same friend discussed her search for a husband with me. As a former track athlete, she considered her search quite successful because she had married a man who was, as she said, "short, fat, and with a bad disposition"—but was a graduate student at the Chinese Academy of Sciences. When she opened the door to receive him at their first meeting, arranged by friends, her initial reaction was, "I don't want to be with him." At the same time, another athlete was courting her, but she had decided to "strive to marry a graduate student."

When American women began participating in bodybuilding competitions in the 1980s, they stimulated a good deal of discussion over whether muscles were "feminine." When I asked a Chinese bodybuilding coach whether Chinese women bodybuilders had trouble finding husbands, he told me a story that he said illustrated Chinese gender ideals very well. One of his students, a 33-year-old with a technical school diploma, had been through three boyfriends, but they had all broken up with her. They thought she was physically attractive, but they broke up with her because she spent too much time training. The coach laughingly commented that this shows Chinese men are more concerned that a woman devote her time to them and to the household than they are with any abstract ideas (like "femininity") in the sport of bodybuilding.

THE EMERGENCE OF ESSENTIALIZED GENDER IN CHINA

In order to make my point, I have oversimplified the Chinese and Western constructions of gender. As Foucault notes, alliance persisted alongside "sexuality" even in the West (1978: 106). There are times when Westerners define gender with reference to social roles and relationships, and there are Westerners who choose mates for their social status rather than their "sexuality." There are also times when Chinese conceptualize gender like Westerners do; I noticed that discussions about sexual intercourse with Chinese men my age often led to blanket abstractions about "women." These sorts of discussions rarely arose with any of my married female friends because they seemed much more concerned with talking about the social status of their husbands, their plans to have a child, or the abortions they had undergone. Women were perhaps slightly more preoccupied with the social status of their mates and with childbearing than men, who were more interested in the appearance of their mates and in the experience of sexual intercourse. However, this does not mean that "sexuality" in the Western sense shapes men's experience of their bodies and their sex. Most Chinese men are also very concerned with the status of their mates. Star sportswomen have very little trouble finding mates, regardless of their appearance. The women's volleyball team was said to receive thousands of love letters as well as photos and gifts that came almost every day (He Lu 1982: 17). Sports fame helps these women make more desirable matches than they would have made otherwise.

Some scholars have remarked that essentialized gender ideals seemed to gain importance in China in the late 1980s. For example, newspaper articles distinguished the thinking of male students (broad, quick, independent) and female students (narrow, easily distracted, trivial, diligent, meticulous) and discussed the character traits of the ideal lover. The attempt to define the manly temperament led to a new magazine devoted entirely to describing it, entitled "Real Man" (*Nanzihan*) (Honig and Hershatter 1988: 101). In analyzing what is happening, it is important to keep in mind three of the points raised in this chapter. The first is that gender ideals play an important role in the political process, so one must ask who is promoting them, in what contexts, and for what purposes. The second point is that gender may be essentialized in different ways in service of political agendas: one must ask what is the logic of the essentialism, to what is it being anchored—to an immutable biology or to fixed social roles, for example? The third point is that a consideration of the first two issues should clarify the degree of complicity of the state in the promotion of certain gender ideals.

A number of explanations for the emergence of essentialized gender have been offered by both Western scholars and the Chinese themselves: it is a return to Confucian ideology, a reaction to the excesses of the Cultural Revolution, or a result of Western influence, among others. If the first explanation is correct, then based on my previous discussion I must argue that the emerging essentialism should differ from that found in the West. While the remaining two factors are important, I believe that the decline of arranged marriage and of the extended family play equally large roles. These changes in the practices of alliance combine with an increasing emphasis on consumption by the state in its promotion of economic modernization.

Arranged marriage has been discouraged by the Communist government, but no custom of interaction between the sexes has emerged to take its place. Today, many young people rely on family and friends for introductions to prospective mates. The process is often conducted much like a job interview. The go-between sets up a meeting, and the prospective partners get together to discuss likes and dislikes, family, profession, and so on. First impressions are important. An example is my friend who opened the door to meet her future husband and immediately thought, "I don't want to be with him." The new style of courtship has led to an increase in the importance of gender-stereotyped self-presentation in finding a mate. Thus, essentializing statements about gender are frequently encountered in discussions about courtship.[8]

The increasing availability of stylish clothes, cosmetics, hair salons, and fitness clubs has given young people the technology for "putting on" their gender. The body techniques by which gender is expressed are often inspired by Western trends. Physical fitness activities such as aerobics and bodybuilding are becoming increasingly popular on college campuses because, as one reporter found, "If you ask college students why they like physical fitness, they say, fitness is popular abroad, society advocates fitness, and when you're looking for a mate it depends on whether or not you are physically fit (*jianmei*)" (Cai Dengbiao 1988a).

Sports have played a role in the changing ideals of gender in China. Female students surveyed at Beijing University in 1985 most often named as their ideal man none other than Yuan Weimin, coach of the world-champion women's volleyball team (Xie Baisan and Zhang Ming 1985). The study concluded on a surprising note: "They most disliked men who are purely scholarly." Nevertheless, the majority of women preferred a man with a Master's Degree, which was the highest degree offered in most disciplines at that time. A paradox is built into the structure of Chinese hypergyny: while physically robust men have a certain appeal, the educated men with the highest social status are often not that type. I cannot say whether many women now place more emphasis on appearance than in the period before the reforms. However, my 29-

---

8. William Jankowiak's study of courtship in Inner Mongolia during the 1980s showed that young Huhhot residents expressed rather essentialized views about sex differences when discussing courtship (1993: 168). He comments that "women and men within the sexual encounter, and especially during courtship, strive to present an image meant to be appealing to the opposite sex" (p. 178).

year-old friend did suggest to me that the appearance of a prospective husband is more important than it used to be because everyone knows about heredity and wants to avoid having ugly children. She offered as proof the story of a male athlete who was very unattractive and went through one broken engagement before finally marrying. The growing awareness of Western scientific biology offers greater opportunity for the naturalization of sexual differences. However, for the moment, when it comes right down to it, women still prefer the educated man.

Western influence is clearly playing a role in the reformulation of Chinese gender. Among urban youths, especially college students, social status is perhaps becoming less important in marriage choices, while more abstract considerations like complementarity and sexual attraction are becoming more important. In their growing attention to physical attractiveness, sexual pleasure, and "microtechniques of the body," as well as to consumption and sexual deviance, urban Chinese (and, to a lesser extent, rural) would seem to be approaching Foucault's description of "sexuality" in the West. However, the effects of alliance are still all-pervasive. Ultimately, most of the state discourse on gender gets channeled back into the service of alliance. Reproduction is still the central sex-related issue for the state because of the birth control policy, and it is still the anchor point for Chinese women's experience of their bodies. My unmarried female friends seemed more concerned with their menstrual periods than with any other aspect of their physiology. They refused to train during their menstrual periods because they believed it would affect their future fertility and also because a regular menstrual cycle was perceived as the key to overall physical and mental health (this is discussed at length in the following chapter). Their second most consuming preoccupation was to avoid getting a dark suntan. Dark skin is associated with outdoor labor and the working class and damages one's chances to marry well (Kong Xiang'an 1988). In contrast to these two aspects of the body, on which agreement was unanimous, the issue of muscles got mixed responses. Some women thought bigger muscles were attractive on women and some did not. This contrasts with my own experience in the United States. I remember that as an adolescent athlete my perception of my body was most influenced by concerns over whether muscles were "feminine" or not. In China, reproduction and class are more potent components of gender symbolism than is an abstract notion of "femininity."

Though sports have played a role in changing perceptions of the body, they have not been used to separate females from males or to support claims to female biological inferiority as in the West.[9] Of course, the successes of Chinese women athletes have precluded this possibility for the time being.

CONCLUSIONS: SPORTS IN THE HISTORY OF THE BODY

A history of sports is an important part of the history of the body because sports are one of the most important genres for publicly performing and dramatizing the body as a cultural artifact. By writing a history of the body in sports, one can begin to write the specific history of the political investment of the body that Foucault called for (1979: 25–26). In writing this history, it becomes apparent that this political investment occurs as much as a result of general social processes as it does from the actions of the narrowly conceived state. In particular, a history of sports in China demonstrates the ways in which considerations of alliance, concepts of the person, and notions of social class constitute bodily experience in a positive way, so that bodies are not simply "crushed between processes of power" (one of Habermas's critiques of Foucault—1991: 285). Rather, people actively pursue the options that are open to them.

I proposed that in Chinese society "alliance" in the Lévi-Straussian sense is still a very important social principle. The effect on gender is that marriage and reproduction are central preoccupations of young people and they are, for the most part, what one's anatomical sex is for. Thus, the measure of sexual normality is whether one is able to achieve the roles of spouse, parent, and daughter- or son-in-law. Though these are essentially the effects of an emphasis on alliance that Foucault predicted, I went beyond Foucault in demonstrating the complex involvement of history, concepts of the person, sex-linked symbolism, and class relationships, as well as alliance, in the production and maintenance of Chinese gender. The effects on perceptions of the body come into focus in the realm of sports. Chinese women calculate whether a sports career will improve their social status and thus make them more desirable as

9. Of course, Chinese people recognize that top male runners can, for example, run faster than top female runners and that this has a genetic component. However, I am describing a widespread belief that if Chinese men trained as hard as Chinese women, they would perform better in competitions with men from other nations. Thus, women's biological disadvantage in physical performance is not used to explain an inferior moral character but, rather, is said to be compensated for by a superior ability to "eat bitterness."

mates. They worry whether sun-tanned skin will be perceived as lower-class and hurt their chances of marriage. They refuse to train during their menstrual periods because they believe menstruation is central to their future childbearing abilities and to their overall health. The elusive standards of normality that preoccupy Americans, making such a secret out of what it means to "be a woman," are considerably less important. American women calculate the effect of sports careers on their "sexuality" and contend with stereotypes of the "masculine," promiscuous, or lesbian female athlete, among others.

The PRC state discourse on nationalism and modernity has also played a different role in sports than did Western state discourses on "sexuality." With China's increasing participation in international sports, the promotion of women's sports came to be more a matter of national pride than of women's liberation. That women's liberation was a secondary consideration is evident in that there was no general outcry over the absence of women in important administrative and coaching positions. By the late 1980s, the popular view of female athletes had come to be a mostly positive one. Sportswomen basked in the tremendous national enthusiasm for the world-champion women's volleyball teams. And even if they were not themselves champions, sportswomen could still enjoy the thought that they were doing their part for China's future generations, because, as the proverb says, "muscular mothers have fat babies" (*mu zhuang*[10] *er fei*). This argument is cited in the authoritative 1980s history of sports as a reason for promoting women's sports (Rong Gaotang et. al. 1984: 122).

The example of Chinese sports shows that, depending on one's point of view, an official and popular emphasis on alliance can place fewer restrictions on women's bodies in the realm of sport than does the emphasis on "sexuality" in the West. Then again, Chinese women's involvement in sport fits the cultural ideal that women can and should endure more "bitterness" than men because of the social roles that are preordained for them. Chinese alliance and Western "sexuality" have each carried their own set of freedoms and restrictions.

10. This character (*zhuang*, fourth tone) is translated as "strong; robust" in *A Chinese-English Dictionary*. I translate it as "muscular" here because I found that in colloquial speech it was the closest equivalent to the English word. Also, like the English "muscular," it has male associations (for example, *zhuangshi*, "hero, warrior").

CHAPTER NINE

Bodies, Boundaries, and the State

THE "SOMATIZATION" OF CHINESE CULTURE

The bodies of all human beings are at the center of a nexus of demands and pressures created by personal desires, material conditions, and social context. All Chinese are subject to these pressures, but athletes' involvement in physical activities concentrates the conflicting demands placed upon the body in contemporary China and brings them into especially sharp focus. Today as well as in the past, Chinese people find themselves caught in a web of interdependencies, the most acute of which are among the individual, the family, and the state. This web of interdependencies is symbolically expressed in conceptions about the body and its physiology; points of conflict receive the most elaboration in the form of body symbolism. This expression of social tensions in bodily metaphors is what I am calling "somatization." In various forms, somatization has characterized Chinese culture since ancient times. Historically, concepts of the body were a part of encompassing beliefs about the cosmos and humankind's place in it. Today, some of the classical beliefs persist in altered form, but in addition the socialist state has added a new twist to conceptions of the body and its relation to the wider society.

This chapter is about the tendency toward somatization in Chinese culture, a tendency that results primarily from the practice of everyday life. Because of their bodily dependency on others, Chinese athletes do not perceive their bodies as entirely their own. Their interconnectedness with their families is primarily expressed through concerns about their reproductive organs; their interconnectedness with their work unit, and by extension the state, is expressed through an obsession with food. Somatization is a way of coping with the stresses of everyday life. For athletes, the main sources of stress are their relationships with their families and with the state. This analysis illustrates how body culture is inculcated because somatization arises out of daily practice while at the same time the bodily metaphors are shaped by a unique cultural tradition that includes classical philosophy and medicine. Thus, body culture occupies a middle space between institutionalized culture and unconscious daily practice.

My concept of somatization draws on the works of Sun Lung-kee and Arthur and Joan Kleinman, but it departs from them in significant ways. In his controversial book *The "Deep Structure" of Chinese Culture* (1983), Sun Lung-kee argued that Chinese grow up in a condition of dependence within a network of social obligations, first and foremost among them being the hierarchical family, which generate a "disorganization of the self." The older generation is overly concerned for the physical well-being of the younger generation, a concern that revolves around the act of feeding (1988: 164). The intergenerational relationship epitomizes the somatization (*shentihua*) of Chinese culture as a whole, which refers to the idea that "the entirety of purposes in life all lead toward the satisfaction of the needs of the body (*shen*)" (p. 21). The satisfaction of physical needs is not for the ultimate pleasure of the individual, however; rather, such pleasure is given and received—or denied—along channels that ultimately reinforce the importance of the collectivity (the family, the nation) over the individual. The most marked aspect of this somatization, Sun argues, is the obsession of Chinese people with oral gratification. Chinese culture as a whole values food like no other, and "'Food' is indeed the pivotal point in Chinese government" (1983: 40). At the same time, Chinese people must be desexualized in order to maintain the harmony between generations because sexual maturity leads to rebellion against authority (1988: 227). In short, in Freudian terms the Chinese individual is fixated in the oral stage and does not experience the stages of personality development that produce a sense of self, "sexuality," and a mature individual. The result is that Chinese do not view their own bodies as belonging first to themselves and then to the world at large. Rather, there is a blurring of boundaries between one's own body and those of others and between psychological states and physical sensations.

Like Sun, I argue that Chinese athletes do not perceive their bodies as entirely their own and that the boundaries between self and family, nation, and state are not delimited in the same way as in the United States. However, to speak of a "disorganization of the self" is to take a Western psychology as the standard while failing to realize that Chinese athletes' conceptions of self originate in very real material conditions. Hence it is slightly dishonest to speak of a "blurring" of boundaries between self and other because these boundaries are culturally constructed in the first place and do not actually exist with the clarity that we in the West might like to believe. Westerners typically conceive of their bodies as inviolable sealed units—a conception that is being profoundly disturbed by the AIDS epidemic. Thus, I reject Sun's Freudian explanation, which traces the roots of this "deep structure of Chinese culture" to childrearing practices. This explanation is insufficient because, as will be seen, this construction of self and of the body is reproduced continually throughout people's lives by the patterns of daily existence. However, Sun's emphasis on a "Chinese" cultural tradition is valuable because classical philosophy and medicine still provide many of the idioms that frame bodily experience.

In their study of depression in Hunan, the Kleinmans also found a high degree of somatization, which they defined as "the expression of personal and social distress in an idiom of bodily complaints and medical help seeking" (1985: 430). While they were interested in the ways that their patients expressed depression through physical symptoms (headaches, dizziness, fatigue), they also acknowledged that somatization can occur in the absence of any medical disorder as a habitual way of coping with social stress (p. 473). They noted that persons who are the most powerless are most likely to somatize (p. 475), and they argued that the social sources of human distress can be found in the microlevel inequalities that result from larger-scale political, economic, and institutional forces (1985: 467; Arthur Kleinman 1986: 2).

This chapter takes the view that the somatization in the context of illness described by the Kleinmans is only one aspect of a general tendency in Chinese culture. While the Kleinmans restricted their research to people who defined themselves as ill, I am concerned with the process of somatization among athletes who are generally very healthy. Like the Kleinmans, I argue that somatization is a way of coping with the stresses of everyday life. For athletes, the main sources of stress are their relationships with their families and the state, and these stresses are expressed in concerns about reproductive and digestive physiology.

THE CLASSICAL CHINESE BODY: FLUID BOUNDARIES

Before proceeding to contemporary China, it is necessary to outline the philosophical and medical traditions that have some influence on contemporary concepts of the body. Utilizing categories developed by Thomas Laqueur (1990) to describe Western conceptions of physiology, it is possible to note three important facets of the classical Chinese conception of the body, which I will call the "cosmic hierarchical model" of the body, the "economy of fluids," and the "one-sex model" of physiology. First, a cosmic hierarchical model (Laqueur 1990: 115–22) dominated the classical Chinese conceptions of biology. The *Yellow Emperor's Classic of Medicine,* the central classic of Chinese medicine since at least the Han (220 b.c.–206 a.d.), assumes a linkage between body and cosmic hierarchy. The human body was perceived as intimately connected with the world around it: the body and the environment mutually influenced each other, each being permeated with essences that circulated throughout the cosmos. The most important influence on both the cosmos and the body was the balance of yin and yang, which were the source of the universe, of life and death, and of health and illness in the individual parts and organs of the body (Ebrey 1981: 36).

In the classical view, the body was also an economy of fluids: fluids (for example, blood, semen) circulate throughout the body, are convertible from one to the other and produce new life when mixed (Laqueur 1990: 25–62). The medical tradition and the Taoist alchemical tradition both conceived of human physiology as based on the circulation throughout the body of four important substances: *jing* ("seminal essence"), *qi* ("vital energy"), *shen* ("spirit"), and *xue* ("blood"). The mouth and digestive system mediated between the internal fluids and the outside world. Common medical prescriptions called for blood, menstrual blood, mother's milk, and placenta as ingredients for restoring an internal balance by adding fluids from the outside (Furth 1986: 47). Domestic remedies for menstrual problems probably included special foods and concoctions (p. 56).

In procreation, a woman's *xue* combined with a man's *jing* to form an embryo. Blood was the "ruling aspect" in females, and a female's "yin blood" was her contribution to reproduction and was the source of menses, breast milk, and the blood that nourished the fetus (Furth 1986: 46). *Qi* was the male principle, and the physiological relationship between *xue* and *qi* expressed the patriarchal social hierarchy: "blood follows *qi*" (p. 45).

The traditional Chinese economy of fluids was an economy of scarcity. The expenditure of semen was a particular concern. The Taoist alchemists believed that *jing* could be either wastefully expelled as semen in intercourse, or, if ejaculation could be prevented, circulated up the spinal column to nourish the brain, promoting longevity (Needham 1983: 125, 209; Van Gulik 1961: 46–47). The concern about the waste of semen appears to have been widespread.

The female economy of fluids was also ruled by scarcity. Childbearing resulted in depletion and loss, so that almost any disease in women was believed to stem from the reproductive functions (Furth 1986: 50). Concern about the congestion of blood led to a focus on menstruation. During this time women were considered particularly vulnerable (p. 51).

Food was an important part of the economy of fluids because eating was the main means for incorporating outside substances into the body, and diet was an important means of regulating the body's internal balance (see Anderson 1988: 229–43). "The merging of boundaries between self and other, or the lack of one's autonomy, is epitomized both in sexual relations and in the human relationship with food" (Kahn 1986: 62). Thus food, like bodily effluvia, is often a focal point for symbolizing social relationships. This has certainly been true in Chinese culture since ancient times. Food was essential to all religious and social rituals: worship of ancestors and gods, festivals, life crisis rituals, feasts, and gift-giving. "This use of food as social lubricant, stimulus, and marker is traceable to the very dawn of Chinese civilization" (Anderson 1988: 245).

Finally, Charlotte Furth's work reveals that a one-sex model of the body (Laqueur 1990: 62) dominated Chinese medical discourse in the sixteenth through nineteenth centuries. This does not mean that people could not tell the difference between men and women; rather, both sexes were believed to share the same essential physiology. The male body was taken as the norm, and the female body was a lesser version of it. As discussed in the previous chapter, woman was not an ontologically distinct category and this was expressed in beliefs about physiological sex differences. Medical texts described both sexes as sharing the vital essences of "seminal essence" and "blood," though females were regarded as sexually deficient (Furth 1986: 45–46; 1988: 23–24). Sexual difference was a matter of degree rather than of kind. Bodies were depicted as capable of changing sex. Stories about males changing into females and vice versa even made their way into the Ming dynastic history (Furth 1988: 9). Gender identity was determined by social role, a central aspect of which was the ability to reproduce according to social expectations. Homosexual behavior did not change a person's gender identity (pp. 6, 14).

The classical Chinese view of the body—with its cosmic hierarchical biology, its economy of fluids, and its one-sex model—was grounded in a social world in which connections among people and the surrounding environment were more important than were individuals as impermeable, inviolable entities. These connections were expressed by the symbolism attached to the substances that flowed between individual bodies and between bodies and the outside world.

The notion of the body as a microcosm began to disappear in the West sometime in the late seventeenth century (Laqueur 1990: 151), and the one-sex model began to change in the eighteenth century (p. 149). As Foucault phrases it, when alliance gave way to "sexuality," then the problematic was no longer one of relations but rather one of flesh, and the "symbolics of blood" gave way to the "analytics of sexuality" (Foucault 1978: 108, 149).

The reasons were many, but certainly one of them was the rise of scientific rationalism, which, as Luce Irigaray (1985) points out, is a logic that grants precedence to solids. The scientific fixation is on homeostasis and equilibrium rather than on fluids (p. 115). Fluids are problematic because they flow between solid bodies and connect them in ways that make them hard to define as individual unities (p. 111). Farquhar asserts that Chinese medicine, by contrast, does not assume the body to be materially stable as does Western medicine; rather, it is "historical and constructed, ever vulnerable to disorganization and in need of continued reinvention" (1994: 93). Westerners tend to be more comfortable thinking of their bodies as closed circuits with impermeable borders, and this resonates with the ways in which "sexuality" is a marker of an essential individual identity. Where alliance relationships are more important, we might find that greater symbolic importance is placed on the substances that link bodies, such as semen, blood, saliva, and food. This is one of the factors contributing to the somatization of Chinese culture.

With this conceptual framework as a starting point, I will now look at some of the preoccupations of athletes in contemporary China.

LIFE STAGES: REPRODUCTION ABOVE ALL

The emphasis on alliance in Chinese society means that it is generally expected that all healthy people will one day marry and have a child. This is the natural course of life and to not do so is considered abnormal. Thus, reproduction is in many ways the central function of the body. Most of the state discourse on gender focuses on maintaining the strict policy of limiting couples to one child; even in discussions of women at work, the central issue is that childbearing conflicts with productivity. Despite the efforts of the government to promote late marriage (in the cities, a man must be twenty-two and a woman twenty to marry), a long tradition of early marriage means that a person who is over twenty-five years old, especially a woman, feels increasing social pressure to marry. Pressure to marry is stronger on female athletes than on males because of notions about life stages. When a woman reaches thirty, she is no longer young and should conduct herself with more decorum. In north China, it is the custom that a woman stop wearing brightly colored clothes at age thirty and put on more somber hues. One young sportswoman told me that this was one reason for women giving up sports after marriage: "People think that once you're married you shouldn't be running around in shorts."

Marriage should lead to reproduction. One former athlete, married with a young child, mentioned that couples are under great pressure to have a child: if the wife doesn't want one, then the husband does; and even if they don't want one, then the parents do. He said, "If you have reached a certain age without having a child, people think something is wrong with you, and keep asking why you haven't had a child." He had heard that ideas were different abroad and asked me if it were so.

In the 1980s most professional teams had regulations forbidding athletes to have romantic relationships with members of the opposite sex. Athletes could not marry while still actively competing. If "love affairs" (*tan lian'ai*) were discovered, one of the athletes could be sent to another team, or one or both athletes could be expelled. Men were not allowed to visit the women's dormitories at will, nor vice versa. On the Zhejiang

Provincial team in 1988, the rule was that athletes could not become engaged (*ding hun*) until after age twenty-four for females and twenty-six for males. Therefore, in order to become engaged or married, many athletes had to retire. Only the top athletes were in a position to bargain for the right to marry while still competing. Active athletes who were married were few in China, though their numbers were increasing. Sexual activity usually did not begin until after marriage ("they aren't that open yet," said one young woman), which added to the restlessness and frustration of some athletes.

The rationale for this prohibition was that sports teams must maintain military discipline so that athletes can focus all of their attention on winning glory for the nation (Zhao Yu 1988c: 181). Also, there were practical problems. Many athletes joined the teams at a young age and virtually grew up there. Their coaches took the place of parents and felt obliged to control their charges even more tightly, perhaps, than the parents would have. In addition, there was the problem that teams were not prepared to provide married athletes with their own apartments. There was also concern that married athletes would have children who would require daycare facilities, which would divert resources away from the primary goal of the team.

In his controversial article "Superpower Dream," Zhao Yu (1988) wrote that these concerns created an atmosphere in which "not a few leaders and coaches of professional sports teams stand guard against love as if they were standing guard against a flood" (p. 182). He used this point to attack China's sports system as a whole. He wrote,

> Inevitably there will be people who will call me to account: So do you want to take a "united, alert, earnest, and lively" sports brigade compound and turn it into a nursery school with infants crying loudly and diapers hung out up high? —Precisely because this cannot be done, we ought to look for the reasons in the sports system, and carry out real reforms. I will also ask in reply: If our sports were for the entire people and the entire society, and were not closed off and operated by the government for a few people, wouldn't this problem be solved? (Zhao Yu 1988c: 183)

He went on to compare the ages of China's top ten male and female athletes with the top ten athletes in the world in track and field. On the whole, the Chinese athletes were younger than the international athletes, and the difference was greater for Chinese women than for Chinese men (p. 183).

When I asked five members of the Beijing City Team what the greatest obstacle was to China's improvement in sports, several answered that the length of athletes' peak years was too short. A judo coach who had married at age twenty-five but continued training until thirty-one said,

> There are not many athletes over 30 years old. At age 25 to 26 they want to quit. At age 24 to 25 they start to want to have love affairs. It used to be felt that athletes shouldn't have love affairs; now it's better, but it's still thought they shouldn't get married . . . It often seems that those who were most restricted by the team don't keep practicing after marriage. This really could be managed better. After they plateau, they feel they can't improve and they can't have love affairs either, so they don't want to practice any more.
>
> . . . It's completely possible to get married and keep training until you are 30. My performance improved after marriage . . . The important thing is that relationships in your family, especially between the wife and mother-in-law, are managed well. (Beijing City Team 1988)

He also noted, "If athletes retire at 25, it's as if you trained them for nothing. It is exactly as if the state is wasting five years, because 25 to 30 is just when they'll do their best."

I was once asked with surprise by a 14-year-old athlete, "At 27 are you still able to train?" An older woman asked me, "At that age isn't it too tiring?" These two were themselves involved in sports, yet they still had clear-cut notions that 27 was too old to train in sports.

Sportswomen who have married and continued competing are few and far between, those with a child even more so. At the 1987 Chinese National Games, two female athletes who were ages 30 and 29, one with a child, won gold medals and attracted quite a bit of attention in the press. Ye Peisu, who won the high jump, had retired, married, and had a daughter. When I asked her why she decided to return to competition, she answered that she didn't have any clear goals: she simply wanted to "try it and see." *Sports News* commented on the significance of the victories by married women:

> On the sports field, the competitive spectacle of "I chase you, you overtake me," and "the dragon flying and the tiger leaping" is especially able to directly attack outdated beliefs and viewpoints in the realm of sports. Internationally, not a few female athletes enter

their second "golden age" after marriage, but we've had difficulty in accepting this and for a long time have emphasized the so-called weaknesses of the Eastern female. Li Meisu, a 29-year-old shotputter from Zhejiang, married for two years and who already has one child [sic—she had no child], this time broke the Asian record and ascended into the ranks of the world's top ten shotput-ters in seventh place. That her performance improved shattered the rigid notion that "On the wedding day / the shoes are put away" and brought enlightenment to top athletes about ex-tending their athletic careers. (Miao Hui 1987)

Another article noted,

Writers were often surprised that so many of our country's female athletes before marriage were "valiant and heroic," "galloping across the battlefield," but once they got married, they went through the "post-wedding 18 changes" [a pun on the eighteen changes of shape of which a folktale character was capable], the radiance of former days suddenly faded, and if they had a child, it was the same as completely saying "bye-bye" to the competition field. (Wang Baosheng 1987)

Why did marriage bring about such an abrupt end to most women's athletic careers? Chinese women usually have their first child right after marriage, especially those who are older, as are most top athletes who have delayed marriage. Despite the efforts of the government, house-work and child-raising are still very much women's work. Many people explained to me that, as a result, a woman's attention becomes divided and her training suffers. Ye Peisu felt she was able to perform well be-cause her mother helped her with childcare. She also occasionally took her daughter to the track, where other athletes played with her during practice.

In general, women's status at work suffered under the reforms, a problem that was much discussed in the press from 1987 to 1989. Work units preferred to recruit male employees over females. Due to their ex-tra burdens of child-rearing and housework, females were perceived as less productive workers. Female graduates of sports institutes looking for jobs encountered this stereotype. One 29-year-old woman was told outright that a work unit didn't want her because she would have a child right after starting work—which was indeed her plan. The prob-lem was especially marked for those who would become physical education teachers. A middle-aged female physical education teacher explained that once they have taken a year's leave of absence to have a child, they have lost much of their fitness and technique and are no longer able to be good physical education teachers. The 29-year-old physical education institute student discussed the problem as follows:

> Actually I think I might just become a housewife. I've thought about this a lot. When you're studying, you have a lot of dreams about realizing your potential, applying your knowledge, and making a contribution to society. But then when you get a job you find that there are all sorts of obstacles. On top of this, women have such a problem. People still look down on women, doubt their abilities, and some work units don't want them. And then someone has to raise the child and look after the household.
>
> It seems like all of my friends who are two years older or so had ambitions, but once they were married they had to deal with reality, raise the children, and all that. And now they really don't have much dedication to their work. All of them were like that.
>
> A lot of my girlfriends attack my attitude, but I feel it's more realistic. It's based on observing the actual situation. They say, "Women have to move into the work force and take on jobs, otherwise men will always look down on them." But, in fact, I've discovered that when I discuss my ideas with men, they really support me. Maybe it's different abroad. Maybe once the economic level has reached a certain point, then women's situation will be different. But right now it's "no go."

Female athletes who continue competing after marriage violate the norms that dictate life stages for women. That they often do not compete successfully is merely symptomatic of the social pressures that are placed on all married women. The cultural ideal is a relatively clearcut transition at around the age of twenty-five from a nonreproductive, physically active youth to a settled, reproductive adult. Because physical activity is considered antithetical to female reproductive functions, women who have continued to compete in sports after marriage and childbirth have attracted a good deal of attention in the press. Although men are also under a good deal of pressure to marry, married male athletes have not attracted nearly so much attention. Closer consideration of cultural conceptions of physiology demonstrates why this should be so.

MENSTRUAL BLOOD, SEMEN, AND SPORTS

Menstruation and Exercise

All of the sportswomen I knew refused to train during their periods because they believed it would affect their childbearing abilities. Few modern Chinese are well-versed in the entire complex of traditional medical ideas about the body, but the concern about menstruation does seem to be quite similar to that found in the ancient medical texts. The Song medical classic *Good Prescriptions for Women* (*Furen liangfang*) stated that "During the menses it is most advisable to protect one's health carefully," and "Hard labor and fatigue at this time will give rise to depleting and hot type disorders, leading further to intolerable pain" (Furth 1986: 51).

As recently as the 1960s, many scientists in the Western and Eastern Bloc countries expressed a sometimes irrational concern about the effects of activity on the reproductive organs, asserting that women should stop training, avoid swimming, and so on, during their menstrual periods. Some suggested that jarring while jumping, landing, and running could damage the female organs. A plethora of scientific studies have failed to turn up conclusive evidence either that sports permanently impair fertility (although the menses may temporarily cease) or that sports performance is negatively affected by the menstrual period (Wyrick 1974: 485–509).

In China, medical studies and propaganda work helped dispel a widespread fear of sterility. When the first women's soccer teams were formed in Xi'an in the early 1980s, for example, it was reported that "Some [conservative people] warned darkly that women who played football would never be able to have children" (Wen Jiao 1982: 58). Studies of women's soccer teams were publicized in order to allay these fears. However, Chinese medical texts still support the view of women as particularly vulnerable during their periods, espousing views similar to those found in Western medical texts of the 1960s and 1970s.

One Chinese sports medicine textbook states that light physical activity may benefit menstruating women, but adds five cautions for female athletes:

1. Suitably reduce the training load; training time should not be too long; especially for adolescent women who have just begun menstruating.

2. During the menstrual period, do not engage in strenuous training, especially movements involving strong shaking or increased abdominal pressure, such as quick running, jumping,
and strength training, to avoid displacement of the uterus or
excessive bleeding.
3. During the menstrual period, avoid the disturbance of heat and
cold, such as cold showers or fierce sun.
4. During the period, do not go swimming, to avoid germs entering the reproductive organs and causing inflammation.
5. Females with painful or irregular menstrual periods should stop
sports activities during their periods. (Zhou Yingnan 1987: pt.
7, p. 5)

Chinese women did not give clear-cut medical reasons for not training during their periods. They simply said that hard training (especially
weight training), all-out sprinting, or sit-ups, could cause cramps or irregular periods. One girl told me that even though the books said it
was okay, she believed that training during her period might result in
difficulty in childbearing later. "It's not that you'll be infertile, but it
will be harder." She had been told so by her mother, who had refused
to let her train during her period when she was younger.

In general, the athletes with whom I trained daily seemed to discuss
menstruation with greater ease than most American athletes. Once I was
sitting on the curb of the track before running a race when one of my
competitors, with whom I had not previously spoken, sat down beside
me. She commented quite casually that she was not feeling well because
her period had arrived. One 17-year-old teammate at the Beijing Institute of Physical Education was concerned about her menstrual period
and discussed it regularly with her coach, including details about its
regularity and the appearance of the flow.

College athletes generally stop training for all five days of their period, perhaps jogging a little. A more serious athlete might do light exercise for the first three days and then resume training. Some provincial
team athletes rest for the first day and then resume training as normal.
Even the toughest coaches, however, do not require the women to train
as normal throughout their periods.

Foreign coaches who have had positions at the national team center
have conflicted with athletes and doctors over this issue. Western
women usually train and compete during their periods. Some top athletes use birth control pills or suppositories to adjust the timing of the

period to avoid the year's major competition; sometimes the adjustment is made up to a year ahead of time. One foreign coach was told that Chinese female athletes do not take birth control pills because they are "unnatural," although the medical text cited here mentions it as an alternative to injections.

In China, if normal training may cause menstrual problems, then all-out competition is even more damaging. The text cited above does note that athletes may adapt to competing during their periods by gradually increasing their training load in regular practice sessions during their periods. However, most people consider it harmful to compete during menses, or at least negative to performance. Hence women whose periods are expected to occur during a major competition are often given injections of progesterone that induce the period early.

When I represented Beijing in the National College Games, the female assistant captain of the team visited all of us to ask when we should get our next periods. She urged everyone whose period was scheduled to occur in the week on either side of their competitions to have the injection. I refused and also advised my roommate against it, reasoning that such a strong dose of hormones was bound to have side effects, although we were told there were none. My roommate agreed and decided not to take the injection either, but was later persuaded by her coach. She was given three injections on three successive days. After the first injection, she felt dizzy and was able to train only lightly. After the second, she felt nauseated and skipped practice. After the third, she had hot flashes, felt dizzy, vomited, and went home for a day. She asked me to tell her coach she was ill and couldn't go to practice, but not to tell him the reason. I told him she was ill. When he asked what was wrong, I said I didn't know, but perhaps the injections he had ordered might be the cause. "This just broke our pre-meet plan to pieces," he said with irritation. "She misses three days of practice and she can't make them up because she has to rest for the meet next week. Females! You don't have to worry about this with males."

The sports medicine text cited above cautions, "Bringing about an 'artificial menstrual period,' disturbing the normal pattern of menstruation, will harm the organism. Therefore, from the medical point of view, it should not be frequently utilized" (Zhou Yingnan 1987: pt. 2, p. 31). In fact, it is frequently utilized by sportswomen and doctors who believe its side effects are preferable to the effects of competing during menstruation.

Semen Loss

Whereas for women the focus is on menstruation, for men it is on the expenditure of semen. Some people still accept the Taoist notion that the expenditure of semen saps a man's strength. This belief was said to be stronger among martial artists, who train their bodies more in accordance with the classical conceptions of physiology. A male member of the Beijing City Team, commenting on athletes who continue training after marriage, said, "The more traditional events have stronger ideas about this. Martial arts athletes still believe you should save your 'original vitality' (*yuanqi*)." One married retired martial artist said that he tried to limit himself to having sex with his wife only once a month as part of his ongoing meditation training.

For most athletes, the effect of sex on performance is a moot point because team rules prevent them from having girlfriends and boyfriends or marrying. Thus, I do not have good information on beliefs about sex and sports. However, I believe that the stringent rules against contact between the sexes and the surprise at those who are able to compete after marriage derive from a fundamental notion about the incompatibility of sexual reproduction and physical prowess. Such ideas were not usually stated openly to me. These ideas, of course, are not so different from Western notions that sex can negatively affect the performance of male athletes, which led to the practice of cloistering teams the night before a big competition. Scientific research has turned up no basis for these beliefs.

In rural China, many male peasants resist sterilization because they believe that a man's strength lies in his semen, hence a vasectomy would affect his ability to labor in the fields. Tubal ligations might also affect a woman's ability to labor, but it is less important for her (Potter and Potter 1990: 247–49). Since all but one of the active male athletes I interviewed were unmarried, the issue of sterilization did not arise. I did not think to ask them what the hypothetical effect of sterilization might be on their performance, but I can imagine that they would consider the idea with distress.

An examination of the beliefs about menstruation and semen indicates an underlying assumption that a man's physical prowess is his most important capacity, while a woman's childbearing ability is her most important capacity. In both cases there are cautionary beliefs against excess expenditures of reproductive and physical energy, but the relationship is inverted for men as compared with women. A man who engages in too much sexual activity may harm his physical vitality; a woman who engages in too much physical activity may harm her reproductive vitality. The physical and reproductive capacities are in a complementary, hierarchical relationship, with the male and female hierarchies as mirror opposites.

These conceptions of bodily function clearly derive from the economic and reproductive duties of men and women within the family. Social and familial pressures to fulfill these duties put young people under a great deal of stress. People cope with this stress by focusing on the body fluids associated with the reproductive organs, over which they can exercise some modicum of control. In short, the concern with women's menstrual blood and men's semen are two examples of how social stresses become somatized in Chinese culture.

FOOD, HUNGER, AND THE STATE
Against a Background of Hunger

Until recently, perhaps the main reason parents wanted their children to attend sports schools was because they received extra food subsidies (*huoshi buzhu*). Food subsidies have been an important part of China's sports effort since the implementation of the sports school system in 1955. Food is not something that Chinese people take for granted; it occupies an important part in their calculations about social relations, future survival, and success. When asked about the benefits of their chosen career, sportspeople are likely to answer that their work is "bitter," their salaries and prestige are average, "but we eat a little better" than people in other occupations. Despite eating better than nonathletes, Chinese athletes at all levels express constant concern that they will not be able to eat enough food to support hard training, that their "nutrition can't keep up" (*yingyang genbushang*). This constant sense of scarcity was puzzling to me since I knew that athletes' diets were far richer than the average Chinese diet. Could the hunger that athletes felt in fact be due to inadequate nutrition?

Certainly there is evidence that malnutrition was still widespread in the 1980s. A national survey of nearly one million Chinese between seven and twenty-two years old from all parts of China concluded that, according to the height-weight ratio established by the World Health Organization, 28.98 percent of male students and 36.60 percent of female students in China suffered from malnutrition. They were, however, taller and heavier than ever before, and rural students were growing faster than urban ones (Wu Jingshu 1988). Iron deficiency was common and was related to the low consumption of meat (*China Daily* 1987d, 1988f).

Moreover, in the not so distant past there were periods of real deprivation. Cao Xiangjun, member of the Beijing City handball team, recalled that after they won the championship in the 1959 National Games, they returned to the dorms for dinner. Tears welled up in her eyes when she saw the pitiful portions they had. One of the courses was the left-over leaf droppings from cabbages, boiled in salt. The kitchen staff felt very badly. They were still hungry when the "victory banquet" was over. Even in 1979, there was a story that the women's national racewalking team all became anemic during a training camp. Their meal allowance was then 1.5 yuan (40 cents) per day. Their coach gathered orange peels and sold them to raise money to buy ginseng and a clay pot with which he boiled the women a medicinal soup (Li Jian 1987). A State Sports Commission document issued in 1981 stated that "some athletes have acquired anemia and other diseases of malnourishment" and tried to rectify the situation by revising nutritional standards (Guojia tiwei zhengce yanjiushi 1982: 872). Anemia is perceived as the most immediate danger of inadequate nutrition. The word for anemia (*pinxue*) literally means "poor blood." That concern about malnourishment focuses on the blood is another example of the way in which complex social situations are condensed into the symbolism of body fluids.

Children must be put into sports schools at a young age in order to receive food subsidies during their most important growth years. Events in which training usually starts at older ages may be affected by early malnutrition. For example, a track and field coach who liked to recruit peasants for their endurance and toughness said that he was careful to examine the family's economic situation before he accepted the child for training. If the family was poor, the child might not have had adequate nutrition when young and might not be able to stand hard training.

In sum, many Chinese, even urban Chinese, actually do experience hunger. And even if they are not experiencing it now, many people have recent and vivid memories of hunger. It has been my experience that people who have known hunger can never forget the importance of food. This is the background for the obsession with food among contemporary Chinese.

However, when one examines the situations of specific individual athletes, it is hard to believe that they are suffering from malnourishment. Since they are obviously in good health, I am inclined to believe that their perception of hunger is not due to outright malnourishment, but rather to the social and cultural frames within which food is distributed. Food is very much a part of an entire hierarchical system, with the state at the top of the food chain and the athletes very close to the bottom.

Food and the State

There are a multitude of phrases in Chinese that portray the relationship between the individual and the state in terms of food. The ubiquitous phrase "eating out of the big pot" is a metaphor for dependence on the state for subsistence and security. To have an "iron rice bowl" is to have the lifelong job security promised by socialism. Sun Lung-kee argues that food is the central problem of any Chinese state: "If only they 'have a bite of food to eat,' the common Chinese people will not revolt" (Sun Lung-kee 1983: 39). In other words, the central problem for the Chinese state is to control its "person-mouths" (*renkou*)—its population.

One of the benefits of being a high official in China is access to more and better food. A high official is often literally a "big man." I was told that the same bureau that supplies food to the national sports team in Beijing also supplies the nation's top leaders. When the Party has attacked governmental corruption, official banquets have been a prime target (Anderson 1988: 245). Banquets are one of the techniques for establishing and maintaining the *guanxi* ("connections") that is perceived as the root of bureaucratic corruption.

In Mayfair Yang's analysis (1989b), food is so important in the establishment of *guanxi* because of the symbolism of incorporating another's substance into oneself. Those who are lower in social status tend to give the banquet and those who are higher in status receive it. To incorporate another's substance is to be possessed by the other and therefore to be beholden to and dependent on the donor (pp. 43–44). Thus, those of lower status use the gift of food as a means of extracting favors from those of higher status. Food is used to transform an outsider into an insider. A familiar person is a *shuren,* which literally means a "cooked or ripe person"; a stranger is a *shengren,* literally a "raw or unripe person." The transformation of the "raw" into the "cooked" makes the establishment of *guanxi* possible (p. 40).

It goes without saying that food is also extremely important within the family. Traditionally in rural China, a family was primarily defined as the group of people who ate food cooked on one stove (see Wolf 1968: 28). A family member was called a "one-mouth-person" (*yikou ren*).

Food is clearly an important expression of social relationships. How then are we to view the effects of state rationing on perceptions of the relationship between the individual and the state?

In the late 1980s, athletes, like coaches and physical education teachers, received a food subsidy from their work unit, with the amount determined both by state policy and by the local cost of food. The subsidy was in addition to the grain rations that all urban Chinese received; athletes received the higher level of grain ration that was reserved for people engaged in hard manual labor (25 kg. per month). According to policy guidelines, the subsidy could not be given directly to the athletes in cash but was calculated into the preparation of food in the communal cafeteria. Eating in the team cafeteria was a prerequisite to receiving the subsidy.

Many athletes left home at a young age to board at sports schools. For them, the locus of food-sharing shifted from the family to the communal cafeteria that dished out food based on athletic performance. Since the food subsidies were set by state policy, athletes were very conscious of the fact that the state provided them with their food. Eating in a communal cafeteria meant that the times of meals and the dishes offered were highly regimented and allowed little room for individual preference. In a pointed critique of the communal cafeterias in sports teams, Yin Weixing referred to the phrase "eating out of the big pot" as a metaphor for dependence on the state and observed, "The true 'big pot' cannot be any more fully embodied than it is inside the sports team cafeteria" (Yin Weixing 1988b: 113). Oversize shotputters and undersize gymnasts all received the same subsidy. So did women and men. Unlike in many other realms of life, with respect to food subsidies the uniform state policy was perceived as discriminating against men since they actually needed more food than women.

The national team athletes received the highest subsidies. One physical education institute student commented that being on the national team was like having an "iron rice bowl"—not like in the United States where you have to pay for your recreation. The national team athletes each received 15 yuan per day, and they also received special foods which could not be bought on the open market. At 600 yuan ($162) per month, this level of nutrition was far beyond the reach of the average monthly wage of 100 yuan; as one professor noted, at this rate even the premier of China could not afford to raise a top athlete. Professional athletes ate more food and higher-quality food than the average person. By a "high-quality" diet, my informants meant primarily two things: more meat or fish and more dairy products (primarily milk and yogurt). Dairy products are not a typical part of the Chinese diet. The emphasis on them for athletes is a result of an awareness that they form a large part of the Western diet, the assumption being that they explain the greater size and musculature of Western athletes.

Provincial and municipal team athletes also ate well, with an allowance of 12 to 15 yuan per day. The amount varies according to the cost of living in the area, which is usually lower than in Beijing, so that provincial athletes claim they eat better than Beijing athletes. Zhejiang Province athletes, for example, got three dishes for lunch and dinner, two of which contained meat. These numbers were fixed by policy. They also received many supplements, such as oranges, apples, and other fruit, and "royal jelly" (a substance made by honey bees which is often used as a dietary supplement). Even with all of these extras, young women on the team laughed about the fact that when they weren't eating they were snacking, so that they actually ate all day long.

The situation of physical education institute students shows the importance of food subsidies. In order to encourage students to become teachers in a country that had frequently denounced teachers (and worse) in the previous decades, the Education Commission gave students in teacher training programs a food subsidy. In 1988 at the Beijing Physical Education Institute, this subsidy was one yuan per day, which at 30 yuan per month was still almost one-third of a lecturer's salary. This subsidy was distributed in the form of vegetable tickets (*caipiao*) to be used in the school cafeteria and was combined with grain ration tickets (*mianpiao*) of 45 *jin* (25 kg.) per month.

Everyone I talked to maintained that this allowance was not enough to maintain hard physical training, and most students required up to 40 yuan extra from their parents. They repeatedly told me they were afraid to train hard because their nutrition "can't keep up." This was despite the fact that many acknowledged they had more grain tickets than they could possibly use. Grain tickets were exchanged for rice and flour products, primarily steamed buns (*mantou*). Students explained that they could only eat so many steamed buns. What they really needed was meat and vegetables.

Nutrition was given as the reason that provincial and national team athletes who came to the physical education institute often saw their performances decline. One athlete had been accustomed to eating 15 yuan per day of food on the Guizhou team and was now eating only four yuan; it was easy to see why she felt deprived, even though she still received more than the one yuan given to most physical education institute students. Her four-yuan subsidy was due to her former status as an athlete and a "model worker." She often fondly recalled the meals on the provincial team. When I asked her if she ate better before coming to Beijing, she replied, "Of course I ate better then. Now I'm paying for my own food." On another occasion, she made a statement that shows how food and emotions are wrapped together. She noted that she felt she could adapt to the inferior nutrition at the physical education institute, she could adapt to living with five other roommates, but the hardest thing was getting used to not being pampered. "I couldn't adapt to that."

One shotput and discus coach at the Beijing Institute of Physical Education complained that food was a particular problem for male throwers. They simply could not eat enough to become big enough to throw well. He complained that in the past, the institute had given a subsidy in addition to the Education Commission subsidy, but now it claimed "economic difficulties." Sweeping his arm toward the new gymnasium being erected for the Asian Games, he asked, "Tell me, what economic difficulties are there?"

If the physical education institute students could not eat their fill, then the regular college student, who received no subsidy at all from the Education Commission, was even worse off. However, members of college teams were given a special subsidy that steadily increased as efforts were made to raise the level of college sports. In 1985, Beijing city gave 0.30 yuan (8 cents) to college athletes for each day of training, based on daily roll taken at team practice. I consistently received more money than the other women because I did not miss practice during my menstrual period (I tried to refuse the money, but my coach explained, "This is the state's money. If you don't take it, it just goes to waste.") This was increased to one yuan per day early in 1986 in preparation for the Second National College Games, but only those selected to participate in the Games received the subsidy. In preparation for the third Games in 1988, the amount was raised to four yuan per day. Food prices had also risen considerably in that time. However, four yuan made a difference, in contrast to the 0.30 yuan in 1985 which, as one athlete complained, "Won't even buy one bottle of yogurt!"

When I participated in the training camp for the 1986 National College Games, a topic of utmost concern was whether or not the cafeteria staff was skimping on our daily six yuan ($2) worth of food. Heated debates at team meetings and repeated complaints resulted in a guarantee that we would get at least one meat or fish dish at lunch and supper and that each supper would include two bottles of yogurt per person. The conflict had caused relationships with the cafeteria staff to deteriorate to the point that the service was very surly. A strategy for rectifying this by giving some "face" to the staff was suggested during a team meeting by one of the Party members on the team. He sneaked into the cafeteria one night to hang a large "commendatory poster" (*biaoyangshu*) on the wall praising the staff for their service to the cause of the Beijing City College Team. When the staff entered the next morning, they were pleasantly surprised and friendly relations were restored.

Twice a day we received cucumbers, tomatoes, green peppers, bamboo shoots, eggplant, or mushrooms stir-fried with eggs, shrimp, beef, pork, or fish. The elements stayed the same, but the combinations changed. Because there was a heat wave, we also received a weekly "nutritional supplement" of twenty-four bottles of lemon-lime or orange soda pop and three watermelons. My teammates were very conscious of the fact that they were not allowed to receive their six yuan directly, but that it was given to the cafeteria, while the coaches and leaders received theirs in cash and then saved some of it by eating at home. Over two months, this would come to 360 yuan, no small sum. A younger coach asked rhetorically,

> Is it fair that they get as much as the athletes, who train hard, put out lots of sweat, experience fatigue? I'm a coach, and I don't think it's fair. And why do you have to have so many coaches? When we go to Dalian [for the National Collegiate Games] at the very least there will be one official for every athlete, if you include all the workers. And *they* will all get a subsidy, too. That's China. It's just the way it is.

In this hierarchical system, the hunger for food was intimately linked with the hunger for athletic success and ultimately for the security that success brings. Most people would be unable to completely fulfill their personal aspirations. Thus, hunger could refer to "the lack of fulfillment of personal aspirations and desires" as much as to real malnourishment (Kahn 1986: 122).

That the food subsidy was based on performance was peculiar to the lives of athletes. However, it was part of a wider pattern that applied to Chinese society as a whole. Food was an important marker of hierarchy and insiderhood long before the current ration system was put into place. This use of food persists, but it has been taken over by the state in both formal and informal ways. In this way the state can partly dictate the hierarchical structure of Chinese society. According to the traditional symbolism of food, by providing food to people the state is reinforcing its superior social position and making its recipients beholden to and dependent on it. Mayfair Yang even suggests it is "possessing" the recipient (1989b: 44). Top state leaders can ensure themselves access to better food. Lower-level officials can expect to be treated to banquets. Even coaches on a municipal college team can set themselves apart from their athletes by taking their meals at home and saving the subsidy while requiring that the athletes eat in the cafeteria. These practices stimulate much resentment. Food and power are intimately linked. Food is one of the main ways in which the Chinese state is symbolically constructed as provider, superior, and incorporated part of the self.

Thus, it is not surprising that food played an important symbolic role in the student demonstrations of 1989. The mass hunger strikes in Tiananmen Square were begun as a way to break away from an authoritarian family that was perceived as acting in complicity with state power. Refusing food was an act of rebellion against the family because in the Confucian scheme of things, to damage the body inherited from one's parents was unfilial (Chiu 1991: 342). At the same time, the students were very conscious that food also symbolized Chinese people's relation to the state. Chiu, a graduate student from Hong Kong, wrote that he had a late night conversation with a group of students in the square in which the question of "who fed whom?" arose. He pointed out to the students that they received monthly subsidies from the state; didn't they owe the state something in return? The students replied, "No! We were taught to think so ever since we were born. And some may still be accustomed to thinking so. But not any more." "To take the Party as our mother and give thanks for its breast-feeding? Not a chance, not any more!" "We finally learned that They don't ever feed anybody. On the contrary, They themselves were fed, and far over-fed all those years" (1991: 341).

Thus, the student hunger strike was an attempt to break away from the family and the state by constructing new boundaries around individual bodies, outlining a new and different conception of self in the process.

CONCLUSIONS: THE BODY CAUGHT IN THE MIDDLE

Because of the nature of their occupation, athletes rely on their bodies as vehicles to improve their lot in life. However, the aspects of their bodies that most preoccupy them are not so much things like bigger muscles or better endurance, but aspects related to reproduction and nutrition. These physiological processes are central to the two most important dependencies in a Chinese person's social life: dependence on family and state. Because a person has little control over these dependencies, the processes attached to them are a subject of much anxiety and calculation.

While reproduction and food have always been central in Chinese culture, many things have changed. Previously, they were embedded in an entire hierarchical cosmology that saw humans and nature as engaging in a never-ending exchange of essences. Human social life was one manifestation of these cosmic exchanges. Today, reproduction and digestion are no longer embedded in an entire "cosmic hierarchical biology," though fragments remain. For example, the 6:30 morning exercises required of physical education institute students, in which inhalation is emphasized, probably stem from the ancient belief that these *yin* hours are best for augmenting one's *qi* (Ware 1966: 139). However, what remains of the classical conceptions of body and cosmos are partial fragments. By contrast, the socialist state and its communist ideology are ever-present in the birth control policy and the food rationing system. Family and class allegiances are sometimes in conflict with the state. The bodies of athletes are caught in the midst of pressures to produce better sports performances for the state and oneself but at the same time to avoid damaging one's ability to marry (and marry well) and to produce children.

One similarity between contemporary and historical China is that the web of dependencies is nearly inescapable because it is so complete. As a result, the boundaries between the body, the family, and the state are more fluid than in the West. The body is not a sealed vessel situated at the center of these social axes, and the person who possesses that body does not do so completely. The "disorganization of the self" described by Sun reflects the social pressures that continuously pull the individual's identity in different directions, while the somatization of Chinese culture reflects the individual's attempt to pull together the fragments of the body that are particularly subject to these centrifugal forces. Because of the importance of food in this process, the student hunger strike in 1989 stands as a powerful symbolic effort to stake out a space for a new and more autonomous self.

PART
•5•

Body Culture in
Social Change

CHAPTER TEN

"Obscene" Bodies, the State, and Popular Movements

Bodybuilding and Old People's Disco

This chapter describes the role of two popular fitness activities—bodybuilding and "old people's disco"—in the political process of the late 1980s. These fads were examples of a subtle contestation of state policies that took place in a seemingly apolitical realm, among a seemingly apolitical group of people, and which focused on the body rather than on explicit discourse. The stories of bodybuilding and disco illustrate the rapid changes in Chinese body culture that were initiated by the growth of consumerism and exposure to international culture under the policies of the Dengist regime. They illustrate the role that body culture can play in the political process. A concrete description of the political context surrounding the growth of each demonstrates this point quite clearly.

BODYBUILDING

The Chinese word for bodybuilding, *jianmei*, literally means "healthy and beautiful" and encompasses both

An earlier version of this chapter was delivered as a paper in the panel on "Popular Cultural Practices in China: Room for Heterodoxy?" (which I co-organized and co-chaired with Louisa Schein) before the American Anthropological Association, San Francisco, 6 December 1992. I would like to thank Ralph Litzinger, Louisa Schein, and Andrew Kipnis for their helpful comments. I also profited from the comments by our discussants, Fred Wakeman and Mayfair Yang.

265

competitive bodybuilding and recreational fitness activities. This chapter concentrates on the competitive sport form, which involves training with weights and on machines in order to develop the muscles. Competition involves fixed poses before a panel of judges, who evaluate the development of specific muscle groups as well as the overall proportion and grace of the body. This necessitates the exposure of most of the body; international rules require men to wear bikini trunks and women to wear two-piece bikinis. The women's bikini was what inspired the greatest debate in China. First introduced to China through Western missionary schools, and revived in the 1980s under Western influence, bodybuilding was the only sport to develop outside of China's state sports system.

From the start, Western missionizing in China involved a conflict between two different cultures of the body. In contrast to the "muscular Christianity" of the missionaries, Chinese culture labeled strenuous exercise as lower-class and the baring of the body as improper. Manual laborers developed muscles and bared their bodies; gentlemen did not. Both cultures supported a stricter concept of modesty for females than for males. Women did not bare their arms and legs, let alone their torsos. A 63-year-old physical education teacher who had been educated in missionary schools in his youth commented to me with a tinge of guilt, "Maybe it's feudal thinking, but I can't get used to female bodybuilders. In my youth at the missionary school, we were taught to appreciate the male body, that developed muscles were beautiful. But I don't feel they suit females. I feel they lose their femininity."

In many rural areas today, peasants still consider the exposure of arms and legs inappropriate.[1] A student who did a teaching practicum in a very poor part of Hebei province in the mid-1980s told me that although the peasants were very eager to learn, he and his classmates encountered taboos against baring the body. The peasant boys didn't like to wear shorts, although it was expected for the physical education class that my friend taught. My friend was himself summoned to the office of the local party leader and criticized for wearing shorts and a short-sleeved T-shirt while jogging; he was told it was not proper for someone of his status. Bare female arms and legs are called a "provoca-

---

1. Andrew Kipnis reminds me that attitudes toward the baring of the body vary by region. In Fengjia, Shandong, where he did his research, older married women went topless on hot summer nights (1992). Urbanites have a tendency to project their own prudishness onto peasants.

tion" or "stimulation" (*ciji*). My friend told me that girls in the village could not wear shorts and short-sleeved shirts at all because the peasants would say they were "bad" (*buhao*).

Thus, the sport of bodybuilding violated the intellectual notions of bodily decorum that were widespread before Western contact and the norms of modesty still prevalent in many places. Exposure to Western ideas, initially through missionary activity, began to change the traditional beliefs among a handful of people.

The following history of bodybuilding was recounted to me by Yi Chenghong, vice-chairman of the Chinese Fitness (*jianmei*) Committee (Yi Chenghong 1988). According to Mr. Yi, bodybuilding began in the 1930s at Hujiang University when Zhao Zhuguang, who had attended a missionary school in Shanghai, translated some American materials on muscle development methods. He also participated in an international correspondence course organized by Americans. He may well have been the original Chinese Charles Atlas: said to have been a sickly forty-kilo (eighty-eight lbs.) weakling, he took up bodybuilding for his health and became quite robust. In 1988, at the age of eighty-one, he was still active in Chinese bodybuilding. Guangzhou and Shanghai were and are the centers of bodybuilding. The director of the National Fitness Committee in 1988 was a 74-year-old who also learned bodybuilding as a youth in Shanghai. Bodybuilding reached the north in the 1940s. Mr. Yi's teacher, Lin Zhuyin, had attended Furen University in Shanghai, where he had read American bodybuilding materials and became acquainted with Zhao Zhuguang. He brought molds for weightlifting plates back from Shanghai and set up a bodybuilding center in the basement of the Beijing YMCA. Bodybuilding also spread to nearby Tianjin. Before Liberation, the sport was popular only with the sons of the wealthy because, of course, others lacked the time, money, or energy to do it. According to Mr. Yi, sometime before 1953, Lin Zhuyin gave an exhibition to China's top leaders in their residence compound in Nanhai; he wore a swimsuit, took off his clothes, and posed for them.

In 1953, bodybuilding was denounced as "bourgeois" and banned. This occurred as the Party began to promulgate a new culture of the body, one that was conceived of in opposition to both the pre-Liberation Chinese culture and the Western culture. The communist body culture was to be egalitarian, militaristic, and proletarian: it was to erase class and gender distinctions, prepare the people for national defense, and promote productive labor. Bodybuilding was "bourgeois" because it was perceived as an unproductive and narcissistic pursuit of beauty originating in the capitalist West. Because women's bodybuilding did not exist at that time, it was not an issue.

GRASSROOTS REVIVAL OF BODYBUILDING

Bodybuilding began to spread in the 1980s as its popularity in Hong Kong spilled over into Guangdong. It received official approval in 1983, when the first formal competitions were held. In 1985, China joined the International Bodybuilding Federation, paving the way for the participation of Chinese athletes in international competitions. With the growth of popular interest, the men who had learned bodybuilding in missionary and other schools found a demand for their knowledge, and they became instrumental in bodybuilding associations. Bodybuilding was different from the other internationally contested sports that were practiced in China in that it did not develop within the framework of the state sports commission system. It continued to spread despite disapproval from the official state apparatus. The state opposed bodybuilding for two reasons: first, state leaders felt that the baring of the body, especially the female body, was "bourgeois" and that it might incite social disorder (luan); second, bodybuilding was not an Olympic sport, so no gold medals could be gained. Despite the official criticism of its bourgeois decadence, bodybuilding actually had the greatest appeal to peasants and workers, which is similar to what we find in the West (see Bourdieu 1984: 210–11). The widespread grassroots enthusiasm for bodybuilding indicated that its popular appeal was not widely affected by its "bourgeois" aspects and that Olympic golds were not the only goal of the masses.

Since bodybuilding athletes initially trained outside of the sports commission system, they relied on private and corporate sponsorship for financial support. A state document had first called for corporate sponsorship of sports in 1984, the year that China competed in the Olympic Games again after a 32-year absence due to the "two China problem." The timing makes it likely that the goal of the document was to promote Olympic sports, but it also paved the way for corporate sponsorship of bodybuilding. A list of the ten winners in different classes in the 1988 National Bodybuilding Championship (sponsored by Xi'an Beer Company) showed that most of them represented corporations; these included North Star Clocks, Phoenix Cosmetics, and Five

Star Beer. (The involvement of beer and cosmetic companies reminds one of the advertising strategies used by American beer and cosmetics corporations.) One winner represented the Locomotive team of the National Railway Industry; sports teams sponsored by state industries represent a small but growing alternative to the state sports commission system. Only one winner came from the sports commission system itself—the Liaoning provincial sports team (Qiu Zutai 1988a). In addition to large corporations, individual factories began to sponsor teams. In October 1987, it was reported that ten work units nationwide had begun to sponsor bodybuilding teams (Dao Jie and Miao Ye 1987); this number has no doubt increased rapidly. Wealthy peasants and *getihu* were especially supportive. In 1986, a *getihu* from Anhui used 50,000 yuan to found a private workout club, and in 1988 his bodybuilders placed well in provincial competitions (Zhang Xiaozhu 1988). Cadres from the Peasants Sports Association told me that bodybuilding had become popular among male peasants in their areas, while females preferred aerobic dancing. They felt bodybuilding would continue to spread because, as one male cadre put it, "everyone thinks muscles are attractive on men." One of the cadres said that one of his students had taken off his clothes

Scene from 1988 Beijing City college weightlifting competition held at Qinghua University.

and posed for him—"His muscles stood out and were quite well developed." They stated that peasants appreciate muscles because they do hard labor.

THE BIKINI DEBATE

In 1985, the year China joined the International Bodybuilding association, women gave an exhibition in the national competition wearing one-piece bathing suits. Actual competitions for women were first held in 1986, when bikinis were worn for the first time. In 1987, aerobic dancing was added to the program (Yi Chenghong 1988). Thus, women's bodybuilding did not lag far behind men's. However, it was the subject of a much more heated debate.

The debate concerned the question of whether or not China's women bodybuilders should be allowed to wear bikinis in competition. The argument against it was that the bikini "did not suit the national conditions" (bu fuhe guoqing). Critics pointed out that Chinese women do not wear bikinis on the beaches, whereas Western women have for years. Many people believed that bikinis would have a "bad social influence," especially on young people.

The bikini is a symbol of Westernization. Chinese sportspeople I met assumed that, in the West, bikinis and nudity are everyday practices that arouse no particular interest. A 35-year-old woman who was doing bodybuilding in her spare time told me that many Chinese girls do not like bodybuilding because they don't want to wear bikinis in front of the judges. I told her that I would feel the same way, and she expressed surprise. She said she had always assumed that Westerners felt no embarrassment about showing their bodies. After digesting my statement for a moment, she concluded that perhaps all people felt that way.

In general, Chinese women feel shy about baring their bodies. In urban areas, more women are wearing shorts in the summer, but even athletes do not like to bare their legs except when they must compete in their assigned uniforms. Most of my female teammates at Beijing University wore their long sweatpants even when the weather was extremely hot and humid. Rather than remove the pants, they would roll them up to their knees. When asked why they always wore their long pants, they replied that they kept their legs warm. I once pressed a teammate further, and she admitted that she preferred not to show her legs in practice. My training partners at the Beijing Institute of Physical Education were sometimes shy about removing their sweatshirts when they felt their tops were too tight or transparent. We discussed the fact that bras are uncomfortable but that, as our coach put it, even if you have a small bust you have to wear one because of men. The national-team athletes who wore the skin-tight lycra that was the international style told me that they were able to do so because they had "become used to it," but not everyone was accustomed to wearing or even looking at lycra. One 19-year-old at the Beijing Institute of Physical Education said she thought lycra running briefs for women were ugly because they "split the legs" (in the United States these briefs are called "bun huggers"). Clearly, there were widespread feelings of modesty about baring the body even among athletes.

The argument for the bikini was that it was required for international competitions and was necessary to observe the athlete's torso muscles for fair judging; Chinese women would be excluded from international competitions if they could not wear them. It was rumored that the topic was debated by the Central Committee itself (Schell 1988: 78). According to Mr. Yi, the top state leaders, the National People's Congress, and the Ministry of Culture opposed the bikini, while most of the leaders of the State Sports Commission supported it. It was only because of this support that the women were finally allowed to wear bikinis.

The Sports Commission was thus more "progressive" than Party leaders, the National People's Congress, or the Ministry of Culture. The impression was that the State Sports Commission preempted criticism by announcing that women would wear bikinis in the national contest before other state organs had fully taken a stand. The Communist Party did not officially express its approval until a front-page article appeared in the *Guangming Daily* a few months later (Mann 1986). In my interpretation, the support of the Sports Commission can be attributed to two main reasons. First, bodybuilding had become popular without the state's support; incorporating it into the sports commission system would strengthen the popular base of the State Sports Commission and give it one more international stage upon which to perform. Success in the international arena had been the force behind the State Sports Commission's gains in prestige and power since the beginning of the era of reform. Beginning with the victories of the women's volleyball team, and followed by Olympic successes, the State Sports Commission had managed to improve its position relative to the State Education Commission and the Ministry of Culture. These are the two organizations most closely linked to the Sports Commission, and with which it must both negotiate and compete.

In my analysis, a second reason for the Sports Commission's support derives from the life experiences of many members of the sportsworld. Many influential sportspeople had been educated in the West or in missionary schools. They suffered persecution during the Cultural Revolution, when "medals-and-trophyism" was labeled a counter-revolutionary mindset and the Sports Commission was a particular target of attack. Indeed, not just those with Western connections, but large numbers of other sports professionals suffered as well. The resentment felt by sportspeople toward these memories is so strong that it is even quite evident in the official history of sport written after the reforms (Rong Gaotang et al. 1984). Thus, the Sports Commission's support of bodybuilding not only expressed the move toward modernity, but also the reaction against the stifling egalitarianism and militarism of the Cultural Revolution body culture (see Honig and Hershatter 1988). This critique of the Cultural Revolution had become a permissible discourse by that time.

Clearly this situation cannot be described as a "state" versus "society" opposition. One cannot pinpoint a site of state power here because the state was fragmented, and because the individuals in the State Sports Commission themselves brought viewpoints to their arguments that derived from their bitter life experiences under the preceding regime. The State Sports Commission is a small but upwardly mobile government organ that has been propelled upward by the popular enthusiasm over international sports victories. It utilized social support of bodybuilding to bolster its prestige and power within the state apparatus—and this was a social support with which many members of the State Sports Commission sympathized.

The State Sports Commission's publicly expressed argument for bodybuilding was that it represented an attack on "feudalist thinking," a move toward internationalism, and that it allowed individual expression through the "pursuit of beauty." These were all consonant with the orthodox Party discourse of the time. The bikini debate was not expressed as a primarily feminist issue, which would have been more problematic in relation to the Party line; as several scholars have noted, the commitment of the Party to women's liberation is ambivalent at best (Wolf 1985; Honig and Hershatter 1988; Anagnost 1989).

Bodybuilding could develop in the cracks between state and society because it was not clearly identified (by the Party, the people, or the Western press) as a form of political resistance. In fact, the State Sports Commission made every effort to identify the main issue as that of following international rules rather than of transforming cultural beliefs; this was obviously part of its strategy for calming the furor. The emphasis on following the international rules deflected attention from the more important fact that the body culture promoted by the Party since its inception was being attacked and dismantled.

The first officially approved bikinis were worn in October, 1986, at the National Hercules Cup Invitational held in Shenzhen. Since Shenzhen is a special economic zone more open to the outside world than any other area in China, it was considered the proper place for the "experiment."

The event attracted remarkable nationwide attention. Journalists from seventy-one news and press agencies (including "Blind People's News"), sixteen broadcasting stations, fourteen television stations, and three movie companies were present. They totalled 813 people, more than Xinhua agency sent to the Asian Games (Xiao Tian 1987). The spectators numbered between five and six thousand (*Time Magazine* 1986; Shi Yumei 1987: 22). According to Mr. Yi, all of the binoculars in the area were sold out before the competition. He also noted that the women's competition was not broadcast in Beijing except for a very brief, distant shot of the winner.[2]

Once the novelty wore off, people lost interest, and after the first day the competition was not so well attended. During the course of the competition, sports cadres paid great attention to crowd reaction. They concluded that the reaction was "normal" and that the event had attracted a lot of people who were "alarmed at something perfectly normal" (*dajing xiaoguai*) (Xiao Tian 1987). The politically correct attitude was reflected by the all-around women's champion:

> She believes that each sports event has its specified clothing. For example, a fencer couldn't wear a bikini, but has to protect himself from top to bottom. Bodybuilding competitions aren't like that; they require the beauty of the body's muscles to be presented openly. If you wear a one-piece swimsuit, then won't the lines of those muscles that you took great pains to achieve be covered up? Then what can you see? As far as this specified clothing goes, if

2. Mr. Yi stated that this was because of the influence of the Ministry of Culture, which had not approved the bikini. However, since China Central Television was under the control of the Ministry of Radio, Film, and Television, it is possible that this ministry also opposed the bikini. Regional television stations are more autonomous from the ministry (Lull 1991: 26), so it is possible that there was more coverage in other parts of the country. Jeff Olson (1992) recalls seeing many close-up shots of the women on television in Guangzhou.

you love the career of bodybuilding, then it's quite natural to wear it. (Shi Yumei 1987:23)

In an article in "Health and Beauty" magazine, Mr. Yi wrote,

Although judgments varied, praise exceeded criticism. From looking at competitions held in different places where everything was orderly, it can be said to reflect one aspect of the efforts of the Chinese people toward human advancement; they have a good ability to support the effort. . . . [Bodybuilding] is not only a prerequisite for developing sports, but also is a prerequisite for the construction of socialist spiritual civilization. Therefore it is beyond reproach. (Yi Chenghong 1987)

In 1987, the national competition was attended by only a hundred-odd reporters, and the audience showed a "normal" reaction. However, bikinis could not appear at every competition. They still must pass the approval of the municipal or provincial sports commission for a lower-level competition and the State Sports Commission for a national competition. As of 1988, the Ministry of Culture still had not given its stamp of approval, so that no organs under its auspices were permitted to hold bodybuilding competitions with bikinis. This meant that such competitions must always be held in sports arenas and gymnasiums rather than in theatrical stages and auditoriums.

THE STATE, PORNOGRAPHY, AND BODYBUILDING

Chinese policy assumes that "pornography" incites young people to crime. Most of the objections in the bikini debate revolved around its influence on young people. "There must be some control," commented my advisor, Guo Jiaxing. "Every nation has some controls. Not everyone views it [the bikini] with the same perspective. They don't want to let in chaos; then there will be a terrible social influence."

In fact, bodybuilding and other sports provided a channel for a degree of relaxation in state controls on "spiritual pollution." Regulations against "spiritual pollution" in the media prohibited body-revealing photos, including bikini calendars—although some were available on the black market. As discussed in chapter 3, magazine censorship in China is less strict than for other media and tends to be self-imposed by the writers and editors. They apparently took the national bodybuilding contest as a go-ahead sign. *Liberation Daily* complained that since women were allowed to wear bikinis in the contest, magazine editors felt "emancipated" to use bikini-clad women on their covers (Schell 1988: 76). Sporting photos in magazines, calendars, and on postcards were the only officially acceptable way the public could satisfy its curiosity about the human body, especially the Western female body. Pictures of Western women bodybuilders were popular items for the front and back covers and the central color photo sections of sports magazines and of many magazines having little to do with sports. Calendars featuring Western sportswomen or Chinese gymnasts in various athletic poses were popular fixtures on household walls.

Sports were perhaps the major medium for transmitting the "modern" concepts of the body that were supposed to accompany China's move into modernity and consumer culture. The official view was that Chinese people must be taught to appreciate human nudity at more than a prurient level. An example of the didactic approach taken in many periodicals is an article, entitled "Nudity Does not Equal Obscenity," in which the author stated,

> Whether statues, paintings, and dance, or gymnastics, ice skating, and bodybuilding—in their artistic discovery of the beauty of the human body, all these have not only given the human form unique aesthetic value, but also, by using the beauty of form to reveal the human spirit, have caused outward and inward beauty to attain a harmonious unity. This undoubtedly has an active, positive effect in shaping people's aesthetic awareness and transforming their ideas. (Zhang Fuyang 1987)

The ubiquitous presence of bodybuilding photos in the popular media undoubtedly contributed to its popularity. This was a crack in the Party's front on "pornography" which contributed to the growth of bodybuilding. It seemed clear that magazine editors were eager to take advantage of the crack in order to sell magazines which sometimes had little relevance to bodybuilding. Led by the Sports Commission, the state was a somewhat reluctant accomplice, nevertheless recognizing that an aesthetic appreciation of the body contributed to the growth of consumerism.

"RESISTANCE"?

Did women bodybuilders conceive of themselves as "resisting" either state or societal oppression?

According to Mr. Yi, the first bikini was exhibited in August of 1986 in a competition staged in Guangdong by a "bodybuilding family." The head of the family was a *getihu,* and the grandfather was an Overseas Chinese. The daughter wore a bikini for her demonstration during a men's competition. It seems likely that the family's Hong Kong connection and the father's economic independence from the state, as a private entrepreneur, contributed to their pioneering spirit. Again according to Mr. Yi, in September a university student wore a bikini in a competition in the Northeast.

I talked to some of the young women at the Beijing Institute of Physical Education who had begun to train in the newly instituted bodybuilding class. I asked them why they had begun bodybuilding, expecting to hear some rebellious feminist responses. I didn't get them. Instead, they uniformly gave very practical reasons. They were typically former weightlifters, track and field athletes, or other athletes whose performances had peaked. When they realized their potential was limited, they began to consider other career paths. They saw that women's bodybuilding was in its early stages, making it easier to be a champion than in more well-established events. These sorts of reasons were very common in newspaper articles on top bodybuilders as well. The 1987 national grand champion was a former acrobat who, at twenty-seven, was past her peak (Shi Yumei 1987: 24). When *Sports Illustrated* caught up with her in 1988, she had started her own business of aerobics and bodybuilding classes (Swift 1988: 46).

The young bodybuilders I met claimed that they were not concerned about negative reactions. However, newspaper reports tended to emphasize that champions had overcome the objections of parents and boyfriends. The grand champion of the first national exhibition contest is reported to have said, "Weak people fear gossip and I am not weak!" (Luo Pan 1988); and the winner of the 1987 competition reportedly said, "I myself have my own ideas; whoever says something, I just let it blow by my ear, but my husband really loves face" (Shi Yumei 1987: 24).

Apparently, bodybuilding repeated the class patterns found in other sports. Those who saw in it a path of social mobility were inclined to take it up. In this sense, female bodybuilding, like male bodybuilding, was an expression of the peasant and working-class ethos. It was hard to detect an attitude of organized resistance to the state or, on the part of women, to "feudal" attitudes. On the other hand, as I sat in the weightroom and observed the young bodybuilders watching themselves in the mirrors, I was struck by their un-self-conscious pleasure in their own bodies and couldn't help but feel that some sort of awakening was taking place. Already they were enthusiastically discussing where one could buy the nicest bikinis. Consumerism did not lag far behind this newly discovered culture of the body.

WHY WERE OLD PEOPLE DISCO DANCING?: OLD AGE AND REBELLION THE CHINESE WAY[3]

Disike is a phonetic approximation of our word "disco" (interestingly, the character for *di* means "to enlighten or guide"). It was the name of a fitness activity that emerged around 1985 and became very popular over the next few years. It bore a little resemblance to aerobic dancing or jazzercize and a lot of resemblance to the radio broadcast exercises it had supposedly replaced. The types of body movements characteristic of disco were Western-inspired. Hip-swiveling and shoulder-rolling were key defining elements, but they appeared to lack explicit sexual connotations. Other Western movements were also used, such as hand-clapping and cross steps. The music tended to be slightly outdated Western pop music, which was lively by Chinese standards of the time. Chinese people perceived disco dancing to be a vigorous, exciting activity, and newspaper articles expressed concern about disco injuries to older people who might not be up to such demanding movements.

While young people were discovering their bodies and the joys of consumption, the elderly were not sitting idly by. At the same time that bodybuilding and disco were becoming popular among the young, "old people's disco" was said to be one of the "Three Hots," or three biggest crazes, in China along with billiards and *qigong*.

The "old people" to whom I refer were retirees around age sixty and older. It is hard to say whether or not they were participating in larger numbers than other age groups, since dancing exercises were substituted for the morning and mid-day broadcast exercises in many schools and work units. Formerly, these exercises were performed to the accompaniment of a musical broadcast from the national radio station. Disco, on the other hand, was often danced to the accompaniment of a large cassette player provided by one of the dancers. If the elderly were dancing in greater numbers, then it could be attributed in part to their having more leisure time than other groups. However, it was clear that old

---

3. An earlier version of this section of the chapter was delivered in the panel, entitled "When Life Is Hard: Cultural Forms of Coping and Healing," before the American Anthropological Association, Washington, DC, 19 November 1989.

"Young people's disco," opening ceremonies of 1988 Beijing University Sports Meet. Note the shoulder-rolling motion.

people doing disco attracted more media attention and public curiosity than other age groups.

It was reported that in Shanghai over 100,000 people participated in disco dancing (*Tiyu bao* 1988). Handfuls of older disco dancers clustered around a large cassette player could be found in almost every Beijing park in the early morning hours, and the same was true in other cities. Beijing's most popular gathering place was the Sun Temple (*Ritan*) Park. It was reported that 600 people assembled there for early-morning disco, wearing heavy coats during the cold winter months (*China Daily* 1988d). Old people's disco developed such drawing power that a performance was broadcast by the national television station on the eve of the 1987 Chinese New Year, during the most-watched television program of the year. It featured the disco performance of a Shanghai club founded by a 70-year-old woman.

The opening ceremonies of the 1988 Beijing University sports meet included an old people's disco performance and attracted more spectators than the competitions themselves, with the crowd numbering several thousand. This group of middle-aged and retired staff members had 224 dancers, 48 of whom were men. At the closing ceremonies of the 1988 Beijing City Sports Meet, approximately 600 members of the

Beijing Institute of Physical Education staff practicing "disco" during the midmorning work break.

"Old people's disco," opening ceremonies of 1988 Beijing University Sports Meet.

Qinghua University staff, about 30 of whom were men, gave a disco display. In both of these groups, the women outnumbered the men by quite a bit, which was usually true.

"RETURNING THEIR YOUTH"

There were two intriguing aspects to the disco fad. The first is captured in the question of one journalist, who noted that in the past people felt

"when a person became old, if he could eat and drink a little, then his entire life counted as full of good fortune." But today, old people have also begun to pursue the "latest fad" . . . Why would these old people, who in the past didn't even know how to do broadcast exercises, suddenly become this "modernized"? (Guo Bowen 1988)

If you asked elderly dancers why they liked to dance, they said that they were concerned about their health, and disco was simply more fun than other forms of exercise such as tai chi, broadcast exercises, and jogging. Disco was new, different, "modern," and "stimulating." They commonly mentioned that disco made them feel younger, it made them "glow with youthful vigor" (huanfa qingchun). One 56-year-old woman explained, "This activity most easily arouses the child's heart in the old person" (huanqi tongxin) (Guo 1988).

Two more commonly stated reasons provide greater insight into the social significance of disco and its relation to the problems of the elderly. One reason the elderly participated in disco dancing was that they were retired and thus had more leisure time than other age groups. Many of them had feelings of uselessness, which dancing was said to combat. An example was an 83-year-old male disco dancer who said:

[W]e can still suggest ideas to young people in the midst of the reforms, we can still do a little beneficial social activity. We old people long to show that "old age has a purpose, has a use" (lao you suo wei, you suo yong). (Guo Bowen 1988)

It is perhaps significant that the speaker was a man, because women were less likely to mention feelings of uselessness after retirement from the working world. They were more likely to mention the easing of tensions with their daughters-in-law as a motivation for dancing. Since most elderly disco dancers were female, this problem is worth considering at greater length.

ELDERLY WOMEN DISCO DANCERS

One of the main sources of conflict in Chinese society has always been the relationship between the mother and daughter-in-law in the patrilocal extended family. Margery Wolf hypothesized that this conflict stems from the attempt of both women to guarantee their status within the family by controlling the son (husband). The mother-in-law resents her daughter-in-law's sexuality because, as Wolf phrased it, "women in their fifties recognized that . . . they could not compete with the woman in their son's bed" (Wolf 1985: 11). With this in mind, it is interesting that older women often said they were urged to disco dance by their daughters-in-law, even borrowing brightly colored clothes from them to do it. Sometimes daughters-in-law were urged to dance by their mothers-in-law. Those who were formerly engaged in constant bickering said they found that they could get along better when they had a common hobby and that disco shrank the distance between generations. How often this actually happened is hard to say, but according to the mythology, disco reduced intergenerational conflict, especially between mothers- and daughters-in-law.

There is a custom among most of the Han majority that children and unmarried girls wear brightly colored clothes, especially the color red. Red is an auspicious color used on festive occasions, and it is the traditional color of the bride's wedding gown. When a woman reaches the age of thirty, she is supposed to adopt more somber colors, but there is no reason to assume that she was ever happy about giving up the symbols of her youth. For example, Chinese friends in their mid-twenties advised me that my clothes were too dark and that I should wear brighter clothes while I still could because soon it would be too late. This custom is changing in Beijing, and disco-dancing is part of the reason. Elderly female disco-dancers often put on brightly colored, red, or shiny beaded or silk blouses to dance, sometimes borrowing them from their daughters-in-law. When an older woman wears a bright blouse, she is breaking a taboo by adopting the trappings of youth, and this is regarded with much amusement by the spectators. When I was watching the Chinese New Year broadcast with a Chinese family, for example, they all laughed and commented on the brightly colored clothes of the dancers.

When an older woman put on her daughter-in-law's brightly colored blouse and did decadent modern disco, she symbolically became young again and attracted much attention from spectators, many of whom were male. The change in ideas evident in the television broadcast of old people's disco was commented on by a middle-aged, female scholar as follows:

All of the women were sixty to seventy years old, with white hair, and some with a little extra weight. Their bodies weren't that beautiful, but they put on brightly colored clothes and got up there and danced. In the past, disco dancing, especially swiveling the rear end, was considered very ugly. But now these old women stand on stage and are considered the "height of refinement" (*ya-guan zhi tang*). (Cao Xiangjun 1988)

The taboo against bright clothing was not the only taboo they were breaking. There were also taboos on bodily deportment. Sports scholar Lu Yuanzhen described these in an article on disco:

Traditional Chinese culture prescribed a rigid model for the behavior of old people: we expect them to be sedate and slow, "tai-chi style," leaning on a walking-stick, carrying a birdcage. But when they are wearing sweatsuits and tight pants, hopping and jumping, at first we feel they are lunatics, "getting naughty with old age," overstepping their bounds. This is really an intolerable social attitude and an oppressive public sentiment, harmful not only to the elderly but also to ourselves. We will also get old. Old people's disco comes from a foreign culture; it is different from traditional customs. No wonder that it doesn't look right when you are first learning it; but the longer you dance, the more beautiful it becomes. (Lu Yuanzhen 1988b)

Lu pointed to his first exposure to old people's disco as an incident in the film "On Golden Pond," in which Katharine Hepburn's character expressed her love of life through dancing. That this minor part of the movie attracted his attention in itself shows the difference between Chinese and American norms for behavior of the elderly.

AGE IN THE CULTURE OF THE BODY

These examples illustrate the age-graded nature of body culture in China. Elderly disco dancers were breaking some strongly held taboos on their behavior: they should not wear brightly colored clothes, sweatsuits, or tight pants, nor should their movements be bouncy and energetic. These taboos were the product of traditional Confucian norms, which made sedate behavior an essential element of one's "face." The breaking of these taboos was what stimulated the most public discussion about disco.

Chinese are often embarrassed to try new things because they are afraid of "losing face." This is a very real fear because, on the other side of the fence, people often greatly enjoy watching someone make a fool of himself. At the Beijing University Meet display of old people's disco, the spectators were almost as zealous as they had been for the visit of the world champion women's volleyball team. I could only get a view by standing in the middle of a large mud puddle. Wherever old people's disco was practiced, there were likely to be more spectators than participants. It might take a long time before an observer got up his or her nerve to participate. There was even a little jingle which summarized the four steps in accepting disco: "can't bear the sight / stand on the side / give it a try / together they writhe" (Wang Jintang 1988).

A second aspect of the disco fad was that it was an activity formerly banned as decadent, bourgeois, and Western. The social and political significance of the disco craze cannot be appreciated unless one understands that even a few years prior, disco was viewed askance by the authorities. Since the Cultural Revolution, dancing had often been forbidden. At the more progressive universities, student dance parties were a focal point for seesawing conflicts between university leaders and the students. Sometimes they were allowed, sometimes they weren't. Even when they were allowed, sedate ballroom dancing was the acceptable dance form. Commercial ballrooms had been allowed in other cities since around 1984, and in Beijing only since May of 1987; but "close dancing and obscene music" were still forbidden (Zeng Lingtong 1987). In a 1988 newspaper article, the author observed that he had written an article on disco in the Year of the Ox (1985) but hadn't published it "because some friends said it was inadvisable to promote disco" (Wang Jintang 1988). Two years later, he marveled that disco dancing "has already everywhere vigorously replaced the broadcast exercises systematized for over thirty years."

The breaking of modern political taboos was not as openly acknowledged as the breaking of traditional Confucian taboos, yet obviously this was going on. In this context, it is important to note that the disco craze began with the intellectuals, though it rapidly become popular among workers and peasants. This was the usual path by which foreign popular culture entered Chinese culture, because intellectuals had more exposure to Western ideas. One reporter who did casual surveys at many

Beijing city parks found that 60 to 70 percent of the dancers were doctors, teachers, and technical workers. Most colleges and universities started disco clubs for students and staff, and this seems to have been the origin of the fad.

As discussed in chapter 7, concern for the health of older intellectuals had arisen due to the state survey that showed they had a life expectancy almost ten years lower than the national average, over half of them dying between the ages of forty and sixty (He Zhenliang 1988). The officially given reason was that intellectuals did not get enough physical exercise because of the nature of their work. However, a perhaps more important factor was that they were the ones who suffered most during the Cultural Revolution when they were sent to the countryside to do manual labor. The malnourishment and physical hardships they endured then extracted a toll on their health. In the 1980s, they continued to live under heavy stress because their social status and salaries were comparatively low, and the burden of restoring social science and graduate departments fell on their shoulders. In the 1980s, a great deal of China's social stress fell on the shoulders of the intellectuals, especially older intellectuals, hence it was not surprising that some sort of movement would arise among this group.

Many of these educated people who discoed the most vigorously were the same cadres and Party members who opposed such practices the most vigorously a few years previously, a fact at which people often marveled. As one sport cadre commented to me, "Many middle-aged and elderly cadres are joining in, and this is really amazing because they have been most strongly influenced by the feudal tradition" (Yi Chenghong 1988).

Although the elderly disco dancers did not claim to be the vanguard of a political movement, the effect of their dancing on their own thinking and that of the onlookers should not be underestimated. As one commentator wrote,

> The significance of old people accepting disco far and away surpasses the physical activity itself. If you say this is a revolution in ideas, if you say this is modern rhythm making inroads into traditional consciousness, you probably wouldn't be exaggerating! (Wang Jintang 1988)

In conclusion, old people's disco became significant under the conditions of social stress produced, among other things, by contact with the dominant, industrial West. Disco blended Chinese and Western body culture, producing a form of activity that was nevertheless uniquely Chinese. Although disco had distinctly Chinese characteristics, it was perceived to be a foreign, Western practice. No one seemed to be aware that this was not a popular thing for the elderly to do in the West. That so much attention could be given to old people's disco in China indicates the higher status of the elderly in Chinese society, bolstered by the Confucian norms which were then changing. Reverence for the elderly and strong intergenerational ties made the elderly less willing to step aside from the stream of progress. Instead, they took a symbolic step right into the stream of progress.

Both China and the elderly were trying to cast off rigid traditions and old taboos in order to "put new life into the system." The analogy is what made old people's disco "good to think" in this time of social change. Disco was, in a sense, the rehearsal of the new order, and this is why disco was said to express the "feeling of the times."

BODY CULTURE AND THE "POLITICAL"

But in what sense can we say that bodybuilding and disco were "political" at all? And how could these seemingly frivolous recreational activities have any power to influence the course of social change?

Let me end by theorizing "the political" and "recreational activities" in a way that allows us to see the role of body culture in social change.

Practice theory provides a way to explain the importance of the body in social change by showing how everyday body techniques are actually the main means by which the existing social order is produced and maintained; it follows that they must be important sites for challenging and transforming the social order when change does occur. However, because social scientists have failed to ascribe importance to the mechanisms that are capable of reproducing the social order without conscious intention, they have typically excluded everyday practice from the study of "legitimate politics" (Bourdieu 1977: 189). Yet this is precisely the level at which any thorough and durable social change will occur. This book has already set out many examples of the centrality of body culture in the political process. It has also suggested some of the reasons for the centrality of body culture in the Chinese political process in particular, such as the rethinking of the relationship between body and nation that occurred with exposure to social Darwinism and Western imperialism, the focus on the body in the growth of consumer culture, and the tendency toward somatization in Chinese culture as a whole due to a person's dependence on the family and state. This chapter adds a final piece to this picture by making the point that in the late 1980s the culture of the body was a unique realm in which subtle contestations of the state were possible when such opportunities were not available in other realms.

Jean Comaroff notes that under an authoritarian state, resistance often takes place in seemingly apolitical realms (Comaroff 1985: 261), and contests over symbols may predominate in the place of contests over actual structural issues (pp. 196–97). In this kind of political context, combined with a social context in which cosmological beliefs are shaped more by everyday practice and less by explicit discourse, resistance may tend to focus on the body (1985: 9, 80, 167, 171, 197).

Bourdieu's and Comaroff's views were echoed in the views of Chinese people on bodybuilding and disco. Everyone that I talked to felt that the acceptance of bodybuilding—especially women's bodybuilding—and disco represented a transformation of the traditional "feudal" concepts of the body as well as of the concepts promoted until the end of the Cultural Revolution. They recognized that a transformation was taking place before their eyes, one which had important political implications, but it was not being played out in an arena clearly demarcated as "political." Though some people expressed fear that the women's bikini might let in social "chaos," no one perceived the sport as primarily an expression of political resistance. As a spectator at the first competition in which bikinis were permitted told a reporter, "If you say that the bikini is some kind of breakthrough, you are really assigning it a bit too much value" (Xiao Tian 1987). Likewise, the widespread recognition that old people's disco indicated a "revolution in ideas" did not go so far as to propose that the individuals doing it were expressing their resistance toward the political regime. Sports scholar Lu Yuanzhen wrote that disco dancing was "merely a kind of recreational fitness activity, and has no political connotations" (Lu Yuanzhen 1988b). It was precisely because this was the widespread conception that its participants could break the rules that they did. If disco had been explicitly labeled "political," it is doubtful that the fad would have been officially tolerated. It would also probably not have attracted so many older participants, because this class of people, in their twilight years, was not interested in suffering again.

In this world of the subpolitical, gender occupied a central but unacknowledged place. The debate over the bikini was at one level a debate over sex and class, though it was never overtly phrased as such. In my opinion, the fear of chaos unleashed by displays of the female body echoed the fear of violence discussed in chapter 6. It was a fear that was felt by urban men who attributed to themselves a self-control that they did not attribute to younger, less educated men. Thus, the debate over the bikini was really a debate among men about how to control other men. The popularity of disco dancing among elderly women was related to the age-old attempt of older women to control younger women (especially daughters-in-law) by reasserting a claim to youthful energy and sexuality. These conflicts originated close to the heart of the Chinese social order—the generation/gender axis—a realm which is not quite open yet to political debate because it is the ultimate source of power of the elderly patriarchs who still rule China.

BODY CULTURE AND LIMINALITY

Another characteristic of bodybuilding and disco contributed to the ambivalent popular views which did not readily identify the activities themselves as "political" or "revolutionary." This ambivalence characterizes liminal activities. As leisure, or non-work, activities engaged in for the purpose of enjoyment, they fit Victor Turner's "genres of free-time activity" (fine arts, literature, sports, and many others), which he describes as possessing liminal qualities (1982: 86; 1974: 16). This is because leisure is a "liminal," or in-between, period set off from the normative social structure represented by the world of work (1982: 40). The liminal quality of leisure activities means they can potentially bring new social structures into existence (1974: 16). They do this by allowing the members of a society to experience moments of detachment from the processes of everyday life when they can reflectively examine their own customs, choosing to discard old ones and adopt new ones, if they wish.

Bodybuilding and disco provide striking examples of how liminal activities may provide a "frame" set apart from everyday life in which new behaviors may appear and potentially spread. Bodybuilding became a "frame" within which a particular Western costume—the bikini—was acceptable, allowing a change in customs that will doubtless take years to penetrate everyday life, if at all. The extensive propaganda promoted the idea that bikinis were acceptable for female bodybuilders within the context of bodybuilding competitions, but there was no discussion or encouragement of females wearing them on beaches. Disco was also practiced within a frame set off from everyday activities and characterized by what Turner calls the "what if," or subjunctive, mode of thought. It invited onlookers to think, "What if Chinese body culture were such that old people could wear bright clothes and jump around?" Since it was only play, the participants could break the rules, knowing quite well that if they were to wear bright clothes and walk energetically down the street every day, they would suffer the disapproval of their neighbors.

In sum, bodybuilding and disco contributed to the social changes of the 1980s for two reasons: they were not defined as political activities and hence were less apt to be restricted by the Party-state, and they occupied a liminal space that allowed for experimentation with everyday norms. However, a deeper analysis of these changes shows that they were driven by long-standing class, gender, and generational power differences which, in fact, had not changed very much at all.

CHAPTER ELEVEN

"Face" and
"Fair Play"

*Sports and Morality in the
Economic Reforms*

Americans who observed early efforts to teach Western sports to Chinese people in the early 1900s often commented that the Chinese students were poor losers. According to Edward Ross (1911), "Bob" Gailey in Beijing told him that, at first, his students hung back in athletic contests because they were afraid of "losing face" if they lost. Sometimes a soccer team would quit when the game was going against them. Ross notes that gradually, however, "they are being brought around to the spirit of sportsmanship" (p. 339).

In 1913, Eugene Barnett, director of the Hangzhou YMCA, added Gene Turner to his staff to organize an interscholastic soccer league. It was a new sport in Hangzhou and instruction began from scratch. Barnett recalls,

> More difficult to inculcate than the skills and rules were the meaning and the requirements of team play and sportsmanship, whether in victory or defeat. Team effectiveness rather than the display of individual prowess was a norm which had to be learned. It was not uncommon in the early days for the losing team and its schoolmates to seek retrieval of their lost face by launching bodily assaults on the winning team

and its supporters! "A sound mind in a sound body," "team play," and "good sportsmanship" were exciting new ideas, not tired cliches, and we saw more clearly than ever before the relevance of the qualities they connoted to good citizenship in a democratic society. (1990: 89)

Is it any wonder that one of Barnett's close friends, David Yui (later National General Secretary of the Chinese YMCA), recalled to Barnett that in his boyhood the mission school teachers practically had to drive the students from their books to the sportsfields? And is it not naive when Ross writes smugly, "None of them suspect us of sinister designs in inciting their youth to make the most of the body. But athletics will strengthen the character of Young China as well as the body" (1911: 340)? By 1921, Communist Party members denounced the YMCA: "What kind of an organization is the YMCA? It is an organization, a very successful one, which employs games, amusements, and sports as stimuli to satisfy certain crude senses and instincts of the young people" (Barnett 1990: 149–50). In 1925, radical students attacked the YMCAs because they "constantly use athletics, popular education, etc., to do evangelistic work so as to smother the political thought of the youth" (Garrett 1970: 179). By the late 1920s, Chinese sportspeople had begun to take over the organization of sports meets.

John MacAloon argues that contemporary international sports have become what he calls an "empty form." By this he means that they have been emptied of the cultural and historical content that characterized them in their original (often Western European or North American) context. "As pure, that is purely empty forms for the constitution of intercultural spaces, they present themselves to the human groups interconnected by them for refilling with diverse cultural meanings" (1994b: 20). He argues that this emptying process has three aspects (1994a: 3–4). First, histories of sports are appropriated by rival groups and reinvented. Second, sports are naturalized when their foreign—frequently imperial and colonial—origins are forgotten or neutralized. Third, sports forms of different origins are mixed, as when East Asian martial arts are popularized in the West. I described these processes in chapter 2. Histories of sports were reinvented to suggest ancient Chinese roots; colonial origins were neutralized by suggesting that the Communist Party-State perfected the flawed sports system introduced by the imperialists; the indigenous martial arts were "mixed" with Western sport when they were turned into a competitive sport following the Western model and promoted internationally.

The accounts that open this chapter illustrate that sports were not an empty form when they were introduced into China. In particular, those who taught them invested them with rules of fair play and sportsmanship that were not easily understood by Chinese students, whose participation was governed by their own logic of "face." Because the missionary schools and YMCAs were backed by governments then more powerful than the Chinese, they were in a position to attach their own cultural meanings to sport. These meanings were not fully open to different interpretations until the power structure changed.[1]

Over time, the explicit morality that Western sportspeople attached to sport forms was challenged and differently interpreted in China. As Chinese took control of their sports, they began the process of emptying them of this morality and replacing them with meanings more in tune with their own culture. This chapter looks at two conflicts between the Western and Chinese sporting morality that seemed most striking. The first conflict was between the English conception of "fair play" and the Chinese notions of "face." The second conflict, related to the first, was between the Western and Chinese attitudes toward the competitive spirit.

"FAIR PLAY" AT THE TURN OF THE CENTURY

At the turn of the century, when sports were being introduced into China, the concept of "fairness" or "fair play" was perhaps the central moral value attached to Western sports. In England, the morality of "fair play" was used to justify sport as a means of character training in schools. In nineteenth-century British public-school literature, "by far the most popular moralistic exhortation was 'play the game'" (Mangan 1981: 200). The phrase "reverberated throughout the pages of journals in which secular and clerical missionaries either sought to set the world to right, or strove to maintain its rightness, through the simple expedient of propagating the public school ethic of "playing the game" (p. 202). A sense of fair play was sometimes extolled as a national character trait. A 1927 book, entitled *Character and Sportsmanship*, stated that

---

1. See Arjun Appadurai (1991) for a similar discussion of cricket's evolution in India from a "hard" cultural form to a "softer" form.

"We must be worthy of our heritage. We shall keep it through that sense of fair-play which is bred in our bones and courses through our blood, which makes a boy play the game" (Mangan 1981: 202).

Fair play was strongly emphasized by Coubertin, who was inspired by the English public school sports. In 1908, he stated: "The Olympic idea is in our view the conception of a strong physical culture based in part on the spirit of chivalry, which you [the English] so attractively call 'fair play' and in part on an aesthetic idea, the cult of beauty and grace" (1967: 19).

The concept of fair play is loaded with connotations derived from its background in English culture, specifically in English sport. *Webster's New Collegiate Dictionary* defines "fair" with such synonyms as "just," "impartial," "unbiased," and notes that it "implies an elimination of personal feelings." It is a legalistic concept, and indeed the early proponents of sport often interchanged it with the word "justice." In German, the word for "justice" (*Gerechtigkeit*) was used until eventually the English word "fair" gained popular usage.

Fair play is a complex concept, the meanings of which differ through time and among different social groups. However, one of its central tenets is that of sportsmanship, which refers, above all, to the idea that one should win and (especially) lose graciously. As Alain Caille states, "[A] game is impossible if the victor does not make it understood that the loser could have, or could in the future be the victor in his turn . . . Equally, in a game, the respect shown by the loser gives the victory its value" (1993: 4–5). A game is a social relationship that particularly resembles gift exchange in that, in order for the relationship to be successful, the participants must give and receive in a way that adds to the honor and dignity of both. Viewed in this way, good sportsmanship is not so different from the Chinese ethic of gift exchange described in chapter 9; this ethic is governed by the logic of "face." One might expect, then, that the missionary school students would have easily comprehended the rules of fair play and would have been humble losers. After all, as Johan Huizinga pointed out, "Competition for honor may also take, as in China, an inverted form by turning into a contest in politeness . . . one demolishes one's adversary by superior manners, making way for him or giving him precedence" (1970: 87). However, as Ross and Barnett noted, the Chinese did not accept defeat easily. And, as chapter 6 illustrated, leaders in Chinese sports recognize this as a continued problem today that must be combatted with thought education to inculcate civilized manners. The riots after China's loss to Hong Kong on 19 May 1985 gave unfortunate international exposure to what was known to be a potential problem. I believe that the fear of a breakdown in order also accounts for the strict adherence to sporting rules. I found that the international rules were more closely adhered to in Chinese track and field than was the case in analogous American events.[2]

In spring of 1986, I observed an event at Beijing University that brought home to me how strongly the students felt about their intramural sports. Several months after the first wave of demonstrations had subsided at Beijing University, the university's intramural championship soccer game was held. The final game between the mathematics and biology departments attracted perhaps the most avid interest of any college sports event that year; in Chinese universities, intramural sports commonly attract more interest among the student population than intercollegiate sports. Before the final game, Yuan Weimin appeared and made a speech, demonstrating the importance assigned to it by the authorities. The game was not refereed to the satisfaction of the losers, the biology department, who vented their feelings by pasting up the big-character posters that several months earlier had called for greater democracy in China. This time, however, the posters described the alleged wrongs against the biology department team and challenged anyone to come out onto the field any time and play them. The posters were pulled down within hours, and the incident did not go any farther than that.

Why is defeat sometimes difficult for Chinese to accept in silence?

THE DIFFICULTY OF TRANSLATING "FAIR PLAY" INTO CHINESE

The English concept of "fair play" does not seem to have a significant equivalent in the Chinese language.

In 1947, anthropologist Fei Xiaotong identified "fair play" as a crucial measure of moral judgment in English and American culture that did

2. Every Chinese meet I competed in was conducted according to the international rules (which dictate, among other things, that athletes cannot enter the competition area until twenty minutes before the start of their event; this helps keep order on the field). In fifteen years of competition in the United States, I only competed under international rules once (in the 1984 Olympic Trials).

not have a Chinese equivalent. A student of Malinowski, he had lived for some years in England and later, inspired by Margaret Mead's book *And Keep Your Powder Dry* (sold in Europe under the title *The American Character*), he recorded his observations on cultural differences between Chinese and Americans in his book on *Meiguorende Xingge* [*The American Character*] (1947). In it, he discussed the difficulty of translating "fair play" into Chinese:

> We have used the original word directly because it is indeed difficult to translate it. This word is a little similar to our character *li*, but after it we can add the character *rang* ["give way or yield"], while fair play is more active and can be followed by the word "to contend." With *li*, we cannot imply raising a hand to strike out, while fair play is fully accompanied by movements, one of which is the use of force. . . . Fair play also contains this meaning: that a victory not gained according to the rules is a moral loss. (Fei Xiaotong 1985: 186)

Fei's choice of *li* as the closest equivalent of "fair play" is interesting because of the ways in which these concepts were central in Chinese and Western morality, respectively. However, closer analysis shows that while they may have been functionally equivalent as guiding principles, they cannot be considered similar. *Li* was based on a notion of proper social hierarchy, while "fair play" was based on the ideal of a "level playing ground" (of course, in practice many people were kept off the playing ground in the first place). In addition, "fair play" was closely related to the existence of codified rules.[3] To "play the game" implied playing by the rules. Fei also noted the importance of rules when he stated that "fair play" means "that a victory not gained according to the rules is a moral loss." *Li*, on the other hand, is more closely tied to adherence to custom than to codified rules. The *Modern Chinese Dictionary* defines *li* as "the rites commonly observed by everyone in social life, which were shaped by habitual customs (*fengsu xiguan*)" (*Xiandai Hanyu cidian* 1987: 692). Beyond exhortations to athletes to be civilized and polite (*wenming limao*), *li* is not an important element in contemporary discourses about sport.

Fei does not even mention the closest Chinese translation of "fair,"

---

3. The discussion of "fair play" in this section is based on research by and discussions with my assistant Ren Hai.

gongping. Literally, it means "level public." It connotes selflessness and is often used in reference to economic exchange. Two common phrases refer to trade: *maimai gongping,* "be fair in buying and selling," and *gongping jiaoyi,* "a fair deal" (*A Chinese English Dictionary* 1986: 235; *Hanyu da cidian* 1988: 57). "Fair play" is often translated into Chinese as *gongping bisai* ("fair or equal competition").

I do not think that fairness was a key cultural concept in China in the 1980s. This came to my attention through my own attempts to apply the word *gongping.* There were many things about Chinese society that I thought were "unfair," but when I commented on them to my friends, I noticed that my use of *gongping* did not provoke much reaction. In the United States, to say something is "unfair" is a rather damning accusation, while an action that is "fair" is highly justified. In the past few years I have heard "fairness" used by American politicians to justify everything from the Gulf War to new taxes. *Gongping* did not seem to have quite the same moral force in Chinese. Phrases containing the characters for "right" (*dui*) or "upright" (*zheng*) probably had more moral force (for example, *bu zheng zhi feng*).

In sum, there is some (admittedly anecdotal) evidence that fair play was not a concept that was easily grasped by the Chinese: Western sports teachers in the early 1900s found it at first difficult to teach it to their Chinese students; one of China's most insightful social commentators was struck by its absence in China before the communist period; and in the late 1980s, displays of "poor sportsmanship" did occur, and the authorities exerted quite a bit of effort to forestall them.

One of the objectives of the International Olympic Committee is to promote fair play as one of the "universal, fundamental ethic[s]" mentioned in the definition of Olympism (Caille 1993: 4). That the promoters of the Olympic Movement regard fair play as a natural, universal ethic was clearly brought home to me during a conference at the International Olympic Academy in Olympia, Greece. After I suggested in my presentation that fair play does not easily cross the cultural boundary into Chinese, several members of the audience told me that they had never considered that this might be a problem.

Instead of fair play, there is a notion that permeates Chinese sports discourse in the same way that fair play and sportsmanship permeate Western sports discourse. This is the notion of "face." Thus, this serves as an example of the way in which local meanings have been added to the moral content of international sports in China.

"FACE" IN CHINESE SPORTS

There are two kinds of "face" (Hu Hsien Chin 1944). The first, expressed by the word *lian,* emphasizes the moral reputation of a person more than outward achievements. This kind of face is less common in discussions of sports. When it is necessary to distinguish the two kinds of face, I will call this kind of face "moral face." The second kind, *mianzi,* refers to "a reputation achieved through getting on in life, through success and ostentation" (p. 45). This is the kind of face that predominates in discussions of sports. I will call this "prestige face."

Moral Face: *lian*

An analysis of the logic of moral face suggests that sports success may actually violate some of the standards of the Chinese moral order. This contrasts with the righteous English statements about the moral value of "playing the game." Why are sports more morally ambiguous in the Chinese scheme? To answer this question, I will offer a popular comedy routine as an illustration of the moral problems inherent in sports from the Chinese point of view.

Crosstalk (*xiangsheng*) is the main form of stand-up comedy in China. It consists of a rapid dialogue between a comedian and his straight man. "A Hundred Ways to Boast" (*baichuitu*) was recorded by the well-known comedian Ma Ji and his sidekick Zhao Yan in 1985 and seemed to be the most popular crosstalk in China at that time. Male college students repeated the jokes to each other and the recording was played during the entertainment hour on almost every long train trip. Its popularity had not yet abated in 1988. A discussion of this comedy shows why it had such appeal to the Chinese people, for it satirized the very basis of Chinese social relationships in an extremely subtle and clever way by setting up an equivalence between bragging and sports.

The comedy begins thus (Beijing shi yinxiang chubanshe 1985):

Ma: Let's us two, right here, have a sports contest.
Zhao: Where?
M: Ah, on the stage.
Z: Sports are allowed on the stage?
M: We won't do a large-scale sport.
Z: Then what will we do?
M: Let's . . .
Z: Chess?
M: They can't see us play chess.

Z: Then shall we play tug-of-war?

M: Tug-of-war is a group event. Can two people do it?

Z: Then shall we box?

M: Boxing—it doesn't matter who's boxing who, it's all inappropriate.

Z: Then what shall we compete in?

M: Let's us two, right here, have a boasting match.

This is a key point of laughter. What is so funny? The word used here for boasting is *chui niu*, literally "blowing the bull" (the Chinese don't just "blow their horn"—they blow the whole bull). Boasting is a popular activity among same-age male friends in Beijing. They especially like to boast about their drinking abilities, but may engage in friendly boasting on any topic. However, boasting is very much a "counter-discourse." It violates the dominant public notions of decorum and, therefore, is only engaged in among close friends in a private setting. What is funny above is that Ma Ji proposes to boast in public as if it were a sports contest. The equivalency is a source for later jokes when Ma Ji rephrases the guiding slogans of Chinese sports to apply to boasting:

Zhao: But I don't have any experience in boasting matches.

Ma: That's not important . . . Practice makes perfect. Just boast your best and boast hard; before you've been boasting too long, I guarantee you'll boast your way out of Asia and advance on the world.

The original sports slogans are "Train your best and train hard" and "Break out of Asia and advance on the world."

And later:

M: Let's have a friendly competition. We won't keep points or places.

This is a pun on the "friendly competitions" that were so strongly emphasized during China's era of ping pong diplomacy.

Z: Fine.

M: We have to boast to our potential and boast with good sportsmanship.

This is a pun on the slogan "Compete to your potential, compete with good sportsmanship."

Ma Ji also establishes another important relationship—that between boasting/sports and moral face:

M: You should have confidence, you've got talent.

Z: What talent do I have?

M: Just wait a while and see, your face is pretty thick-skinned.

Z: Who's thick-skinned? I can't compare with you!

M: Don't be polite. . . .

People who act in immoral ways, as if they don't care what others think, "don't want face" (*bu yao lian*) or "have thick skin on their faces" (*lianpi hou*). Therefore, Ma Ji is pointing out that to engage in a public competition resembling a sports event is to demonstrate that one does not care for one's moral reputation. This point is brought home again at the very end of the crosstalk:

Ma: Let me tell you, I'm really tall. Real tall.

Zhao: I'm taller than you.

M: I'm two meters 78 tall.

Z: I'm three meters 69 tall.

M: I'm still taller.

Z: I'm still taller.

M: I'm as tall as the Long White Mountain Hotel.

Z: I'm two stories taller than that hotel.

M: I'm taller.

Z: I'm taller.

M: Airplanes fly into my back here.

Z: Satellites hit my feet as they go by.

M: I'm taller.

Z: I'm taller.

M: The top of my head touches the sky when my feet are standing on the earth. There's no way you can be taller than that!

Z: I'm still taller! My upper lip touches the sky and my lower lip touches the earth.

M: Ah, your upper lip touches the sky and your lower lip touches the earth. Then where is your face (*lian*)?

Z: We braggarts don't want face!

M: Right!

This crosstalk brings to the surface a cultural bias with a long history in China: people who display themselves publicly are a bit morally suspect. Naturally, there is an elitist, class-based component to this judgment. It explains, in part, the historically outcast status of actors and actresses in the imperial social order. This is a bias that has probably weakened a great deal in the last century, and certainly in the last decade. It was not an issue that I heard discussed in sports circles in those terms, though people did comment on the ways in which scanty sports clothing and vigorous movements violated concepts of proper decorum. However, the success of "A Hundred Ways to Boast" seems to indicate that people still identify with the underlying logic.

The central issue in contemporary sports is not a concern with the morality of public display per se, but rather a concern that what is displayed reflects well on the groups represented. This is reflected in the concern about the other kind of face—*mianzi*.

Prestige Face: *Mianzi*

Mianzi is a facade of personal dignity that may by extension apply to a group. It is sometimes translated as "reputation or prestige." When one's dignity is violated through exposure of weakness or embarrassment, it is said that one has "lost face" (*diu mianzi*), one's "face is ugly" (*mianzi bu haokan*). On the other hand, when one's reputation is enhanced, it is said that "a glow is added to the face" (*gei mianzishang tian guang*). When an athlete performs well in a competition, it is said that she has added a glow to the face of her coach or leaders. The word for "glow" can also be translated as "honor" or "glory," as in "winning glory for Beijing." *Mianzi* is hierarchical because people with higher status have more prestige face than those with lower status, though not necessarily more moral face.

People who are overly concerned with promoting their own reputations are said to "love face." Like the love of "fair play" which was sometimes portrayed as a national characteristic of the English, Chinese people often mentioned that "Chinese people love face," as if it were a part of the national character. This is because the notion of prestige face shapes the behavior of individuals, influences relationships between groups, and even pervades China's actions as a nation. It is interesting that, while most of the talk about the "face of China" uses the word *mianzi*, it also possible to speak of the *lian* of China: during the student demonstrations in Tiananmen Square in 1989, one banner was held aloft that read, "Li Peng, you have completely lost China's face (*lian*)." Of course, this implied a strong judgment on Li Peng's moral character.

The discourse on "face" is an unofficial discourse. In the official language, the words for honor and dignity are substituted for the colloquial phrases about face. For example, according to Chinese sport theory,

International sports competitions and the friendly communication between all nations, high or low levels in sports technique, not only reflect the state of sports, but also are measures of a nation's economic, technological, cultural and educational levels of development, and a people's physical and mental conditions. They are connected to a nation's international honor and dignity. (Quanguo tiyu xueyuan jiaocai weiyuanhui 1987: 13)

In colloquial speech, people often attribute the desire of state leaders to win Olympic medals to the fact that medals reflect well on the face of China, which in turn gives face to state leaders. For this reason, state leaders take the face of China quite seriously in international sports as well as in other realms of the international public sphere. This was evident in such events as the debate over how the film *Red Sorghum* reflected on the face of China and the Chinese responses to accusations of human rights violations during Beijing's bid for the 2000 Games (described in the Epilogue). For the 1988 Olympic Games, only athletes with a chance of placing in the top eight were chosen for the Chinese Olympic team. Up-and-coming young athletes were not allowed to participate simply for the experience. The reason was that Chinese athletes should not be seen in last place.

Another example of this attitude is the story told to me by a 400-meter runner who was originally told he had been chosen to compete in the World University Games. Unlike most of the Chinese representatives, he was a real student at a regular university (Qinghua) and had been chosen because of increasing pressure to send at least a few regular students instead of a complete contingent of professional athletes. He was instructed to begin training and did so, but a few days later the team leaders decided to send a swimmer instead. Although no one told him so, he felt the reason might be that swimmers only wear tiny little bathing suits and when they get out of the water people cannot easily see which country they represent. But if he, as a runner, placed last in his heat, with "China" in big characters on the front of his shirt, everyone would know. He said this attitude is illustrated by the saying, "Family shame should not be made known to outsiders" (*jiachou bu wang wai yang*).

Andrew Kipnis conducted interviews on the topic of face shortly after the conclusion of the 1992 Olympics. He noted that his informants often brought up the idea that having a child win a gold medal would increase their face (*lian*) more than almost anything they could imagine (Kipnis 1993: 23).

Olympic gold medals are also very important. An example is the restoration of boxing in 1980 after years of prohibition as a "bourgeois" sport that appealed to base instincts. Its restoration was strongly debated, and when it was finally accepted, an important reason was that forty-eight medals were awarded in boxing in the Olympics, so that "In world and continental multi-sport competitions, the winning or losing of boxing competitions influences the nation's overall placing to a large extent" (Bo Fei 1987). Similarly, there was great concern about building up China's swimming and track and field because these sports award a large number of medals; some people said team sports should be deemphasized because they require many people for only one medal (Shen Yanping 1988b).

The Chinese press keeps both a point score and a medal score for the Olympic Games, though neither is recognized by the International Olympic Committee. In fact, the Olympic Idea forbids official scoring for the Olympic Games. The general public is not aware that these are unofficial, and they talk frequently of the Soviet Union "beating" the U.S.A. Of course, the U.S. press also keeps a medal count as well, but a point system is not used.

One of China's most popular fiction writers in the early 1990s, Wang Shuo, utilized the national concern for face as the basis of a novel called *No Man's Land*. The story features Tang Yuanbao, a cab driver/martial artist who is chosen to restore the national reputation after an international sports loss. Tang is victorious in a series of bizarre competitions, one of which involves castrating him so he can compete in a women's event. In the final event, Tang cuts his face and peels it off to win an Olympic medal (WuDunn 1993: 3). Wang's satirical point is clear: in trying to win at all costs, China has not only castrated itself; in the final tally, it has lost its face.

Despite Coubertin's noble idea that "The important thing in these Olympiads is less to win than to take part in them" (1967: 20), Chinese sports leaders recognized that the concern for face could be used as a motivational force. They instituted a point system for the 1987 National Games to determine provincial rankings. There was general agreement that it motivated provincial leaders to pay more attention to sports, especially those whose provinces were at the bottom of the hierarchy. This was explained as an appeal to the leaders' fear of losing face.

Analysis of the two kinds of face shows that sports occupy a morally ambiguous position in the Chinese cultural scheme. This is a striking contrast with the concept of "fair play," a central organizing principle in the conception of modern Western sports. "Fair play" focuses on the morality of the process by which the winner and loser are determined. In the Chinese case, sports competitions are closely tied to the desire for superficial prestige (*mianzi*) but are rather more distant from considerations of personal morality (*lian*). If anything, the public display of the body and the competitive spirit in sports may violate notions of morality. The emphasis on prestige means that the Chinese cultural focus is much more on the end result—the hierarchy—than it is on the rules-regulated competition that leads to it. This hierarchy is taken very seriously.

This provides us with a final piece to the puzzle of why Chinese are often not "good sports." Bourdieu reminds us that fair play is "the way of playing the game characteristic of those who do not get so carried away by the game as to forget that it *is* a game" (1978: 824). However, in China sports are not "just a game." Sports losses and victories have concrete repercussions in the realm of face—for China as a nation, they are just as real as military defeats, economic accomplishments, or political reversals. The gain or loss of face has very real social consequences in China, and the link between face and sports means that Chinese people may actually take their international sports more seriously than those who first brought them to China.

THE IDEA OF COMPETITION IN THE CULTURAL REVOLUTION

The discourses of face and fair play are also inseparable from the discourses on the notion of competition. This notion has had a tortured history since it was first introduced by Yan Fu a century ago. In Yan Fu's social Darwinism, the emphasis was on the competition between groups of people or nations, not between individuals. Individual goals were to be subordinated to the good of the group, a tendency that continued to the late 1980s. Chairman Mao, though he valorized physical strength, never fully embraced the competitive spirit in sports. Instead, he made it subservient to the collective spirit and correct ideology (Hoberman 1984: 222–25). According to official ideology, physical culture was part of the "all-around education," which included moral education. The role of physical culture in education was expressed as follows:

. . . in service of socialism, physical culture ought to ultimately be expressed in the cultivation of the individual; it should insure that the members of society are all "both red and expert," that they become individuals with ideals, morals, culture, discipline, and good health; it should develop qualified, capable people for the construction of socialism. (Cao Xiangjun 1985: 196)

During the most extreme period of socialist ideology, the Cultural Revolution (1966–76), competitive sports all but ceased and the competitive spirit was denounced as "medals-and-trophyism" (*jinbiaozhuyi*). This was an attack that had first been raised by communist revolutionaries in the 1920s against the practice of giving special financial awards to top athletes in missionary schools. During the Cultural Revolution, it came to refer to an overemphasis on winning and a neglect of sports ethics. Of course, the ethics of the time were the communist political ethics that were promoted in all walks of life. Like other workers, athletes were to be both "red" and "expert."

At the height of the Cultural Revolution, Mao's wife Jiang Qing, who seemed to have a special vendetta against the State Sports Commission, dismantled the commission and placed it under the control of the military from 1968 to 1971. The popular first chairman of the commission, Marshal He Long, was harassed to death, as were outstanding sports figures throughout the nation. Sports institutes were closed, teams disbanded, fields plowed under and planted. Deng Xiaoping was denounced once for playing bridge, and again for advocating "revisionism" when he told the Chinese squad before the Asian Games in 1976, "Improve your sports skills, strive for good performances" (Rong Gaotang et al. 1984: 22–25).

With the advent of Ping Pong Diplomacy in 1971, the phrase "Friendship first, competition second" became the guiding slogan of sports. The humility of Chinese athletes in international meets disarmed some Western opponents, who felt they were being mocked when they could not tell if the Chinese were playing seriously (Hoberman 1984: 222).

THE IDEA OF COMPETITION IN THE ERA OF REFORM

The attitude toward competition has changed dramatically since the end of the Cultural Revolution and the beginning of the period of reform. After his rise to power in 1978, Deng Xiaoping, who was still very fond of bridge, initiated a broad program of economic change. "Competition" (*jingzheng*) became a key buzzword as China moved toward a competitive market economy and job market and away from rigid state planning and guaranteed lifelong jobs.

Much of the discourse resembled the social Darwinist discourse at the turn of the century: competition is good because it selects the fit and weeds out the weak; China traditionally lacked a competitive spirit and this must be changed in order for China to be successful in the worldwide competition between nations. There were also significant departures, however. The discourse on competition focused much more on the national economy and much less on national military strength. More emphasis was placed on individual competitiveness—the "competitive spirit"—and less on individual sacrifice for the good of the group. Lastly, the discourse on competitiveness was more completely integrated into an entire worldview that included concrete technologies for inculcating the competitive spirit, such as sports. Sports served as both a disciplinary technology and a metaphor for a properly operating free market economy, functions which they did not have in the social Darwinist discourse.

Under the economic reforms, competition was believed to "promote activism" by eliminating the apathy produced by a system that equally rewarded freeloaders and hard workers. Competition was to be "the source of vitality" in the reforms. "It was precisely this spirit of competition that shattered 'the big pot,' stirred back to life a pool of stagnant water" (Gui Jia 1988).

At the start of the 1988 Olympic Games, a reporter waxed eloquent with his interpretation of the Olympic Message:

> The life of all things on earth lies in competition, comes out in the midst of competition, exists and develops in the midst of competition. The life of the Olympic Games also lies in competition; it is only through fair competition that the goal of "swifter, higher, stronger" can be realized. (Lu Guang 1988)

Articles in the press portrayed an outdated, "traditional" Chinese mentality of "contending with one's lot" that must be changed. One social scientist noted, "In her long history, China has never seen normal competition that works to regulate and spur the economy and social life" (Li Honglin 1988). There seemed to be a general feeling that Chinese people were unprepared to deal with competition. "If we decide to encourage competition, we have to look reality in the face and try to avoid an undesirable psychological response from the public," noted a sociologist from the Chinese Academy of Sciences (Zhan Guoshu 1988). He proposed that the "competitive mentality" is necessary to combat feelings of insecurity.

In 1988, a series of articles in *China Women* (*Zhongguo Funü*) magazine discussed the growing problem of women's place in a competitive economy. "'*China Women*' hopes that through this . . . sincere inquiry, it can strengthen females' awareness of competition . . . create for females an equal starting point for a competitive environment" (Ma Lizhen and Song Meiya 1988).

Unlike at the turn of the century, however, sports were much better integrated into the philosophy of competition. In a book on sport theory, competition itself was said to be good for the character: "Sports are characterized by heated confrontation. This kind of confrontation is both a contest of technique and strategy, and a contest of the contestants' will, character, and fighting style" (Quanguo tiyu xueyuan jiaocai weiyuanhui 1987: 14).

Sports scholar Lu Yuanzhen argued that sports training could help transform the "traditional" mentality:

> In a self-sufficient, natural economy and society, people don't need competition, going so far as to abolish and oppose competition, because competition can disturb people's peaceful, idyllic existence. And so sport, with its extreme competitiveness, will not emerge in this kind of society . . .
> Modern society cannot separate itself from competition . . .
> In traditional Chinese culture, Confucian thought advocated, "If only man would not contend, then all under heaven would not contend," respectful humility, a yielding and shrinking national spirit, and a social attitude of diluting competition, denigrating competition; this is extremely disadvantageous to a market economy society and the education of young people in a modernized society. In a sense, competitive sport not only has actual significance in stimulating the national spirit, but also has a deep value in shaping the character of a new generation of the people. (Lu Yuanzhen 1988a)

In the discourse on competition, sports were sometimes cited as a model of how a competitive economy should work. For example, a social scientist asserted that normal competition is dependent on freedom, quality, and openness; rules should be fair and institutionalized. He illustrated his point by using a running race as a metaphor:

> It is to widen the gaps between people's abilities that competition is introduced. It is very much like a race. Putting the athletes on the same starting point is meant to decide who is the first, second and so on, instead of letting them march abreast like soldiers in a martial parade. (Li Honglin 1988)

When competition became the method of choice for promoting activism, a competition craze swept across China. It was suddenly as if people wanted to turn everything into a contest. In late 1987 and early 1988, national newspapers announced a storytelling contest for primary- and middle-school students; a quality contest for state-made lightweight vehicles; a fire department sports meet ("utilize the form of the sports meet to improve techniques of fire prevention and fire extinguishment"); the Second National Violin Manufacture Contest; a lantern riddle contest; a young people's contest of labor technique and technological manufacture; a packaging contest; and the Contest of Demonstrating Ideals and Comparing Sacrifices of Engineers and Technicians from National Industrial Enterprises; not to mention a plethora of fashion and photography contests, plus the first beauty contest since Liberation. There was even a "Healthy Children Contest" in which children between the ages of three and six were judged on their bodies and intelligence; the contest was "aimed at helping create a more healthy and competent generation of the nation's people" (Zou Hanru 1988).

One kind of contest that became extremely popular was the "knowledge contest" or quiz show. These were sometimes intended to promote public education about certain subjects. In late 1987, there was a nationally broadcast contest with such categories as "building and cultivating materialism," "the patriotic viewpoint," and "turning oneself into a New Socialist Person." There was another quiz show on "Population, Family, and Society." The *Guangzhou Evening News* published a criticism of quiz shows, noting that some sponsors of the contest published the questions in newspapers beforehand. Then the leaders in factories, government departments, or schools selected the brightest of their subordinates and gave them time off to memorize the answers so that they could win honor for the factory or department. This defeated the purpose of the contest, the article argued, which was to promote creative understanding of the issues. Instead, rote memorization stifled creativity

(Jin Shaoren 1987). The spirit of the contest was circumvented in order to bring glory to the face of the leadership.

CHENGBAO: A KIND OF BETTING

In the initial stages of the reforms, a kind of contractual arrangement that dated back to Imperial times was resurrected and reshaped to serve the needs of the changing economy. *Chengbao* ("contract") referred to an agreement between two parties, usually leaders and subordinates, establishing a goal the subordinates must accomplish. If they succeeded, they received a bonus, and if they failed, they forfeited the "risk money" (*fengxianjin*), or security deposit, that they had had to pledge. Sometimes the security deposit was set aside at the beginning of the endeavor; other times it would be subtracted from future wages and bonuses in the event of failure. The practice began in factories and construction and typically involved the setting of a deadline and cost limit for completion of a construction project, or production quotas for the manufacture of a product. One or several people signed a contract guaranteeing completion of the terms and were then given a high degree of autonomy in controlling the project.

The unique and clever feature of *chengbao* was that, as in Imperial times, it allowed parties to enter into agreements in the absence of a reliable system of contract law. Failure to fulfill the contract brought with it its own sanctions in the form of economic loss rather than legal sanctions. As practiced in the 1980s, it resembled speculation or betting. It was praised because it brought the "mechanism of competition" (*jingzheng jizhi*) into play. Newspaper articles argued that *chengbao* wrapped risk, responsibility, control, and benefit into one, thus stimulating activism and allowing talent to distinguish itself (Xu Yaozhong 1988; Zhang Zhenguo 1988).

The sportsworld was one of the first to implement the practice of *chengbao*. One would think that sports performances are less controllable than factory performances, but this did not deter the practice. In some ways, it may have been easier to institute the practices in sports because the standards of success and failure were absolute.

As practiced in sports work units, *chengbao* was not unlike sports gambling. An example was the case described to me of five university coaches. A contract was drawn up between the cadres of the university's physical culture office and five of the track and field coaches. The administrators agreed to allow the coaches to recruit a certain number of athletes with low scores on the national college entrance exam, to give some financial subsidy to the athletes, and to upgrade facilities. The coaches pledged to improve the university's placing in the annual city collegiate sports meet by one place over the seventh place achieved in the previous year. If the coaches succeeded, they would receive 2,000 yuan; if they failed, they would have to pay 500.

Many examples were given in the press. A fairly complex contract was set up between the Beijing City Sports Commission and the Xiannongtan Sports Technique School. The latter pledged that, together, several coaches would win one gold, one silver, and one bronze medal at the Seventh Games in 1993. The risk money ranged from three to five thousand yuan. After two years, the contractors would undergo a review, and if they had failed to uphold the contract thus far they would lose 50 percent of the risk money. If they failed in the end to meet the medal quota, they would lose all of the risk money. Those who succeeded would be returned twice the risk money as a bonus. This type of arrangement was said to be a way of changing the unfair situation of equal rewards regardless of coaching performance (Yang Mali 1988).

Another example was that of the Hubei provincial track team coaches, who entered into a five-year contract with the head of the provincial sports training center. They pledged to win forty points at the Seventh National Games (up from twenty in 1987). The leaders pledged to provide the coaches with a certain quota of athletes they could recruit, the necessary facilities and equipment, medical care, competitions, scientific backup, and other conditions; the coaches would be responsible for recruiting, training, and managing the athletes and overseeing their competitions, tests, and political and ideological education; they also pledged to win between one and six points each in the Seventh Games. Each coach put up risk money of 1,000 yuan. If they succeeded, they would be returned from 1.5 to 3 times over the deposit; also, for each point over one that their athletes won, they would receive 20 percent of the risk money as a bonus. If they failed, they would forfeit the deposit (Qian Deng 1988).

In the spirit of reform and competition, one especially ambitious coach approached the head of his provincial training center and proposed that if the team head would give him a yearly operating budget of 10,000 yuan (a fraction of the current budget) and turn the track and field team over to him, he would pledge to win twice as many points in the Seventh Games as the team had won in the Sixth Games. The team leader pointed out that the coach couldn't possibly put up enough risk money, and the coach replied that he would be willing to forfeit all of his future salary and bonus money for the rest of his life. The leader turned down the offer. If the coach had succeeded, it would have caused the team to lose face. But the coach had made his point: there was an incredible waste of money in the team; many coaches were so apathetic that they never went to practice but still drew salaries. If he, a single person, controlled the team, he could do it at a fraction of the cost and get better results as well.

SPORT IN THE ECONOMIC REFORMS

The State Sports Commission was at the forefront of China's shift toward a more competitive economy. When Li Menghua became chairman of the State Sports Commission in 1981, he was one of the first state leaders to "break the big pot" by instituting a new incentive system. He said his philosophy was, "Give bonuses until eyes turn red [with jealousy]; fine them until their hearts hurt" (Li Xiaofei 1987). In addition to *chengbao,* sports teams also implemented the new practices of voting for managers (in this case head coaches), giving out letters of appointment (*pinshu*) for jobs, and instituting "democratic management" of teams. The last had become a necessity as athletes' star status increased and they became less willing to obey orders. One innovation was by Zhejiang province, which set up insurance policies for top athletes to remove their worries about serious injury (Lin Nan 1988).

Reviving some of the social Darwinist imagery from a century ago, *Sports News* summarized the role of sport in the reforms as follows:

> Opening up to the outside world in a basic sense is allowing us to enter into a worldwide competition, and also allowing us to become victors in this kind of competition. It was precisely China's sports, this world competition for "survival of the fittest," and the many sports which gained victory in the competition, which caused old concepts like "eating out of the big pot," "lining up for wages according to seniority," "suffering because of your [young] age," etc., to first lose their market in the realm of sports. (Zhang Yaohong 1988)

At the highest levels of government, the competitive spirit characteristic of sport had made an impression. The Minister of Culture, Wang Meng, cited the Sports Commission as a model for other state ministries and commissions in his discussion of the implementation of mechanisms of competition in the fine arts world. He remarked,

> In the past few years there was a lot of discussion in society, asking, why has our sport had a comparatively successful development? Beside the fact that the state has adopted many measures, established many organs, and started children at a young age, many comrades feel that the mechanism of competition in sport is comparatively well developed, that the competition is fierce, moreover that results cannot be disputed. For example, go king Nie Weiping cannot be disputed. Then there is the renewal of the team; due to the nature of sports activity, this replacement of old with new cannot be disputed nor resisted, you might even say it is "merciless replacement." Naturally, the arts and sport are different; for example, the arts don't have publicly recognized standards. But the realm of arts is full of competition, full of opportunities, full of risk, likewise requires the fighting spirit, requires one to fulfill his highest potential . . . (*Zhongguo tiyu bao* 1988)

CONCLUSIONS:
INTERNATIONAL SPORTS AS AN EMPTY FORM

Across the time period from the introduction of sports into China by Western Christian organizations, to the apex of socialist collectivism in the Cultural Revolution, to the market reforms of the 1980s, it is possible to chart the ways in which sports were emptied of their muscular Christian moral content and replaced with contents that suited the needs of politics and the tenor of the times in China. The muscular Christian morality of fair play, citizenship, and democracy was replaced over time with Chinese discourses about national prestige and international competition. While the physical structure of modern sports is fixed by international rules, there is quite a bit of room for variability in the cultural beliefs that accompany them. An example of this variability was the importance of the logic of "face" in Chinese sports and the difficulty of translating the concept of "fair play" into Chinese. However, this variability is not limitless. Modern sports and the free market economy share some rules of formation. In China, this point was illustrated by the incompatibility of sports with the collective socialist mentality of the Cultural Revolution followed by the glorification of sports in the era of reform.

This diversity within a unified framework reiterates the point I made in the first chapter: There is no unified world culture of the body, but there is more unity than there used to be. The unity stems from the fact that once one accepts the vision of China as one nation among others in a worldwide competition, then there are certain ground rules that must be obeyed in order to compete. If a nation "wins" by obtaining Olympic gold medals or a higher per capita income level, then it must follow certain international codes to do so. There are those, like the novelist Wang Shuo, who believe that in order to do so China must castrate itself and tear off its face. There are others, like the supporters of economic reform, who believe that by entering into this competition China will bring itself back to life. In reality, there is no black-and-white resolution to the conflicts introduced by nationalist thinking and the transnational flow of culture which since the turn of the century have caught up China, like the rest of the world, in a maelstrom of change.

EPILOGUE

Beijing's Bid for the 2000 Olympic Games

On 23 September 1993, the host city for the Olympic Games to be held in the year 2000 was decided by a vote of the International Olympic Committee. The winner was Sydney, Australia. This was the first year that a PRC city had bid for the Games, an event that attracted global media attention. In 1964, the Tokyo Olympic Games had marked Japan's emergence as a world power; in 1988, the Seoul Olympic Games had marked South Korea's emergence as a world power; Beijing's hosting of the 2000 Games was to mark China's emergence as a major player on the world stage. Beijing campaigned zealously to host the 2000 Games and appeared to have a very good chance of winning (see table 12.1); it led the vote counts until the last round, when most of the votes for Manchester, which had been eliminated in the previous round, moved over to Sydney.

All over the country, Chinese people watched the live broadcast of the announcement of the winning bid. Despite a mistranslation that led them at first to think they had won, they accepted the defeat with a calm that surprised observers. Many people had feared that a loss would spark a riot like that after the China-Hong Kong soccer game in 1985, or ill-feeling like that after China won only five medals in the 1988 Olympic

Table 12.1 Numbers of IOC Votes for the Host City of 2000 Olympics

Olympic Host City	Round			
	1	2	3*	4*
Beijing	32	37	40	43
Sydney	30	30	37	45
Manchester	11	13	11 (out)	
Berlin	9	9 (out)		
Istanbul	7 (out)			

*one abstention

Games. Although they were bitterly disappointed, people seemed to accept the loss with resignation. Lu Yuanzhen commented to me that they went back to work the next day as if nothing had happened. He observed, "This demonstrates that China has matured."

The course of events leading up to Beijing's bid and its loss to Sidney serve as a postscript to summarize the main themes of this book. In particular, it reveals the changing representations of the Chinese nation that circulated within China and abroad and the key role that gender played in them.

OLYMPIC GAMES: SELLING A NATIONAL IMAGE TO THE WORLD

Beijing's bid has to be viewed against the changing global political economy that was a backdrop to the event. The Olympic Games now attract a larger world audience than they ever have, and the bidding process is more hotly contested than ever before. Hosting an Olympic Games is viewed as a way of projecting an image of a city and a country to a global audience and advertising them to an increasingly accessible world market. With the demise of the Cold War and the revolution in global telecommunications, the Olympic Games increasingly serve as an arena for debate about modern nationhood and international relations. As John MacAloon notes, "Being a nation, having a culture, are the chief requirements for claiming a rightful and autonomous place in the global system." And, "To be a nation recognized by others and realistic to themselves, a people must march in the Olympic Games Opening Ceremonies procession" (1991a: 42).

The opening ceremonies for the 1992 Barcelona Olympic Games were produced by one of Catalonia's premier advertising agencies, Bassat, Ogilvy and Mather. Luis Bassat, chair of the division that created and produced the opening ceremonies, said that they had won the contract by telling the Barcelona Olympic organizing committee that instead of making a ceremony, they would make a commercial about Barcelona and Spain for the world. They calculated that a three-hour advertisement of Barcelona broadcast simultaneously worldwide would cost 30 billion dollars in order to make their point that this was an opportunity to promote the reputation of Barcelona that, outside of the context of the Olympic Games, could not be bought (Bassat 1993).

Likewise, Beijing in its bid emphasized the tremendous market that would be opened to Olympic sponsors and the gigantic potential Chinese television audience, said to be one billion. The Chinese Olympic Committee enlisted the top American producer of inspiring sports documentaries, Bud Greenspan, to produce three promotional videos to be shown to IOC members. Like other marketing efforts, these videos avoided the human rights issues and focused on China's ancient culture, rapidly developing economy, and recent sports successes.[1]

In sum, the Olympic Games have become the world's largest single event for the production of national culture for international consumption.

China's preparations for its Olympic bid had begun with its National Sports Games in 1987, which were attended by Juan-Antonio Samaranch, president of the IOC. As discussed in chapter 4, starting with those games, representations of the nation underwent a rapid transition that must be attributed to China's increasing openness to the outside world and associated desire to shape an image of itself for foreign consumption. As in the Soviet Union and other socialist countries, the opening ceremonies for the National Games had always been an occasion for the demonstration of mass calisthenics on a scale not seen in the West since World War II. (In the West, this performance genre was discredited by the Nazi mass displays. For this reason West Germany has not had a national sports games since the war.) Mass calisthenics visually represented the militaristic, egalitarian, and collective body culture of the Maoist era. Six national games were held in China between 1959

1. I appeared in two brief cameo interviews in one of the videos (for which I and other interviewees were not compensated). Although I had reservations about the adequacy of Beijing's infrastructure, I personally felt that hosting an Olympic Games could bring positive changes to China, so I took this as an opportunity to describe some of the contributions that sport has made to China's political and economic development.

and 1983 in which mass calisthenics as a way of representing the nation were not challenged. Most of those mass calisthenics shows had revolutionary themes: one of my favorites is the 1965 act entitled "Tightly Grip the Gun in your Hand."

The 1987 National Games were the first games in which the choreographers debated doing away with mass calisthenics in the opening ceremonies and attempting a more "artistic" show such as they had seen on television during the 1984 Los Angeles Olympics. In 1987, the militaristic body was on its way out and the consumer body was on its way in under the policies of economic reform and opening-up. The Games almost marked a turning point, but in the end the mass calisthenics were kept because the choreographers were more confident in their ability to succeed with them.

However, the choreographers considered the 1987 mass calisthenics innovative because of their combination of "traditional" and modern elements. The traditional elements represented local Guangdong culture to the rest of China and included a bamboo pole dance borrowed from a minority group, a dragon dance, and the act entitled "Pride." This act took the audience into China's mythical past, with girls dancing in pastel dresses with scarves and boys performing southern-style martial arts in black-and-white military costumes. It stood out from the other acts for its strong degree of sexual differentiation in dress and style of movement. The placard section showed scenes from China's history, such as the Great Wall and the Yellow River. Afterwards, the choreographers were well aware that on the whole it was the best received act in the show.

In the year following the 1987 National Games, opening ceremonies in sports meets around Beijing showed a new development: "disco" became the preferred performance genre. As discussed in chapter 10, disco performances were substituted for mass calisthenics in the 1988 Beijing University sports meet and the Beijing City college meet. The similarity between disco and the innovative act in the National Games was that gender appeared as a central symbol in both. The difference was that, in the first instance, it was inspired by a Western practice and, in the second, by the resurrection of a romanticized Chinese past.

When they began work on the show for the 1990 Asian Games, the choreographers were determined to use "traditional" Chinese elements more fully than had yet been done. As one of them explained to me afterwards, the artistic program was the culmination of a course of development that traced its roots to the 1975 National Games. The choreographers had found the militaristic mass calisthenics of those games, which were held during the Cultural Revolution, so unsatisfactory that they had spent the years since then searching for a better way to express the spirit of the Chinese people. By 1990 they were ready to bring their ideas to fruition. Three of the six acts for the Asian Games opening ceremonies used motifs that were announced as "folk traditions" (*minzu chuantong*); their titles were "Festival Drum Dance," "Lotus Swaying on Water," and "Chinese *wushu* [martial arts]." They utilized the costumes and dances of "national minorities," huge drums and racks of bells, and placard sections showing imperial symbols such as the Summer Palace, the Great Wall, dragons, horses, and so on. The ceremonies emcee repeated several times that "China is an ancient people (*gulaode minzu*)." The transition that had taken place from 1987 to 1990 continued a trend in changing representations of the nation. The revolutionary mass calisthenics had never been described as a Chinese tradition grounded in Chinese history. The techniques had been borrowed primarily from Czechoslovakia in the 1970s. Although many in the PRC audience were nevertheless moved by the performances, Overseas Chinese in Hong Kong and elsewhere often regarded them with distaste because they provided a powerful visual image of the imposition of communist disciplinary techniques upon the bodies of the populace. In the late 1980s, with exposure to disco, breakdancing, the Los Angeles Olympics, and other forms of international popular culture, it began to occur to some Chinese that the Chinese body on the whole was rather "stiff" and that mass calisthenics were one manifestation of it. Two people who commented on this used the word for "dead" (*si, siban*) to describe this rigidity, and one person located it particularly in the hip area.

The 1990 Asian Games show, on the other hand, made use of symbols that, as the choreographers had discovered in 1987, evoked positive emotions among the majority of Chinese people. They were much more an expression of a popular nationalism. This shift was precipitated by the National Games being mainly a representation of the Chinese nation to itself, while the Asian Games were a representation of China to the rest of Asia and the outside world. Even the newly constructed National Olympic Sports Center utilized architecture with "Chinese characteristics"—something that was never considered important before. As one of the choreographers later wrote to me, "We wanted to publicize to the world the shape of our country's political and economic affairs under the reforms and opening-up and our splendid national culture (*minzu wenhua*)" (Liu Xiyu 1994). The Asian Games occurred in a socio-political context in which such expressions were increasingly permissible and emotional.

The same core members of a national team of choreographers designed the opening ceremonies for the Asian Games and the previous three National Games. The choreographers are not usually subject to direct control by the top state leaders. Thus, the move toward popular expressions of nationalism was not directly controlled by the state leaders, but involved an entire hierarchy of producers of international and national culture.

A final point is that this move was accompanied by a greater emphasis on gender symbolism in the opening ceremonies. In the acts that made use of "tradition," most of the choreography and costuming for the men had a decided military flavor while the women performed more delicate moves in dresses with nonmilitary props such as fans. This was mitigated somewhat by having both girls and boys perform the martial arts in one of the acts. Overall, however, the Asian Games ceremonies took a huge step away from the androgynous military mass calisthenics in which both the men and the women had tightly gripped their guns.

Thus, gender occupied a prominent position in the rejection of the old communist body culture that I have outlined from 1987 to 1990. This was evident both in the disco dancing that was utilized in local ceremonies and in the so-called traditional elements used in the National and Asian Games. In the first case, a Western practice was appropriated and reinterpreted; in the second case, historical and non-Han practices. This difference in itself reflected a trend in public culture, in which the rejection of communism was first associated with an infatuation with things Western, and which then moved toward an effort to rediscover things Chinese as China strove to preserve an identifiable (and marketable) national culture as it moved into the global arena.

NATIONAL SYMBOLS IN THE INTERNATIONAL ARENA

This new representation of the nation must also be placed in the context of the PRC's multiplying links with Overseas Chinese. The "Two China Question" has often been played out in major sports events; until 1987, Taiwan was represented as a province by PRC athletes who marched in the Parade of Athletes at the National Games (they were said to have kinship connections in Taiwan), and performances by Taiwanese athletes were recognized as PRC national records. In the 1980s, sports events served as a focal point for diplomatic efforts by PRC leaders toward Taiwan: Taiwan was invited to the 1987 National Games and its failure to respond was symbolically represented for the first time by the absence of a "Taiwan" team in the Parade of Athletes. Beijing offered to allow Taiwan to host some of the events in the 2000 Games. Large numbers of Overseas Chinese groups came out in favor of Beijing's bid. In New York, Paris, and the Netherlands, organizations of Overseas Chinese came together to write letters of support (*China Daily* 1993a). *China News Digest,* an electronic mail network started by Chinese students in American and Canadian colleges, with some 30,000 subscribers worldwide, advertised a campaign to send a letter of support to the IOC. Many organizations were formed in Hong Kong to support the bid, and Hong Kong developer Timothy Fok offered $300 million toward a new Olympic stadium to be named after him. I. M. Pei, the Chinese American architect, agreed to design it.

Not all Overseas Chinese shared the PRC's revolutionary history; in fact, many left the mainland to escape it. When PRC leaders made overtures to them in the 1980s in an effort to secure international goodwill and global capital, it was necessary to find a repertoire of national symbols with significance to Overseas and Mainland Chinese alike. The result was that the international influence contributed toward the reinvention of "national" symbols that borrowed from the "traditional" and imperial history rather than the communist. Brackette Williams has pointed out that "the position of a national elite in the international arena is part of what structures and delimits its ability to authenticate cultural forms in its national arena" (1990: 113). PRC leaders' desire to court Overseas Chinese limited the sorts of national symbols that could be used at sports events.

MARKET FORCES IN THE BIG RED MACHINE

As the day of the vote on the host country for the 2000 Olympics neared, six Chinese women runners shocked the world of track and field by taking six of nine medals in the long distance events at the world championships in Stuttgart. In the Eighth National Games less than three weeks later, seven women shattered the world records in the

10,000, 3,000, and 1500 meters. Perhaps the location of the world championships in Stuttgart contributed to the unusually open accusations against the Chinese of drug use. The rage of the fans and journalists crystallized around the idea that China was now carrying on the worst traditions of the former East Germany.[2]

In the Western press, the idea of the PRC as the heir to East Germany had begun to congeal at the 1992 Olympic Games when the extremely muscular Chinese women had suddenly dominated the swimming events. In a phone interview with me after the runners' record-breaking performances, an American reporter repeatedly mentioned the "East German coaches" now coaching in China. Finally, I asked him if he actually knew of any East German coaches, and I told him that to my knowledge—and this was also reiterated by Chinese officials—the last East German coach had worked with Chinese swimmers in 1986–87. I had been told this by Günther Lange, a West German running coach who was a visiting coach at the national team center in 1987. In those days before the fall of the Berlin Wall, West Germany collected intelligence on the East German sports system, whose training methods were classified as state secrets. Lange was West Germany's response to East Germany's swim coach in a sort of competition in sports diplomacy. Since he had worked with young middle-distance runners, it was far more logical to think that it was *his* expertise, not that of the East German swim coach, that had led to the current successes. Funded by Krupp Steel, he had brought with him several very expensive pieces of sports medicine equipment. The journalist responded to my question by saying that while there were no East German coaches at the national team center, they could be out in the provinces.

All but one of the runners who performed so well trained on the Liaoning province team, not the national team—a sign of the decentralization that has occurred in sports. Given the rivalries between provincial teams and the national team center, even if there were a systematic use of drugs on professional teams, it is highly unlikely that the program would be centrally administered as it was in East Germany. This is a point that the international sporting press failed to adequately grasp.

2. Academic budgets don't always allow us to hobnob with the producers of international culture. My understanding of the debates that circulated in the international press is based on conversations with an American reporter and a member of the Atlanta Committee for the Olympic Games who were in Stuttgart, my reading of periodicals, and discussions with European sports scholars.

Allen Richardson, chair of the International Swimming Federation medical committee, echoed this inaccurate view with his statement, "This [China] is a country with a totalitarian governmental system, which is just the right milieu for either terrorism or organized drug use" (Hersh 1993: 1). Under the reforms, the center's control of the periphery has increasingly weakened in the state sports system, like other systems. The coach of the Liaoning runners openly discussed his training methods in press conferences. Showing how far the sportsworld has moved from the days of the East German state secrets, he said he could not discuss his methods in detail *because he wanted to patent them!* And setting up an almost comic "exotic oriental" stereotype, he held up a box of herbal medicine and explained that his women athletes drank a tonic made from Chinese caterpillar fungus. In addition, he had studied the running motion of horses and dogs, but "It's from deer and ostrich that I found the key to success in distance running" (*China Daily* 1993b). He was reported in the Beijing Evening News to have sold a secret formula to the Today Group, a maker of health drinks, for 10 million yuan ($1.15 million) (*Track and Field News* 1994a: 60). Other reports were that he dismissed one of his athletes because, among other things, she had refused to share with him the Mercedes she received for her world championship and that he had threatened to resign from his job as provincial coach unless he was paid the $150,000 in bonus money promised to his team after their outstanding performances (*Track and Field News* 1994b: 66). Although it was hard to verify these reports, which were often contradictory and were culled from the Chinese press, it seemed that the "mercurial" Ma Junren was no straight-line Party man. The point is that Ma and his athletes were not simply cogs in a socialist sports machine. On the contrary, it was the loosening of state control that made it possible and lucrative for an ambitious man like Ma to exploit female athletes to benefit himself (and them—at whatever cost). This was not centralized socialism run rampant—it was free enterprise run rampant. This same situation occurs in the United States and closely resembles the relationship between a certain American track and field coach and his female athletes in the 1970s to mid 1980s, which eventually resulted in the coach being banned from coaching for life by the U.S. track and field federation.[3]

---

3. Several of my competitors trained under this coach, who was the model for the coach featured in the feature film *Personal Best* (1981). It has been suggested that I should say some-

In any case, it was clear that with the end of the Cold War, American sports journalists had some trouble adapting their reporting styles. Old paradigms die hard, and as China became a "world sports power," sports journalists found it all too easy to slip China into the slot of the "Big Red Machine" formerly occupied by the Eastern Bloc sports teams. What was important to the Western press was not the nature of social changes in any one country, but the replication of a set of international oppositions that had taken on a life of their own.

The amazing thing about the women runners was that they had performed well beyond what had been conceived as possible even for Soviet, German, or American women who were on steroids. One of the world records that was broken belonged to a Soviet who had herself tested positive for steroids several years after setting the record; it is not unlikely that steroids had aided her record performance. The implication seemed to be that even if they were taking known drugs, there must be something else at work, too. Some reports mentioned the point raised by Bill Sweetenham, Hong Kong's national swim coach: "In their defense, the motivation for the Chinese to succeed is 20 times that of athletes in the Western world . . . Chinese athletes are much more willing to pay a higher price in enthusiasm, dedication and willingness to train" (Hersh 1993: 8). However, none of the reports delved into the *gendered* nature of this dedication. As I discussed in chapter 8, rural Chinese women's "willingness" to "pay the price" is, in part, a product of their limited opportunities outside of sports and the perception that they are better adapted to bitter lives.

---

thing about my own experience as an elite athlete who probably would have been ranked higher nationally if all of my competitors had been drug-free (though, of course, I never knew for certain). Indoctrinated as I was into the "win-at-all-costs" mentality, my primary feeling toward these athletes was awe at the thought that they would be willing to make the ultimate sacrifice—their bodies—in order to win. At that time, I thought that winning did not mean enough to me, hence my choice not to use steroids was actually due to my not being willing to "pay the price." It is only now, in retrospect, that I realize that my rather long career of competition at the national level (thirteen years, in which I finished every pentathlon/heptathlon that I started) demonstrated *more* dedication than was possessed by most of my pharmaceutically enhanced rivals. I cannot view steroid-users simply as "cheaters" because I know the kinds of social pressures and constructed realities that make steroids seem like the ultimate test of one's dedication to the pursuit of excellence. On the other hand, in both China and the United States, I heard secondhand rumors about athletes (including athletes coached by the man mentioned above) who unknowingly took steroids from coaches who had told the athletes they were being given vitamins. I find this a far more deplorable situation.

WOMEN WHO REPRESENT THE NATION

The gender stereotypes that emerged from Western accusations and Chinese responses could almost be arranged as a dialogue:

> Western press: "Why are the women suddenly so good while the
> men remain so average? . . . because anabolic steroids work bet-
> ter on women than men." (*Track and Field News* 1993: 74)
> Chinese press: "The Chinese female athletes can withstand hard-
> ships better than the men" (*China Daily* 1993c, quoting the
> deputy secretary general of the Chinese Association of Sports
> Medicine). "All the runners I chose are from rural areas. They
> are used to enduring difficulties. Otherwise how could they
> bear to run a marathon a day at the high altitude of 2,236 me-
> tres? Who else in the world does this?" (Coach Ma Junren,
> *China Daily* 1993b)

The repeated assertions by Chinese officials that they had discovered Chinese women could train harder than men, and the disbelief expressed by Western sportspeople and in letters to the editors of *Track and Field News,* serve as evidence for the different constructions of gender in Chinese and Western sports, as discussed in chapter 8.

The controversy over the Chinese women runners reveals the different ways in which women "represent" the nation in Chinese and Western sports. In the West, it is obvious that female athletes often do not "represent" the nation in the same way that males do. MacAloon (1995: chap. 3) describes the participation of women in the modern Olympic Games as being in tension with an underlying Western cultural logic which dictates that young women should be the prizes for the male victors. He observes that young women present the medals at the victory ceremonies, and no ceremony has ever involved young men presenting medals to women. The lone exception was the Melbourne Olympics in 1956, in which medals were borne by Boy Scouts—who, however, were not young marriageable men.

The outrage that the Western sportsworld expressed against the Chinese distance runners was probably enhanced by the fact that they were women. What was so disturbing was the specter of a state—thought to be now dead—whose disciplinary techniques penetrated equally the bodies of women and men, and the sight of the "Ma-family soldiers," whose bodies might be sacrificed for national glory in a way that Western cultural logic would reserve only for men. And unlike in the West, the financial rewards for the Chinese women would have been the same if they had been men.

The 1993 Chinese National Games were scheduled to conclude just before the IOC vote on the Olympic host city. These Games were to showcase all that is best about Chinese sports, and the Chinese hailed the women's breaking of the world records as a way of attracting the world's attention. Instead, the victories worked against Beijing when people cited the Big Red Machine image as one more reason that Beijing should not get the Games.

And, of course, for a variety of reasons Beijing did not get them. Human rights groups had campaigned against the bid as a protest against the killing of workers and students in the 1989 Tiananmen uprising, the continued imprisonment of political dissidents, the systematic denial of freedom of religion and speech, the use of prison labor, and the suppression of the separatist movement in Tibet. The U.S. House of Representatives passed a resolution calling on the IOC to reject Beijing's bid, and sixty senators signed a similar letter to the IOC. Many observers felt that this meddling by the U.S. government might backfire, given the IOC's commitment to preserving its own autonomy. However, the Chinese government released many imprisoned dissidents and priests, a move that was perceived as hypocritical by many Western observers. When a Chinese delegation sought out a member of the Atlanta team that successfully bid for the 1996 Games for advice, they were told outright that they would have to overcome a severe public relations problem. However, success was all in how they marketed themselves; they had to focus on their strong points.

The strongest point in the bid was the argument that a truly international Olympic Movement would have to encompass the non-Western world: to date, only the Tokyo and Seoul Olympics had been held outside of Anglo-European countries. President Samaranch had developed strong Chinese ties since coming to office, which was rumored to be part of his strategy for gaining a Nobel Peace Prize for the IOC.

After the decision, and amidst rumors that they would boycott the Atlanta Games in retaliation, the Chinese hastened to assert that they would be in Atlanta and would bid again for the 2004 Games. There is a possibility that Beijing will win the 2004 Olympic Games and, if it does, then we may observe a Chinese political economy that seems to approach nearer to Western ideals of human rights, the free market economy, and political openness, while at the same time we may observe the most dazzling display to date of the cultural diversity that lies under the umbrella of the Olympic Movement. In other words, we may observe what Marshall Sahlins calls "the creation of difference in the very process of integration" (1990: 79). Whatever happens, the Olympic Movement and international sports will continue to be a primary channel through which global cultural forms flow into and out of China.

SELECT GLOSSARY OF CHINESE TERMS AND NAMES

an shen	安身	To settle down.
baichuitu	百吹图	"A Hundred Ways to Boast." A popular crosstalk comedy.
Bao Sushan	包苏珊	Chinese name of Susan Brownell.
baogao hui	报告会	Lit., report meeting. A type of public event in which a team discusses how it achieved an important sports victory.
baogao wenxue	报告文学	Reportage literature; an important genre in the Democracy Movement of 1989.
Beijing ribao	北京日报	*Beijing Daily.*
bentou	奔头	Lit., way out; refers to social mobility through sports.
biaoshuai	表率	Lit., model, example. Refers to the role Party members and coaches should play on teams.
biaoyangshu	表扬书	Certificate of commendation; a reward for meritorious behavior.
Bingbai Hancheng	兵败汉城	"Defeat of the Troops in Seoul." Controversial piece of reportage by Zhao Yu.
bu dong shi	不懂事	Lit., doesn't understand things. Naive; said of peasant athletes.
bu fuhe guoqing	不符合国情	Lit., does not suit the national conditions. Said of bikinis worn by women bodybuilders.
buhao	不好	Lit., not good. Bad.

bu yao lian	不要脸	Lit., doesn't want face. Immoral.
bu zheng zhi feng	不正之风	Lit., incorrect wind; refers to violations of state policy.
caipiao	菜票	Tickets exchanged for meat and vegetable dishes in communal dining halls.
Cao Xiangjun	曹湘君	Professor and Chair of the Sport Management Department at the Beijing Institute of Physical Education.
chahua hui	茶话会	Lit., tea and talk meeting. Public event in which selected people meet with political figures and sports stars.
changshan jieji	长衫阶级	Lit., long-gown class. Referred to the scholar-official class in imperial times.
chengbao	承包	Lit., contract. A method of economic reform that gave individuals greater responsibility for the outcome of projects.
Chen Hongmou	陈宏谋	Statesman (1696–1771), author of works on women and the family.
chibaole chengde	吃饱了撑的	Lit., to eat until one is stuffed. A peasant insult referring to useless activities engaged in by people with too much leisure, formerly applied to sports.
chiku nailao	吃苦耐劳	Lit., eat bitterness and endure hard labor. An ability attributed to female athletes, especially peasants.
chuantong	传统	Tradition. Opposed to things that are *xiandaide*.
chuantong tiyu xiangmu zhongxue	传统体育项目中学	A regular middle school that is traditionally strong in a few sports events and receives state support for them.
chui niu	吹牛	Lit., to blow the bull. To brag or boast, a popular pastime among Chinese men.
chulu wenti	出路问题	The exit problem. Refers to athletes' difficulty in finding good jobs after retiring from sports.
chushen	出身	Class background.
ciji	刺激	Stimulation, provocation; said of females who bare their arms and legs.
cu	粗	Vulgar, boorish.

daibiao	代表	To represent; said of both athletes and political figures who represent entire groups.
daibiaotuan	代表团	Delegation; a team chosen to represent a group.
dajing xiaoguai	大惊小怪	To be alarmed at something trivial; said of the reaction to women bodybuilders.
Dangdai	当代	*Contemporary Times*, a magazine.
daoluan fenzi	捣乱分子	Lit., chaotic element. Label applied to soccer fans.
Daotai	道台	An official title in imperial times.
Da Qing Huidian	大清会典	Statutes of the Qing. Instructions for conducting rituals of state.
de-zhi-ti (mei)	德智体 (美)	Moral, intellectual, physical, (aesthetic); describes the all-around education.
dian	典	Celebration conducted by the state, non-familial ritual; a type of public event.
dianli	典礼	Same as above.
ding hun	定婚	To become engaged to be married; forbidden on sports teams.
disike	迪斯科	Phonetic approximation of English "disco." A kind of fitness dancing popular among the elderly.
diu mianzi	丢面子	To lose face.
dong	动	Movement, activity; in the early 1900s, said to be characteristic of the West and opposed to the *jing* of China.
dongren	动人	Emotionally moving.
dongya bingfu	东亚病夫	"Sick Man of East Asia." An insult that the Chinese believed was applied to them by Japan and the West; a goal of international sports successes was to disprove it
dongyuan gongzuo	动员工作	Lit., mobilization work. Refers to efforts made to persuade reluctant parents to allow children to enter sports schools.
duanlian shenti	锻炼身体	Train the body. An exhortation linked with the goal of strengthening the Chinese nation.
Duanwu	端午	Dragon Festival; an important festival in the lunar calendar, celebrated with boat races.

dui	对	Correct, proper; used to refer to social justice more frequently than *gongping*.
exi	恶习	Bad habit; refers to (mostly male) athletes who smoke, engage in premarital sex, and look at pornography.
fa	法	Law; in Confucian statecraft, opposed to *li*, ritual.
fazhan tiyu yundong, zengqiang renmin tizhi	发展体育运动, 增强人民体质	"Develop physical culture and sports, strengthen the people's physiques." An endorsement penned by Mao which became the guiding slogan in sports.
Fei Xiaotong	费孝通	Noted anthropologist, cultural critic.
fei zhengchangde qudao	非正常的渠道	Lit., irregular channel. Used by dissident students in 1985 to refer to the use of a xeroxed pamphlet to spread their message.
fen	分	Social role; a concept used by Chen Hongmou.
fengsu xiguan	风俗习惯	Customs and habits.
feng xian fei	凤先飞	Lit., the phoenix takes off first. Refers to the success of Chinese women in international sports relative to the failures of Chinese men.
fengxianjin	风险金	Risk money, security deposit; used in the practice of *chengbao*.
fenjin	奋进	Vigorous progress.
Furen liangfang	妇人良方	*Good Prescriptions for Women.* Song Dynasty medical classic.
fuwu renyuan	服务人员	Service personnel such as hotel employees or drivers.
ganqing	感情	Feelings, emotions.
gei mianzishang tian guang	给面子上添光	To add glory to one's face. Sports victories do so for the team leaders and cadres responsible for them.
getihu	个体户	Private entrepreneur; a newly prospering class under the economic reforms, they were notorious sports fans, despised for their lack of culture.
gongfu	功夫	Kungfu, martial arts; daily practice, honest effort.

gongping	公平	Fair.
gongping bisai	公平比赛	Lit., fair or equal competition; fair play.
gongping jiaoyi	公平交易	Fair deal.
guanti	官体	The system of body organs.
guanxi	关系	Lit., connections. Refers to social connections used to obtain desirable goods and services.
gulaode minzu	古老的民族	Ancient people; referred to the Chinese folk traditions performed in the 1990 Asian Games opening ceremonies.
guocui tiyu	国粹体育	National Essence Physical Culture. Label applied to martial arts in the 1910s and 1920s.
guojia	国家	State.
guojia lingdao	国家领导	State leaders.
Guojia Tiyu Yun-dong Weiyuanhui	国家体育运动委员会	State Physical Culture and Sports Commission, the ministry-level organization responsible for the administration of sports.
Guo Jiaxing	过家兴	Professor and Chair of the Sports Training Department, Beijing Institute of Physical Education.
guoji jianjiang	国际健将	International Master of Sports. The highest grade in the athlete ranking system.
guoqing	国情	National conditions; the technological capabilities and sentiments of the nation at a given period in time.
Guoqingjie	国庆节	National Day, 1 October; celebration of the founding of the PRC.
guoshu	国术	The national art; *wushu*.
guoti	国体	Lit., the national system.
Han	汉	Han; the ethnic majority in the PRC.
haose zongyu	好色纵欲	To lust after women and give in to carnal desires. One of the behaviors forbidden to participants in the 1933 Republican National Games.
hen	狠	Ruthless.
hengfu	横幅	Horizontal banner; a type of banner with writing on it, used at public events.

Heshang	河殇	"River Elegy," a TV series that was an inspiration in the 1989 student demonstrations; it contained a scene about sports and nationalism.
hexin	贺信	Congratulatory letter; often read aloud at the openings of sports meets or at the ceremonies celebrating sports victories.
He Zhenliang	何振梁	IOC member in China, 1981 to present.
huanfa qingchun	焕发青春	To return one's youth; a power attributed to old people's disco.
huanqi tonxin	唤起童心	To arouse the child's heart; a power attributed to old people's disco.
huansong hui	欢送会	Send-off meeting; held for teams before they depart for an important competition.
huanying hui	欢迎会	Welcoming meeting; held for teams returning from an important competition.
huanying yishi	欢迎仪式	Welcoming ceremony; held for teams when they arrive at the airport on their return from an important competition.
hui	会	Gathering, assembly, meeting; a type of public event.
huiqi	会旗	Association banner or flag; groups rally behind them at public events.
Hujiang	沪江	Hujiang University, site of the first bodybuilding association in the 1930s.
huoshi buzhu	伙食补助	Food subsidy, an important part of the Chinese sport system.
jiachou bu wang wai yang	家丑不往外扬	Lit., family shame should not be made public. Refers to the effort to maintain face; said to be one reason that athletes with no chance for a medal are sometimes not taken to international competitions.
jiang wenming	讲文明	Lit., pay attention to civilization. Refers to obeying rules of etiquette and sportsmanship.
jianjiang	健将	Master of Sport, the second-highest grade in the athlete ranking system.
jianmei	健美	Lit., healthy and beautiful. Label for bodybuilding and fitness activities.

Jiao nü yigui	教女遗规	*Advice Handed Down for Educating Women*, by Chen Hongmou.
jiaoxue minzhuhua	教学民主化	Democratization of educational methods; advocated in reforming the authoritarian relationship of coach over athletes.
jiaoyu wenti	教育问题	Lit., the education problem. Refers to the low educational level of many athletes, who stop taking classes at a young age.
jie	节	Festival; a type of public event.
jie	界	World, social circle.
jieling	节令	Seasonal cycle of festivals.
jieqing	节庆	Festival.
jieri	节日	Festival day.
jieshao	介绍	To brief, introduce; describes the talks given by athletes just back from major competitions.
jilü	纪律	Discipline; an important means of constructing spiritual civilization.
jin	斤	unit of weight; one-half kilo or 1.1 pounds.
jinbiaozhuyi	锦标主义	"medals-and-trophyism." An insult used in the early 1900s and during the Cultural Revolution to denounce the competitiveness and elitism of sports.
jindai tiyu	近代体育	Modern sports.
jing	精	Semen, seminal essence. In Taoist physiology, one of the four vital bodily substances. Its conservation was the key to male strength; some sportsmen today have similar beliefs.
jing	静	Still, tranquil; in the early 1900s, said to be characteristic of China, and contrasted with *dong*.
jingcai	精采	Splendid.
jinggong	静功	Quiet meditation; criticized by early Communists and the New Culture Movement as a kind of traditional exercise that should be discarded. See *jingzuo*.
jingji tixiao	竞技体校	Sports school.
jingji tiyu	竞技体育	Competitive sports.

jingshen mianmao	精神面貌	Lit., mental attitude. Morality, ethics; said to be on display at major sports events.
jingshen wenming	精神文明	Lit., spiritual civilization; a code of public morality and etiquette.
jingshen wenming jianshe	精神文明建社	Lit., construction of spiritual civilization; refers to the Communist Party's promotion of a code of public morality and etiquette that is to serve economic modernization.
jingshen wenming yundongyuan	精神文明运动员	Lit., spiritual civilization athlete. A spirit award for athletes who display good discipline and sportsmanship.
jingzheng	竞争	Competition; extolled by social Darwinists in the early 1900s and by economic reformers in the 1980s.
jingzheng jizhi	竞争机制	Mechanism of competition.
jingzuo	静坐	Quiet sitting; see *jinggong*.
jinqi	锦旗	Silk banner inscribed with calligraphy; given as an award or gift.
jinru jiaose	进入角色	To enter one's role. Refers to mental preparation for sports competition.
jishi	集市	Country fair.
jufu biaoyu	巨幅标语	Large vertical banner with calligraphy; used at public events.
kai guo da dian	开国大典	Ritual celebrating the founding of a new state.
kailang	开朗	Open-minded, sanguine; attributed to athletes.
kanbuguan	看不惯	Lit., can't bear the sight of. To dislike.
Kong Xiang'an	孔祥安	Professor at the Tianjin Institute of Physical Education, sport sociologist.
kouhao	口号	Shouted slogan.
ku	苦	Bitter, difficult; said of sports as a career.
Lang Ping	郎平	Star spiker of the Chinese women's volleyball team in the 1980s.
laoshi	老师	Teacher (term of respect).
laoxinzhe zhi ren, laolizhe zhiyu ren	劳心者治人，劳力者治于人	Those who work with their brains rule, those who work with their brawn are ruled (attributed to Mencius).

leitai	擂台	Lit., platform fighting. Kick-boxing, an indigenous sport.
li	礼	Familial ritual; a type of public event. Also, ritual, etiquette, manners; a central concept in the Confucian theory of statecraft. In Fei Xiaotong's opinion, the equivalent of "fair play" in England and the United States.
li	力	Strength.
lian	脸	(Moral) face; a reputation based on one's morals.
lian min jinhai, gu min xueqi	练民筋骸, 鼓民血气	Lit., train the people's tendons-bones, arouse the people's blood-*qi*. Train the people's bodies, arouse the people's courage. Advocated by Yan Fu.
Liang Qichao	梁启超	(1873–1929) Writer, social Darwinist, advocate of national strength.
lianpi hou	脸皮厚	Lit., thick-skinned face; insensitive to one's reputation.
Li Menghua	李梦华	Reform-minded director of the State Sports Commission, 1981 to 1988.
Lingyunzhi	凌云志	"Great Aspirations" (title of mass calisthenics in 1987 Chinese National Games).
lixing jingshen	理性精神	Spirit of reason; advocated by Su Xiaokang.
longzhong	隆重	Solemn, ceremonious. Used to describe opening ceremonies of major sports events.
luan	乱	Disorder, chaos.
Lu Yuanzhen	卢元镇	Associate Professor, Beijing Institute of Physical Education; sport sociologist.
Ma Liang	马良	Commander under the Northern Warlords (1912 to 1927), founder of *xin wushu*.
maimai gongping	买卖公平	Fair business deal.
mantou	馒头	Steamed bun. Along with rice, the main foods exchanged for grain tickets in communal eating halls.
mei	美	Beautiful.
Meiguorende Xingge	美国人的性格	*The American Character*, a book by Fei Xiaotong.

meiyou wenhua	没有文化	Lacking culture, uneducated, crude.
mendang hudui	门当户对	Lit., doors match; said when a woman and man of equal social status get married.
mianpiao	面票	Ration ticket for grain products.
mianzi	面子	(Prestige) face; a reputation based on outstanding achievements.
mianzi bu haokan	面子不好看	Lit., one's face is ugly; said when one has been humiliated.
miaohui	庙会	Temple fair.
minde	民德	The people's morals; along with strength and intellect, part of the tripartite formula advocated by Yan Fu.
minli	民力	The people's strength. See above.
minzhi	民智	The people's intellect. See above.
minzu chuantong	民族传统	Folk tradition.
minzu wenhua	民族文化	Folk culture.
mu zhuang er fei	母壮儿肥	Lit., muscular mothers have fat babies. One reason that women should keep physically fit.
nanxing	男性	Male character, masculine.
Nanzihan	男子汉	*Real Man*, a colloquial phrase and magazine title.
nanzi qi	男子气	Masculine.
naoli laodongzhe	脑力劳动者	Mental worker; refers to white-collar workers such as doctors, engineers, scientists, writers, teachers, officials, accountants, secretaries, and librarians.
nongmin tixie	农民体协	Peasant Sports Association
nüxing	女性	Female character, female.
nüzi qi	女子气	Feminine.
pangde	胖的	Fat, plump.
Pingjiang bu Xiao Sheng	平江不肖生	The Unworthy Man of Pingjiang, pen name of Xiang Kairan.
pinshu	聘书	Letter of appointment; under the economic reforms, these began to replace the system of job assignment and lifelong job security.

pinxue	贫血	Poor blood, anemia.
piping bao	批评报	Poster of criticism; put in a public place to announce the name and deed of an athlete who has violated team rules.
piping tongbao	批评通报	An announcement of criticism.
qi	气	Breath, vital energy (Taoist physiology).
Qiangguo meng	强国梦	"Superpower Dream," article by Zhao Yu criticizing the Chinese sport system.
qigong	气功	Meditational breathing and exercise.
Qing ming	清明	Pure Brightness, a festival in the lunar calendar.
quanshu	拳术	Fist-fighting, one of the categories of martial art.
qunzhong tiyu	群众体育	Mass physical culture; label for popular, nonelite sports.
rang	让	To give way or yield.
renao	热闹	Festive; bustling and noisy.
renkou	人口	Population; consists of the characters for person and mouth.
Renmin Ribao	人民日报	*People's Daily*; the leading state newspaper.
Renmin tiyu chu-banshe	人民体育出版社	People's Sports Publishing House.
routi	肉体	Lit., flesh-body. The physical body, contrasted with *shenti*.
shehui gejie daibiao	社会各界代表	Lit., representatives of various social circles; people selected to attend meetings with political leaders.
shehuihua	社会化	Lit., societization; key word in the state's call for sports to rely more on nongovernment support.
shen	身	Person-body; animate, subjective body; contrasted with *ti*.
shen	神	Spirit.
shenfen	身分	Status.
shenghui	盛会	Grand Assembly, solemn occasion.
shengren	生人	"Raw person"; refers to a stranger.

shenti	身体	The body. Combines characters for subjective and objective body.
shentihua	身体化	Somatization; used by Sun Lung-kee to describe the deep structure of Chinese culture.
shenti jiaoyu	身体教育	Literal translation of English "physical education," seldom used; contraction *tiyu* is used instead.
shenti wenhua	身体文化	Literal translation of English "physical culture," almost never used; *tiyu* is used instead.
shi	市	Market; one of the kinds of public events.
shi	式	Ceremony; one of the kinds of public events.
shikong	失控	Loss of control; refers to displays of poor sportsmanship and outbreaks of violence.
shiti	尸体	Dead body, corpse.
shuren	熟人	Lit., cooked person; refers to a friend or acquaintance, a person with whom one has established *guanxi*.
si	死	Dead; used to describe mass calisthenics.
siban	死版	Dead, rigid, stiff; used to describe mass calisthenics.
sixiang jiaoyu	思想教育	Lit., thought education; refers to the effort to shape political and ethical opinions through group study seesions, slogan-shouting, singing and other means.
sizhi fada, tounao jiandan	四支发达头脑简单	Lit., four developed limbs and an undeveloped brain: said of athletes.
Sun Lung-kee	孙隆基	Cultural critic, author of *Zhongguo Wenhuade Shenceng Jiegou*.
Su Xiaokang	苏晓康	Leading writer of reportage literature; author of *Heshang*.
tan lian'ai	谈恋爱	To court, fall in love; forbidden on professional sports teams.
tantu koufu	贪图口福	Be greedy for gourmet food; forbidden to athletes at the 1933 Republican National Games.
ti	体	The body; inanimate, objective, instrumental body; the character most fre-

quently used in words having to do with sports and physical education.

tiao	挑	To carry with a carrying pole resting across the shoulders; requires a flat-footed gait so the pole doesn't bounce off the shoulders.
ticao	体操	Gymnastics, calisthenics, physical exercises.
tihui	体会	To personally experience.
tili	体力	Physical strength; advocated by Yan Fu and Liang Qichao in the early 1900s as necessary for saving the Chinese nation from Western Imperialism.
tili laodongzhe	体力劳动者	Lit., physical workers; refers to manual laborers such as factory workers, peasants, and *getihu*.
tipo	体魄	Physique, body.
tiqi	体气	Lit., body-*qi*. Physical vigor.
tixing	体形	Physique, build.
tiyan	体验	To learn through personal experience.
ti-yong	体用	Lit., substance-application or body-action; referred to the idea in the early 1900s that the essence of Chinese culture could be preserved while Western culture could be practically utilized.
tiyu	体育	Physical culture (the broad meaning); embraces high-level sports, popular fitness activities, and physical education in the schools. Physical education (the narrow meaning).
Tiyu bao	体育报	*Sports News*, the premier sports newspaper; in 1988, its name was changed to *Zhongguo tiyu bao*.
Tiyu bolan	体育博览	*Sports Vision*, a magazine.
tiyu jia	体育家	Sports family; a family in which several members participate in sports, or whose members make up a single team.
tiyu xianjin xian	体育先进县	Advanced physical culture county; designation awarded by the State Sports Com mission to counties that achieve a set standard of sports facilities and participation.
tiyu yundong	体育运动	Physical culture and sports.

Tiyu zhi Yanjiu	体育之研究	"A Study of Physical Culture," essay by Mao Zedong.
tizhi	体质	Physique, constitution.
tongxinglianren	同性恋人	Lit., persone who loves someone of the same sex. Homosexual.
tongxuemen	同学们	Fellow classmate.
tu	土	Indigenous, native; earthy, countrified.
tu yang tiyu zhi zheng	土洋体育之挣	The conflict between indigenous and foreign sports; a heated debate in the 1920s and 1930s.
Wang Zhenya	王振亚	Author of one of the first post-1949 histories of Republican-era sports.
wang zi cheng long	望子成龙	Hoping your children become dragons; refers primarily to parental hopes for academic achievement.
Wan Li	万里	Vice-premier of the PRC in 1987, he lit the torch at the beginning of the torch relay for the National Games and gave the opening speech at the games.
wei Beijing zheng guang	为北京争光	Win glory for Beijing; said of victorious athletes.
weisheng	卫生	Health and sanitation.
wei . . . tici	为 . . . 题词	Lit., to offer words; to endorse an event by writing a short saying in one's own calligraphy.
Wei Zhenlan	魏振兰	Director of the Guangdong Provincial Sports Commission, leader in the reforms instituted for the 1987 National Games.
wen	文	Letters, literacy, culture; opposed to *wu*.
wenhua	文化	Culture; tends to take educated urbanites as the standard, while uneducated and rural people are said to lack culture.
wenhua shuiping	文化水平	Cultural level, years of schooling; athletes are often said to have a low cultural level.
wenhua tiyu zhongxin	文化体育中心	Culture and sports center; recreational center.
wenhua zhan	文化站	Cultural center; a recreational center, often including simple sports facilities.

wenming	文明	Civilization, culture; refers to the cumulative material and spiritual achievements of a nation or region of the world; Beijing is often portrayed as the center of Chinese civilization.
wenming gongzuo	文明工作	Civilization work; refers to the effort to shape the manners and morals of the populace.
wenming limao	文明礼貌	Civilization and manners; refers to observance of proper etiquette.
wu	武	Martiality, things associated with war; opposed to *wen*.
wudan	武旦	Female martial artist; a popular character in operas.
wuguan	武馆	Martial arts hall; place for learning martial arts.
wushu	武术	Martial arts, kungfu.
wuxia xiaoshuo	武侠小说	Martial arts novel, knight-errant novel. A popular literary genre.
wuyi	武艺	Lit., martial skills. Premodern word for military-related sports.
wuyong	武勇	Lit., military valor. Premodern word for military-related sports.
wuzhi wenming	勿质文明	Wealth, material civilization; contrasted with spiritual civilization.
xiandaide	现代的	Modern; contrasted with *chuantong*.
xiandaihua	现代化	Modernization.
xiangsheng	相声	Crosstalk; a form of stand-up comedy involving a comic and a straight man.
Xiang Kairan	向恺然	Advocate of *guoshu* and premier author of martial arts novels; a key figure in the martial arts revival of the 1910s to 1930s.
Xiayi Yingxiong Zhuan	侠义英雄传	*Lives of Chivalrous and Altruistic Heroes*, martial arts novel by Xiang Kairan.
xinghai	形骸	Skeleton, body. Premodern word for physique.
xingti	形体	Physique, body.
Xinhua Wenzhai	新华文摘	*New China Digest*.

xin tiyu	新体育	Lit., new physical culture; label for Western sports in the early 1900s.
Xin Tiyu	新体育	*New Sports*, magazine published by the State Sports Commission.
xin wushu	新武术	New Martial Arts; invented by Ma Liang in the 1910s.
xiong	凶	Fierce, ferocious.
xitong	系统	Lit., system; used to designate all organizations under the control of a certain state ministry or commission, such as the Sports Commission system.
xiu shen	修身	To cultivate one's moral character; includes Taoist and Buddhist meditational exercises.
xiyang tiyu	西洋体育	Lit., western physical culture; label for Western sports in the early 1900s.
xuandu	宣读	To read aloud, proclaim; *hexin* are commonly read aloud at public events.
xue	血	Blood. In Taoist physiology, one of the four vital bodily substances; particularly important for women.
xueke	学科	Academic discipline, branch of knowledge.
xueli	学力	Academic attainments; desirable in a husband.
xueqi	血气	Lit., blood-*qi*. Vigor, courage.
xueqitili	血气体力	Lit., blood-*qi*-body-strength. Vigor and strength.
xuerou	血肉	Lit., blood-flesh. Flesh and blood, the body.
xuexiao tiyu	学校体育	School sports, physical culture in the schools.
yaguan zhi tang	雅观之堂	The height of refinement.
yamen	衙门	A government office in imperial times.
Yan Fu	严复	The leader of social Darwinism in China at the turn of the century; advocate of strengthening the nation.
yang	阳	*Yang*, the male principle, culture, the hierarchical superior in a dyad; opposed to *yin*.
yang	洋	Foreign, Western.

yangcheng	羊城	City of the Rams, Guangzhou.
Yang Duo	杨铎	Vice-director of the Beijing Workers' Sports Technique School; member of the Beijing City Sports Commission.
yang sheng	养生	Lit., to cultivate life; a Taoist label for physical exercise.
yang sheng zhi dao	养生之道	Lit., the way of life-cultivation; refers to Taoist meditational and body practices intended to lead to longevity. A holistic approach that contrasts with the limited focus on an alienated body in Western sports.
yanjing	燕京	Yenching University; established by Americans on the site of the present Beijing University.
yeyu tixiao	业余体校	Spare-time sports school.
Yi Chenghong	裔程洪	Vice-chairman of the National Body-building and Fitness Committee of the Chinese Weightlifting Association.
yi qun wei ti, yi bian wei yong	以群为体, 以变为用	Take the group as your body and take change as your action. Social Darwinist notion espoused by Kang Youwei.
yikou ren	一口人	Lit., one mouth-person; a family member.
yin	阴	*Yin*, the female principle, nature, the hierarchical inferior in a dyad; opposed to *yang*.
yingyang genbu-shang	营养跟不上	Lit., nutrition can't keep up; refers to athletes' fear that they cannot eat enough to support hard training.
yinian tu, ernian yang, sannian buren die he niang	一年土, 二年洋, 三年不认爹和娘	Lit., One year later—rustic, two years later—foreign, three years later—won't acknowledge Dad and Mom. A rhyme said to characterize peasant athletes after they are selected to a provincial sports team and move to the city.
Yin Weixing	尹卫星	Author of "*Zhongguo tiyu jie.*"
yishi xingtai	意识形态	Ideology; official, politicized discourse promoted by the Communist Party.
you wenhua	有文化	To have culture; be educated, cultured. College-educated urbanites generally taken as the standard.

yuanqi	元气	Original vitality, a Taoist concept.
Yuan Qiang	原强	"The Source of Strength," an essay by Yan Fu.
Yuan Weimin	袁伟民	Coach of the world champion Chinese women's volleyball team and vice-director of the State Sports Commission.
Yun Daiying	恽代英	Early communist revolutionary who criticized Western-organized sports.
yundong	运动	Activity; (political) movement; (political) campaign; sports.
yundonghui	运动会	Sports competition.
Zhao Yu	赵瑜	Author of "Superpower Dream"; leader in the 1989 Tiananmen demonstrations.
Zhao Zhuguang	赵竹光	Founder of bodybuilding in China in the 1930s.
zheng	正	Upright, correct. Used to refer to social justice more often than *gongping*.
zhengmingshu	证明书	Certificate; given in recognition of meritorious behavior.
zhengzhi mianmu	政治面目	Political affiliation, such as Communist Party member or Communist Youth League member; important determinant of leaders and captains of sport teams.
zhixing	致性	Essential nature; notion found in Chen Hongmou's discussions of gender.
Zhongguo Funü	中国妇女	*China Women*, a magazine.
Zhongguo Qingnian Bao	中国青年报	*China Youth News*, a newspaper.
Zhongguo Tiyu Bao	中国体育报	*China Sports News*, the leading daily sports newspaper; until 1988 a four-day per week paper called *Tiyu bao*.
Zhongguo tiyu jie	中国体育界	"The Chinese Sportsworld," three-part article by Yin Weixing.
Zhongguo zhi wu-shidao	中国之武士道	"China's Bushido," essay by Liang Qichao.
Zhonghua Renmin Gongheguo Yun-donghui	中华人民共和国运动会	National Games of the People's Republic of China.
zhong shen	终身	Lifelong.

zhong wen qing wu	重文轻武	Lit., esteem literacy and despise martiality. Said to be an enduring characteristic of Chinese culture that accounts for the low regard for sports.
zhongyang	重阳	Zhongyang; a festival in the lunar calendar.
zhuangde	壮的	Muscular, robust.
zhuangshi	壮士	Warrior, hero.
ziwo jianding	自我鉴定	Self-evaluation; a highly formulaic assessment of one's performance and mental attitude, submitted for consideration as a "spiritual civilization athlete."
ziwo piping	自我批评	Self-criticism; one of the sanctions for rules violations on professional teams.

REFERENCES

A Chinese-English Dictionary
1986   Beijing: Shangwu yinshuguan.

Abu-Lughod, Lila
1991   "Writing Against Culture." In Richard G. Fox, ed., *Recapturing Anthro-pology: Working in the Present*, pp. 137–62. Santa Fe, NM: School of American Research.

Anagnost, Ann
1993   "Constructions of Civility in the Age of Flexible Accumulation." Paper presented at the panel on "Popular Cultural Practices in China: Room for Heterodoxy?" American Anthropological Association Meetings, San Francisco, 6 December 1993.
1989   "Transformations of Gender in Modern China." In Sandra Morgen, ed., *Gender and Anthropology: Critical Reviews for Research and Teaching*, pp. 313–42. Washington, DC: American Anthropological Association.

Anderson, Benedict
1991   *Imagined Communities: Reflections on the Origin and Spread of Nationalism.* London and New York: Verso.

Anderson, E. N.
1988   *The Food of China.* New Haven: Yale University Press.

Appadurai, Arjun
1991   "Decolonizing the Production of Culture: Cricket in Contemporary India." In Kang Shin-pyo, John MacAloon, and Roberto DaMatta, eds., *The Olympics and Cultural Exchange: The Papers of the First International Conference on the Olympics and East/West and South/North Cultural Exchange in the World System*, pp. 163–90. Seoul: Hanyang University Press.

345

Appadurai, Arjun, and Carol Breckenridge
1988   "Why Public Culture?" *Public Culture: Bulletin of the Project for Transnational Cultural Studies* 1, no. 1 (Fall): 5–9.

Asia Watch
1994   *Detained in China and Tibet: A Directory of Political and Religious Prisoners.* New York: Human Rights Watch.

Bai Guanglin and Ju Shirong
1987   "Dui Baoyingxian chengxiang renmin tiyu shenghuode chouyang diaocha" [A Sample Survey of the Physical Culture Life of the Urban People of Baoying County]. In *Jiangsu sheng tiyu shehuixue yanjiuhui* [Jiangsu Provincial Sport Sociology Association], *Lunwen diaocha baogao xuanbian* [Selected theses and survey reports], vol. 2, May, pp. 177–88.

Barlow, Tani
1991   "Theorizing Woman: *Funü, Guojia, Jiating* [Chinese Women, Chinese State, Chinese Family]." *Genders,* Special Issue on Theorizing Nationality, Sexuality, and Race 10: 132–60.

Barnett, Eugene E.
1990   *My Life in China, 1910–1936.* East Lansing, MI: Asian Studies Center, Michigan State University.

Barney, Robert K.
1991   "For Such Olympic Games: German-American Turnfests as Preludes to the Modern Olympic Games." In Fernand Landry, Marc Landry, Magdaleine Yerles, eds., *Sport . . . The third millennium: Proceedings of the International Symposium,* pp. 697–706. Quebec, Canada, 21–25 May 1990. Sainte-Foy: Les Presses de l'Université Laval.

Bassat, Luis
1993   "The Barcelona '92 Opening Ceremonies." Lecture delivered before the International Symposium on Television and the Olympic Games: Cultural Exchanges and the Understanding of Olympic Values. International Olympic Academy, Olympia, Greece, 2–7 July.

Beijing City Team
1988   Interview with five athletes and coaches from the Beijing City Team, Xiannongtan, 6 February.

Beijing daxuesheng daibiaotuan mishuzu [Beijing College Team Secretariat]
1986   *Saiqian xuzhi* [Things to Know before the Meet]. July.

Beijing Review
1986   "Sports in China Has Ancient History." *Beijing Review* 29, no. 5 (April): 32–33.

Beijing shi yinxiang chubanshe [Beijing City Sound Recording Publishing House]
1985 *Ma Ji, Zhao Yan xiangsheng wanhui* [An Evening of Crosstalk with Ma Ji and Zhao Yan]. Cassette.

Black, Alison H.
1986 "Gender and Cosmology in Chinese Correlative Thinking." In Caroline Walker Bynum, Stevan Harrell, and Paula Richman, eds., *Gender and Religion: On the Complexity of Symbols,* pp. 166–95. Boston: Beacon Press.

Bleicher, Josef
1990 "Struggling with *Kultur.*" *Theory, Culture and Society* 7: 97–106.

Bodman, Richard W., and Pin P. Wang
1991 *Deathsong of the River: A Reader's Guide to the Chinese TV Series "Heshang."* Ithaca, NY: Cornell East Asia Series.

Bo Fei
1987 "Weishemma huifu yeyu quanji?" [Why Restore Amateur Boxing?]. *Beijing ribao [Beijing Daily]* 9 October.

Bonavia, David
1985 "Frustration pitch . . ." *Far Eastern Economic Review,* 6 June, p. 46.

Bourdieu, Pierre
1990 *In Other Words: Essays Toward a Reflexive Sociology* (1987). Translated by M. Adamson. Stanford: Stanford University Press.
1988 "A Program for the Comparative Sociology of Sport." In Kang Shin-pyo, John MacAloon, and Roberto DaMatta, eds., *The Olympics and Cultural Exchange: The Papers of the First International Conference on the Olympics and East/West and South/North Cultural Exchange in the World System,* pp. 67–83. Seoul: Hanyang University Press.
1984 *Distinction: A Social Critique of the Judgement of Taste.* Translated by Richard Nice. Cambridge: Harvard University Press.
1978 "Sport and Social Class." *Social Science Information* 17, no. 6: 819–40.
1977 *Outline of a Theory of Practice.* Translated by Richard Nice. Cambridge: Cambridge University Press.

Brownell, Susan E.
1993 "Qing Dynasty Grand Sacrifice and Communist National Sports Games: Rituals of the Chinese State?" *Journal of Ritual Studies* 7, no. 1 (Winter 1993): 45–64.
1991 "The Changing Relationship between Sport and the State in the People's Republic of China." In Fernand Landry, Marc Landry, Magdaleine Yerles, eds., *Sport . . . The third millennium: Proceedings of the International Symposium,* pp. 295–301. Quebec, Canada, 21–25 May 1990. Sainte-Foy: Les Presses de l'Université Laval.

Bruner, Edward M.
1986   "Experience and Its Expressions." In Victor W. Turner and Edward M.
          Bruner, eds., *The Anthropology of Experience*, pp. 3–30. Urbana: Univer-
          sity of Illinois Press.

Butler, Judith
1990   *Gender Trouble: Feminism and the Subversion of Identity.* New York:
          Routledge.

Cai Dengbiao
1988a   "Mei, qiang, ya, le, zhi" [Beautiful, Strong, Refined, Happy, Intelligent].
          Tiyu bao [Sports News], 2 February.
1988b   "Bushi guanjunde 'guanjun'" [He's not a Champion's "champion"].
          Tiyu bao [Sports News], 20 February.

Caille, Alain
1993   "The Concept of Fair Play." In *Olympic Centennial Congress Bulletin*, pp.
          4–8. Lausanne, Switzerland: XII Olympic Congress Media Ad Hoc Com-
          mittee of IOC.

Calhoun, Craig
1989   "Tiananmen, Television and the Public Sphere: Internationalization of
          Culture and the Beijing Spring of 1989." *Public Culture* 2 (1): 54–71.

————, ed.
1992   *Habermas and the Public Sphere.* Cambridge: MIT Press.

————, Edward LiPuma, and Moishe Postone, eds.
1993   *Bourdieu: Critical Perspectives.* Chicago: University of Chicago Press.

Cao Xiangjun
1988   "Tiyu gailun" [A General Theory of Physical Culture]. Lecture at Beijing
          Institute of Physical Education, 5 January.
1987   "Tiyu gailun" [A General Theory of Physical Culture]. Lecture at Beijing
          Institute of Physical Education, 15 September.
1985   *Tiyu gailun [A General Theory of Physical Culture].* Beijing: Beijing tiyu
          xueyuan chubanshe.

Cao Yuchun
1987   "Yangcheng ban liuyunhui xinzhao" [New Tricks in Guangzhou's Han-
          dling of the Sixth Games]. *Xin tiyu,* November, pp. 14–15.

Chatterjee, Partha
1990   "A Response to Taylor's 'Modes of Civil Society.'" *Public Culture: Bulletin
          of the Center for Transnational Cultural Studies* 3, no. 1 (Fall): 119–32.

Chen, Nancy
1994   "Urban Spaces and Experiences of *Qigong.*" In Deborah Davis, ed., *Ur-
          ban Spaces.* Cambridge: Cambridge University Press.

Chen Jia
1986   "Wrestling in Old China." *China Daily,* 22 May.

Chen Mengsheng
1987   "Lijie quanyunhui zongheng tan" [On Past National Games in Length and Breadth]. *Xin tiyu,* November, p. 11.

Chen Yuanhui, Jun Dexin, Wang Bingzhao, eds.
1981   *Zhongguo gudaide shuyuan zhidu* [*Ancient China's Academy System*]. Shanghai: Shanghai jiaoyu chubanshe.

China Daily
1993a   "Overseas Chinese the World Over Join on Supporting Bid," 15 September, Special Supplement.
1993b   "Star Coach Reveals His Secrets," 13 September.
1993c   "Chinese Official Denies Drug Accusations," 8 September.
1988a   "Sichuan Arrests Six People for Soccer Riot," 2 June.
1988b   "Soccer Fans Held," 31 May.
1988c   "Guangzhou Meet Blazed Way," 23 February.
1988d   "Elderly Waking Up to Disco Beat," 4 February.
1988e   "China's Top 10 Exporters," 3 February.
1988f   "Iron Deficiency Affecting Babies," 5 January.
1987a   "National Games," 4 December.
1987b   "CD News," 27 November.
1987c   "Viewers Ask for Better TV Dramas," 9 November.
1987d   "Children's Diet Improved—Report," 3 November.

China Sports
1983   "Confucius as Physical Culture Promoter." 2 (February): 24–27.

Chiu, Fred Y. L.
1991   "The Specificity of the Political on Tiananmen Square, or A Poetics of the Popular Resistance in Beijing." *Dialectical Anthropology* 16 (3–4): 333–47.

Chu Zi
1987   "Rexin Zhongguo tiyude Meiguo guniang" [The American Girl who Warmly Loves Chinese Sports]. *Tiyu bolan* [*Sports Vision*], March, pp. 26–27.

Cleverley, John
1985   *The Schooling of China: Tradition and Modernity in Chinese Education.* Sydney: George Allen and Unwin.

Cohen, Myron
1991   "Being Chinese: The Peripheralization of Traditional Identity." *Daedalus* 120 (2): 113–34.

Comaroff, Jean
1985   *Body of Power, Spirit of Resistance.* Chicago: University of Chicago Press.

Coubertin, Pierre de
1967   *The Olympic Idea: Discourses and Essays.* Carl-Diem-Institut an der Sport-
          hochschule Köln, eds.; translated by John G. Dixon. Schorndorf bei
          Stuttgart: Karl Hoffman.

Croll, Elizabeth
1981   *The Politics of Marriage in Contemporary China.* New York: Cambridge
          University Press.

DaMatta, Roberto
1988   "Hierarchy and Equality in Anthropology and World Sport: A Perspec-
          tive from Brazil." In Kang Shin-pyo, John MacAloon, and Roberto Da-
          Matta, eds., *The Olympics and Cultural Exchange in the World System,* pp.
          15–66. Seoul: Hanyang University Institute for Ethnological Studies.

Dang Li
1988   "Shiyijie sanzhong quanhui yilai woguo tiyu qude juda chengjiu"
          [Since the Third Plenum of the 13th Party Congress, China's Physical
          Culture Has Made Tremendous progress]. *Tiyu bao,* 21 October.

Dao Jie and Miao Ye
1987   "Xi'ai jianmei yundongde ren yue lai yue duo" [More and More People
          Like Bodybuilding]. *Tiyu bao,* 30 October.

d'Aquili, Eugene G., and Charles Laughlin
1979   "The Neurobiology of Myth and Ritual." In Eugene d'Aquili, Charles
          Laughlin, John McManus, eds., *The Spectrum of Ritual: A Biogenetic Struc-
          tural Analysis,* pp. 152–82. New York: Columbia University Press.

DiKötter, Frank
1992   *The Discourse of Race in Modern China.* London: Hurst Co.

Dilling, Margaret Walker
1990   "The Familiar and the Foreign: Music as Medium of Exchange in the
          Seoul Olympic Ceremonies." In Koh Byong-Ik, ed., *Toward One World,
          Beyond All Barriers: The Seoul Olympiad Anniversary Conference,* pp. 357–
          77. Seoul: Seoul Olympic Sports Promotion Foundation.

Dong Hua
1987   "Yige chaoji qiumide bange gushi" [Half of the Story of a Super-soccer
          Fan]. *Tiyu bolan,* August, pp. 4–5.

Dunning, Eric
1986   "Sport as a Male Preserve: Notes on the Social Sources of Masculine
          Identity and Its Transformations." In Norbert Elias and Eric Dunning,
          Quest for Excitement: Sport and Leisure in the Civilizing Process, pp. 267–83.
          Oxford: Basil Blackwell.

Ebrey, Patricia Buckley, ed.
1981   *Chinese Civilization and Society: A Sourcebook.* New York: The Free Press.

Eichberg, Henning
1993   "Der Dialogische Körper: Über einen dritten Weg der körperanthropo-
        logischen Aufmerksamkeit" [The Dialogical Body: On a Third Kind of
        Attentiveness in the Anthropology of the Body]. In Knut Dietrich and
        Henning Eichberg, eds., Körpersprache: Über Identität und Konflikt [Body
        Language: On Identity and Conflict], pp. 257–308. Butzbach: Afra.
1989   "Body Culture as Paradigm: The Danish Sociology of Sport." Interna-
        tional Review for the Sociology of Sport 24 (1): 45–61.
1977   "Den einen Sport gibt es nicht—Das Beispiel West-Sumatra Zur Kritik
        des olympischen Universalismus" [There Is Not Just One Sport—The
        Example of West Sumatra as a Critique of Olympic Universalism]. Sport
        und Kulturwandel [Sport and Culture Change], pp. 72–78. Stuttgart: Insti-
        tut für Auslandsbeziehungen.
1973   Der Weg des Sports in die industrielle Zivilisation [Sport on Its Way into In-
        dustrial Civilization]. Baden-Baden: Nomos Verlagsgesellschaft. (English
        language summary on pp. 165–72.)

Elias, Norbert
1978   The History of Manners, vol. 1 of The Civilizing Process, 2 vols. (1939).
        Translated by Edmund Jephcott. New York: Pantheon Books.

Elvin, Mark
1989   "Tales of Shen and Xin: Body-Person and Heart-Mind in China during
        the Last 150 Years." In Michel Feher, ed., Fragments for a History of the
        Human Body, part 2, pp. 266–349. New York: Zone Books.

Esherick, Joseph W., and Jeffrey N. Wasserstrom
1990   "Acting Out Democracy: Political Theater in Modern China." The Jour-
        nal of Asian Studies 49 (4): 835–65.

Farquhar, Judith
1994   "Multiplicity, Point of View, and Responsibility in Traditional Chinese
        Healing." In Angela Zito and Tani Barlow, eds., Body, Subject and Power
        in China, pp. 78–99. Chicago: University of Chicago Press.

Featherstone, Mike
1991   "The Body in Consumer Culture." In Mike Featherstone, Mike Hep-
        worth, and Bryan S. Turner, eds., The Body: Social Process and Cultural
        Theory, pp. 170–96. London: Sage.

Fei Xiaotong
1985   Meiguorende xingge [The American Character] (1947). Republished in the
        compilation Meiguo yu Meiguoren [America and Americans] (Beijing: San-
        lian shudian), pp. 155–215.

Feuchtwang, Stephan
1977   "School-Temple and City God." In William Skinner, ed., The City in Late
        Imperial China, pp. 581–608. Stanford, CA: Stanford University Press.

Foucault, Michel
1979   *Discipline and Punish* (1975). Translated by Alan Sheridan. New York: Vintage Books.
1978   *The History of Sexuality, Volume I: An Introduction* (1976). Translated by Robert Hurley. New York: Vintage Books.

Frank, Manfred
1992   "On Foucault's Concept of Discourse." In Timothy J. Armstrong, trans., *Michel Foucault: Philosopher*, pp. 99–116. New York: Routledge.

Furth, Charlotte
1988   "Androgenous Males and Deficient Females: Biology and Gender Boundaries in Sixteenth and Seventeenth-Century China." *Late Imperial China* 9 (2): 1–31.
1986   "Blood, Body and Gender: Medical Images of the Female Condition in China, 1600–1850." *Chinese Science* 7:43–66.

Fuss, Diana
1989   *Essentially Speaking: Feminism, Nature and Difference.* New York: Routledge.

Gamble, Sidney D.
1921   *Peking: A Social Survey.* New York: George H. Doran Company.

Garnham, Nicholas
1992   "The Media and the Public Sphere." In Craig Calhoun, ed., *Habermas and the Public Sphere*, pp. 359–76. Cambridge: MIT Press.

Garrett, Shirley
1970   *Social Reformers in Urban China: The Chinese YMCA, 1895–1926.* Cambridge: Harvard University Press.

Geertz, Clifford
1980   *Negara: The Theatre State in Nineteenth-Century Bali.* Princeton, NJ: Princeton University Press.
1973   *The Interpretation of Cultures.* New York: Basic Books.

Gruneau, Richard
1991   "Sport and 'Esprit de Corps': Notes on Power, Culture and the Politics of the Body." In Fernand Landry, Marc Landry, Magdaleine Yerles, eds., *Sport . . . The third millennium: Proceedings of the International Symposium*, pp. 169–86. Quebec, Canada, 21–25 May 1990. Sainte-Foy: Les Presses de l'Université Laval.

Gui Jia
1988   "Cong 'kuai bei bifengle' shuo kaiqu" [Starting from "almost forced to insanity"]. *Zhongguo tiyu bao*, 16 April.

Guo Bowen
1988   "Ai tiao disike de laonian ren" [Old People Who Love to Dance Disco]. *Tiyu bao*, 29 January.

Guojia tiwei zhengce yanjiushi [State Sports Commission Policy Research Division]
1982 *Tiyu yundong wenjian xuanbian 1949–1981* [*Selected Physical Culture and Sport Documents, 1949–1981*]. Beijing: Renmin tiyu chubanshe.

Guojia tongjiju shehui tongjisi [State Statistical Bureau, Social Statistics Division]
1985 *Zhongguo shehui tongji ziliao* [*China Social Statistics Data*]. Beijing: Zhongguo tongji chubanshe.

Gu Shiquan
1990 "Introduction to Ancient and Modern Chinese Physical Culture." In Howard G. Knuttgen, Ma Qiwei, and Wu Zhongyuan, eds., *Sport in China*, pp. 3–24. Champaign, IL: Human Kinetics Books.

Guttmann, Allen
1986 *Sports Spectators*. New York: Columbia University Press.
1978 *From Ritual to Record: The Nature of Modern Sports*. New York: Columbia University Press.

Habermas, Jürgen
1992 "Further Reflections on the Public Sphere." In Craig Calhoun, ed., *Habermas and the Public Sphere*, pp. 421–61. Cambridge: MIT Press.
1991 *The Philosophical Discourse of Modernity* (1985). Translated by Frederick G. Lawrence. Cambridge: MIT Press.
1989 *The Structural Transformation of the Public Sphere: An Inquiry into a Category of Bourgeois Society* (1962). Translated by Thomas Burger. Cambridge: MIT Press.
1974 "The Public Sphere: An Encyclopedia Article" (1964). *New German Critique* 1 (3): 49–55.

Hall, Stuart, Chris Critcher, Tony Jefferson, John Clarke, and Brian Roberts
1988 *Policing the Crisis*. London: Macmillan.

Handelman, Don
1990 *Models and Mirrors: Towards an Anthropology of Public Events*. Cambridge: Cambridge University Press.

Hanyu da cidian [*Great Chinese dictionary*]
1988 Vol. 2. Hong Kong: Sanlian shudian.

Hausen, Karin
1981 "Family and Role-Division: The Polarisation of Sexual Stereotypes in the Nineteenth Century—An Aspect of the Dissociation of Work and Family Life." In Richard J. Evans and W. R. Lee, eds., *The German Family: Essays on the Social History of the Family in Nineteenth- and Twentieth-Century Germany*, pp. 51–83. Totowa, NJ: Barnes and Noble.

He Lu
1982   "World Champions." *China Reconstructs*, 15–17 February.

Hersh, Phil
1993   "China's Swimming Success Raises Specter of East Germany." *Chicago Tribune*, 16 November, section 4, pp. 1, 8.

Hevia, James L.
1990   "Making China 'Perfectly Equal.'" *Journal of Historical Sociology* 3, no. 4 (December): 379–400.

He Zhenliang
1988   Jiji fazhan tiyu, nuli banhao Yayunhui [Actively Develop Sport, Diligently Prepare for the Asian Games]. *Tiyu bao*, 9 April.

He Zhuoqiang
1988   "Wo ke bushi 'shentong'" [I'm Certainly Not a "Child Prodigy"]. *Tiyu bao*, 1 January.

Hoberman, John M.
1984   *Sport and Political Ideology.* Austin: University of Texas Press.

Hong Qingbo, ed.
1988   "Wenxuede shuangfeng kuayue" [Leaping Across the Twin Peaks of Literature]. In *Bingbai Hancheng: Zhao Yu tiyu wenti baogao wenxue ji* [Defeat of the Troops in Seoul: Collected Reportage by Zhao Yu on Physical Culture Problems], pp. 192–203. Beijing: Zhongguo shehui kexue chubanshe.

Honig, Emily, and Gail Hershatter
1988   *Personal Voices: Chinese Women in the 1980s.* Stanford, CA: Stanford University Press.

Hsiao Kung-chuan
1960   *Rural China: Imperial Control in the Nineteenth Century.* Seattle: University of Washington Press.

Huang He
1987a   "Yiyi chaoguo tiyu fanwei" [The Significance Surpassed the Bounds of Physical Culture]. *Tiyu bao*, 9 December.
1987b   "Xi'ai tiyu guannian zai bianhua" [Concepts about Liking Physical Culture Are Changing]. *Tiyu bao*, 29 November.

Huang Yawen
1987   "Sanfen xunlian qifen guan" [Three Parts Training, Seven Parts Management]. *Tiyu bao*, 5 December.

Huang Zhenzhong
1988   "Qiye weihe yu tiyu 'jieqin'" [Why Does Enterprise "Get Married" with Physical Culture]. *Renmin ribao*, 4 March.

Hu Hsien Chin
1944   "The Chinese Concepts of 'Face.'" *American Anthropologist* 46 (1) pt. 1: 45–64.

Huizinga, Johan
1970   *Homo Ludens: A Study of the Play Element in Culture.* New York: Harper and Row.

Illich, Ivan
1982   *Gender.* New York: Pantheon.

(IOC) International Olympic Committee
1991   *Olympic Charter.* Lausanne, Switzerland: International Olympic Committee.
1984   *The Olympic Movement (January 1985).* Lausanne, Switzerland: International Olympic Committee.

Irigaray, Luce
1985   *This Sex Which Is Not One* (1977). Translated by Catherine Porter with Carolyn Burke. Ithaca: Cornell University Press.

Jankowiak, William
1993   *Sex, Death, and Hierarchy in a Chinese City: An Anthropological Account.* New York: Columbia University Press.
1989   "Sex Differences in Mate Choice and Sexuality in the People's Republic of China." *The Australian Journal of Chinese Affairs,* no. 22: 54–74.

Jin Shaoren
1987   "Knowledge Contests Go Too Far." *China Daily,* 10 October.

Kahn, Miriam
1986   *Always Hungry, Never Greedy: Food and the Expression of Gender in a Melanesian Society.* Cambridge: Cambridge University Press.

Kang Bing
1988a   "New Look for China's Games." *China Daily,* 23 March.
1988b   "Check those Olympic Badges." *China Daily,* 23 January.

Kang Shin-pyo
1991   "The Seoul Olympic Games and Dae-Dae Cultural Grammar." In Fernand Landry, Marc Landry, Magdaleine Yerles, eds., *Sport . . . The third millennium: Proceedings of the International Symposium,* pp. 49–64. Quebec, Canada, 21–25 May 1990. Sainte-Foy: Les Presses de l'Université Laval.

Kanin, David B.
1978   "Ideology and Diplomacy: The Dimensions of Chinese Political Sport." In B. Lowe, D. B. Kanin, and A. Strenk, eds., *Sport and International Relations,* pp. 263–78. Champaign, IL: Stipes Publishing Co.

Kapferer, Bruce
1988   *Legends of People, Myths of State: Violence, Intolerance, and Political Culture in Sri Lanka and Australia.* Washington: Smithsonian Institution Press.

Kelly, William
1990   "Japanese No-Noh: The Crosstalk of Public Culture in a Rural Festivity." *Public Culture: Bulletin of the Center for Transnational Cultural Studies* 2, no. 2 (Spring): 65–81.

Kenyon, Gerald S.
1966   "The Significance of Physical Activity as a Function of Age, Sex, Education, and Socio-Economic Status of Northern United States Adults." *International Review of Sport Sociology* 1: 41–57.

Kipnis, Andrew
1993   "'Face': An Adaptable Discourse of Social Surfaces." Unpublished manuscript.
1992   Letter, personal communication with author. December 10.

Kleinman, Arthur
1986   *Social Origins of Distress and Disease: Depression, Neurasthenia, and Pain in Modern China.* New Haven: Yale University Press.

———, and Joan Kleinman
1985   "Somatization: The Interconnections in Chinese Society among Culture, Depressive Experiences, and the Meanings of Pain." In Arthur Kleinman and Byron Good, eds., *Culture and Depression: Studies in the Anthropology and Cross-Cultural Psychiatry of Affect and Disorder,* pp. 429–90. Berkeley: University of California Press.

Kolatch, Jonathan
1972   *Sports, Politics, and Ideology in China.* Middle Village, NY: Jonathan David Publishers.

Kong Xiang'an
1988   Interview, Tianjin Institute of Physical Education, 16 January.

——— and Zhang Zhidong
1987   "Zuqiuchang baoli chengyin yu fangfan" [Components of Soccer Violence and Prevention]. In Jiangsu sheng tiyu shehuixue yanjiuhui [Jiangsu Provincial Sport Sociology Association], *Lunwen diaocha baogao xuanbian* [*Selected Theses and Survey Reports*], vol. 2, May, pp. 13–23.

Kramer, Michael
1989   "Free to Fly Inside the Cage." *Time,* 2 October, pp. 30–79.

Kristof, Nicholas D.
1992   "China Leaders Stress Both Market and Orthodoxy." *New York Times,* 13 October, p. A-3.

Landor, A. Henry Savage
1901   *China and the Allies*. New York: Charles Scribner's Sons.

Lang Ping
1985   "Lang Ping riji" [Lang Ping's Diary]. *Xin tiyu*, December, pp. 22–24.

Laqueur, Thomas
1990   *Making Sex: Body and Gender from the Greeks to Freud*. Cambridge: Harvard University Press.

Larson, James F., and Heung-Soo Park
1993   *Global Television and the Politics of the Seoul Olympics*. Boulder, CO: Westview Press.

Laughlin, Charles D., John McManus, and Eugene G. d'Aquili
1979   "Introduction." In Eugene d'Aquili, Charles Laughlin, John McManus, eds., *The Spectrum of Ritual: A Biogenetic Structural Analysis*, pp. 1–50. New York: Columbia University Press.

Lavely, William
1991   "Marriage and Mobility under Rural Collectivism." In Rubie S. Watson and Patricia Buckley Ebrey, eds., *Marriage and Inequality in Chinese Society*, pp. 286–312. Berkeley: University of California Press.

Lee, Leo Ou-fan, and Benjamin Lee
1990   "A Chinese 'Public Sphere': Reflections on the Tiananmen Democracy Movement." Chicago: Center for Transnational Studies.

Levenson, Joseph R.
1964   *Confucian China and Its Modern Fate:* vol. 2, *The Problem of Monarchical Decay*. Berkeley: University of California Press.

Lévi-Strauss, Claude
1969   *The Elementary Structures of Kinship*. Translated by Rodney Needham. Boston: Beacon Press.

Liang Qichao
1959   "Zhongguo zhi wushidao" [China's bushido] (1916). In *Yinbing shi quanji [Collected Writings from the Ice-drinker's Studio)*, vol. 44, pp. 43–49. Taipei: Wenguang tushu gongsi.

Li Honglin
1988   "Social Scientist Sees Good Side of Competition." *China Daily*, 5 May.

Li Jian
1987   "Xia yige mubiao: sanlianguan!" [Set a Goal—Three Championships in a Row!]. *Nanzihan [Real Man]*, May.

Li Lijiang
1987a   Shenti lixing shang saichang" [Earnestly Practicing What They Advocate, They Take to the Competition Field]. *Tiyu bao [Sports News]*, October 7(?).

1987b	"Gaige, kaifangde songge" [An Ode to Reform and Opening-up]. *Beijing ribao [Beijing Daily]*. 21 November.

1985a	"Zhuhe nüpai ticao weiqi dui qude youyi chengji" [Congratulations to the Women's Volleyball, Gymnastics, and Go Teams for Achieving Excellent Results]. *Tiyu bao*, 27 November.

1985b	"Zhongguo weiqidui dao Beida Qinghua zuo baogao" [Chinese Go Team Visits Beijing U. and Qinghua to Give a Report]. *Beijing ribao*, 24 November.

1985c	"Nüpai guniang zaiyu huijing shoudao relie huanying" [The Women's Volleyball Girls Return to the Capital Loaded with Glory and Receive a Warm Welcome]. *Beijing ribao*, 22 November.

Lingyunzhi [Great Aspirations]
1987	"Program for Group Calisthenics of Sixth National Games of PRC," Guangzhou, 20 November.

Lin Nan
1988	"Zhejiang youxiu xuanshou xiangyou tuiyi baoxian" [Zhejiang Athletes Enjoy Retirement Insurance]. *Renmin ribao*, 13 February.

Lin Nan and Xie Wen
1988	"Occupational Prestige in Urban China." *American Journal of Sociology* 93 (4): 793–832.

Lin Yutang
1939	*Moment in Peking: A Novel of Contemporary Chinese Life*. New York: John Day.

Lippe, Rudolf zur
1988	*Vom Leib zum Körper. Naturbeherrschung am Menschen in der Renaissance (From [subjective] body to [objective] body. Nature's domination of man in the Renaissance)*. Hamburg: Reinbek.

Liu, James J. Y.
1967	*The Chinese Knight-Errant*. Chicago: University of Chicago Press.

Liu, James T. C.
1985	"Polo and Cultural Change: From T'ang to Sung China." *Harvard Journal of Asiatic Studies* 45 (1): 203–24.

Liu Fuhe and Sun Zhonghua
1988	"Wanhu nongmin wenjuan diaocha" [A Questionnaire Survey of Ten Thousand Peasant Households]. *Renmin ribao*, 12 April.

Liu Shun and Lei Wenbing
1987	"Guojia jiaoweide jueding pinbu zhihou . . ." [After Issuance of the Decision by the State Education Commission . . .]. *Tiyu bao*, 12 October.

Liu Xinwu
1985	"5-19 chang jingtou" [Distant Shot of May 19]. *Renmin wenxue [People's Literature]*, no. 7.

Liu Xiyu
1994   Letter, personal communication with author. March 20.

Li Xiaofei
1987   "Tiyu gaigede daitouren" [A Leader in the Physical Culture Reforms].
         Tiyu bao, 22 November.

————, and Zhang Xiaozhu
1988   "Shijia yundongyuan" [Top Ten Athletes]. *Tiyu bao,* 30 January.

Li You
1985   "Qingxiede zuqiu chang: 5-19 zhi ye" [The Tilted Soccer Field: The
         Night of May 19]. *Renmin wenxue [People's literature]* vol. 7.
1978   "Yangmei jian chushao" [Proudly Draw Your Sword]. *Renmin ribao
         [People's Daily]* 11 June.

Lu Guang
1988   "Baxian guo hai" [The Eight Immortals Cross the Sea]. *Zhongguo tiyu
         bao,* 16 September.

Lull, James
1991   *China Turned On: Television, Reform, and Resistance.* London: Routledge.

Luo Pan
1988   "Shizongde jianmei guanjun" [The Bodybuilding Champion Who Dis-
         appeared without a Trace]. *Tiyu bao,* 9 April.

Lüschen, Günther, and George H. Sage, eds.
1981   *Handbook of Social Science of Sport.* Champaign, IL: Stipes Publishing Co.

Lu Xun
1973   "Suiganlu 37" [Random Thoughts, no. 37] (1918). In *Refeng [Hot Wind]*,
         p. 17. Beijing: Renmin wenxue chubanshe.

Lu Yuanzhen
1988a   "Renlei jiben jiazhi guanniande hongyang" [The Spread of Basic Hu-
         man Values]. *Zhongguo tiyu bao,* 30 September.
1988b   "Guanyu 'laonian disike' duihua" [A Dialogue about "Old People's
         Disco"], *Renmin ribao,* 5 June.

MacAloon, John J.
1995   *Brides of Victory: Nationalism and Gender in Olympic Ritual.* London:
         Berg (forthcoming).
1994a   "Humanism as Political Necessity? Reflections on the Pathos of Anthro-
         pological Science in Pluricultural Contexts." In James Fernandez and
         Milton Singer, eds., *The Conditions of Reciprocal Understanding.* Chicago:
         International House (forthcoming).
1994b   "Interval Training." In Susan L. Foster, ed., *Choreographing History.*
         Bloomington: Indiana University Press (forthcoming).

1992   "The Ethnographic Imperative in Comparative Olympic Research." *Sociology of Sport Journal* 9, no. 2 (June): 104–20.

1991a   "The Turn of Two Centuries: Sport and the Politics of Intercultural Relations." In Fernand Landry, Marc Landry, Magdaleine Yerles, eds., *Sport . . . The third millennium: Proceedings of the International Symposium*, pp. 31–44. Quebec, Canada, 21–25 May 1990. Sainte-Foy: Les Presses de l'Université Laval.

1991b   "Are Olympic Athletes Professionals?" In Paul D. Staudohar and James A. Mangan, eds., *The Business of Professional Sports*, pp. 264–97. Urbana: University of Illinois Press.

1990   "Steroids and the State: Dubin, Melodrama and the Accomplishment of Innocence." *Public Culture* 2, no. 2 (Spring): 41–64.

1988   "Encountering Our Others: Social Science and Olympic Sport." In Kang Shin-pyo, John MacAloon, and Roberto DaMatta, eds., *The Olympics and Cultural Exchange: The Papers of the First International Conference on the Olympics and East/West and South/North Cultural Exchange in the World System*, pp. 15–42. Seoul: Hanyang University Press.

1987a   "Missing Stories: American Politics and Olympic Discourse." *Gannett Center Journal* 1, no. 2 (Fall): 111–42.

1987b   "An Observer's View of Sport Sociology." *Sociology of Sport Journal* 4, no. 2 (June): 103–15.

1987c   "Festival, Ritual, and Television." In R. Jackson and T. McPhail, eds., *The Olympic Movement and the Mass Media: Past, Present and Future Issues*, International Conference Proceedings, session 6, pp. 21–40. The University of Calgary, Alberta, Canada, 15–19 February 1987. Calgary: Hurford Enterprises Ltd.

1984   "Olympic Games and the Theory of Spectacle in Modern Societies." In John MacAloon, ed., *Rite, Drama, Festival, Spectacle: Rehearsals Toward a Theory of Cultural Performance*, pp. 241–80. Philadelphia: Institute for the Study of Human Issues.

1981   *This Great Symbol: Pierre de Coubertin and the Origins of the Modern Olympic Games*. Chicago: University of Chicago Press.

———, and Kang Shin-pyo

1990   "*Uri Nara:* Korean Nationalism, the Seoul Olympics, and Contemporary Anthropology." In Koh Byong-Ik, ed., *Toward One World, Beyond All Barriers: The Seoul Olympiad Anniversary Conference*, pp. 117–59. Seoul: Seoul Olympic Sports Promotion Foundation.

Ma Lizhen and Song Meiya

1988   "1988—nürende chulu?" [1988—Women's Future?]. *Renmin ribao*, 11 January.

Ma Mingshan

1984   "Woguo bufen youxiu yundongyuande jingshen xuyao yu manzu—diaocha 68ming quanguo guanjun he shijie guanjun" [The Spiritual Requirements and Satisfaction of a Selection of China's Top Athletes—A Survey of 68 National and World Champions]. In Tianjin tiyu xueyuan jiaowuchu [Tianjin Institute of Physical Education Dean's Office], *Tiyu shehuixue wenji* [*Collected Sport Sociology Papers*], vol. 1, pp. 109–17.

Mangan, J. A.
1981   *Athleticism in the Victorian and Edwardian Public School: The Emergence and Consolidation of an Educational Ideology.* Cambridge: Cambridge University Press.

———, and Roberta J. Park
1987   "Introduction." In J. A. Mangan and Roberta J. Park, eds., *From "Fair Sex" to Feminism: Sport and the Socialization of Women in the Industrial and Post-Industrial Eras.* London: Frank Cass.

Mann, Jim
1986   "The Bikini Breakthrough." *The Washington Post,* 29 November, p. D3.

Mao Zedong
1917   *Tiyu zhi yanjiu* [*A Study of Physical Culture*]. Stuart R. Schram, *Une étude de l'education physique.* Paris: Mouton. Originally in *Xin qingnian* [*New Youth*] 3, no. 2 (April).

Mauss, Marcel
1979   "Body Techniques." In *Sociology and Psychology: Essays* (1935), translated by Ben Brewster, pp. 97–105. London: Routledge and Kegan Paul.

McNay, Lois
1991   "The Foucauldian Body and the Exclusion of Experience." *Hypatia: A Journal of Feminist Philosophy,* Special Issue on Feminism and the Body 6 (3): 125–39.

Mead, Margaret
1963   *Sex and Temperament in Three Primitive Societies* (1935). New York: Morrow Quill.

Miao Hui
1987   "Bushi jinpai shengguo jinpai" [It Wasn't Gold Medals Surpassing Gold Medals]. *Tiyu bao,* 4 December.

Miura, Kunio
1989   "The Revival of *Qi*: Qigong in Contemporary China." In Livia Kohn, ed., *Taoist Meditation and Longevity Techniques,* pp. 331–62. Ann Arbor: Center for Chinese Studies, University of Michigan.

Modern China
1993   Symposium: "Public Sphere"/"Civil Society" in China? Paradigmatic Issues in Chinese Studies, III. Vol. 19, no. 2 (April).

Moragas Spa, Miquel de
1993   "Olympic Values and the Television Broadcast of the Inaugural Ceremony at Barcelona in 1992." *Olympic Centennial Congress Bulletin,* pp.

42–48. Lausanne, Switzerland: XII Olympic Congress Media Ad Hoc Committee of IOC.

Moran, Thomas
1995 "Preface." In Thomas Moran, ed., *Unofficial Histories: Chinese Reportage from the Era of Reform*. Boulder, CO: Westview (forthcoming).
1993a Personal communication with author. June.
1993b "A Certain Class of Ideas: The Discourse of Contemporary Chinese Reportage." Unpublished manuscript.

Murdock, George Peter
1945 "The Common Denominator of Cultures." In Ralph Linton, ed., *The Science of Man in the World Crisis*, pp. 123–42. New York: Columbia University Press.

Naquin, Susan
1976 *Millenarian Rebellion in China: The Eight Trigrams Uprising of 1813*. New Haven: Yale University Press.

Needham, Joseph
1983 *Science and Civilization in China*, vol. 5, pt. V. Cambridge: The University Press.

New World Press
1986 *Sports and Games in Ancient China*. Beijing.

Nie Lisheng
1988 "China Tops World TV ratings." *China Daily*, 27 January.

Niu Xinghua and Feng Jianxiu
1986 "Woguo dazhong chengshi butong chanye tiyu renkou jiegou taishi" [Trends in the Sports Population of Different Industries in China's Large and Medium Cities]. In Tianjin tiyu xueyuan jiaowuchu [Tianjin Institute of Physical Education Dean's Office], *Tiyu shehuixue wenji* [*Collected Sport Sociology Papers*], vol. 2, pp. 9–19.

——, Li Shuyi, Su Lianyong
1986 "Tamen zhichi zijide zinü congshi zhuanye jingji yundong ma?" [Do They Support Their Children in Following Careers in Professional Sports?]. In *Tianjin tiyu xueyuan jiaowuchu* [Tianjin Institute of Physical Education Dean's Office], *Tiyu shehuixue wenji* [*Collected Sport Sociology Papers*], vol. 2, pp. 59–64.

Olson, Jeff
1992 Personal communication with author. December.

Ortner, Sherry
1975 "Is Female to Male as Nature Is to Culture?" In Michelle Zimbalist Rosaldo and Louise Lamphere, eds., *Woman, Culture, and Society*, pp. 67–88. Stanford: Stanford University Press.

Ostrow, Ronald L.
1983   "Hu Na Wins Long-Awaited Asylum as Chinese Protest." *Los Angeles Times*, 21 March, I:1,17.

Ozouf, Monique
1988   *Festivals and the French Revolution*. Translated by Alan Sheridan. Cambridge: Harvard University Press.

Park, Roberta J.
1987   "Biological Thought, Athletics and the Formation of a 'man of character': 1830–1900." In J. A. Mangan and James Walvin, eds., *Manliness and Morality: Middle-class Masculinity in Britain and America, 1800–1940* pp. 7–34. New York: St. Martin's Press.

Peasant Sports Association Cadres
1988   Interview with six Peasant Sports Association cadres, Beijing Institute of Physical Education, 10 March.

People's Sports Publishing House
1986   *Sports in Ancient China*. Beijing.

Perry, Elizabeth J.
1992   "Casting a Chinese 'Democracy' Movement: The Roles of Students, Workers, and Entrepreneurs." In Jeffrey N. Wasserstrom and Elizabeth J. Perry, eds., *Popular Protest and Political Culture in Modern China: Learning from 1989*, pp. 146–64. Boulder, CO: Westview Press.

Ping Yuan
1987   "Jiejue sanda kunnan: changdi zijin huanjing" [Solving Three Big Difficulties: Sports Fields, Capital, Environment]. *Tiyu bao*, 16 November.

Pocock, J. G. A.
1964   "Ritual, Language, Power: An Essay on the Apparent Political Meanings of Ancient Chinese Philosophy." *Political Science* 16 (1): 3–31.

Postone, Moishe, Edward LiPuma, and Craig Calhoun
1993   "Introduction." In Craig Calhoun, Edward LiPuma, and Moishe Postone, eds., *Bourdieu: Critical Perspectives*. Chicago: University of Chicago Press.

Potter, Sulamith Heins, and Jack M. Potter
1990   *China's Peasants: The Anthropology of a Revolution*. Cambridge: Cambridge University Press.

Pusey, James Reeve
1983   *China and Charles Darwin*. Cambridge: Council on East Asian Studies, Harvard University Press.

Qian Deng
1988   "Hubei tianjingdui yinjin jingzheng jizhi, shixing 'fengxianjin chengbao zerenzhi'" [Hubei Track and Field Utilizes the Mechanism of Com-

petition, Implements the "risk money contract responsibility system"]. *Tiyu bao*, 15 April.

Qiu Zutai
1988a "Quanguo jianmei guanjunsai yuanman luomu" [The Curtain Closes on a Successful National Bodybuilding Championship]. *Zhongguo tiyu bao*, 28 September.
1988b "Xi'an zhigong liansai chuxian jiti oudou" [A Worker's League Match in Xi'an Ends in a Brawl]. *Tiyu bao*, 29 April.

Quanguo tiyu xueyuan jiaocai weiyuanhui [National Committee on Teaching Material for Physical Education Institutes]
1987 *Tiyu lilun* [*Physical Culture Theory*]. Beijing: Renmin tiyu chubanshe.

Qu Beilin
1987 "Zhong, ri qingshaonian shenti suzhi chayi" [Differences in the Physical Health of Chinese and Japanese Youth]. *Beijing ribao*, 26 December.

Qu Guangli
1988 "Sporting Chance for China." *China Daily*, 24 May.

Rankin, Mary Backus
1990 "The Origins of a Chinese Public Sphere: Local Elites and Community Affairs in the Late Imperial Period." *Etudes Chinoises—Bulletin de l'Association Française d'Etudes Chinoises* IX (2): 12–60.
1975 "The Emergence of Women at the End of the Ch'ing: The Case of Ch'iu Chin." In Margery Wolf and Roxane Witke, eds., *Women in Chinese Society*, pp. 39–66. Stanford: Stanford University Press.

Rao Hu
1982 "An Old People's Long-Distance Running Team." *China Reconstructs*, August, pp. 34–35.

Rawski, Evelyn S.
1988 "A Historian's Approach to Chinese Death Ritual." In James L. Watson and Evelyn S. Rawski, eds., *Death Ritual in Late Imperial and Modern China*, pp. 20–34. Berkeley: University of California Press.

Reilly, Rick
1988 "Here No One Is Spared." *Sports Illustrated*, 15 August, pp. 70–77.

Renmin ribao [*People's Daily*]
1988 Untitled (p. 3). 3 February.

Renmin tiyu chubanshe [People's Sports Publishing House]
1985 *Zhongguo jindai tiyushi* [*History of sports in modern China*]. General use text for physical culture departments. Beijing.

Riordan, James
1977 *Sport in Soviet Society: Development of Sport and Physical Education in Russia and the USSR.* Cambridge: Cambridge University Press.

Rivenburgh, Nancy K.
1993   "Images of Nations during the 1992 Barcelona Olympic Opening Ceremony." In *Olympic Centennial Congress Bulletin*, pp. 32–39. Lausanne: XII Olympic Congress Media Ad Hoc Committee of the IOC.
1992   "National Image Richness in US-Televised Coverage of South Korea During the 1988 Olympics." *Asian Journal of Communication* 2 (2): 1–39.

Robinson, John P.
1967   "Time Expenditure on Sports Across Ten Countries." *International Review of Sport Sociology* 2: 67–87.

Rofel, Lisa
1992   "Rethinking Modernity: Space and Factory Discipline in China." *Cultural Anthropology* 7 (1): 93–114.

Rong Gaotang et al., eds.
1984   *Dangdai zhongguo tiyu* [*Contemporary Chinese Sports*]. Beijing: Chinese Academy of Social Sciences Press.

Ross, Edward Alsworth
1911   *The Changing Chinese: The Conflict of Oriental and Western Cultures in China*. New York: The Century Co.

Rowe, William R.
1992   "Women and the Family in Mid-Ch'ing Social Thought: The Case of Ch'en Hung-mou." *Late Imperial China* 13, no. 2 (December): 1–41.
1990   "The Public Sphere in Modern China." *Modern China* 16 (3): 309–29.

Ru Qi
1987   "Guoren zhi yuxia" [The Nation's Leisure Time]. *Tiyu bao*, 23 December.

Sahlins, Marshall
1990   "China Reconstructing or Vice Versa: Humiliation as a Stage of Economic 'Development,' with Comments on Cultural Diversity in the Modern 'World System.'" In Koh Byong-Ik, ed., *Toward One World, Beyond All Barriers: The Seoul Olympiad Anniversary Conference*, pp. 78–96. Seoul: Seoul Olympic Sports Promotion Foundation.

Schein, Louisa
1992   "Reconfiguring the Dominant: Multidimensionality in the Manufacture of the Miao." Paper presented in the panel on Popular Cultural Practices in China: Room for Heterodoxy? Annual Meeting of the American Anthropological Association, San Francisco, 6 December.

Schell, Orville
1988   *Discos and Democracy: China in the Throes of Reform*. New York: Pantheon Books.

Schwartz, Benjamin
1964   *In Search of Wealth and Power: Yen Fu and the West*. Cambridge, MA: The Belknap Press of Harvard University Press.

Shenghui bolan [*Overview of the Grand Occasion*]
1987   Special publication of the Sixth National Games of the PRC.

Shen Yanping
1988a   "Kids Like Sports, But Parents Don't." *China Daily,* 17 March.
1988b   "The Medal Tally Is What Counts." *China Daily,* March 17.

Shi Chunming
1987   "Yangcheng tiyu yongpin gouxiao liangwang" [Brisk Buying and Sell-
          ing of Guangzhou Sports Products]. *Tiyu bao* [*Sports News*], 2 December.

Shi Yumei
1987   "Meide huashen" [The Embodiment of Beauty]. *Xin tiyu,* January, pp.
          22–24.

Smith-Rosenberg, Carroll, and Charles Rosenberg
1987   "The Female Animal: Medical and Biological Views of Women and
          Their Role in Nineteenth-century America." In J. A. Mangan and Ro-
          berta J. Park, eds., *From "Fair Sex" to Feminism: Sport and the Socialization
          of Women in the Industrial and Post-Industrial Eras,* pp. 13–37. London:
          Frank Cass.

Spence, Jonathan
1990   *The Search for Modern China.* New York: W. W. Norton.

Steel, Richard A.
1985   *Through Peking's Sewer Gate: Relief of the Boxer Siege, 1900–1901.* New
          York: Vantage Press. Edited and with introduction by George W. Car-
          rington.

Stocking, George W., Jr.
1987   *Victorian Anthropology.* New York: The Free Press.

Strand, David
1990   "Protest in Beijing: Civil Society and Public Sphere in China." *Problems
          in Communism* 39 (May–June): 1–19.

1989   *Rickshaw Beijing: City People and Politics in the 1920's.* Berkeley: Univer-
          sity of California Press.

Strathern, Marilyn
1980   "No Nature, No Culture: The Hagen Case." In Marilyn Strathern and
          Carol MacCormack, eds., *Nature, Culture, and Gender,* pp. 174–223.
          Cambridge: Cambridge University.

Sun Lung-kee
1988   "The Deep Structure of Chinese Culture (excerpts)." In Geremie Barme
          and John Minford, *Seeds of Fire: Chinese Voices of Conscience.* New York:
          Hill and Wang.

1983   *Zhongguo wenhuade "shenceng jiegou"* [*The "Deep Structure" of Chinese
          Culture*]. Hong Kong: Jixianshe.

Su Xiaokang
1988   "Zhao Yu jianying" [Sketch of Zhao Yu]. In *Bingbai Hancheng: Zhao Yu tiyu wenti baogao wenxue ji* [*Defeat of the Troops in Seoul: Collected Reportage by Zhao Yu on Physical Culture Problems*], pp. 210–16. Beijing: Zhongguo shehui kexue chubanshe.

Swift, E. M.
1988   "Sleeker, Stronger." *Sports Illustrated,* 15 August, pp. 44–51.

Takenoshita Kyūzo
1967   "The Social Structure of the Sport Population in Japan." *International Review of Sport Sociology* 2: 5–18.

Taylor, Stuart
1983   "China's Tennis Player Gets Asylum in U.S.; Peking Aide Protests." *New York Times,* 5 April, A:1,10.

Thompson, John
1990   *Ideology and Modern Culture: Critical Social Theory in the Era of Mass Communication.* Stanford: Stanford University Press.

Time Magazine
1986   "China's Fear of the Bikini," 15 December, p. 48.
1985   "Old Wounds." 2 December, p. 50.

Tiyu bao [*Sports News*]
1988   "Shiba sheng, shi, qu chengli nongmin tixie" [18 Provinces, Municipalities, and Regions Found Peasant Sports Associations], 6 January.
1987a   "Liuyunhui qishi lu" [On the Insights of the Sixth Games], 6 December.
1987b   "Quanyunhui longhu bang" [List of Dragons and Tigers from National Games], 6 December.
1987c   "Tiyu jiangjuan" [Lottery Tickets], 22 November.
1987d   "Yi zui jia jingshen zhuangtai jinjun yangcheng" [Enter Guangdong with Superior Mental Preparation], 31 October.
1987e   "Shenti hegelu zhunian xiajiang burong hushi" [The Progessive Yearly Drop in the Physical Standards Is Not Easy to Ignore], 10 October.
1985a   22 November (title unknown).
1985b   25 November (title unknown).

Tocqueville, Alexis de
1956   *Democracy in America.* New York: Mentor (1835). Edited and abridged by Richard D. Heffner.

Track and Field News
1994a   "Get Faster Quick!" p. 60 (April).
1994b   "No Dating Allowed," "Ma Wants Bonus Money," p. 66 (March).
1993   "Chinese Raise Questions," p. 74 (November).

Turner, Victor W.
1988   *The Anthropology of Performance*. New York: PAJ Publications.
1982   *From Ritual to Theatre: The Human Seriousness of Play*. New York: Performing Arts Journal Publications.
1974   *Dramas, Fields, and Metaphors: Symbolic Action in Human Society*. Ithaca: Cornell University Press.
1969   *The Ritual Process: Structure and Anti-Structure*. Ithaca: Cornell University Press.
1966   "Colour Classification in Ndembu Ritual: A Problem in Primitive Classification." In Michael Banton, ed., *Anthropological Approaches to the Study of Religion*, pp. 47–84. ASA Monograph No. 3. London: Tavistock.

————, and Edward M. Bruner, eds.
1986   *The Anthropology of Experience*. Urbana: University of Illinois Press.

TV Guide
1993   "Yang Weiguang's Speech at Reception in Celebration of 35th Birthday of CCTV." In *Guide to Foreign Language Programs in China* 2 (3) (total no. 69), (27 September–3 October), published 13 September, p. 1.

Van Gulik, R. H.
1961   *Sexual Life in Ancient China: A Preliminary Survey of Chinese Sex and Society from ca. 1500 B.C. till 1644 A.D.* Leiden, Netherlands: E. J. Brill.

Wakeman, Frederic, Jr.
1973   *History and Will: Philosophical Perspectives of Mao Tse-Tung's Thought*. Berkeley: University of California Press.

Wang Baosheng
1987   "Mama xuanshoude huimaqiang" [Mama Athletes Return to the Battlefield]. *Tiyu bao*, 9 December.

Wang Jintang
1988   "Laonian disike xiaxiang" [A Reverie on Old People's Disco]. *Renmin Ribao*, 5 June.

Wang Zhenya
1987   *Jiu Zhongguo tiyu jianwen* [*Information on Sports in Old China*]. Beijing: Renmin tiyu chubanshe.

Wan Li
1987   "Zai liujie quanyunhui kaimushishangde jianghua" [Speech at the opening ceremonies of the Sixth National Games]. *Guangzhou ribao* [*Canton Daily*], 21 November.

Ware, James R., trans.
1966   *Alchemy, Medicine, and Religion in the China of A.D. 320: The Nei P'ien of Ko Hung*. New York: Dover.

Wasserstrom, Jeffrey
1991   *Student Protests in Twentieth-Century China: The View from Shanghai.* Stanford: Stanford University Press.

Watson, James L.
1988   "The Structure of Chinese Funerary Rites: Elementary Forms, Ritual Sequence, and the Primacy of Performance." In James L. Watson and Evelyn S. Rawski, eds., *Death Ritual in Late Imperial and Modern China*, pp. 3–19. Berkeley: University of California Press.
1985   "Standardizing the Gods: The Promotion of T'ien Hou ('Empress of Heaven') Along the South China Coast, 960–1960." In David Johnson, Andrew J. Nathan, and Evelyn S. Rawski, eds., *Popular Culture in Late Imperial China*, pp. 292–324. Berkeley: University of California Press.

Webster, James B.
1923   *Christian Education and the National Consciousness in China.* New York: E. P. Dutton.

Wechsler, Howard J.
1985   *Offerings of Jade and Silk: Ritual and Symbol in the Legitimation of the T'ang Dynasty.* New Haven: Yale University Press.

Wen Jiao
1982   "Women's Football Makes the Grade." *China Reconstructs*, December, pp. 58–59.

Whyte, Martin King, and William L. Parish
1984   *Urban Life in Contemporary China.* Chicago: University of Chicago Press.

Williams, Brackette
1990   "Nationalism, Traditionalism, and the Problem of Cultural Inauthenticity." In Richard G. Fox, ed., *Nationalist Ideologies and the Production of National Cultures*, pp. 112–29. American Ethnological Society Monograph Series, No. 2. Washington, DC: American Anthropological Association.

Williams, E. T.
1913   "The State Religion of China During the Manchu Dynasty." *Journal of the Royal Asiatic Society, North China Branch* 44: 11–45.

Wolf, Margery
1985   *Revolution Postponed: Women in Contemporary China.* Stanford: Stanford University Press.
1968   *The House of Lim: A Study of a Chinese Farm Family.* Englewood Cliffs, NJ: Prentice-Hall.

Wu Dong
1987   "Tiyu buhege zhongxuesheng bude baokao gaoyiji xuexiao" [Students Who Fail Physical Culture May Not Test into the Next Highest Level School]. *Beijing ribao*, 24 September.

Wu Jingshu
1988   "Youngsters Taller but Still Facing Nutrition Problems." *China Daily*, 9 May.

Wu Wenrui
1932   *Lun "jinhou Guomin tiyu wenti" shuhou* [Postscript on "Past and present problems in national physical culture"]. *Dagong bao*, Tianjin, August 23.

WuDunn, Sheryl
1993   "The Word from China's Kerouac: The Communists Are Uncool." *New York Times Book Review*, 10 January, pp. 3, 23.

Wyrick, Waneen
1974   "Biophysical Perspectives." In Ellen W. Gerber, Jan Felshin, Pearl Berlin, and Waneen Wyrick, *The American Woman in Sport*, pp. 403–515. Reading, MA: Addison-Wesley Publishing.

Xiandai hanyu cidian [*Modern Chinese Dictionary*]
1987   Beijing: Shangwu yinshuguan.

Xiao Tian
1987   "Bubi da jing xiao guai" [It's Not Necessary To Be Alarmed at Something Perfectly Normal]. *Xin tiyu*, January, p. 24.

Xie Baisan and Zhang Ming
1985   "Nüdaxuesheng bitan nanxingmei: meixue xinli diaocha" [Female College Students Discuss the Masculine Ideal: A Psychological Aesthetics Survey]. *Beijing daxue xiaokan* [*Beijing University School Newspaper*], vol. 91, October.

Xie Lingzheng
1988   *Shixi Zhongguo jindai tiyushishangde "tu yang zhi zheng"* [*A Preliminary Analysis of the "Conflict between Indigenous and Foreign Physical Culture" in Modern Chinese History*]. Master's Thesis, Beijing Institute of Physical Education.

Xie Siyan
1932   "Ping 'Dagong bao' qiri sheping" [A Critique of the Editorial in 'Dagong News' on the Seventh]. *Tiyu zhoubao* [*Physical Culture Weekly*] 30 (August 27): 1.

Xie Yanmin
1988   "Shenyang qiumi julebu chengli" [The Shenyang Soccer Fan Club Is Founded]. *Renmin ribao*, 1 February.

Xu Yaozhong
1988   "Chengbao zhongdian shi yinru jingzheng jizhi" [The Focus of the Responsibility System Is Introducing the Mechanism of Competition]. *Renmin ribao*, 13 February.

Xu Yongchang
1983   *Zhongguo gudai tiyu* [*Ancient Chinese Sports*]. Beijing: Beijing Shifan daxue chubanshe.

Xue Tongshe
1985   "Yingle qiu huanying, shule qiu ye huanying" ["Popular after winning the ballgame, also popular after losing the ballgame"]. *Tiyu bao*, 29 November.

Yan Fu
1959   "Yuan qiang" [The Source of Strength] (1898). In Zhou Zhenfu, ed., *Yan Fu Shiwen Ji* [*Yan Fu's Collected Poems and Essays*], pp. 14–52. Beijing: Renmin wenxue chubanshe.

Yang Duo
1988   Interview, Xiannongtan, 6 February.

Yang Mali
1988   "Beijing pinren jiaolian changshi xin fangfa" [Beijing Tries a New Method in Appointing Coaches]. *Tiyu bao*, 19 March.

———— and Huang Weikang
1985   "Relie qingzhu wo nüpai ticao weiqi dui huo youyi chengji" [Warm Congratulations to our Women's Volleyball, Gymnastics, and Go Teams for Obtaining Outstanding Results]. *Tiyu bao*, 27 November.

Yang, Martin C.
1945   *A Chinese Village: Taitou, Shantung Province.* New York: Columbia University Press.

Yang, Mayfair Mei-hui
1989a   "Between State and Society: The Construction of Corporateness in a Chinese Socialist Factory." *The Australian Journal of Chinese Affairs* 22 (July): 31–60.
1989b   "The Gift Economy and State Power in China." *Comparative Studies in Society and History* 31 (1): 25–54.
1988   "The Modernity of Power in the Chinese Socialist Order." *Cultural Anthropology* 3 (4): 409–27.

Yang Xuewei
1987   "Wan Li dianran liuyunhui xiongxiong huoju" [Wan Li Lights the Raging Torch of the Sixth Games]. *Tiyu bao*, 18 November.

Yang Yingming
1987   "Huoju, dangdai Zhongguode xiangzheng; huoju, dianran weilaide xiwang" [The Torch, Symbol of Contemporary China; The Torch, Lighting Hope for the Future]. *Tiyu bao*, 21 November.

Ye Hongsheng
1985   Introductory essays. "Pingjiang buxiao sheng" [The Unworthy Gentleman from Pingjiang]. In *Jianghu qixia zhuan* [*Extraordinary Knights Roaming over Rivers and Lakes*]. Taibei: Lianjing.

Yeh Wen-Hsin
1990   *The Alienated Academy: Culture and Politics in Republican China, 1919–1937.* Harvard East Asian Monographs 148. Cambridge: Council on East Asian Studies, Harvard University.

Yi Chenghong
1988   Interview, Beijing Institute of Physical Education, 1 March.
1987   "Nüzi jianmei bisai zhi wo jian" [The Women's Bodybuilding Competition as I See It]. *Jian yu mei*, no. 5, September 10, p. 30.

Yin Weixing
1988a   "Zhongguo tiyujie" [The Chinese Sportsworld], part 2. *Huacheng* [*Flower City*] 2: 57–74.
1988b   "Zhongguo tiyujie" [The Chinese Sportsworld], part 2. *Huacheng* [*Flower City*] 1: 104–41.
1987   "Zhongguo tiyujie" [The Chinese Sportsworld], part 1. *Huacheng* [*Flower City*] 6: 78–119.

Yuan Weimin
1988   *Wode zhijiao zhi dao* [*My Way of Teaching*]. Beijing: Renmin tiyu chubanshe.

Yun Daiying
1925   "Dadao jiaohui jiaoyu" [Overturn Missionary School Education]. *Zhongguo qingnian* [*China Youth*] 60 (January 3): 159.

Zeng Hong and Zhou Meng
1988   "Tiyujie lianghui daibiao ying zhenxi canzheng yizheng jihui" [Representatives to the Two Congresses from the Sportsworld Ought to Treasure the Opportunity to Participate in Government and Express Their Views]. *Tiyu bao*, 8 April.

Zeng Lingtong
1987   "Beijing Gets Ballrooms." *China Daily*, 19 October.

Zhang Fuyang
1987   "Luoti budengyu huangse" [Nudity Does Not Equal Obscenity]. *Jian yu mei*, 4, 10 July, p. 2.

Zhan Guoshu
1988   "Some People Fear Competition." *China Daily*, 10 March.

Zhang Xiaozhu
1988   "Zou xiang weilai" [Advancing Toward the Future]. *Tiyu bao*, 16 March.

Zhang Yan
1986   "Yige Meiguo qingniande tiyu guannian" [An American Youth's View of Physical Culture]. *Xin tiyu* [*New Sports*], February, pp. 16–17.

Zhang Yaohong
1988   "Jiangjin zai zheli yiweizhe gongzheng" [Here Bonuses Signify Fairness]. *Tiyu bao*, 26 February.

Zhang Yinzeng
1988   Photo caption. *Renmin ribao*, 16 April.

Zhang Zhenguo
1988   "Chengbao chu rencai" [The Responsibility System Brings Out Talent]. *Renmin ribao*, 4 February.

Zhao Lihong
1987   "Renjian shenhua" [A Real-life Fairytale]. *Tiyu bao*, 22 November.

Zhao Yu
1988a   "Da *Tiyu bolan* jizhe wen" [Reply to Questions of the *Sports Vision* Reporter]. In *Bingbai Hancheng: Zhao Yu tiyu wenti baogao wenxue ji* [*Defeat of the Troops in Seoul: Collected Reportage by Zhao Yu on Physical Culture Problems*], pp. 217–26. Beijing: Zhongguo shehui kexue chubanshe.
1988b   "Bingbai Hancheng" [Defeat of the Troops in Seoul]. *Wenhui yuekan* [*Encounter Monthly*] no. 12: 2–12.
1988c   "Qiangguo meng" [Superpower Dream]. *Dangdai*, February, pp. 163–98.
1986   "Zhongguode yaohai" [A Key Issue for China]. *Reliu* [*Warm Current*] no. 2.

Zhong Yang and Yi Xianhe
1985   "Beida jihui qingzhu woguo qishou huosheng" [Beijing U. Assembles to Congratulate Our Nation's Victorious Go Players]. *Tiyu bao*, 23 November.

Zhongguo tiyu bao [*China Sports News*]
1988   *Wang Meng tan jingzheng jizhi* [Wang Meng discusses the mechanism of competition], August 20.

Zhou Yingnan, ed.
1987   *Yundong Yixue* [*Sports Medicine*]. Beijing Institute of Physical Education Correspondence Course Text. Beijing: Beijing Institute of Physical Education, September.

Zhou Yixing, ed.
1989   *Dangdai Zhongguode Beijing* [*Contemporary China's Beijing*] vol. 1. Beijing: Zhongguo shehui kexue chubanshe.

Zhu Minzhi
1984   "How Top Leaders Keep Fit." *China Reconstructs*, February, pp. 12–14.

374 REFERENCES

Zito, Angela Rose
1984   "Re-Presenting Sacrifice: Cosmology and the Editing of Texts." *Ch'ing-shih Wen-t'i* 5 (2): 47–78.

Zong He
1987   "Jingshen wenming jianshe jie shuoguo" [Outstanding Fruits Netted in the Construction of Spiritual Civilization]. *Tiyu bao,* 4 December.

Zou Hanru
1988   "Our Healthy Babies." *China Daily,* 31 May.

INDEX

Abu-Lughod, Lila, 14
Actors, 181, 298
"Advice Handed Down for Educating
Women" (Chen Hongmou), 219, 331
Aerobic dancing, 270
Age: in the culture of the body, 282–85. *See
also* Elderly, the
Alliance: emphasized in Chinese society,
219; and gender, 232, 236–37; and mate
selection, 231; and sexuality, 24–25,
215, 216–18, 232, 235, 237, 243
American Character, The (Fei Xiaotong), 294,
333
Anagnost, Ann, 69n.1, 156, 221
Anderson, Benedict, 93n
Anemia (*pinxue*), 254, 335
An shen, 16, 325
Appadurai, Arjun, 291n
Archery, 223
Arnold, Thomas, 45n
Arranged marriage, 233
Arts, 116
Asian Games (1990), 132, 315–16
Athletes: and the body, 6–8; bonuses for,
106–7, 169, 185; children of workers as,
194; in China, 22–23; Chinese women
athletes' chances of finding a mate,
213–14; Chinese women athletes more
successful than the men, 226–27, 229,
322; Chinese women runners, 318–22;
clothing for women athletes, 270–71;
conflict with coaches, 177–78; conflicting demands on bodies of, 238, 239,
240; considered stupid, 193; in the Cultural Revolution, 272; discipline for,
157–67; drug abuse by, 319–21, 321n;
education levels of top athletes, 200;
the education problem, 197–200, 331;
the exit problem, 200–201, 205, 326;
exploitation of female athletes by
coaches, 320; female athletes who refuse to train during menstruation,
250–51; and food, 23, 253, 256–61; and
foreign currency, 185–86; as lacking culture, 174–75; living conditions of,
183–86; lowering admissions standards
for, 169, 198, 199; marriage prohibited
for, 244–46; marriage prospects of,
182–83; married women athletes,
246–48; at missionary schools, 48–49;
as occupational class, 35; open-
mindedness of, 174–75; parental opposition to their children becoming, 201–8;
peasant attitudes toward, 195–96, 197;
photographs of Western women athletes, 275; as representatives, 29, 95–96,
97; and reproduction, 23, 244–48; retired athletes becoming coaches, 200,
201; and social change, 209; and socialist spiritual civilization, 178; social
standing of, 27–28, 181–83, 209; and
the state, 23, 96, 97, 155, 239, 261;
State Sports Commission training system, 58–59; team officers, 166; and

375